John Lloyd

The Book of Joshua

A critical and expository commentary of the Hebrew text

John Lloyd

The Book of Joshua
A critical and expository commentary of the Hebrew text

ISBN/EAN: 9783337316372

Printed in Europe, USA, Canada, Australia, Japan

Cover: Foto ©Lupo / pixelio.de

More available books at **www.hansebooks.com**

THE BOOK OF JOSHUA.

A Critical and Expository Commentary

OF THE

HEBREW TEXT.

BY THE REV.

JOHN LLOYD, M.A., F. R. Hist. Soc.,

RECTOR OF LLANVAPLEY, MONMOUTHSHIRE;

Author of "Analysis of Hebrew Text of Gen. i. to xi.," "Analysis of Hebrew Text of Ecclesiastes," etc.

London:
HODDER AND STOUGHTON,
27, PATERNOSTER ROW.

MDCCCLXXXVI.

Printed by Hazell, Watson, & Viney, Ld., London and Aylesbury.

PREFACE

THE following Commentary comprises notes grammatical, exegetical, historical, and ethical. The Grammar followed is that of Gesenius, not only in the syntax, but the orthography; for thus, when Hebrew words are written in their corresponding English letters, ק is always expressed by *q*, and צ by *ts*, instead of by *k* and *z* respectively, as in many grammars. Further, in giving the derivation and meaning of the Hebrew names of persons, places, towns, etc., the Lexicon of Gesenius has been chiefly consulted. Many also of the renderings which differ from those in the Authorised Version will be found to agree with those in the Revised Version, which had not been published when this work was finished. The author acknowledges his obligations to the Commentaries of Keil, Rosenmüller, Knobel, Fay, and others, for much help in the exegesis of the Hebrew text; and to Dean Stanley's *Sinai and Palestine*, Robinson's *Palestine* and *Later Biblical Researches*, Walton's *Negeb*, Smith's *Dictionary of the Bible*, and many other works, for illustrations of the history and geography of the book. The ethical remarks, which are interspersed here and there throughout the notes, are, in a great measure, drawn from Bishop Wordsworth's *Commentary*, who has done more perhaps than any other recent expositor to call attention to the typical and spiritual meaning of the "Book of Joshua."

It is well known that the Palestine Exploration Fund has been successful in discovering the probable sites of many of the towns mentioned in this book, which had been previously unrecognised. Some allusions to these will be found in this Commentary, but many of the positions assigned cannot be established according to the boundaries of the tribes as marked out in existing maps. Such is the case with regard to the *Biblical Atlas*, which the author of this Commentary has mainly followed, and which is that of Clark, edited by that eminent historiographer, Sir George Grove, who has written many of the articles on Scripture places in Dr. Smith's *Dictionary of the Bible*.

It only remains for the author to add that, having taken much pains to render this work useful to biblical students, he devoutly hopes that the blessing of the Great Head of the Church, the true Joshua, may rest upon it.

INTRODUCTION.

THE title of this book does not necessarily imply that Joshua was its author, for, like the books of Ruth and Esther, it may have been named from its subject-matter, as giving an account of the deeds of Joshua, by whom God, according to His promise, brought His people into Canaan, and portioned it out among them. It has, however, been most generally ascribed to Joshua, in accordance with the testimony of the early Hebrew Church, which says, "Joshua scripsit librum suum et octo versus in lege" (Tr. *Bava Bathra*, fol. 14, c. 2). Certainly, none could have been better fitted to write it than Joshua, who was not only present in all the great transactions which it records, but received personal communications from Jehovah, which no one but himself could, in the first instance, have divulged to others; who also spoke the speeches recorded in chapters xxiii., xxiv., and is expressly said to have added to the Book of the Law some account of his own acts (xxiv. 26). As, however, Joshua could not have recorded his own death (xxiv. 29), whoever added that account might have written the rest of the book, mainly from records left probably by Joshua himself. Thus the authorship has been attributed to Phinehas (Lightfoot), or to one of the elders who survived Joshua (Keil). Though the exact date of its composition cannot be fixed, it is clear that the book must have been written before the time of David (see notes on xv. 63 and xi. 8); also by one who was living at the time when Rahab was still alive (vi. 25). The oft-repeated expression, "to this day,"[1] does not necessarily denote a long period, not at farthest more than twenty-five or thirty years (comp. the use of the same phrase in Matt. xxviii. 15). The writer speaks of himself as one of those who had crossed over Jordan (v. 1),[2] and to whom the land had been promised (v. 6); describes Gibeon "as one of the royal cities" of Canaan (x. 2); and mentions the Canaanitish names of the towns at the time of the invasion, *e.g.*, Kirjath-Arba, afterwards called Hebron (xiv. 15), Kirjath-Sepher, afterwards Debir (xv. 15). Other indications of an early date are furnished by the *style and diction* of the book. Thus, the *scriptio defectiva*, which is the ancient form,[3] prevails far more throughout than the *scriptio plena*. Old forms of words occur which are not found in the later books, *e.g.*, תְּמוֹל (iii. 4, iv. 18, xx. 5), as in the Pentateuch, for אֶתְמוֹל (1 Sam. iv. 7; 2 Sam. v. 2);

---

[1] See iv. 9, v. 9, vi. 25, vii. 26, viii. 28, 29, ix. 27, xiii. 13, xiv. 14, xv. 63, xvi. 10, xxii. 3, 17, xxiii. 8, 9.

[2] "The reading of the Q'ri עָבְרָם (till *they* were passed over) is nothing but an arbitrary and needless conjecture, and ought not to have been preferred by Bleek and others, notwithstanding the fact that the ancient versions and some MSS. also adopt it" (Keil). The majority of the MSS. read עָבְרֵנוּ׃

[3] Ges., *Gram.*, § 8, 4 b.

אֶתְמוּל (Micah ii. 8; Isa. xxx. 33); אֶתְהֶן (xxi. 9), cf. אֶתְהֶם (Gen. xxxii. 1), רְאִיָּה (xxi. 10), only used again in Job xv. 7; אֲרָרוֹת (x. 40); זֵג (x. 19), cf. Deut. xxv. 18; יִלּוֹנוּ from לוּן, to murmur (ix. 18), found only besides in the books of Exodus and Numbers; the unusual form אִישֵׁי (xiii. 14); שׁ for אֲשֶׁר, though it occurs as early as Judges, is not found in Joshua. The old suffix ־ָם is repeatedly used, but the later form ־ֵיהֶם, only in xi. 6, 9, xviii. 21. Phrases common to the Pentateuch are occasionally met with, such as "wrought folly in Israel" (vii. 15); "people even as the sand shore for multitude" (xi. 4); "a land flowing with milk and honey" (v. 6); "heads of the fathers," or "of the house of the fathers" (xiv. 1, xix. 51, xxii. 14), etc.

But though the book thus bears resemblance to the Pentateuch in its style and diction, it is quite independent or distinct from it. This is evident from the references made in it to the Pentateuch (cf. Josh. xiii. 14, 33, xiv. 4, with Numb. xviii. 20; Deut. xviii. 1, 2), and its repetition, but with additional particulars, of the conquest of the country on the east of Jordan. Also from the fact that certain archaisms in the Pentateuch are not found in it, e.g., הוּא, used as a fem. (Ges., Gr., § 32, 6); הָאֵל for אֵלֶּה (§ 34); נַעַר for נַעֲרָה (§ 2, 3 Rem.) Again, Jericho, which throughout the Pentateuch is spelt יְרֵחוֹ, is always spelt in Joshua יְרִיחוֹ, or יְרִחוֹ; the form כְּמִלְבַת, used in the Pentateuch, is changed to כְּמִלְבוּת in Josh. xiii., where it five times occurs. The following forms also are not found in the Pentateuch, viz., שִׁבִּיעַ (Josh. vi. 27, ix. 9); קָנוֹא (xxiv. 19); יָרֵא (xxii. 25); גִּבּוֹרֵי הַחַיִל (i. 14, vi.

2, viii. 3), but בְּנֵי חַיִל (Deut. iii. 18); נאד, a bottle (ix. 4, 13), for חֵמֶת (Gen. xxi. 14, 15, 19); הִצִּית, to set on fire or burn (viii. 8, 19); צָנַח, to spring down (xv. 18); קָצִין, a prince or leader (x. 24); יָקַט, to rest (xi. 23, xiv. 15). Thus the book may be said to occupy in style and diction a middle place between the Pentateuch and the books which follow. It affords also internal evidence of being the composition of *one* author, and not of several; for on no other supposition can we account for the easy flow of the narrative in the historical part, where event follows event, if not always in the exact order of time, yet of thought; and the whole is narrated with a vividness which bespeaks an eye-witness of the various scenes depicted. It is true that there is a difference in the style of that portion of the book which records the partition of the land, and that which relates its conquest; but this is what might be expected from the nature of the subject-matter, and from the fact that this portion of the book was apparently in the main derived from written surveys, made previously to the apportionment of the conquered territory (see ch. xviii.) Yet in this part, as well as in the foregoing, there is connection and method, the transactions following one another in chronological order, and all serving to show (what was evidently a principal design of the author) the fulfilment of God's promise to give the land of Canaan to His people Israel. Hence the supplementary theory of Ewald, Knobel, and others, according to which the hand of several authors is traceable in the book, does not seem at all applicable to it.

The Divine authority of this book is established by the references made to it in Holy Writ[1]; also by the fact of its having been included in the Canon of Scripture by the early Hebrew Church, and tacitly acknowledged by our Saviour, when, " beginning at Moses and the Prophets, He expounded to His disciples in all the scriptures the things concerning Himself."

Various objections, indeed, have been raised to its credibility, and, therefore, to its Divine inspiration. One of these is drawn from the *apparent discrepancies* which are met with in the book, as, *e.g.*, the statement in xi. 23, xxi. 43-5, that the whole land was subjugated; whereas in xiii. 1-3 and xviii. 3 we read that a great part was yet unoccupied by the Israelites; for an answer to which the notes on those passages in the annexed commentary may be consulted. Again, the statement, in xi. 21, that Joshua cut off the Anakim from Hebron, Debir, etc., is not irreconcilable with their subsequent extirpation, recorded in xv. 13, 14 (see note on x. 37). Nor is the promise of God that the boundaries of Israel should extend to the Euphrates (i. 4) at variance with the fact that the country which Joshua divided does not reach so far (xiii. 6; see note on i. 4). Another and more serious objection is the alleged injustice of depriving the Canaanites of their country, and dooming them all to destruction. This has been satisfactorily answered by many commentators (see especially Dr. Fairbairn's *Typol.*, vol. ii., chap.

---

[1] See, *e.g.*, 1 Kings xvi. 34; 1 Chron. ii. 7; Psalm cxiv. 3, 5; Isa. xxviii. 21; Hab. iii. 11-13; Acts vii. 45, xiii. 19; Heb. iv. 8, xi. 30-1, xiii. 5; James ii. 25.

iv.). Here it may suffice to remark that God is the supreme Ruler and Judge of the universe, and, being infinitely just and holy, must do right. It was His command that the Canaanites, on account of their flagrant and long-continued enormities,[1] should, when the cup of their iniquity was full, be extirpated from off the earth. The Israelites were but instruments in executing the Divine purpose; and they had been forbidden by God to spare those nations or to receive them into covenant.[2] They were thus emphatically warned against the great sin of idolatry, to which they were themselves but too prone; and so far were they from being rendered hard-hearted and sanguinary by the work of vengeance in which they were employed, that we find from the history that they executed their commission with reluctance, and far less completely than they ought; nor were they allowed by God to wage aggressive war on other nations besides the Canaanites. The fact that innocent children were involved in the fate of their guilty parents is analogous to what happens in other judgments, such as a plague or earthquake, and can present no difficulty to the minds of those who believe in a future state, where all apparent inequalities in God's dealings now will be redressed. No less futile is the objection which has been raised to

---

[1] See Lev. xviii. 21-25; Deut. xii. 30, 31.
[2] Deut. vii. 1, 2; Exod. xxiii. 32, xxxiv. 12. God, however, made a marked distinction between the inhabitants of Canaan and other neighbouring nations; peace might be made with the latter, if they submitted, but not with the former (see Deut. xx. 10-18). The case of the Gibeonites does not prove the contrary; for the fact that they obtained peace by fraud shows that they were aware that they had no hope of escaping destruction in any other way (see ix. 24).

the historical fidelity of this book on account of the *miracles* recorded in it. The whole history of God's people is miraculous, and the Book of Joshua does but continue that series of wonders which we meet with in the Pentateuch. Miracles were necessary in order to put the Israelites into possession of the Promised Land, for otherwise it is difficult to see how, being scarcely more numerous than the Canaanites, and inferior to them in military skill and equipment, having neither horses nor chariots, nor warlike engines for attacking the great and fortified cities, they could possibly have proved successful. Moreover, nothing could have more tended than God's visible interposition in their behalf, to encourage and strengthen their faith in Him, and to convince them that in the subjugation of Canaan they were doing His work rather than their own. This objection, however, to miracles proceeds from those only who deny the continued agency of an Omnipotent and Personal God, Who, at His own good pleasure, may depart from those settled laws whereby He governs the universe (cf. John v. 17).

But further, to be rightly understood the Book of Joshua must be regarded, not only as a literal, but as a prophetic and spiritual history. It was classed by the Jews as the first of those books called by them " The early Prophets," נְבִיאִים רִאשׁוֹנִים, not only as written by inspired men or prophets, but as prophetical and typical of God's dealings with His Church, or people, to the end of time. Thus, Joshua means the same as Jesus ('Ιησοῦς), Jehovah-Saviour; and in his office as general of the armies of Israel he was a type of Jesus, the Captain of our salvation

(Heb. ii. 10). The Canaan, into the possession of which he brought the children of Israel, was a type of heaven, and also of the state of true believers here on earth, whilst they are yet carrying on a warfare with their spiritual enemies, but are, at the same time, "seated together with Christ in heavenly places," and have "their conversation" (or citizenship) "in heaven." It must not be forgotten that the Israelites who were brought by Joshua into Canaan were very different in character from those who perished in the wilderness. The long course of discipline which they had undergone during their thirty-eight years' wanderings, the instructions of Moses, and, above all, the influence of Divine grace, seem to have humbled and inclined them readily to obey the will of God.[1] With these, therefore, God renewed His covenant, as we read in Deut. xxix. 1; and these, under the conduct of Joshua, having passed through the Jordan, and having been circumcised, and partaken of the Passover (v. 10), entered at once on the work of conquest to which they were called. In all which we may see a prophetic reference to Christians now, who, having been baptized into Christ, circumcised with the true circumcision of the Spirit, and strengthened by the Bread of Life, are both qualified and pledged to fight, under the banner of their Divine Leader, against His and their spiritual foes, and, as far as in them lies, to establish His empire here on earth. Viewed in this light, there is a striking parallel between the Book of Joshua and St. Paul's Epistle to the

---

[1] This their character seems clearly indicated in this book; see, *e.g.*, the note at the end of xxii. 34.

Ephesians, where the great privileges which all Christ's followers already enjoy by union with Him, their risen Head, and their corresponding spiritual duties, are forcibly delineated. But Canaan, as has been already said, was a type also of heaven itself, whither Christ has gone before " *to prepare a place* " for us. As Moses, who typified the Law, could not bring the Israelites into the Promised Land, so " *by the deeds of the Law shall no flesh be justified; but now the righteousness of God without the Law is manifested, even the righteousness of God which is by faith of Jesus Christ, unto all and upon all them that believe* " (Rom. iii. 20-22). This spiritual character of the Book of Joshua has, however, been often dwelt upon by Christian commentators, and it may suffice, therefore, to refer to such well-known works as Bishop Pearson, *On the Creed*, art. ii., pp. 115–118; Dr. Barrow, *Sermons on the Creed*, ser. xvii., p. 230; Mather, *On the Types*, vol. i., pp. 134-7; and of more ancient authors, Origenis *Opera*, tom. ii., pp. 397—457, ed. Benedict, Paris, 1733.

The number of years comprised in this history cannot be exactly determined, for we know not certainly the age of Joshua at the time of the invasion, nor the length of his war with the Canaanites, nor of his life after that war was ended. Some light, however, is thrown on this subject by Joshua xiv. 7, 10. There Caleb, who not improbably may have been of the same age as Joshua, who is called a young man in Exod. xxxiii. 11, declares himself to have been forty years old when he was sent by Moses from Kadesh to spy out the land, but eighty-five when, after the conquest of Canaan, he came before Joshua to claim Hebron for his possession. As, then, the mission of the spies took place in the second year after the exodus (Numb. xiii. 20), and the period from the exodus (B.C. 1491, Usher) to the crossing of the Jordan (B.C. 1451) was forty years, Caleb must have been thirty-eight years old when he passed through the Red Sea, and seventy-eight when he passed through Jordan. Thus, a period of seven years is left for Joshua's conquest of Canaan[1]; and, as Joshua died at the age of one hundred and ten (xxiv. 29), he must, if of the same age as Caleb, have survived the conquest twenty-five years, which, added to the seven years, would embrace a period of thirty-two years as comprised in this book, and quite bear out the assertion in xxiii. 1, that "a long time after that the Lord had given rest, Joshua waxed old and stricken in years." Josephus, however, says (*Ant.*, v., 1., 19) that the war with Canaan lasted five years, and in *Ant.*, v., 1., 29, that Joshua lived forty years with Moses before the invasion of Canaan; and after Moses' death was head over Israel for twenty-five years; which, since he lived to the age of one hundred and ten, would make him to have been forty-five years old at the time of the exodus (*e.g.*, $45 + 40 + 25 = 110$). This view is adopted by Ewald, Knobel, and Fürst, and is not very different from the first-mentioned, if we suppose Caleb to have used round numbers. Others (*e.g.*, Theoph., *Ad. Autol.*, iii., 24; Clem. Alex., *Strom.*, i., 21; Euseb., *Chron.*, i.) reckon twenty-seven years as

---

[1] Theodoret, C. a Lap., Keil, and most modern commentators think this was the length of the war.

the length of Joshua's government. Eupolemus (ap. Euseb., *Præp. Evang.*, ix., 30, x., 14) names thirty years. C. a Lap., on xxiv. 29, says that the two most generally supported views are those which assign to his government seventeen (or eighteen) or twenty-seven years.

The book may be divided into two parts. The first has reference to the conquest of the land, and contains : 1, The campaign against the south (i.—x.); 2, The campaign against the north (xi. 1—18); 3, The war against the Anakim (xi. 21-23); 4, A general summary of the conquest (xi. 23 to the end of xii.). The second describes the division of the land and the settlement of the tribes: 1, The territory assigned by Moses to the trans-Jordanic tribes, and Caleb's inheritance (xiii., xiv.); 2, The allotments of Judah, Ephraim, and Manasseh (xv.—xvii.); 3, The setting up of the tabernacle at Shiloh, and the distribution of territory among the remaining seven tribes (xviii., xix.); 4, The cities of refuge (xx.); 5, The cities of the priests and Levites (xxi.); 6, The dismissal of the trans-Jordanic tribes to their homes (xxii.); 7, The two last addresses of Joshua, renewal of the covenant, Joshua's and Eleazar's death.

CHAPTER I.

Vers. 1-9.—*Introduction to the Book.*

JOSHUA, before Moses' death, had been nominated as his successor (Numb. xxvii. 18, etc.), and had received a solemn charge from Jehovah; but now, Moses being dead, he is called to the active performance of the duties of his office. Jehovah renews to him His promises, and, as a condition of their fulfilment, requires of him a faithful observance of His law.

Ver. 1.—וַיְהִי, "*And it came to pass*": ו consec. (Ges., *Gr.*, § 49, 2), connecting this book with the close of Deuteronomy (see Dr. Pusey, *On Daniel*, p. 309, and note ‡ of Ges., *Gr.*, § 49, 2), but not so intimately as to indicate a sameness of authorship (cf. Ruth i. 1, where the "Vav" has the same power in reference to Judges, of which Ruth is an appendix). "*After the death of Moses*": *i.e.*, after the expiration of the thirty days' mourning for Moses (Deut. xxxiv. 8). "*The servant of the Lord*": *i.e.*, one commissioned by Jehovah and sent by Him to do His work. It was, therefore, Moses' regular official title (see Deut. xxxiv. 5; Josh. i. 13, 15, viii. 31, 33, ix. 24, xi. 15, xii. 6, xiii. 8, xiv. 7, xviii. 7, xxii. 4, 5), applied to Joshua also, after he had succeeded Moses

(Josh. xxiv. 29 with Judges ii. 8), a higher title than that of מְשָׁרֵת, borne by Samuel when a boy (1 Sam. ii. 11, iii. 1). Dean Perowne on Psalm xviii. (inscription of) remarks that the title עבד יהוה is never applied by the individual to himself, and in this respect, therefore, differs from the δοῦλος Θεοῦ (Χριστοῦ) of the New Test. (Phil. i. 1 ; Titus i. 1). "*The Lord spake unto Joshua*" : Either in a dream or vision, or through the intervention of the High Priest by means of the Urim and Thummim, or by a direct revelation to his mind; for it is not said that God *appeared* to him. The occasion being one of great importance, it is likely that the address was immediate and personal. "*Joshua*": A prince of the tribe of Ephraim, and originally named Hoshea, הוֹשֵׁעַ (Numb. xiii. 8), *i.e.*, *help*, to which Moses, on some occasion not mentioned, prefixed the name יָהּ, whence, by contraction, יְהוֹשֻׁעַ, "Jehovah-help" (Numb. xiii. 16), written יֵשׁוּעַ (Neh. viii. 17) ; Sept. Ἰησοῦς, so in Greek Test. (Acts. vii. 45 ; Heb. iv. 8) ; a type of the Messiah, Whose name Jesus, therefore, means a Divine Saviour (Matt. i. 21). בִּן־נוּן, the form "bin" for "ben" is rare (Ges., *Gram.*, § 96, 2), but always used when followed by the pr. n. "Nun" (Ges., *Lex.*). "*Moses' minister*" : The piel participle is here used as a noun in construc. (Ges., *Gr.*, § 135, 1, 2). The term is never equal to עֶבֶד, and is translated in the Sept. by ὑπουργὸς or λειτουργὸς (see here), or ὁ παρεστηκὼς (Exod. xxiv. 13, and cf. Deut. i. 38, where מְשָׁרֵת is interchanged with הָעֹמֵד לִפְנֵי, one who stands before another, waiting instructions), but never by δοῦλος. It might be rendered "assistant," and answer to our word adjutant or aide-de-camp. When a young man, Joshua filled this office, and continued in it up to the time of Moses' death. Having thus been long trained to obedience, and being intimately acquainted with the counsels of Moses, and eminent for his courage, skill, and fidelity (see Exod. xvii. 8, etc.; Numb. xiv. 6-14), he was better fitted than any other to be Moses' successor.[1] As the minister of Moses he was also a type of Christ, Who was "*made under the Law*" (Gal. iv. 4).

Ver. 2.—וְעַתָּה, "*And now*": Sept. νῦν οὖν (cf. A. Ver.). The adverb seems to be here not so much a particle of time, as of inference, as frequently the Greek νῦν. With the imperative it has an hortatory power (cf. Gen. xxxi. 13; Isa. xxx. 8; Micah iv. 14). "*This Jordan*": The pronoun is used δεικτικῶς, as the Jordan was within sight of Shittim, where the Israelites were encamped; הַיַּרְדֵּן, always with the art. in prose, prop. "the Descender;" from יָרַד, to descend (Ges., *Lex.*; Reland, *Pal.*, iii., 63), so called from its rapid descent. The Arabic name is now *Esh-Sheriah*, the watering-place, or *Sheriat el Khebir*, the great watering-place, to distinguish it from *Sheriat el Mandhur*, the Hieromax. Between the Sea of Galilee and the Dead Sea is its most rapid descent; but, though its course for that distance is

---

[1] In Eccles. xlvi. 1 he is called the successor of Moses in *prophecies* (cf. Joseph, *Antiq.*, iv., c. 7, 2, and Sherlock, *On Proph. Disc.*, vi., p. 128). Had he, however, been strictly a prophet, it is strange that he should have been directed to seek the Divine will through Eleazar, the priest (Numb. xxvii. 21). Most probably he was only qualified by Divine wisdom to be the leader and governor of Israel after the death of Moses.

only sixty miles, it is increased to two hundred[1] by its multiplied windings (Dean Stanley's *Sin. and Pal.*, pp. 283-4, note 2). It rises in Antilebanon, flows into the Dead Sea, and forms the eastern boundary of Canaan proper. "*Thou and all this people*": The Reubenites, Gadites, and half tribe of Manasseh, who had received their possessions on the east side of Jordan, being excepted, though under the conditions mentioned in vers. 12-15 (cf. Numb. xxxii.). "*Which I do give*": The Vulg. renders by "*quam dabo*," but the present נֹתֵן, "*am giving*," implies that the bestowal of the gift had already begun. אָנֹכִי is emphatic; and the fact that Canaan was thus God's own gift shows that the Israelites were not chargeable with the crime of unjustly invading it. בְּנֵי יִשְׂרָאֵל, at the end of the verse, is explanatory of the succeeding suff. הֶם (cf. Exod. ii. 6). "*She saw him, the child*": It may throughout this book be rendered *sons*, rather than *children*, of Israel, because, in a political sense, *males* were regarded as representatives of the whole nation. Note that in this verse, as in the preceding, there is a typical reference to Christ, Who brings all true believers into the heavenly Canaan, thus doing what the Law, of which Moses was the representative, could not do, owing to the weakness, *i.e.*, depravity, of man (see Rom. iii. 19, etc., vii. 4, viii. 3).

Ver. 3.—בְּכָל־מָקוֹם, a nom. absol. (*Gr.*, § 145, 2 ; cf. xiii. 6). "*On which the sole of your foot shall tread*":

---

[1] So Lieutenant Lynch (*Official Letter*, p. 265, *of Narrat.*), who published the first authentic account of this river, after actual survey; some, however, make the distance to be increased to only 113 miles.

The expression implies, as in xiv. 9, possession in its utmost entirety. "*I have given it*": The perfect denotes the certainty of the gift (*Gr.*, § 126, 4). In the last clause the reference is to Deut. xi. 24, where the same promise is given from God by Moses, nearly word for word as here and in the next verse. "*I spoke*": On the distinction between דִּבֶּר and אָמַר, see Ges., *Lex.*, under the latter verb.

Ver. 4.—The general statement, "*Every place that the sole*, etc." (ver. 3) is here explained by a delineation of the farthermost boundaries. "*From the wilderness*": *i.e.*, the Arabian desert, the southern boundary. "*This Lebanon*" (the white): The Sept. has Antilebanon, but both are parts of the same mountain, and formed the northern boundary;[1] 'this' indicates that the mountain was within sight of the Israelitish camp. "*Unto the great river*": The Euphrates (Heb. Perath) was so called κατ' ἐξοχήν (cf. Gen. xv. 18, Deut. i. 7); also simply הַנָּהָר (Gen. xxxi. 21; Exod. xxiii. 31; 2 Sam. x. 16, etc.); נָהָר always means a constantly-flowing stream, like the Euphrates or Nile, and is never used of fleeting brooks or torrents; rt. נָהַר, to flow. The Heb. Perath is derived by Ges. (*Lex.*) from "parath," an unused rt., meaning in Syr. and Chal. "to break;" but in Arab., "to be sweet;" Sept. Εὐφράτης; in Old Persian, Ufrâta, "the good and fertile stream" (Delitzsch); now "Frath." *The great sea*": *i.e.*, the Mediterranean, called "great" in contrast to the Dead Sea and Lake of Genesa-

---

[1] The Arabic poets say of this mountain, "He bears the Winter on his head, the Spring on his shoulders, in his bosom the Autumn, and Summer slumbers at his feet" (Volner, i., 243).

reth. הַשֶּׁמֶשׁ מְבוֹא, accusative of place (*Gr.*, § 118, 1), literally "at the entrance," *i.e.*, the setting, "of the sun" (cf. Deut. xi. 30 ; Psalm l. 1) ; hence the *West.* "*Your coast*": The Hebrew word גְּבוּל denotes properly the cord by which the limit of a field or region is marked out, rt. גָּבַל, to twist, or to wreathe, hence "a boundary." The intermediate statement "*all the land of the Chittites*" (see note on iii. 10) has occasion the difficulty. The Sept. omits the words, and the Arabic version must have read עַל for כֹּל, for it renders " *ultra terram Chittæorum.*" But probably the words were intended to mark out the limits of the land of Canaan strictly so called, the Chittites, as one of the principal nations of Canaan, being taken as a representative of the rest ; yet we need not with Keil regard the broad description of the land given in this verse as *rhetorical, i.e.*, as merely indicating, in a general way, certain well-known points within which the land to be given to the Israelites would lie. In the reign of Solomon the kingdom reached to Eloth and Eziongeber, on the Œlanitic gulf of the Red Sea (1 Kings ix. 26), and to Tiphsah on the river, *i.e.*, the Euphrates (1 Kings iv. 24), having for its western boundary the sea of the Philistines (Exod. xxiii. 31), *i.e.*, the Mediterranean, and for its southern boundary the Desert, *i.e.*, the wilderness of Shur and Paran.[1] God's promise, however, of this enlarged dominion was *conditional* (Deut. xi. 22-4), and it was His people's sinfulness which, after Solomon's death, deprived them of it ; yea, as regards the Canaan strictly so-called, we are

---

[1] Probably identical with the desert of Et Tih (*Grove*).

told that in consequence of their sloth and wickedness they could not, after Joshua's death, fully drive out their enemies (Judges ii. 20-1).

Ver. 5.—In this and the next verse the order of events in the book is briefly indicated, viz., 1, The Conquest ; 2, The Division of the Land. With the first clause cf. Deut. xi. 25, where the same promise is made to all the people. יִתְיַצֵּב לִפְנֵי, literally "*shall place himself before*," is varied to יִתְיַצֵּב בִּפְנֵי (Deut. vii. 24, xi. 25), "*all the days of thy life*": for after Joshua's death the Canaanites, owing to the supineness and sinfulness of the children of Israel, re-established themselves in many places, whence they had been driven out (Judges i. 27, etc). "*I will be with thee*," *i.e.*, I will assist thee (cf. v. 17). דָּךְ, in pause for דָּךְ (§ 103, 2 *a*). "*I will not fail thee*" (Auth. Vers.) : רָפָה, used intrans., means properly "to be let down or relaxed," and is applied to the letting of the hands hang down (Zeph. iii. 16) ; hence it may be used metaphorically of the mind, and be rendered here in Hiphil, "*I will not let thee despond.*" Better, however, "*I will not relax my hand from upholding thee*" (cf. Deut. iv. 31, xxxi. 6 ; 1 Chron. xxviii. 20 ; Heb. xiii. 5, οὐ μή σε ἀνῶ).

Ver. 6.—"*Be strong and of a good courage*" (Auth. Vers.). The first verb חָזַק means lit. "to hold fast," *i.q.*, אָפַף (Ges., *Lex.* [2], p. 72) ; hence "to strengthen," but more often "to be or to become strong," and like רָפָה (ver. 5), is used of the hands (Judges vii. 11 ; 2 Sam. xvi. 21 ; Isa. xxxv. 3). The second verb, אָמֵץ, "to be alert," and hence "to be firm," refers primarily to alertness of the feet (Ges., *Lex.*), or to strength of knees (see Isa. xxxv. 3). The two expressions together denote firmness and resolution of mind (cf. Deut. xxxi. 7, 23). The concluding words of the verse do not imply a *reason* for firmness and resolution, viz., that without such qualities Joshua could never put the people in possession of Canaan, but are rather a promise to inspire him with courage (cf. Deut. i. 38, xxxi. 7, 23). תַּנְחִיל, Hiph. imperf., "*thou shalt cause to inherit*," with an accus. of person and of thing (§ 139, 1 ; cf. Deut. i. 38), from נָחַל, primarily "to receive as a possession," "to possess," but spec. "to receive as an inheritance"; and in Hiph., "to cause to inherit," which latter, according to Keil and Fay, is the meaning here (cf. Auth. Vers.). אֶת־הָאָרֶץ: Some MSS. read אֶל for אֶת, whence Maurer thought that they must have read also תַּנְהִיל, *thou shalt lead*, but as נָהַל in Hiph. is applicable rather to the leading of a flock than of an army, it would not here be suitable, and doubtless אֶל is the emendation of a transcriber.

Ver. 7.—רַק, "*only*," here implies a condition. The two following verbs are repeated from the first clause of ver. 6, but are rendered more forcible by the addition of מְאֹד to the latter verb. "*Turn not from it to the right hand and to the left*" (cf. Deut. v. 29 [Heb. Bib.], xxviii. 14): סוּר here answers to נָטָה in Numb. xx. 17. The masc. suffix in מִמֶּנּוּ may refer either to the foregoing words, "which Moses . . . commanded thee," or to כְּבָר, understood before הַתּוֹרָה. The "Vav" before שְׂמֹאול is better rendered "*and*" than "*or*," which, however allowable in some passages (see Ges., *Lex.* [3], p. 235), here rather weakens the sense. The allusion is to travellers who avoid all paths deviating from the main road. לְמַעַן תַּשְׂכִּיל, "*That thou mayest act wisely*": Sept., ἵνα συνῇς ; Vulg., "ut intelligas" but Chald. and Auth. Vers., "*that thou mayest prosper.*" As wisdom in conducting affairs is connected with prosperity, the word שָׂכַל sometimes denotes "to prosper" (see, *e.g.*, Prov. xvii. 8), but here the primary meaning "to be wise" (in Hiph., "to make wise," "to act wisely") seems preferable, because in ver. 8 תַּשְׂכִּיל is distinguished from תַּצְלִיחַ. In the last clause, בְּכֹל is = בְּכָל־דְּרָכֶיךָ, "in all thy ways," *i.e.*, in all thy actions (cf. 1 Sam. xviii. 14).

Ver. 8.—הַזֶּה may refer to the Book of the Law as having been already mentioned, ver. 7; or, perhaps, indicates that Jehovah was addressing Joshua from the Holy of Holies in the Tabernacle, where the Pentateuch was deposited. The frequent allusions to the Book of the Law throughout this Book of Joshua are a testimony to the genuineness of the former. "*Shall not depart out of thy mouth*": *i.e.*, Joshua's judgments and orders were to be in accordance with the Divine Law; on all occasions he was to speak in accordance with it; and evidently he had a written copy of the Law, as the kings afterwards were required to have (Deut. xvii. 18, 19). "*And thou shalt meditate in it day and night*": *i.e.*, he was to be continually pondering it in his mind with a view to compliance with all its directions; Psalm i. 2 appears to allude to this verse. "*For then shalt thou make thy way prosperous, and then shalt thou act wisely*" (see note on ver. 7).

Ver. 9.—הֲלֹא is here equal to a strong positive assertion (§ 153, 2. Rem.). It is generally employed by those who wish to infuse into another courage and alacrity. The Sept. uses הִנֵּה in place of it, translating by ʼΙδού. תֵּחָת, Niph. imperf. 2 p. m. s. in pause, from חָתַת, to break or to be broken, used here metaphorically of a mind broken by terror. This and the preceding verb, with the negative אַל, give greater force to the foregoing positive injunction, "*Be strong*," etc. (cf. Deut. xxxi. 6, 8).

Let us remember that the same encouragements which were given to Joshua are also given to ourselves in our spiritual warfare. God will be with us (Heb. xiii. 6) to aid us in our conflicts, and to bring us ultimately into possession of the heavenly Canaan. Only we, like Joshua, must be very courageous, and firm in rendering an undeviating obedience to the revealed will of God (Matt. vii. 21; John xv. 14).

VERS. 10-18.—*Joshua's Command to the Overseers of the People, and his Appeal to the Reubenites, Gadites, and Half Tribe of Manasseh.*

שֹׁטְרִים, lit. *scribes*, from שָׁטַר, to write; Sept. γραμματεῖς; so the Syriac and Samaritan versions. The rendering "*overseers*" or "*superintendents*," though not etymologically correct, perhaps sufficiently expresses the meaning. They appear to have been Hebrews, who drew up the Hebrew genealogies, and were generally in attendance on the elders, captains, and judges. Joshua employed them on this occasion to convey his orders to the people, and to see them executed. On Egyptian monuments they are frequently represented giving in written accounts to their immediate superiors. Passages in which they are mentioned are Exod. v. 6; Numb. xi. 16; Deut.

xvi. 18, xxix. 10, xxxi. 28; Josh. viii. 33, xxiii. 2, xxiv. 1. After the death of David it would seem that they, as well as the judges (to whom the genealogical knowledge of the *shoterim* must have been highly useful in determining cases relating to property, etc.), were chosen from the Levites (1 Chron. xxiii. 4; 2 Chron. xix. 11, xxxiv. 13).

Ver. 11.—" *Pass through the midst of the camp* " (cf. Vulg., "transite per medium castrorum"). צֵדָה, properly "*flesh which is taken in hunting,*" from צוּד, to hunt; also any food, but especially " *provision for a journey* " (Gen. xlii. 25; Exod. xii. 39). The manna had not yet, as Keil asserts, ceased (see Josh. v. 12), but when Joshua issued this command, he doubtless knew that the manna would cease when the people had crossed the Jordan (Exod. xvi. 35), and because it would not keep fresh beyond the first day, and there may have been no time to collect and prepare it, he commanded other food to be gathered. Indeed, manna never formed the sole sustenance of the people (see Deut. ii. 6, 26-28); and the country of Sihon and Og, which they had lately conquered, would furnish them with the supplies they now needed. " *Within yet three days* " (cf. Gen. xl. 13), Sept. ἔτι τρεῖς ἡμέραι : A question has been raised whether the three days here mentioned are identical with those in iii. 2. Most commentators think so, and suppose that this chapter anticipates the regular course of events; in other words, that we have the order of *thought* rather than of *time*. The sacred writer, having a *religious*, rather than an historical, design in view, may have wished to put prominently forward God's faithfulness in the performance of His promise to give Canaan for an inheritance to His people, and, therefore, mentioned first God's command to Joshua, and Joshua's immediate proceedings thereupon, and then returned in the second chapter to state what had taken place before this command of God to Joshua, and immediately after the thirty days' mourning for Moses (Deut. xxxiv. 8), viz., the sending forth of the spies to Jericho, etc. On any other supposition it is difficult to understand how the collecting of provisions for the vast host of the Israelites, the sending forth and return of the spies, and the removal of the camp from Shittim to Jordan, could all have been accomplished within the period mentioned (i. 11). According, however, to the above view, the order of events was probably the following: On the third of the first month, Abib, or Nisan, the spies were sent out (ii. 1), on the sixth they return (ii. 23), on the seventh the camp is removed from Shittim to Jordan (iii. 1), and the command (i. 11) is issued, and on the tenth the river is crossed (iv. 19).

For other views, viz., those of Keil, Maurer, Knobel, etc., see note in Keil's *Comment.*, pp. 72—75, Clark, pub. 1857. לְרִשְׁתָּהּ, "*to possess*," or "*to take possession of*": Sept., κατασχεῖν; Vulg., "ad possidendam" (cf. 1 Kings xxi. 15). This is the primary meaning of יָרַשׁ, whence the secondary meaning "*to inherit*" (Gen. xxi. 10; see Gesen., *Lex.*).

Ver. 12.—The tribes here mentioned had received their inheritance on the east of Jordan (Numb. xxxii.)

Ver. 13.—The infin. absol. זָכוֹר is here used for the imperative (§ 131, 4 *b*). "*The word*," but also in

Hebrew "*the mandate*"; so in Esther i. 19 and in Exod. xxxiv. 28, Deut. iv. 13, x. 4, the "ten *words*" mean the "ten commandments." The quotation which follows is not literal, and bears a greater resemblance to Deut. iii. 18-20 than to Numb. xxxii. 20, 29. מֵנִיחַ, Hiph. part. (is), "*giving rest*," *i.e.*, by assigning to them settled habitations in place of a wandering life.

Ver. 14.—"*Your little ones*": From טָפַף, to trip along. The sing. טַף is often used, as here, collectively (§ 108, 1). The "*wives and little children*" were to dwell in fenced cities for protection from the inhabitants of the land (Numb. xxxii. 17). מִקְנֶה, "*cattle*": From קָנָה, to possess (cf. κτήνη from κτάομαι). Wealth in early times chiefly consisted in them.—בְּעֵבֶר הַיַּ, "*on the other side of the Jordan*," Sept. πέραν τοῦ Ἰορδάνου, is explained in ver. 15 by "toward the sun-rising." The Auth. Vers. here and in Numb. xxii. 1; Deut. i. 5, iii. 8, etc., renders it "*on this side Jordan*," but in Deut. iii. 20, 25, "*beyond Jordan*," as the Sept. and other versions generally. The phrase means lit., "*at the side, or passage, of Jordan*," and was usually applied to the district east of Jordan, and corresponded closely to the Greek name *Peræa*. Here, and often elsewhere, it is used quite irrespectively of the actual position of the speaker or writer. חֲמֻשִׁים is derived by Ges. from תָּמֵשׁ, nearly allied to the roots חָמַס and חָמֵץ, "to be eager or sharp;" hence "eager, or ready prepared, for fighting"; Aq. ἐνωπλισμένοι; Symm. καθωπλισμένοι; Vulg. *armati*. But perhaps a better rendering is "*arrayed*," Arab. *instructi, marshalled*, lit. with their loins girt (cf. Eph. vi. 14; 1 Peter i. 13), from הָמֵשׁ, *lumbus*, synonymous with חֲלוּצִים (Numb. xxxii. 32; Deut. iii. 18), from הַחֲלָצַיִם (only in the dual), "*the two loins*," Sept. εὔζωνοι. Ewald (*Gesch. des Volkes Israel*, ii., p. 54) would render it "*arrayed in five divisions*," from חָמֵשׁ, *five*, whence perhaps the strange rendering of the Sept., πέμπτῃ γενεᾷ (Exod. xiii. 18), but this rendering, says Keil (*Comment.*, A.D. 1857), assumes the reading הַחֲמִשִׁים to be correct, the evidence for which is less than that for חֲמֻשִׁים or חֲמוּשִׁים. לִפְנֵי, "*before*" (Auth. Ver.), Sept., Vat., πρότεροι τῶν ἀδελφῶν ὑμῶν, but Masius and Drusius "*in the presence of*," as the word means in Exod. vii. 10, which rendering seems less suitable here, for it was obviously fitting that these tribes, in return for the concessions made to them by Moses, should be exposed more than the others to the brunt of battle. כֹּל גִּבּוֹרֵי הַ׳, "*all the strong heroes*" (§ 108, 3, cf. vi. 2, viii. 3) : The expression is not found in the Pentateuch; in Deut. iii. 18 we have כָּל־בְּנֵי חַיִל. It is incredible that *all* the armed men from these tribes are here included. The number of fighting men in each of these tribes is given in Numb. xxvi. 7, 18, 34, and their aggregate number was 136,930 men, of twenty years old and upward, able to go out to war (Numb. xxvi. 2). כֹּל, therefore, is not to be taken here in its full sense. The real number which passed over is stated in iv. 13 as forty thousand.

Ver. 15.—"*Until the Lord have given . . . rest*" (cf. Deut. iii. 20, and see note on ver. 13. "*Then ye shall return*" (Auth. Ver.). ו begins the apodosis (§ 155, 1 *a*, 3rd par.) For the form יְרִשְׁתֶּם, see § 69, 3, *Rem.* 4, and cf. xxiii. 5; for יְרֻשָּׁה we have אֲחֻזָּה, in Josh. xxii. 4, 9. The words "*toward the sun-rising*" qualify the preceding "*on this side Jordan*," and deter-mine their sense, for the phrase is in itself ambiguous, being sometimes used of cis-Jordanic, sometimes of trans-Jordanic, territory (cf. Josh. ix. 1 with Numb. xxii. 1, xxxii. 32).

Ver. 16.—"*And they answered*," etc.: The "*they*" does not include *all* the tribes, but only the two tribes and a half whom Joshua had just been addressing, for such is the natural and obvious reference.

Ver. 17.—בְּכֹל אֲשֶׁר, "*in all respects as*": רַק, "*only*": here expressing with what follows not a condition but a wish.

Ver. 18.—יַמְרֶה, Hiph. imperf., "*shall rebel against.*" "*Thy commandment*" (cf., for this meaning of פִּי, Eccles. viii. 2). Usually, as Keil remarks, הִמְרָה, followed by this noun, is used of rebellion against God (see Deut. i. 26, 43, ix. 23; 1 Sam. xii. 14), but here of rebellion against a ruler. יוּמָת, Hoph. (in pause), "*shall be put to death*": So the Jewish law prescribed (Deut. xvii. 12). The words "*only be strong*," etc. (cf. ver. 6) further show the desire of these tribes to encourage Joshua in his undertaking, and their resolve to aid him and their brethren.

Several of the Christian Fathers saw in these two tribes and a half a type of true believers under the Old Testament dispensation. Reuben, Gad, and Manasseh were all elder sons, and the conduct of their descendants, as here recorded, shows remarkable faith in the promises of God and ready obedience to His will. But as these two and a half tribes had their inheritance assigned only to them by Moses, but were put into actual possession of it by Joshua, so the believers under the Old Testament dispensation inherited the promises not through the Law, but by faith in the Messiah (Heb. xi. 39, 40). See Origen, *Hom.* 3 and 16; Bede, *Qu. in Josh.*, c. 4; Theodoret, in *Josh. Qu.*, 16.

CHAPTER II.

VERS. 1-7.—*The Mission of the Spies to Jericho.*

Ver. 1.—וַיִּשְׁלַח: Though not grammatically a pluperfect, yet is so as to sense, since it refers to what had occurred prior to i. 11 (see note). "*Shittim*" (lit., the acacias), mentioned in connection with the history of Balaam (Numb. xxv. 1; Micah vi. 5). It was not far from Jordan (sixty furlongs, says Josephus), and was the last place in which the Israelites encamped in the plains of Moab. It is called אָבֵל הַשִּׁטִּים, "*the acacia meadow*" (Numb. xxxiii. 49), and Josephus is supposed to refer to it under the name *Abila* (*Abel*, " meadow," or " moist place "), *Antiq.*, iv. 8, 1, v. 1, 1; *Bel. Jud.* iv. 7, 6. אֲנָשִׁים is rendered by the Sept. νεανίσκους, under the idea that they were probably young and active men, which, though not implied here in the Hebrew word, accords with vi. 23. מְרַגְּלִים, Piel part. from רָגַל, to go, to tread, and hence "to explore" (cf. Gen. xlii. 9; 1 Sam. xxvi. 4; 2 Sam. xv. 10). חֶרֶשׁ, lit. "*silence*," but here used as an adverb, "*secretly*" (§ 100, 2 *b*); the conjunctive accent shows that it is to be construed with לֵאמֹר, *i.e.*, Joshua gave these spies their directions in secret, fearing, perhaps, that the people, if they knew of their mission, would be alarmed, as in the time of Moses

(Numb. xiv. 1), by the tidings they might bring. רְאוּ, "*view ye*": *i.e.*, explore ye (cf. Gen. xlii. 9). "*Even Jericho*" (Auth. Ver.) : The וֹ has perhaps the force of *especially* (Ges., *Lex.*, (*c*), p. 234). יְרִיחוֹ, always so written in this book, but in the Pentateuch יְרֵחוֹ; once יְרִיהֹה (1 Kings xvi. 34). The word means, according to some, "a place of fragrance," from רוּחַ, to breathe ; הֵרִיחַ, to smell ; being celebrated for its palms and balsam (Pliny, *Hist. Nat.*, lib. xii., cap. 25) ; but the older Commentators and Gesenius derive it in the form יָרֵחַ from יָרֵחַ, the moon, which was the principal deity there worshipped [1] (cf. Heliopolis, city of the sun). It was situated in a plain, and was a key to the entrance of Canaan on the southeast side (Joseph., *De Bel. Jud.*, iv., cap. 8, § 2, 3 ; Robinson's *Pales.*, ii., p. 523, etc., and 544, etc.) Every trace of the ancient town has disappeared, but the present dirty and miserable village, called *Eriha*, or *Riha*, by the Wady Kelt, is supposed to be near the site. אִשָּׁה זוֹנָה, "*a woman, a harlot*" : Written without אִשָּׁה in Gen. xxxviii. 15 ; Deut. xxiii. 19 ; but with it, here and in Judges xi. 1 ; Lev. xxi. 7 ; Sept. γυναικὸς πόρνης ; so the Syriac and Arabic ; and in Greek Testament, ἡ πόρνη (Heb. xi. 31 ; James ii. 25) ; but an "*innkeeper*," πανδοκεύτρια (S. Chrysos., *Epis. to Cor.*; the Targum ; Joseph., *Antiq.*, v., 1, 2 ; and some of the Rabbis and modern Commentators), as though the word was derived from זוּן, to feed or to nourish, a rendering not accordant with the use of the word elsewhere in Scripture, and probably designed to avoid the obloquy implied in

---

[1] Or rather, Ashtoreth, of whom the moon was a symbol, was there worshipped.

the epithet זֹנָה. Women, however, of that class may have kept houses of entertainment, as anciently the women in Egypt (see Herodotus, ii. 35). "*Rachabh*": Meaning "to be wide or spacious" (cf. the name of Japheth, Gen. ix. 27). She is evidently the same as the Rachabh mentioned as the wife of Salmon in the genealogy of the Messiah (Matt. i. 5), and Josephus (*Antiq.*, v., 1) calls her ἡ Ῥαχάβη. The Fathers regarded her as a type of the Christian Church (Clemens, *Rom. ad. Cor.*, § 12; Justin Martyr, c. *Tryphon.*, § 112; Irenæus, iv. 37; Origen, *Hom.*, 3. Probably she was at this time a believer, though she had not openly renounced heathenism; and the spies may have been directed to her house by Joshua, who, having formerly visited the country as a spy (Numb. xiii. 16), may have known something of her faith; at all events, the convenient situation of her house on the town wall, and perhaps the fact that she may have kept a lodging for travellers, easily accounts for their coming thither. "*And they lay down there*": With the intention of sleeping, as they had arrived at the beginning of the night.

Ver. 2.—"*And it was told the king of Jericho*": Josephus (*Antiq.*, v., 1, 2) says the news was brought to the king while at supper. If Rachabh kept a house for travellers, some one lodging there may have informed the king, or, since it was known that the Hebrews were on the other side of Jordan watchers may have been set at the gates to report any suspicious persons who entered in. "*To-night*" (Auth. Ver.), lit. "*the night.*" It appears from ver. 5 that it was the beginning of the night, just before the gates were shut. לַחְפֹּר, properly "to dig," as a well or pit, and hence " to explore " (cf. Deut. i. 22.) אֶת־הָאָרֶץ, " *the land.*"

Ver. 3.—" *Bring forth*": The respect which is paid in the East to women's apartments explains why the king's messengers did not search the house. " *Who have come to thee* ": These words are omitted in the Sept. and Syr., perhaps to avoid tautology.

Ver. 4.—" *And the woman took . . . and hid them* ": לָקַח here means, as in Esther ii. 8, 16, to bring or to conduct. Probably Rachabh did this before the king's messengers arrived, for to have kept them waiting at the door would have excited suspicion. But this is no reason for rendering the verbs as pluperfects. " The historian," says Keil, " has merely arranged the particular occurrences in such a manner that he describes first what was done by the king, and then all that was done by the woman. The king sent to Rachabh, and commanded her to deliver up the spies, but she took them and concealed them, and then said to the servants of the king, and so on." If Rachabh suspected that information had been sent, or might be sent, to the king, she would naturally at once hide the spies. The sing. suffix in תִּצְפְּנוֹ is distributive, meaning each of them (cf. Deut. xxi. 10; Jer. xxxi. 15). כֵּן, *so,* or *it is true.* הָאֲנָשִׁים, " *the men* ": *i.e.,* those referred to. מֵאַיִן, " *whence* ": Everywhere else this word is used as an interrogative. True that in Psalm cxxi. 1 the Auth. Vers. renders it as a relative, "*whence* cometh my help," but there also the interrogative sense is better.

Ver. 5.—לִסְגּוֹר . . . וַיְהִי, " *and when the gate was about to be shut* " (see for this construction § 132, 3;

Rem., I, 2): Less accurately the Sept. renders by ἐκλείετο, "was being closed"; for, had the closing actually begun, the spies in going out could scarcely have escaped observation. בַּחֹשֶׁךְ, "*when it was dark*" (Auth. Vers.), not "when it grew dusk" (De Wette): In the East there is very little twilight, and the Hebrew word for it, viz., נֶשֶׁף, sometimes means night (see Isa. v. 11, xxi. 4, lix. 10). "*Pursue ye quickly*": The infinitive מַהֵר is here used as an adverb. More often the finite verb which governs the infinitive is so used (see Exod. ii. 18, and § 142, 4, Rem. i.).

The deceit of Rachabh cannot be justified on the ground of expediency, or of the goodness of her motives. All falsehood must be sin; but, being in her case a sin of weakness and ignorance, it was doubtless pardoned by reason of her faith and devotion to the cause of God and His people.

Ver. 6.—Her mode of concealing the spies is here described. The roof was *flat* (cf. 2 Sam. xi. 2; Matt. x. 27; Acts x. 9). The word used throughout the Sept. for גָּג is δῶμα, which is also used in Luke v. 19, xii. 3, xviii. 31; Acts x. 9. By the law it was required that, for safety's sake, the roof should have a battlement (Deut. xxii. 8). בְּפִשְׁתֵּי הָעֵץ, lit. "*in the flaxes of wood,*" *i.e.*, "*in the stalks of flax*": Sept. ἐν τῇ λινοκαλάμῃ, "the flax which is not yet removed from its stalk"; Vulg., *stipulâ lini ;* less fitly, "*tree-flax,*" or "*pods of cotton*" (Arab. Vers.).[1] The flax (פִּשְׁתָּה or פִּשְׁתֶּה) was ripe at that season (the month Nisan) in Egypt (Exod. ix. 31), the climate

---

[1] So Gesenius (*Lex.*, p. 595), but the season was early spring, and cotton is not gathered till autumn; it is improbable also that cotton was cultivated in Palestine at so early a period.

of which is nearly similar to that of Canaan; and in both countries it grows more than three feet in height, with a stalk as thick as a cane. Rachabh was probably a manufacturer of linen. הָעֲרֻכוֹת לָהּ, "*which were set in order for her upon the roof*": viz., for the purpose of being dried in the sun;[1] לָהּ is here a *dativus commodi*.

Ver. 7.—"*And the men*": *i.e.*, those sent by the king of Jericho. דֶּרֶךְ הַיַּ, "*the way of the Jordan*": Accus. denoting the direction taken (§ 118). עַל הַפְּ: The prep. עַל does not here denote "*beside*" or "*near to*," nor עַד, "*as far as*," nor אֶל־, "*towards;*" but retains its primitive meaning "*over*" (Keil). The words should be connected with the foregoing, *e.g.*, "*The way of the Jordan over the fords*," *i.e.*, which led over the fords; Vulg., "per viam quæ ducit ad vadum Jordanis." The fords meant were opposite Jericho, and are called in Judges iii. 28 "*the fords of Jordan towards Moab.*" It is, however, improbable that the pursuers crossed the fords, for the Israelitish camp was in the vicinity. סָגָרוּ, "*they shut*": The indeterminate third person (§ 137, 3). אַחֲרֵי כַּאֲשֶׁר is an unusual form for אַחֲרֵי־אֲשֶׁר (§ 155, 2 *c*; cf. אַחֲרֵי־כֵן אֲשֶׁר, Gen. vi. 4). The gates were shut in case the spies should be yet in the town, but the narrative which follows shows how useless was such a precaution.

VERS. 8-21.—*Rachabh helps the Spies to escape, having first stipulated with them for the Security of Herself and Family.*

Ver. 8.—טֶרֶם, "*not yet*": Lit. "a cutting off," fol-

---

[1] This custom is alluded to by Josephus, *Ant.*, v., 1, § 2.

lowed by an imperfect coming within the sphere of the past, "*and they had not yet laid down*" (§ 127, 4, *a*; and Ges., *Lex.* [3], p. 325): It seems that they intended to sleep upon the roof, a common practice in the East.

Ver. 9.—The כִּי, which thrice follows יָדַעְתִּי in this verse, means "*that*" = *quod*, as often after verbs of knowing (§ 155, 1, *c*, 3rd par.). "*Jehovah*": This covenant-name of the God of Israel she may have heard of by report, and may here use without a knowledge of its import: see ver. 11, where she only speaks of Jehovah as a God (Elohim) "*in heaven above and upon the earth beneath.*" "*Your terror*": *i.e.*, that of which you are the object, or which you inspire (§ 121, 5). נָמֹגוּ, "*have melted away*": Niph. of מוּג, to flow, to flow down, a metaphor taken from the melting of ice or snow, or of wax before the fire. Like expressions to those in this verse are found in Exod. xv. 15, 16, where we have a prophecy of which we here see the fulfilment. מִפְּנֵיכֶם, "*because of you*" (Auth. Vers.): or "*from the face of you*," *i.e.*, "*before you*" (cf. ver. 10, where the Sept. has ἀπὸ προσώπου ὑμῶν).

Ver. 10.—כִּי, "*for*": This verse gives the reason why Rachabh knew that Jehovah had given the land of Canaan to the Israelites, viz., the great miracles which He had wrought for them, two of the most striking of which are here mentioned. אֶת אֲשֶׁר (see § 155, 1, *c*, 3rd par.) יַם־סוּף, lit., "the sea of weeds," Coptic, Schari-sea (weedy, or reedy sea), *i.e.*, the Arabian Gulf, which abounds in seaweed; always in the Sept. ἡ ἐρυθρὰ θάλασσα, except in Judges xi. 16, where סוּף is rendered Σίφ. "*Sichôn*," lit., "a sweeping away," *i.e.*, a leader carrying everything before him, rt. בּוּס, *i.q.*, כָּהָה, to wipe away. "*Ogh*": Hebrew עוֹג, perhaps contracted from עָנָג, עָנָק, *i.e.*, in stature, long-necked, gigantic (Ges., *Lex.*). Hercules, thought to be the same with Joshua, is by Lucian (*In Hercule*) called Ogmius, from slaying Og, as is supposed (Dickenson, *Delph. Phœnic.*, c. 4, p. 44). הֶחֱרַמְתֶּם, "*ye devoted*," or, "*ye put under a ban*," from חָרַם, properly, "to shut up" (cf. חֵרֶם, a net), hence "to prohibit to common use," "to consecrate;" and in Hiphil, "to dedicate to God in an irredeemable manner," whence "to extirpate," "to destroy utterly" (cf. Auth. Vers.), because the unholy object so dedicated was abominable to God, and could not be used in His service (Lev. xxvii. 29; Deut. vii. 23, etc.). For the events alluded to in this verse, see Exod. xiv. 15, etc.; Numb. xxi. 24-35; Deut. ii. 31, iii. 10.

Ver. 11.—יִמַּס, Niph. imperfect from מָסַס, to melt, to flow down (see on מוּג, ver. 9, and cf. v. 1, vii. 5). וְלֹא־קָמָה, "*and there remained not*": קוּם, "to stand," and hence "to remain." רוּחַ, "*courage*" (Auth. Vers.); or, more simply, "*breath*," from רוּחַ, to breathe. In 1 Kings x. 5, nearly the same expression is used of great astonishment.

In her confession at the end of the verse Rachabh seems to contrast the supremacy of Jehovah with that of the heathen deities, who were supposed to preside over particular localities only; but she was not yet so enlightened as to acknowledge Him the one only true God (cf. Deut. iv. 39). Note, however, the different effect produced upon her and her countrymen by the reports they had heard: in her they wrought faith; in them terror and astonishment (cf. Luke ii. 34; 2 Cor. ii. 16).

Ver. 12.—כִּי is either here causal, and = *because* ["since" (Auth. Vers.)], or, is introductory to the oath and = *that*, e.g., "*swear unto me . . . that I have shown you kindness, and ye will also show kindness*" (i.e., according to the English idiom, "that as I have shown kindness to you, so you will also show kindness," etc.), *and will give me a token of truth, and will save alive . . . and will deliver,*" etc. Here all the verbs which follow הִשְׁבְּעוּ are subordinate to it, and dependent upon כִּי, though the three last may be rendered as imperatives [e.g., "*and give,*" "*and save alive,*" etc.], and, therefore, as co-ordinate with הִשְׁבְּעוּ, and independent of the כִּי. אוֹת אֱמֶת, "*a sign* (or token) *of truth*": Keil identifies this token with the oath itself, which the spies were required to take, but thus there seems to have been no occasion for mentioning it separately, as it would have been implied in the words, "Swear unto me by the Lord." Rather, אוֹת means here, as often in Scripture, something outward and visible (cf. 2 Kings xx. 8, 9 ; Isa. vii. 11, 14, xxxviii. 7, 22 ; and σημεῖον in Luke ii. 12 ; 2 Thess. iii. 17), and was the token referred to in ver. 18. True that the spies were let down from the window by Rachabh *before* she had received this token, but this may be easily accounted for on the supposition that after their oath (ver. 14) she was satisfied, and at once lowered them, whereupon they gave her the outward pledge which assured safety to herself and relatives.

Ver. 13.—This verse explains more fully the expression "my father's house" in ver. 12, and indicates that she had neither husband nor children. וְהִחֲיִתֶם, "*and* (that) *ye will save alive*" (cf. note on ver. 12).

The usual pointing (ְ ֲ) is changed to the shorter (ְ ִ)
(§ 27, Rem. 5), after ו consec. בָּל־אֲשֶׁר לָהֶם: Not their
material property, but the children and other relatives
of her brothers and sisters (see vi. 23, 25). נַפְשֹׁתֵינוּ:
The plural suffix shows that, though in the previous
part of the verse she speaks of her relatives only, she
included herself among them. Yet her *unselfishness*,
which is one of the signs of a true conversion, beauti-
fully appears in this part of the narrative.

Ver. 14.—לָמוּת ... נַפְשֵׁנוּ, lit., "*our life instead of
you to die*": A form of oath by which they invoked
the vengeance of Jehovah on themselves if they proved
false to their word. A more frequent form is "*as thy
soul liveth*" (1 Sam. i. 26, xvii. 55, xx. 3; 2 Kings
ii. 24). The pl. m. suffix in תַּחְתֵּיכֶם refers to Rachabh
and her father's house. To this oath is annexed the
condition, "*if ye tell not* (lit., if ye bring not to light)
this our business." וְהָיָה, "*and it shall be*" (§ 126, 6,
Rem. 2), בְּתֵת יְהוָה, "*when Jehovah shall give*" (§ 132, 2).
The infinitive here expresses future time. וְעָשִׂינוּ: The
ו equals *then*, and introduces the apodosis. חֶסֶד וֶאֱמֶת,
"*mercy and truth*": Not an hendiadys for "sincere
kindness," which rendering weakens the sense, but
kindness together with fidelity in the performance of
their promise.

Ver. 15.—בַּחֶבֶל, the article in the prep. may refer,
says Lyra, to a rope by which Rachabh had before
been wont to draw up or let down those who visited
her. בְּעַד, *through* (Auth. Vers.): This prep., according
to Ges. (*Lex.*), is derived from an obsolete verb בָּעַד,
"to be without" (opposed to "to be within"), "to be
near or beside." Often it may be rendered "*behind*,"
as in Gen. xxvi. 8; Judges iv. 23; and so perhaps

here, as implying that Rachabh stood behind the window (הַחַלּוֹן) whilst lowering the spies. Prof. Lee says (*Heb. Lex.*) that the cognate word in Arabic means "after" or "behind." Cf. the account of the escape of David (1 Sam. xix. 12), and of St. Paul [2 Cor. xi. 33, where the words διὰ θυρίδος (through a little door or aperture) ἐχαλάσθην, are similar to the Sept. Vers. here, viz., κατεχάλασεν αὐτοὺς διὰ τῆς θυρίδος]. St. James (ii. 25) alludes to this window or aperture, when he speaks of Rachabh as "having thrust forth (ἐκβαλοῦσα) the spies ἑτέρᾳ ὁδῷ, "*by another way*," *i.e.*, other than that by which they had come. בְּקִיר הַחוֹמָה, "*on the side of the wall*": קִיר here answers to the Latin *paries*, Greek τοῖχος, but חוֹמָה to *murus* and τεῖχος. In Exod. xxx. 3, קִירֹת is rendered "*sides*" by English version. The city wall appears to have formed the back wall of Rachabh's house. הִיא יוֹשָׁבֶת, "*she was dwelling*." The opinion of Masius and others that this verse has been transposed, and ought to follow verse 20, is not reconcilable with the use of the perfect "*thou didst let us down*" (ver. 18), which shows that the spies had been let down before the conversation recorded in vers. 16-20.

Vers. 16.—הָהָרָה, "*to the mountains*": The sing. הַר is here used coll. Jericho was surrounded by mountains on the north, south, and west; those here referred to were probably situated on the northern side, and were the jagged range of the white limestone mountains of Judæa, afterwards called *Quarantania* (Arabic, *Kuruntul*), from the belief that they were the scene of our Lord's forty days' temptation; they rise from 1,200 to 1,500 feet above the sea, and abound in caves (Robinson, ii., p. 289 ; Dean Stanley, *Syria and Palestine*, p. 307-8). וְנַחְבֵּתֶם, "*and hide yourselves*" : Niph. perf. with ו consec. of the imper., from חָבָה, *i.q.*, to hide ; (־) for (׃) before the guttural ח (§ 22, 2, *a*).

Ver. 17.—"*We (are) free from this thy oath which thou hast made us to swear*" [supply, "unless thou observest the following conditions] ; נָקָה (in the passive) "to be cleansed or freed from pollution," hence "to be accounted innocent or guiltless ; " here, therefore, נְקִיִּם followed by מִן means pure or free from the guilt of having violated our oath (cf. ver. 19 ; Gen. xxiv. 8, 41 ; Numb. xxxii. 22). זֶה, with a fem. noun is an anomaly, explained by the fact that זֶה is often used without regard to gender (Ewald, *Lhrb.*, § 183, *a*). הִשְׁבַּעְתָּנוּ : The more usual form of the 2nd pers. sing. f. with suffix would be הִשְׁבַּעְתִּינוּ, or, without י הִשְׁבַּעְתֵּנוּ (cf. Jer. xv. 10 ; Cant. iv. 9 ; Exod. ii. 10) ; but the masc. form is here used (§ 59, 4, with Parad. C., p. 280-1), or the suffix נוּ ִ is joined to the fem. form, הִשְׁבַּעְתְּ (Lee's *Heb. Gr.*, Art. 209, 8).

Ver. 18.—בָּאָרֶץ . . . הִנֵּה, lit. "*Behold! we coming into this land,*" *i.e.*, when we shall have entered into this land : The apodosis follows in the next clause. הִנֵּה . . . אֶת־תִּקְוַת, "*the line of this crimson thread,*" *i.e.*, this line spun out of crimson thread : The gender of the pronoun is here determined by the *nomen rectum* (Ewald, *Lehrb.*, § 307, *c*). תִּקְוָה is = קַו or קָוֶה, a line, rt. קָוָה, to twist ; in Psalm xix. 5, according to Ges. and Simonis, "the string of a harp," whence the Sept. φθόγγος, but more usually "a measuring line." Here, probably, not identical with the cord or rope by which Rachabh had lowered the spies, for which a different term (חֶבֶל)

is employed. So J. D. Michaelis, Schulz, Maurer, and Keil (*Comment.*, 1857). The spies may have given this line to Rachabh by fastening it to the rope by which they had been lowered, which she then drew up to the window where she was standing. שָׁנִי equals תּוֹלַעַת שָׁנִי (Exod. xxv. 4), the cochineal or coccus ilicis, an insect from which this crimson colour is procured. אֲשֶׁר refers to the "window," not the "cord" (cf. Sept.). In הוֹרַדְתֵּנוּ, the (..) takes the place of (.) (§ 59, 4). The bright crimson colour of this rope would render it a very conspicuous object, but it was *more* than a pledge of the preservation of the life of Rachabh and her relatives. Christian expositors, from the days of the Apostles, have regarded it as a type of salvation by the blood of Christ. See, for the use of scarlet in rites of purification for sin, Levit. xiv. 4, 6, 51 ; Numb. xix. 6.

Ver. 19.—וְהָיָה (cf. note ver. 14). With the expression דָּמוֹ בְרֹאשׁוֹ, cf. דָּמָיו בּוֹ (Lev. xx. 9, 11-13, 16). The fuller form used here by Joshua occurs also in Ezek. xxxiii. 4.

Ver. 21.—כֵּן הוּא, "*so it is*," *i.e.*, so let it be. וַתְּשַׁלְּחֵם, "*and she dismissed them*": Not meaning, as some think, that she lowered them from the window, for that had been already done (see note ver. 12). "*And she bound*," etc.: Perhaps not immediately, but when the Israelites advanced against the city; for, though a crimson line would have been less conspicuous than a crimson cord, yet it might have excited suspicion, and, moreover, as a means of security was not at once necessary. The historian, says Keil, mentions the circumstance here for the purpose of bringing the subject to a close.

VERS. 22-24.—*Return of the Spies to Joshua.*

Ver. 22.—הָהָרָה, see on ver. 16.

Ver. 23.—וַיַּעַבְרוּ, "*and crossed over*," viz., the Jordan, as is evident from the context. כָּל־הַמֹּצְאוֹת אֹתָם, "*all that befell them.*" מָצָא, followed by an accus. of the person, often means "to overtake," or "to befall any one" (Ges., *Lex.*, 3, p. 499; cf. קָרָה, Gen. xlii. 29).

Ver. 24.—כִּי, "*truly*" (Auth. Vers.): But rather "*that*," *quod*, as often in quotations (§ 155, 1, *c*, *a*; cf. 1 Sam. x. 19; Ruth i. 10). וְגַם, "*and also*," rather than "*for even*" (Auth. Vers.): The words following are a quotation of those of Rachabh (ver. 9).

CHAPTER III.

VERS. 1-6.—*Preliminary Regulations for the Passage of the Jordan.*

Ver. 1.—This verse properly belongs to chap. ii. וַיַּשְׁכֵּם, the verb is used in Hiph. only, and is a denom. of שְׁכֶם, and means lit. "to put a load on the shoulder of beasts of burden," which among nomads was done very early in the morning. The word is sometimes used without בַּבֹּקֶר (*e.g.*, in Gen. xix. 2; Exod. xxxii. 6; Josh. viii. 14), sometimes with, as here and in Gen. xix. 2, 27, xx. 8, xxii. 3. Here perhaps בַּבֹּקֶר is used to signify that the removal of the camp took place in the twilight or early dawn. וַיִּסְעוּ, "*and they broke up their encampment*": נָסַע, to pull up the stakes of a tent. מֵהַשִּׁטִּים (see ii. 1). עַד־הַיַּ': The prep. can here mean only "*near to*," not "to the actual brink;" otherwise the distance of two thousand cubits between

the ark and the camp could not have been kept
(ver. 4). וַיָּלִ֫ינוּ, "*and they tarried*": Vulg., "morati
sunt," viz., for three days (ver. 2). לִין, properly, " to
pass the night," frequently means " to tarry " (cf.
Prov. xv. 31 ; Psalm xxv. 13, xlix. 13 ; Job
xli. 14).

Ver. 2.—יָמִים . . . מִקְצֵה, lit., "*from the end of three
days*," *i.e.*, after three days, or at the end of the third
day (see note on i. 11). הַשֹּׁטְרִים (see i. 10). בְּקֶרֶב הַמַּ׳,
"*through the midst of the camp*" (cf. i. 11).

Ver. 3.—בִּרְאֹתְכֶם : Some MSS. read כִּרְאֹתְכֶם. Of the
two particles בְּ prop. expresses indefinite time, "*when
ye see*," or, " *at the sight of ;* " כְּ definite time, " *whilst
ye see*" (Ewald, *Lehrb.*, § 221 and 327, *c.*) ; yet this
distinction is not always observed. "*Ark of the
covenant*": The symbol of the Divine Presence (Numb.
x. 33), called the ark of the covenant, because it
contained the Law, which was the covenant between
God and the people. "*The priests—the Levites*,"
(cf. viii. 33). Vulg., "sacerdotes Leviticæ stirpis ;"
the Sept., Chald., Syr., and several Hebrew MSS.
arbitrarily interpose ו ; but the word " Levites " is
evidently put in apposition to the word " Priests,"
probably to distinguish the priests of true Levitical
descent from the unlawful, non-Levitical priests, who
may at this time have sprung up. For the same
reason, perhaps, the like expression so often occurs in
the book of Deuteronomy, whereas in the earlier
books of the Pentateuch the priests and Levites are
generally mentioned apart. To bear the ark was
indeed one of the duties of the Levites, but that it
was sometimes undertaken by the priests is evident
not only from this passage, but from vi. 6 ; 2 Sam.

xv. 24; 1 Kings viii. 3. וְנָסַעְתֶּם, lit., "*then ye shall break up*" (cf. ver. 1).

Ver. 4.—אַךְ, *only*. רָחוֹק is generally used as an adjective, but here as a substantive, of the form כָּבוֹד, (*Parad.*, iii.), "a distance" (cf. the use of ἐσχάτου in a substantive sense, 1 Peter i. 20; Alford). The Kᵉthibh בֵּינוֹ, is probably more correct than the Qᵉri בֵּינָיו, the plural בֵּינֵי being almost exclusively restricted to those cases in which the suffix also has the plural sense (Ewald's *Lehrbuch*, § 266, *a*). "*About two thousand cubits*," which, according to rabbinical tradition, was the distance between the Tabernacle and the furthest point of the camp in the wilderness, and the prescribed distance for the suburbs of Levitical cities (Numb. xxxv. 5); afterwards called a Sabbath-day's journey (Acts i. 12). This, if we reckon the cubit at twenty-one inches, would be five furlongs and twenty feet, or a little more than five-eighths of a mile. This distance was to be observed not merely out of reverence for the ark, but that, as they came down the heights above the Jordan, they might see the direction they were to take, and how a way for them through the waters would be miraculously opened. מִתְּמוֹל שִׁלְשׁוֹם, lit., "*since yesterday and* (the third day, *i.e.*) *the day before yesterday*" (Ges., *Lex.*; cf. *Gr.*, § 155, 1, *a*). The form אֶתְמוֹל, which occurs in 1 Sam. iv. 7, x. 11, xiv. 21, xix. 7; 2 Sam. v. 2; Micah ii. 8; Isa. xxx. 33, is not found in the book of Joshua, nor in the Pentateuch (see Gen. xxxi. 2; Exod. iv. 10, v. 8; Deut. xix. 6; Josh. iv. 18, xx. 5). The expression refers not merely to time just past, but to any more remote period, as in Gen. xxxi. 2, 5; Ruth ii. 11, etc.; cf. χθίζα καὶ πρωΐζα, (*Il.*,

ii. 303), where the reference is to many years past. The "way" here meant is that miraculous passage which the ark would open for the Israelites.

Ver. 5.—"*Sanctify yourselves*," cf. Exod. xix. 10, though we may suppose that there, as here, the command relates to spiritual, as well as outward, purification, viz., to that preparation of the heart implied in a belief of God's promises, and a readiness to do His will. "*To-morrow*": Which, according to iv. 19, would be the tenth day of Abib or Nisan. נִפְלָאוֹת is used also in Exod. iii. 20, xxxiv. 10, concerning the miracles which God covenanted to perform for His people (cf. Psalm ix. 1).

Ver. 6.—The command issued by Joshua in this and the previous verse, and the prediction of the miracle (ver. 5) show that he had already received his instructions from God. The concluding sentence of the verse anticipates the course of events, for it is unlikely that the command of God to Joshua (vers. 7, 8), and Joshua's address to the people (vers. 9-13) were delivered after the priests had once set forward with the ark. It is a custom, says Keil, peculiar to Hebrew historical literature, to mark the close of each section by a sentence embracing the whole transaction, and forming a temporary conclusion. Hence the repetitions which occur in this and the next chapter.

VERS. 7, 8 (*Jehovah encourages Joshua*).—Ver. 7.—אָחֵל, "*I will begin*": Hiph. future of הָלַל. The passage of the Jordan was the first of that series of wonders which Jehovah was about to perform, in order to put His people into possession of the Promised Land. One great design of it is here intimated, viz., the establishment of the authority of Joshua (iv. 14), just as the miracle at the Red Sea established the authority of Moses. A second design is mentioned in ver. 10, and a third may be inferred from v. 1. אֲשֶׁר, "*in order that.*"

Ver. 8.—וְאַתָּה, emphatic. קְצֵה, lit., "*the extremity of,*" refers not to the opposite bank, but to that on the east side, at which the Israelites were; here equal to "*the border,*" or "*beginning of*" (cf. ver. 15 with Exod. xvi. 35). "*Ye shall stand still*": The object of their doing so was not to mark out to the Israelites the ford by which they were to pass, but to form a dam, as it were, against the force of the water, which was miraculously arrested in its course, and piled up in a heap. The command itself was a trial of the faith of the priests; and the safety of the ark, which they carried on their shoulders, may be regarded as typical of the safety of Christ's Church amid the dangers which surround it.

VERS. 9-13 (*Joshua encourages the People*).—Ver. 9.—גְּשׁוּ for גְּשׁוּ (cf. Ruth ii. 14; 1 Sam. xiv. 38), from נָגַשׁ, the accent retracted, because the following word is accented on the penultima (§ 29, 3, *b*); the half vowel (ְ) gives place to וּ (§ 29, 4, *b*).

Ver. 10.—A second design of the miracle (see on ver. 7). בְּזֹאת, "*by this,*" viz., the miracle announced in ver. 11. אֵל, from אוּל, to be strong, is used of the true God in two hundred and four passages of the Old Testament. חַי, "living," opposed to idols which are אֱלִילִים, "nothings" (Psalm xcvi. 5) and הֲבָלִים, "breaths" (Deut. xxxii. 21; cf. 1 Cor. viii. 4, x. 19). Render "a Living God" (cf. Psalm xlii. 2, lxxxiv. 2; Hosea i. 10; the only other places where the same form of expression occurs). This Living God is a personal Being, and, therefore, very different from "*Chance*," or the "*Order of Nature*." בְּקִרְבְּכֶם, "*in the midst of you*," *i.e.*, so as to protect and to powerfully aid you. "*And will certainly drive out*" (see for this force of the infin. absol., § 131, 3, *a*). הוֹרֵישׁ, "to cause a person to possess," and hence "to drive out another in order to make room for him." "*The Kenaanite*" (lit., a lowlander, rt. כָּנַע), used here coll. (§ 109, 1), though the Hebrews have also the form כְּנַעֲנִים. In its widest sense the term includes all the people of Canaan, but here is limited to the tribe which dwelt on the Mediterranean coast, and in the valley on the west of Jordan (cf. Numb. xiii. 29; Deut. xi. 30; Josh. v. 1). "*The Chittite*": A people who dwelt at first in the south of the Promised Land, chiefly in the mountainous parts, near to Hebron (Gen. xxiii. 3, 7), and perhaps extended as far as Beersheba (Gen. xxvi. 33, 34). In Numb. xiii. 29 they are mentioned as inhabiting the hill country. At a still later period they, or at least a portion of the tribe, seem to have been settled in the north of Palestine, on the borders of Syria (see Judges i. 26; 1 Kings x. 29; 2 Kings vii. 6). These have been supposed identical with the *Katti*, mentioned in the Assyrian inscriptions as dwelling in the valley of the Orontes (see Art. on Hittites in Dr. Smith's *Bib. Dict.*). In Josh. i. 4 they are put for all the nations of Canaan. "*The Chivvite*," from חָוָה = חָיָה, a family or tribe (Ges., *Lex.*); they dwelt near to Shechem (Gen. xxxiv. 2), and at Gibeon (Josh. ix. 7, xi. 19), also at the foot of Hermon and Antilibanus (Josh. xi. 3 ; Judges iii. 3). They appear to have been a peaceable people, addicted to the pursuits of trade and commerce. "*The Perizzite*": A people not mentioned in Gen. x. among the descendants of Canaan, and, therefore, perhaps not of Hamitic origin, though frequently enumerated among the nations inhabiting Canaan (see Gen. xiii. 7, xv. 20 ; Exod. iii. 8, 17). Gesenius and Hengstenberg suppose them to have had their name from their living originally in unwalled villages (פְּרָזוֹת, from פָּרַז, to separate), and addicting themselves to agriculture and the rearing of cattle ; but they also appear to have lived in mountains and woods (see xi. 3, xvii. 15). The *Girgashite* ["dwelling in a clayey soil" from גֶּרֶשׁ, clay (Ges., *Lex.*)], mentioned in Gen. x. 16, xv. 21 ; Deut. vii. 1; Josh. xxiv. 11 ; 1 Chron. i. 14; Neh. ix. 8; but nothing is known as to their exact position and character (Joseph., *Antiq*, i., 6, § 2). According to an Armenian tradition they migrated in the days of Joshua to Armenia. It would seem from Josh. xxiv. 11 that they were on the west of Jordan. The *Emorite* (Gen. x. 16) : Mountaineers or highlanders, from אֱמֹר, elevation (Simonis and Gesen.), for thus they are frequently described as dwelling in the mountains (Numb. xiii. 29 ; Deut. i. 20, 44 ; Josh. x. 6, xi. 3). They were the most powerful of all the nations of Canaan, and first inhabited the mountainous region afterwards occupied by the tribe of Judah, where they were subject to five kings (Gen. xiv. 7, 13) ; and thence many of them passed over Jordan, made war on the Ammonites and Moabites, and seized on Heshbon and Bashan, and all the country between the rivers Jabbok and Arnon, which lands Moses wrested from them, and gave to the tribes of Reuben and Gad, and to the half-tribe of Manasseh (Numb. xxi. 26-29 with Deut. xxix. 7, 8). The prophet Amos (ii. 9) speaks of their gigantic stature and strength. Frequently their name is used to denote the Canaanites universally (Gen. xv. 16, xlviii. 22; Josh. xxiv. 18; Judges vi. 10, etc.). *The Y^ebhûsite* (Gen. x, 16): A small mountain tribe, whose principal city was Y^ebhûs, (lit., "a place trodden down," as a threshing floor," rt. בוס, to tread with the feet; or meaning in Canaanitish "the waterless" hill), afterwards Jerusalem, from the fortress or citadel of which they could not be expelled till the time of David (2 Sam. v. 6). With a slight variation in the order, the same list of seven races is given in Deut. vii. 1 (see also Josh. ix. 1, xi. 3, xxiv. 11). The remnants of five of them are mentioned in 1 Kings ix. 21 as forced to labour for Solomon.

Ver. 11.—"*The ark of the covenant of the Lord of the whole earth*": So the Sept., Vulg., Syr., and Arab., but since in the Hebrew there is a great distinctive accent over הַבְּרִית, Masius takes אֲדוֹן as a noun in apposition to the foregoing "ark of the covenant;" it seems, however, inappropriate to speak of the ark, though a symbol of the Divine Presence, as "The Lord of the whole earth." Others, as Kimchi, repeat אֲדוֹן before אֲדוֹן, e.g., "the ark of the covenant, the ark of the Lord," etc.; but Keil rightly remarks that the words are all dependent on one another, but the first two are drawn more closely together, so as to express a single idea, and are specially defined by the article, whilst the connexion between the second member of the constructive state (אֲדוֹן כָּל־הָאָרֶץ) and the first is slackened in consequence, which the punctators indicated by the zaqeph-qaton between the two members. The title here given to God, viz., "The Lord of the whole earth," occurs elsewhere five times only in the Old Testament, viz., in v. 13; Micah iv. 3; Zech. iv. 14, vi. 5. It was well suited to encourage the Israelites when about to enter on the conquest of Canaan. בַּיַּרְדֵּן, "*into* (Auth. Vers.), not *through* (as Vulg.) *the Jordan*": For the ark did not go before the Israelites from one bank of the Jordan to the other, but remained stationary in the river (see vers. 8, 15).

Ver. 12.—Though the command in this verse appears again in iv. 2, there is no reason to suppose (as Meyer) that it has been here inserted by the mistake of some ancient copyist, or that the author anticipated the order of events. Joshua gave the command doubtless by God's direction, for the next verse shows that he was divinely inspired. עַתָּה is emphatic, denoting the time when the election was to take place, viz., before the crossing began, that the twelve men, as representatives of the people, might be eyewitnesses of the miracle, and, having taken their station near Joshua and the bearers of the ark of the covenant, might be at hand to execute the orders afterwards given them (iv. 3). So Keil. קְחוּ, "*take ye*," *i.e.*, "choose ye," imper. of לָקַח. "*Twelve men out of the tribes of Israel*": In all matters which concerned the entire nation we find that all the tribes were represented (cf. viii. 33; Numb xiii. 2; I Kings xviii. 31). The word שֵׁבֶט, here used for tribe, means literally a *rod* or *sceptre ;* it is employed in the historical portions of this book to denote a tribe in its political or corporate sense, as being under one sceptre, and is thus distinguished from מַטֶּה, a term used in the geographical chapters of the book, and denoting a tribe, as genealogically descended from one stem or root. The different meaning, therefore, of these words furnishes no ground for the supposition of some that the history was compiled from the narratives of two different authors.

Ver. 13.—הַמַּיִם וגו׳ are put in apposition to מֵי הַיַּרְדֵּן. Render "*the waters of Jordan shall be cut off, viz., the waters which come down from above, and they shall stand in one heap*" (or, "as one heap"). So the Chald., Arab., and Luther, though the two latter for perspicuity omit the words מֵי הַיּ׳. Less fitly the Sept. and Vulg. regard המים הי׳ כלמ׳ as a nom. absol., and ו before יַעַמְדוּ as a sign of the apodosis or subordinate clause; *e.g.*, "*as to the waters which come down from above, they shall stand*," etc. "*Shall be cut off,*" *i.e.*, so as no longer to flow down from above. נֵד אֶחָד: Accus. (§ 118), defining the shape the waters assumed. Gesenius renders "like one heap" (*Lex.*); the expression is evidently poetic, and taken from Exod. xv. 8 (cf. Psalm xxxiii. 7, lxxviii. 13), where it is used of the waves of the sea.

VERS. 14-17.—*Commencement of the Passage.*

The apodosis to vers. 14, 15 begins at ver. 16. In the second hemistich of ver. 14 either the substantive verb should be understood before the participle, *e.g.*, "*and the priests* (were) *carrying*," etc., or בִּנְסֹעַ should be repeated, *e.g.*, "*and when the priests set out carrying*," etc. On the construction נֹשְׂאֵי ... הַבְּרִית, see § 110, 2, *c*. Some, as Prof. Lee (*Heb. Gr.*, Art. 221, 6), suppose an ellipsis of אֲרוֹן before הַבְּרִית, "*the bearers of the ark, the ark of the covenant*" (cf. Exod. xxxviii. 21).

Ver. 15.—In the second clause the construction is changed from the infinitive to the finite verb (נִמְבְּלוּ), as frequently in Hebrew (§ 132, Rem. 2 ; cf. iv. 18, x. 20). The meaning of the last clause is correctly given by Auth. Vers., "*for the Jordan overfloweth*[1] *all its banks.*" עַל means "*over*,"[2] not "against," or "up to," implying merely (according to the rendering of the Sept. and Vulg.)³ that the Jordan ran with full banks, or was brimful. "There are, as it were, two banks to the Jordan. The first is that of this river in its natural state, the second is that of its overflowings" (Calmet's *Dict.*) So Kitto : "On leaving the Lake of Gennesareth the river enters a very broad valley or Ghor, within which valley there is a lower one, and within that, in some parts, another still lower, through which the river flows ; the inner valley is about half a mile wide, and is generally green and beautiful, covered with trees and bushes, whereas the upper or large valley is for the most part sandy or barren. In the season of flood, in April and early in May, the river is full, and sometimes *overflows* its lower banks, to which fact there are several allusions in Scripture (Josh. iii. 15 ; 1 Chron. xii. 15 ; Jer. xii. 5, xlix. 19, l. 44)." (*Encyclop. of Bib. Lit.*) כָּל־יְמֵי קָצִיר, "*all the days of harvest*" (accus. of time, § 118, 2) : Barley-harvest

---

[1] Or literally, "*was filled over*" (Keil); cf. Ges., *Lex.*, on מָלֵא (2), p. 473.

² As in Isa. viii. 7, the Euphrates "*shall come up over* (עַל) *all its channels and go over* (עַל) *all its banks.*"

Sept., ἐπλήρου καθ᾽ ὅλην τὴν κρηπίδα αὐτοῦ ; Vulg., "Jordanis autem ripas alvei sui tempore messis impleverat."

is meant, which took place in the month called
Abib, the month of ears, חֹדֶשׁ הָאָבִיב (Exod. xiii. 4),
and afterwards Nisan (Neh. ii. 1; Esther iii. 7),
beginning at the new moon of April, the first month
of the old year, as instituted when the Israelites
came out of Egypt (cf. Exod. xxiii. 15; Deut.
xvi. 1). The overflow of the Jordan is owing to
the melting of the snow of Hermon during the hot
days of April. When the melted snow has filled the
lakes of Merom and Tiberias, the flood is discharged
in a torrent through the Jordan into the Dead Sea.
At such a season the river is impassable by any of
the usual fords, and, therefore, the passage of the
vast host of the Israelites through it was clearly
miraculous.

Ver. 16.—גְד־אָחָד (see ver. 13). According to Keil
and others, the Kᵉthibh בְּאָדָם, "at," or "near Adam,"
is a better rendering than the Qᵉri מֵאָדָם, "from
Adam," the meaning being (say they) that the
waters stood in a heap, very far from the spot where
the Israelites crossed, near Adam. The Qᵉri, however, is followed by the Auth. Vers., the Vulg.,
and other ancient versions, and expresses the more
general and popular view, viz., that the waters were
piled up in one continuous heap in the rear of the
place of crossing, where the priests stood with the
ark, and as far as the city Adam, where the current
of the stream from above was arrested. As the bed
of the river lies greatly beneath the level of the
country, such a pile of water may have been
attended with little or no inundation. This view
accords with what Keil himself says on ver. 8 (see
note above), also greatly heightens the impressive-

ness of the miracle, and explains the haste of the children of Israel to effect the passage (iv. 10), which would have been hard to account for, if the waters had receded as far as Adam. This city, the name of which may have been derived from the colour of the clay in the neighbourhood, is now unknown, and is mentioned *here* only; its position is further defined by the words "*the city which is beside Zaretan*" (Tsar^ethan). This latter is probably the same as that in 1 Kings vii. 46, and identical with the modern *Kurn Sartabeh*, a lofty, rocky ridge, about seventeen miles north of Jericho (Robinson, Knobel). As the rocks here on both sides converge and contract the valley to its narrowest point, it seems to have been a suitable place for damming up the waters. Render the next clause, "*and those which were coming down to the sea of the plain, the sea of salt, were altogether cut off.*" תַּמּוּ here serves for an adverb (§ 142, 3, b). "*The sea of the Arabah* (or Desert-plain)," (cf. xii. 3). Sept., τὴν θάλασσαν Ἄραβα; Vulg., "mare solitudinis." The word עֲרָבָה, derived from עָרַב, to be dry, arid, was the name given, in its widest sense, to the Ghor, or deep valley, extending from Mount Hermon even to the Œlanitic Gulf; but in its more limited sense to the district which extends along the valley of the Jordan, from the Dead Sea to the Lake of Gennesareth, about one hundred and fifty miles in length, and now called by the Arabs *El Ghor* (see Dean Stanley's *Sinai and Palestine*, Appendix, p. 487).[1]

---

[1] This deep valley lies 625 feet below the Mediterranean, where the Jordan leaves the Sea of Gennesareth, and 1231 feet where it empties into the Dead Sea. In it there is no tillable

At the present day the Arabs confine the name Arabah to that portion of the Ghor which lies south of the Holy Land (Clarke's *Biblical Atlas*, note p. 13). "*The sea of salt*": The usual and perhaps most ancient name (Gen. xiv. 3). According to Josephus, this sea or lake is five hundred and eighty furlongs in length, and one hundred and fifty in breadth. Now called the Dead Sea (a name not found in the Bible, but first used in Greek by Pausanias, and in Latin by Justin); in Arabic Bahr Lût, the "Sea of Lot" (Smith's *Bib. Dict.*)

Ver. 17.—"*In the midst of Jordan, i.e.*, not in the mid-channel, but in the bed of the river, as opposed to its bank (so in iv. 3, 8, 18), = "*in Jordan*," iii. 8 (cf. Ezek. xxvi. 5, where Tyre is described as "in the midst of the sea," though it was but a short distance from the continent). הָכֵן, "*firmly*," Hiph. infin. absol. taken adverbially (§ 131, 2). גוי: A word often used in the singular to denote the Israelitish nation (see Exod. xix. 6, xxx. 13; Josh. iv. 1, v. 6, 8, x. 13), but in the plural the Gentiles, or nations of the earth, as distinguished from the Jews (*e.g.*, in Psalm ii. 1, ix. 5, 15, 17). תַּמּוּ לַעֲבוֹר, lit., "*had finished crossing*" (cf. iv. 1, v. 8).

---

soil, except at Bethshean, in the north, and about Jericho, at the south end of the Ghor (Von Raumer, p. 58). The word "Arab" comes from the same root, and denotes an inhabitant of a dry, arid region.

CHAPTER IV.

VERS. 1-18.—*Completion of the Passage.*

Ver. 1.—"*And it came to pass . . . that Jehovah spake unto Joshua*": As the command of Jehovah to Joshua (vers. 1-3) has not been expressly mentioned before (see iii. 12), Knobel, Bleek, and Maurer suppose that we have here the blending of two separate accounts; while others, *e.g.*, Kimchi, Calvin, Masius, and Rosenm., regard ver. 1*b*-3 as parenthetical, and render וַיֹּאמֶר in the pluperfect ("Now Jehovah had spoken," etc.), the apodosis to the first hemistich of ver. 1 commencing, according to them, at ver. 4; but, as in i. 11, ii. 1, the order of *thought*, rather than of *time*, seems to be followed, so likewise here. The sacred writer, wishing to give due importance to the particular incident he is about to relate, represents it not merely as having been commanded by Joshua, but, as it really was, by Jehovah Himself.[1]

The Pisqua (o) at the end of the first clause of ver. 1 is an old pre-Masoretic mark, denoting a pause in the middle of the verse (see marg. note), and the commencement of a parashah or section.

---

[1] "So far as the meaning is concerned, Kimchi, Calvin, and many others, were perfectly correct in taking vers. 1*b*—3 as a parenthesis, and rendering וַיֹּאמֶר as a pluperfect, though, grammatically considered, and from a Hebrew point of view, the historical sense with "Vav" consec does not correspond to our pluperfect, but always expresses the succession either of time or thought. This early Hebrew form of thought and narrative is completely overlooked by Knobel, when he pronounces 1*b*-3 an interpolation from a second document, and finds the apodosis to ver. 1*a* in ver. 4."—*Keil*.

Ver. 2.—קְחוּ (cf. iii. 12): Though the command was given to Joshua, the plural is here used, because the twelve men were to be chosen by the tribes themselves (cf. iii. 12), but subject, doubtless, to Joshua's approbation, and, therefore, spoken of in ver. 4 as "*prepared*" by him.

Ver. 3.—מִמַּצַּב, lit., "*the standing place* (of)": From נָצַב, to set, to place. הָכִין, *firmly* (cf. iii. 17): Connected here with מִמַּצַּב, *e.g.*, "*from the spot where the priests' feet stood firm ;*" so Auth. Vers., Maurer, Gesen, Keil. Others, Walton (*Polyg.*), Rosenm., regard it as a gerund, "præparando, aptando," and as referring to the selection of suitable stones ; Sept., ἑτοίμους δώδεκα λίθους; Vulg., "duodecim durissimos lapides ;" Syr., "parate duodecim lapides." "*And lay down,*" lit., "make to rest." "*In the lodging-place,*" *i.e.*, in the place of encampment, viz., Gilgal (ver. 20). אוֹתָם: m. pron. (§ 117, 2) referring to fem. noun [אֲבָנִים, fem. with plural m. ending] (§ 121, 6, Rem. 1) ; cf. זֶה for זֹאת (ii. 17).

Ver. 4.—וַיִּקְרָא, "*and Joshua called*": ו does not commence the apodosis, and = "*then*" (Auth. Vers.), see note on ver. 1. "*Whom he had prepared*": see note on ver. 2. Probably these twelve men had not crossed over with the rest of the Israelites, but remained with Joshua on the hither bank of the river, waiting to receive his orders.

Vers. 6, 7 (*The Object of the Divine Command stated.*) —זֹאת, *this*, viz., their taking of twelve stones with them, and setting of them up. כִּי, "*when your children shall ask,*" etc. (cf. Exod. xii. 26, etc. ; Deut. vi. 20, 21). מָחָר, "*in future time*" (cf. xxii. 24 ; Gen. xxx. 33 ; Exod. xiii. 14). מָה, "*what,*" is rarely pointed with (׳) before a word beginning with ה, as here and in ver. 21 (see § 37, 1, Rem.)

Ver. 7.—אֲשֶׁר, "*that*" (Auth. Vers.); Sept., ὅτι, after a verb of saying (cf. Esther iii. 4); but Vulg. "*quia*," as in Gen. xxxiv. 27; 1 Kings viii. 33. The words "*the waters . . . were cut off*" are repeated for emphasis. "*Shall be for a memorial*" (cf. Numb. xvii. 5 [xvi. 40, A. V.]; Psalm cxi. 4). "*For ever*": *i.e.*, to all posterity.

Ver. 8.—What was done by the twelve men is here ascribed to "*the sons of Israel*," because the former having been chosen, each from a tribe, were representatives of all the people. For the masc. suffix in יַעֲבְרוּם and in יַנִּחוּם, referring to a fem. noun, see § 121, 6, Rem. 1. "*There*," *i.e.*, in Gilgal, as the place of their encampment was afterwards called (ver. 20). The word יַנִּחוּ denotes that at first they only deposited the stones, afterwards they set them up as a memorial (see the word הֵקִים, ver. 20).[1]

Ver. 9.—It is evident that the twelve stones mentioned in this verse were different from those in ver. 8, otherwise the article would not have been omitted, and the verse would have begun with the historical וַיָּקֶם. To mark this difference, the Sept. inserts ἄλλους (Vulg., *alios*) before δώδ. λίθους. These stones may have been collected by the people from the adjacent fields. The verse is not a gloss, as some think, for it occurs in all MSS. and versions (so Keil, p. 120).

---

[1] Besides being a memorial of the literal passage of the Jordan, these stones may have been typical of the testimony borne by the preaching of the twelve apostles to that still greater event, our true Joshua's victorious passage through the Jordan of death, and His opening of the kingdom of heaven to all believers.

"*In the midst of Jordan*," see on iii. 17. "*Unto this day*," *i.e.*, to the time when the writer of this book lived. As a memorial these stones indicated the exact place of the crossing, as those at Gilgal the place where, after the crossing, the Israelites first encamped.[1]

Ver. 10.—"*And the priests*—(were) *standing*." In the next clause הֹם, infin. of תָּמַם, is used intrans. דָּבָר, either "*word*" or "*thing*." "*According to all that Moses commanded*": refers not to any special commands of Moses about the crossing, but indicates that Joshua's obedience to the commands of the Lord accorded with the injunctions given by Moses. "*And the people hasted*," etc.: Such haste was necessary, not only because the priests bearing the ark were to remain standing till all the people should have crossed (Knobel), or because the people may have feared a sudden return of the waters (see note on iii. 16), but because the passage had to be completed by so vast a multitude in one day (Keil).

---

[1] Keil well remarks that "the monument did not fail of its object, even if it only existed for a short time. The account of its erection, which was handed down by tradition, would necessarily help to preserve the remembrance of the miraculous occurrence. Nor can it be absolutely affirmed that these stones would be carried away at once by the stream, so that they could never be seen any more. As the priests did not stand in the middle or deepest part of the river, but just in the bed of the river, and close to its eastern bank, and it was upon this spot that the stones were set up, and as we neither know their size nor the firmness with which they stood, we cannot pronounce any positive opinion as to the possibility of their remaining. It is not likely that they remained there for centuries ; but they were intended rather as a memorial for the existing generation and their children, than for a later age, which would be perpetually reminded of the miraculous help of God by the monument erected in Gilgal."

Ver. 11.—"*In the presence of the people*" (Auth. Vers.): But as לִפְנֵי elsewhere in this book means "*before*" (see iii. 6, 14, vi. 4, 6, 7, 8, 9), the same sense should perhaps be retained here, the meaning being that the priests crossed the river, and passed through the multitude on the opposite bank, till they took up their station in front of the people. Vulg., "*ante* populum."

Vers. 12, 13.—וַיַּעַבְרוּ: The imperfect here with ן consec. denotes not the order of time but of thought (cf. iv. 1). The author, having stated that all the people crossed, while the priests bearing the ark stood in the river, takes occasion here to add that the tribes of Reuben, Gad, etc., had obeyed the commands of Moses (Numb. xxxii. 20, 29) by crossing over before their brethren. חֲמֻשִׁים (see i. 14).

Ver. 13.—"*Prepared for the war*": εὔζωνοι εἰς μάχην (Sept.): The participle חֲלוּצִים is derived by Gesenius from חָלַץ, "to be active," "to be manful;" but see for another derivation note on i. 14. "*The plains of Jericho*" formed the higher terrace of the Ghor or Jordan valley, where, by the retreat of the mountains of Judæa, it widened towards the west, and is about seven miles broad. The plural "*araboth*" is always used without the article (cf. v. 10, xiii. 32; Dean Stanley, *Sinai and Palestine*, Appendix, § 10). From the palm-trees which flourished in those plains Jericho derived its name of "*the city of palms*" (Deut. xxxiv. 3; Judges i. 16, iii. 13; Josephus, *Bel. Jud.*, iv., 8, § 3).

Ver. 14.—Cf. iii. 7 (note).

Vers. 15-18.—The crossing of the priests with the ark had been already recorded (ver. 11), but as a leading feature in the narrative it is again mentioned here with additional particulars, which clearly show that the passage of the Jordan by the Israelites must have been *miraculous*.

Ver. 16.—הָעֵדוּת, "*the testimony*," rt. עוּד, "to say again and again," "to affirm strongly": The name "ark of the testimony" denoted that the Tables of the Law, kept in the ark (Exod. xxv. 16), contained the testimony of Jehovah against sin in man; (cf. what is said of the whole book of the Law, which was laid up by the side of the ark, Deut. xxxi. 26, 27). וַיַּעֲלוּ: The ו = "*that*," Lat., *ut* (§ 155, 1, *c*; cf. Judges xiv. 15; 1 Sam. xi. 12).

Ver. 18.—The verb נִתְּקוּ with אֶל has a pregnant sense, viz., "*were plucked up* (from the muddy channel) *and set on* (the dry ground)," (§ 141). "*As heretofore*" (see note on iii. 4). עַל, over (cf. iii. 15).

VERS. 19-24.—*Erection of the Memorial at Gilgal.*

Ver. 19.—"*The first month*," *i.e.*, Abib, afterwards called Nisan (see end of the note on iii. 15). The year is not mentioned, but it appears to have been the fortieth after the exodus (cf. v. 6). If, therefore, we assume the date of the exodus to be 1491 B.C. (Usher), that of the invasion of Canaan would be 1451 B.C. "*The tenth day*," *i.e.*, the same day of the month on which the paschal lamb was set apart to be killed on the fourteenth (see Exod. xii. 3). Thus the Israelites were reminded that their departure out of Egypt and their entrance into Canaan were owing to God's redeeming mercy. So, under the Gospel, our salvation from first to last is the fruit of Christ's atonement. "*In* [the] *Gilgal*" (lit., a circle or wheel, rt. גָּלַל, to roll, generally with the art. when a place; (see *Gr.*, § 109, 3): So called by anticipation (see v. 9). It was apparently on a hillock or rising ground, and, according to Josephus (*Antiq.*, lib. v., cap. 1, § 4), was fifty stadia, or about five miles (Dean Stanley, *Sinai and Palestine*, p. 307), from the river Jordan, and ten stadia from Jericho. Here the camp of the Israelites remained for some time, and was probably fortified; also the Tabernacle was set up, though afterwards removed to Shiloh (viii. 1).[1]

Ver. 20.—הֵקִים, "*erected*," or "*set up*" as a memorial. The stones had before been merely deposited (ver. 8).

Ver. 21.—אֲשֶׁר, "*when*": Sept., ὅταν, Vulg., quando (cf. Levit. iv. 22), though it less often than כִּי bears this sense (§ 155, 1, *c*). With this verse cf. ver. 6.

Ver. 23.—אֲשֶׁר, "*because*": (Chald. and Syr.)

---

[1] The site thus chosen for the encampment has been fortunately identified, after more than three thousand years, by the intelligent labours of the members of the Palestine Survey. The name Jiljûlieh, which is the same word as Gilgal, still clings to a mound about three miles south-east from the spot where, apparently, the city of Jericho must have stood, near the beautiful fountain known as the Sultan's Spring, and close to the steep background of the limestone hills of Judah. The host of the Hebrews, at the camp thus chosen for them, were about five hundred feet above the bed of the Jordan, and had the stream from the Wady el Kelt close on the south. The river they had crossed lay underneath them, about four and a-half miles to the east. An open plain stretched on all sides, and permitted free movement; the wall of the hills of Judah, rising one thousand feet above the level of the camp, at the distance of about three miles to the west. (Conder's *Tent Work*, p. 201, f.; Palestine Fund Large Map of Palestine, sheet 18; Geikie's *Hours with the Bible*, vol. ii., p. 391).

"quia" (Vulg.). צַד־עָבְרֵנוּ, "*until we had passed over*": The suff. of the infin. refers to the Israelites as being essentially the same nation as that which came out of Egypt.

Ver. 24.—It is here declared that the miracle was to serve a twofold purpose, viz., (1) To impress the heathen with a sense of the omnipotence of Jehovah; (2) To keep the children of Israel steadfast in the fear, *i.e.*, the worship, of their God (cf. Exod. xiv. 31). כָּל־עַמֵּי הָאָ֫רֶץ, "*all the peoples of the earth*": There seems no reason here to limit, with Keil, the term "*erets*" to the land of Canaan, for though in v. 1 the Canaanites are mentioned as an example of the effect produced by the miracle, yet it was one example out of many more to follow. "*The hand of Jehovah . . . mighty*" (cf. Exod. iii. 19, vi. 1): In the last clause, for יְרֵאתֶם Ewald, Maurer, and Knobel would read יִרְאָתָם, the infin. construc., with plur. masc. suffix, "*that they* [the heathen] *may fear;*" but the *perfect*, says Keil, may be here used to express the speaker's certainty of the duty of such holy fear; to which the heathen could not, as the Israelites, be suitably exhorted. Further, all the ancient versions follow the reading in the text. כָּל־הַיָּמִים, "*always*": cf. ἤματα πάντα, in the Greek poets.

CHAPTER V.

VER. 1.—*The Effect of the Invasion on the Inhabitants of the Land.*

Concerning the Emorites and Canaanites, see iii. 10 (note). Here the former stand as the representatives of the highlanders, the latter of the lowlanders. בְּעֵבֶר הַיַּ, "*on the other side of the Jordan*": Not referring to the country on the east side of the Jordan, as in i. 14, 15, but on the west; hence the addition of יָמָּה (cf. ix. 1, xii. 7, xxii. 7). אֵת אֲשֶׁר (cf. ii. 10). עַד־עָבְרֵנוּ, "*until we had passed over*": The Qᵉri reads עָבְרָם, so the ancient versions, and some MSS., but a change of persons is common in Hebrew (§ 137, Rem. 3; cf. v. 6 below). The expression seems that of an eyewitness, but we cannot, says Keil, infer from it either that the book was written by Joshua himself, or that it was composed during his lifetime. The historian may have spoken collectively, just as Joshua (in iv. 23) refers to what he and a few of his contemporaries had witnessed, as though it had been seen by all the people. וַיִּמַּס (cf. ii. 11): They had probably thought that the swollen waters of the Jordan would prove for a time an insuperable barrier to Israel.

VERS. 2-12.—*The Circumcision of the People, and Celebration of the Passover at Gilgal.*

Ver. 2.—"*At that time*": Probably not later than the eleventh of the month Abib, or Nisan, the day after the arrival at Gilgal, for the Passover took place on the fourteenth day of the same month (see ver. 10). חַרְבוֹת צֻרִים, lit., "knives of rocks" (or, of flints): So Sept., Vulg., Syr., and Arab. (cf. Exod. iv. 25). These were the most ancient kind of knives, and were especially used in embalming (Herod., ii., 86) and in emasculation (Juv., *Sat.*, vi. 514; Ovid, *Fasti*, iv., 237, "*acuto silice*"). The Auth. Vers. "*sharp knives*," or "*knives of edges*," though agreeing with the use of צֻר, in Psalm lxxxix. 44, is not here required. Many ancient [1] and modern commentators have seen in the term "rock" a reference to Christ, through whom we receive the circumcision of the spirit (cf. 1 Cor. x. 4; Rom. ii. 29; Col. ii. 11). שׁוּב, "*again*" (§ 142, 4, Rem. 1), the latter of the two verbs is generally put in the abbreviated form (cf. Exod. iv. 19). שֵׁנִית, "*a second time*": Gives a greater force to שׁוּב (cf. Isa. xi. 11), and τὸ δεύτερον (Jude 5): The meaning is not that the same persons should be circumcised a second time, but that all the Israelites, who had not before been circumcised, should now undergo that rite, so that the whole nation should be a circumcised people, as it had been at the exodus from Egypt (cf. Keil, *in loc.*).

Ver. 3.—"*The hill of the foreskins*," *i.e.*, the hill which was afterwards so called, because the foreskins (the emblem of the sins of the flesh, Col. ii. 11-13, iii. 1-6) were buried there. This "hill" (Gibeah) is probably one of the argillaceous hills which form the highest terrace of the Jordan (Dean Stanley's *Sinai and Palestine*, vii., p. 307, note 1).

---

[1] *E.g.*, Tertullian, *adv. Jud.*, c. 9; and *c. Marcion.*, iii., 16; Origen, *Homil. in Jos.*; Justin Martyr, *c. Tryphon.*, § 24; S. Aug., *in loc.*; Theodoret, *Qu.* 4.

VERS. 4-7 (*A Reason given for the Command in ver. 2*).—Ver. 4.—הַדָּבָר אֲשֶׁר, "*the reason that*," or "*why*" (cf. עַל־דְּבַר אֲשֶׁר, Deut. xxii. 24; 2 Sam. xiii. 22). "*All the people that came out of Egypt*," i.e., those who were twenty years old and upward at the time of the rebellion at Kadesh (see Numb. xiv. 29, 32). בְּצֵאתָם מִמִּצְרַיִם, not, "*after they had come out of Egypt*" (Le Clerc and Rosenm.), but "*on their coming out of Egypt*," i.e., during the journey. The words more strongly define the preceding בַּדֶּרֶךְ.

Ver. 5.—כִּי, *for*, not *now* (Auth. Vers.). כֻלִּים הָיוּ: The participle with the substantive verb is not here used as a preterite or pluperfect, but as an adjective, "were circumcised" men (Keil). A general circumcision of the people by Moses, before they left Egypt, is not recorded in Scripture. The statement in the remainder of the verse can refer to those Israelites only who were born in the wilderness, after the rebellion at Kadesh, for all children born in the interval between the exodus and the passover celebrated at Sinai in the first month of the second year, must have been circumcised (see Numb. ix. 1-5 ; Exod. xii. 48).

Ver. 6.—"*Forty years*," a round number, for the period was strictly thirty-eight years (see Deut. ii. 14). "*Till all the nation, the men of war*": The "*men of war*" are specially mentioned, because such were those who had been numbered from twenty years old and upwards (Numb. i. 45), and whose doom was to perish in the wilderness (Numb. xiv. 29-31); יְ ... אֲשֶׁר, not "*because*" (or "*wherefore*") *Jehovah had sworn*" (Rosenm.), but giving a relative sense to לָהֶם (§ 123); Render "*to whom*," etc., as in Auth. Vers., Sept., and Vulg. "*To give to us*": Some

MSS., and the Sept., Syr., Arab., and Chald., read לָהֶם for לָמוֹ, but the Kᵉthibh is preferable, for the word "*fathers*" refers to the patriarchs, to whom and their posterity the promise was made. "*A land flowing with milk and honey*": An expression frequent in the Pentateuch (see Exod. iii. 8, 17, xiii. 5, xxxiii. 3; Levit. xx. 24; Numb. xiii. 27; Deut. vi. 3, etc.), and denoting a land rich in grass and flowers. The same phrase, after its use here in the Book of Joshua, does not re-occur till met with in Jer. xi. 5, xxxii. 22; Ezek. xx. 6, 15.

Ver. 7.—"*And their sons He raised up in their stead, them Joshua circumcised,*" *i.e.*, caused to be circumcised (see the end of note on ver. 8): Many conjectures have been made why circumcision was omitted during the period between the rebellion at Kadesh and the arrival at Canaan; but the true reason appears to be that suggested by ver. 6, viz., that the whole nation, during that period, were under a ban. The iniquity of the fathers was visited on the children. There was a partial and temporary, though not a total and final, rejection of the people; and, therefore, till the allotted period of their punishment was accomplished, they were not admitted to the privileges implied in Circumcision and the Passover (so Calvin, Hengstenberg, and Keil). To the question, why God had not commanded Moses, when the thirty-eight years of wandering were finished, to circumcise the people in the plains of Moab, it has been well replied by Keil, that God delayed the performance of the rite, that He might first give proofs to the people of His power and mercy in the miraculous passage of the

Jordan, and thus render them more inclined to that obedience to which circumcision pledged them. Nor could any occasion be more suitable for their renewal of their covenant with God, than when they were about to enter on a war with foes mightier than themselves. Moreover, this circumcision was typical of that "*made without hands*" (Col. ii. 11), and, therefore, was fitly performed by *Joshua*, a type of Jesus, after he had brought the children of Israel into Canaan, a type of the Christian Church, into which we are introduced by baptism, prefigured by the passage of the Jordan.

Ver. 8.—תַּמּוּ, followed by the infin., with לְ, "*had left off to be circumcised*" (cf. iii. 17, iv. 1, 11). תַּחְתָּם יָשְׁבוּ, lit., "*they sat under themselves*": "The phrase" (says Le Clerc, on Exod. xvi. 29) "seems derived from the custom of the Orientals, who sit on the ground or pavement, for 'to remain under oneself' is, properly, to remain in that place which was under us when we first sat down." "*Till they were whole*" (Auth. Vers.), lit., "till they lived," *i.e.*, till they recovered, cf. 2 Kings i. 2, xx. 7: It appears from Gen. xxxiv. 25 that on the third day after circumcision its effects were still painful, and hence some supposed that on the fourth day the wound was healed, and consequently, if this circumcision of the Israelites took place on the 11th of Abib, the day after their arrival at Gilgal, they would have felt no inconvenience from it on the 14th of Abib, at least none sufficient to incapacitate them from eating the Passover. It has, indeed, been objected that, because at the census taken after the thirty-eight years' wandering the people amounted to nearly a million, it was impossible that the circumcision could have been performed in one day; but it must be remembered that a large number were already circumcised (see note ver. 5), and that, with the assistance of these, the operation could easily have been got over in a day.

Ver. 9.—"*The reproach of Egypt,*" i.e., the reproach which proceeds from Egypt: For the like use of the genitive see Isa. li. 7; Ezek. xvi. 57, xxxvi. 15; Zeph. ii. 8. This reproach was that God had cast them off, and intended to destroy them (cf. Exod. xxxii. 12; Numb. xiv. 13-16; Deut. ix. 28, xxxii. 27); the entrance into Canaan, and the renewal of the covenant, rolled away that reproach. "*Is called,*" lit. in Heb., "*one called*" (יִקָּרֵא), indeter. 3rd pers. sing., § 137. "*Gilgal,*" lit., "a rolling away": From גָּלַל, to roll; not a town, but a site and encampment seem meant.[1] The name is given also to other places (see, e.g., Deut. xi. 30; Josh. xii. 23), and perhaps for reasons which would admit of a different derivation of the word.

Ver. 10.—"*Encamped in Gilgal*"[2]: The spot was well suited for an encampment, as it possessed both shade and water. "*They celebrated* (lit., they made)

---

[1] Though the name Gilgal was thus given in direct allusion to the rolling away of the reproach of Egypt, yet there may have been also an allusion to the circle of twelve stones, raised by Joshua's orders (iv. 8), the first sanctuary of Israel in Palestine. Many similar rings still exist in Moab and elsewhere, and, indeed, such cromlechs and dolmens were associated with the earliest forms of religion in almost every country. The circle of Gilgal seems ultimately to have become the seat of idolatry (see Hosea iv. 15, ix. 15, xii. 11; Amos iv. 4, v. 5). See Geikie's *Hours with the Bible*, vol. ii., p. 392.

[2] Lit., "*the* Gilgal" (cf. iv. 19, note).

the Passover": This was the second Passover since the exodus from Egypt. The first was at Sinai (Numb. ix. 1-14). Calvin thinks that the celebration of the Passover was permitted by God to continue after the rebellion at Kadesh-Barnea; yet it is strange that no record of the fact is found in the Pentateuch, nor is it likely that the covenant festival of the Passover would be observed, when circumcision, the sign of the covenant, was discontinued. It seems clear from Exod. xii. 25, xiii. 5-10, that after its first celebration at Sinai, it was not to be renewed till the people had entered Canaan. "*On the fourteenth day*" (see Exod. xii. 6, 18; Lev. xxiii. 5). "*In the evening*," but more accurately, "*between the two evenings*" (Exod. xii. 6; Lev. xxiii. 5), or "*at the going down of the sun*" (Deut. xvi. 6). "*In the plains of Jericho*" (cf. iv. 13, note). "All the great movements of the ancient Church of God were begun with eating the Passover. The Israelites ate the Passover, and went forth from Egypt, and crossed the Red Sea. They ate the Passover at Sinai, when the tabernacle had been raised, and set forth on their march towards Canaan; and now they ate the Passover under Joshua, and began their march of victory. Here is a lesson to the Christian Church and to every Christian soul in it, not to undertake any great work, especially not to go forth on its way from this world into eternity, without being first strengthened with the Divine viaticum of the Christian Passover, the holy Eucharist." (Bishop Wordsworth, *in loc.*)

Ver. 11.—עֲבוּר: Found here and in ver. 12 only, The Auth. Vers. (after Kimchi and others) renders it "*old corn*," *i.e.*, corn of the past year, from עָבַר, to pass, or to pass by; but the same word in Syr. and Arab. means simply "corn," or "produce," and is frequently used in the Targums as equal to דָּגָן; hence it is probable that the rt. עָבַר has another and original sense, viz., to cover, to impregnate, to produce, and that עָבוּר here is synonymous with תְּבוּאָה in ver. 12 (cf. Lev. xxiii. 39), and means "produce," not of the past, but of the present year. "*On the morrow after the Passover*": This expression (in Numb. xxxiii. 3) means the 15th of Abib, but here apparently the sixteenth (so Keil), because the Israelites could not lawfully eat of the new corn till the presentation of the wave-sheaf on "the morrow after the Sabbath" (Lev. xxiii. 11). The "Sabbath" in that passage means the first day of the feast of unleavened bread (viz., the 15th of Abib), called a Sabbath, because, though not necessarily the seventh day of the week, it was kept as a Sabbath. To it corresponds in this verse the term passover, which sometimes denotes the paschal lamb (Exod. xii. 21), or the paschal meal (2 Chron. xxx. 18), eaten on the evening of the 14th of Abib; sometimes the feast of unleavened bread, beginning on the 15th, and lasting seven days (Deut. xvi. 2). קָלוּי, "*parched*" (*corn*), (A. V.): Put for אָבִיב קָלוּי בָּאֵשׁ, "ears of corn baked by the fire" (Lev. ii. 14), a food much relished still by the Arabs. These and the unleavened cakes (מַצּוֹת) pertained to the produce of the new year, whereas the unleavened bread, which the Israelites ate with the paschal lamb on the fourteenth day of Abib, must have been of old corn of the land. בְּעֶצֶם, "*in this self-same day*" (see § 124, Rem. 3).

Ver. 12.—"*And the manna ceased,*" etc. (cf. Exod. xvi. 35, and see on " Manna " the article in Smith's *Bib. Dict.*) : This total cessation of the manna shows that it had been a *miraculous* gift from God, but was now withdrawn, because it had served the purpose for which it was given. So in the Christian Church miraculous gifts and powers ceased when no longer necessary.

Vers. 13-15, vi. 1-5.—These verses, with the exception of vi. 1, are closely connected, and record the appearance of the Angel of the Lord to Joshua, and the message He gave to him.

Ver. 13.—בִּירִיחוֹ, "*by*" (Auth. Vers.), *i.e.*, near "*Jericho*" : For this meaning of בְּ see § 154, 3, *a*, 2 ; and cf. x. 16, xxiv. 26 ; Gen. xiii. 18 ; Vulg., "in agro Jericho." Keil thinks it implies not only that Joshua was on the outskirts of Jericho, but that in imagination he was already in it, *i.e.*, was occupied with the thought of conquering the town. "*He lifted up his eyes and looked*" : An expression, says Keil, which denotes the unexpected sight of an object (cf. Gen. xviii. 2, xxxiii. 1) ; it may also be classed among the instances of the *pictorial* style of writing, so common to the Hebrews, by which not only the doing of a thing, but the manner of doing it, is stated (cf. such phrases as " *he arose and went,*" " *he opened his lips and spake,*" " *he put forth his hand and took* "). אִישׁ, "*a man*" : Some say a created angel in human form, but the ancient Jewish Church, and the majority of the Christian Fathers, agree in the belief that it was the Second Person of the Ever Blessed Trinity, The Word, He Who said, " No man hath seen God (the Father) at any time. The Only

Begotten, Who is in the bosom of the Father, He hath declared Him" (John i. 18). This view is confirmed by the command to Joshua in ver. 15, and by vi. 2, where the Person Who here appears to him is called *Jehovah*, and issues His commands with authority. "*And His sword drawn in His hand*" (cf. Numb. xxii. 23, 31; Rev. i. 16, ii. 12, 16, xix. 15, 22, where the Son of God is represented as having a sharp two-edged sword). "*And Joshua went unto Him and spoke to Him*": Clearly, therefore, this was not a dream nor vision.

Ver. 14.—לֹא, "*Nay*" (Auth. Vers., Chald., and Vulg.): More suitable than לוֹ, the reading adopted by the Sept. and Syr., and found in some MSS. The Masora does not include this verse among the fifteen examples where לֹא is used for לוֹ. כִּי, "*but*": After a negative (§ 155, 1, *d*, p. 272). אֲנִי includes the subs. verb (§ 121, 1). שַׂר, "*captain* (of)," (A.V.), as in Gen. xxi. 22, or "prince (of)" (cf. Dan. x. 13, 20, xii. 1); "*the host of Jehovah*": This expression does not refer to the Israelitish army, which is never so called, though twice described by the plural, "*the hosts of the Lord*" (Exod. vii. 4, xii. 41); the singular can only refer to the angels, as in Psalm cxlviii. 2 (צְבָאו, K^ethibh); cf. 1 Kings xxii. 19, צְבָא הַשָּׁמַיִם. "*Now I have come*": Either the sentence is abrupt, and He was about to explain the object of His coming, when He was interrupted by Joshua's falling down before Him, and addressing Him (so Keil); or the expression is simply a solemn announcement of His Presence. וַיִּשְׁתָּחוּ[1]: As this word is used of reverence paid to

---

[1] For this form see *Gr.*, § 75, Rem. v., 18.

men (2 Sam. ix. 6, 8 ; 2 Sam. xiv. 33), it does not necessarily imply here Divine worship. Joshua seems at first not to have recognized the true nature of the Being Who appeared to him, for he calls him Adoni, " my lord," not Adonai, " The Lord."

Ver. 15.—שַׁל : Imper. per. aphœr. for נְשַׁל, "pull," or " pluck off." נָעַל : Rt. נָעַל, to bolt or to fasten, means a sandal, or sole attached to the foot by thongs, Sept. ὑπόδημα or σανδάλιον (so in Josh. ix. 5, 13 ; cf. σανδάλια, Mark vi. 9). On this, as an act of Divine homage, see note ver. 13, above. קֹדֶשׁ for אַדְמַת־קֹדֶשׁ, Exod. iii. 5. The ground of Gilgal was the first portion of Palestine which was pronounced holy (Dean Stanley, *Sinai and Palestine*, vii., p. 308).

CHAPTER VI.

VERS. 1-27.—*The Conquest of Jericho.*

Ver. 1.—This verse is parenthetical (see note v. 13-15), and is introductory to ver. 2, being designed to show that so strong a city as Jericho could not have been overcome by the Israelites without the Divine aid. סֹגֶרֶת וּמְסֻגֶּרֶת, " lit., (was) *shutting its gates, and closely shut up*" : The participles express a state of continuance, and the Pual participle, being intensive, denotes that the city was secured with bolts and bars, the Qal part. simply that the gates were shut (Ges., *Lex.*, p. 579). The last clause of the verse is added for emphasis.

Ver. 2.—Here the " Captain of Jehovah's host " is identified with "*Jehovah*," and speaks with authority as such. "*I have given*": The perfect denoting the certainty of accomplishment (cf. i. 3). נָתַ֫תִּי, (cf. i. 14): Put in opposition to Jericho (*i.e.*, the inhabitants) and its king.

Vers. 3-7 (*Instructions how the City was to be taken*). —Ver. 3.—וְסַבֹּתֶם, "*and ye shall compass*" (Auth. Vers.): But here (says Ges., *Lehrgeb.*, p. 767, 5, b) it has the force of an imperative (cf. Sept., περίστησον, Vulg., circuite). הַקֵּיף, "*in going round*": Written more usually הַקֵּף, as in ver. 11. Hiph. inf. absol. of נָקַף, to go in a circle (Ges., *Lex.*, p. 566); here it defines more accurately the preceding verb. "*Once*," lit. in Heb., "one tread or stroke." "*Six days*": The marchings on these six consecutive days, and that which was repeated seven times on the seventh day, were a trial of the people's faith, patience, and obedience (cf. Heb. xi. 30). To mere human reason the means to be employed would have seemed utterly inadequate.

Ver. 4.—The number seven occurring four times in this verse denotes completeness, and was a sacred number;[1] it was, therefore, symbolic of the *Divine agency* in the overthrow of Jericho. "*Before the ark*": The seat of God's special presence. שׁוֹפְרוֹת הַיּ, lit., "*cornets of soundings*," and hence "*cornets of jubilee*." יֹבֵל, according to Gesenius (*Thes.*, ii., 561) is an onomatopoetic word, meaning jubilum, or a joyful sound, formed from the syllable יו, denoting

---

[1] So likewise among the Persians (Esther i. 10, 14); among the ancient Indians (Von Bohlen's *Alt. Indien*, ii., 224, etc.); among the Greeks and Romans to a certain extent, and probably among all nations where the week of seven days was established, as in China, Egypt, Arabia, etc. (Ideler's *Chronol.* i., 88, 178, ii., 473).

"a crying out," like the Greek ἰώ and ἰοῦ, (cf. the name יוּבָל, given to the inventor of stringed and wind instruments, Gen. iv. 21). Others, with Carpzov, derive it from יָבַל, "to flow copiously and with some violence," and hence יוֹבֵל, a rushing, penetrating sound. The Auth. Vers. "*rams' horns*," is from an unused rt. יָבַל, to be compressed, to be hard, strong; whence יֹבֵל or יוֹבֵל, the strong, and in Arab. *a ram;* thus the Chaldee Targum generally translates קֶרֶן יוֹבֵל, "trumpet of ram's horn." But many Arabic scholars deny that יוֹבֵל ever means "a ram" in Arabic, and a ram's horn, being solid, could not emit sound. שׁוֹפָר [so called from its clear and sharp sound, rt. שָׁפַר, to be bright (Ges., *Lex.*)], *i.q.*, קֶרֶן, ver. 5, means a *bent trumpet*, Lat., *lituus*. According to Engel (*Hist. of Music*, p. 292) it is the only Hebrew musical instrument which has been preserved to the present day in the religious services of the Jews, being blown at the Jewish new year's festival, according to the command of Moses (Numb. xxix. 1). The word differs from חֲצֹצְרָה, the silver trumpet used to summon to war (Numb. x. 2), and which was straight in form. Thus these horns of jubilee, associated with occasions of peace, served, like the other particulars mentioned, to teach the Israelites that the conquest of Jericho would be effected by Divine power. יִתְקְעוּ בַּשּׁ׳, "*they shall blow* (lit., shall strike by blowing into) *the trumpets.*"

Ver. 5.—בִּמְשֹׁךְ בְּקֶרֶן, lit., "*when they draw with the jubilee horn*," *i.e.*, when they blow the jubilee horn with long drawn notes (cf. Exod. xix. 13). קֶרֶן may be here taken collec. for שׁוֹפְרוֹת (ver. 4). תְּרוּעָה: Is used specially of a *joyful shout* (1 Sam. iv. 5), and of a *war-*

like shout, ἀλαλαγμός (Jer. iv. 19); this latter may be meant here and in ver. 20. תַּחְתֶּיהָ, lit., "*under itself*": The meaning is not "the city wall shall sink into the earth" (Chaldee Vers., "absorbebitur sub se"), but (as Keil) "*shall be overthrown from the foundations;*" Vulg., "muri funditus corruent civitatis." The Sept. πεσεῖται αὐτόματα τὰ τείχη, κ.τ.λ., though not a literal rendering of the Hebrew, indicates that the overthrow of the wall would be effected not by any assault of the Israelites, but by miraculous agency. נֶגְדּוֹ, "*straight before him,*" *i.e.*, passing over the fallen wall, and keeping as far as possible in the same direction (cf. Joel ii. 7, "they shall march every one on his ways"). עָלוּ, "*shall ascend*": Refers to the ruins of the wall, by passing over which they were to press into the city.

Vers. 6, 7.—Joshua announces first to the priests and then to the people the instructions he had received. In ver. 7 the Qᵉri has "he said" (so the Auth. Vers.) for the Kᵉthibh "they said," but the plural, as being the more difficult reading, was probably altered to the singular, and may be explained by supposing that Joshua issued his commands through the Shoterim (see i. 10, 11, iii. 2). עִבְרוּ, "*move on,*" or "*march forward*": So in the next hemistich, and in ver. 8 (cf. Psalm xlii. 5, Heb. Bib.). הֶחָלוּץ: Used collectively for חֲלוּצֵי הַצָּבָא (iv. 13, see note). Cor. a Lap., Rosenmüller, and Knobel understand the term here to refer to the warriors of all the tribes, and הַמְאַסֵּף (the rereward,[1] Auth. Vers.; see ver. 9) to the rest of the people, or the unarmed multi-

---

[1] An old English word, *i.q.*, rearguard, used also in Numb. x. 25; 1 Sam. xxix. 2; Isa. lii. 12, lviii. 8.

tude, Vulg., "reliquum vulgus ;" but Keil and others, after Kimchi and Rashi, limit the former term to the armed men of the tribes of Reuben, Gad, and half tribe of Manasseh (who may have been intended to take the lead not only on the occasion of the passage of the Jordan [iv. 12], but on all other occasions, till the conquest of Canaan), but include under the latter term the warriors of the other tribes. This view seems to accord with ver. 3, where the command to go round the city is given to "the men of war" only, which command is here, and in ver. 9, more fully stated. Since, however, the tribe of Dan in the march through the wilderness always brought up the rear (Numb. x. 25), הַמְאַסֵּף may possibly refer to that tribe, and הֶחָלוּץ include all the rest of the men of war.

Vers. 8-11 (*The First Day's Procession and Order of March*).—Ver. 8.—וַיְהִי כֶּאֱמֹר יְהֹ׳, "*and it came to pass when Joshua had spoken*" (Auth. Vers.): The Syr. renders, "*And it happened according to the words of Joshua;*" but כְּ prefixed to the infin. often means "when," or "as soon as" (see Ges., *Lex.*, 5, *b*); and וַיְהִי, though generally followed by the imperfect with ו conversive in the second clause, is often followed by the perfect (see, *e.g.*, Gen. xxii. 1; 1 Kings viii. 54; Isa. xxxvii. 38) (Keil). ו before עָבְרָה begins the apodosis (§ 155, 1, *a*, 3rd par.). The art. before נֹשְׂאִים is omitted (cf. ver. 13, and see § 111, 2, *b*). "*Before Jehovah*," *i.e.*, before the ark, which was the symbol of the Divine presence, and also called here "*the ark of the covenant*," because containing the tables on which the covenant was written.

Ver. 9.—The K^ethibh, תָּקְעוּ, requires an ellipsis of

אָוָה (§ 123, 3), and though more often followed by בְּ, here governs an accus., as in Judges vii. 22; Psalm lxxxi. 4; Jer. iv. 5, etc. הַמְאַסֵּף, "*the rereward*" (Auth. Vers.), lit., "*the gathering* (host)": Piel part. with art. used as a noun, from אָסַף, "to collect," and "to bring up the rear," "agmen claudere" (Isa. lviii. 8); so here in Piel (cf. Numb. x. 25; Isa. lii. 12; see note on ver. 7). הָלוֹךְ וְתָ, "*going on and blowing*" (Auth. Vers.), *i.e.*, trumpeting continually (§ 131, 3, *b*): The meaning is that during the march the trumpets (cornets) continued to sound.

Ver. 10.—צִוָּה, "*had commanded*" (Auth. Vers., Rosenm. and Keil): This verse is parenthetical, and throws light on ver. 5. "*Ye shall not shout*": They were to shout on the seventh day only (see ver. 16), for not till that day would the victory be obtained. On the other days the deep silence observed was befitting the solemnity of the occasion, when God Himself, under the symbol of the ark, was going before them, and about to discomfit so signally their enemies (cf. Hab. ii. 20; Zech. ii. 13).

Ver. 11.—וַיַּסֵּב: The Arab. Vers., Kimchi, Masius, Rosenm., and others, render "*and* (Joshua) *caused to go round;*" but as ver. 10 is parenthetical, the nominative "Joshua" can hardly with propriety be borrowed from it, and Hiphil often has an intrans. signification (see, *e.g.*, הָסֵב in 2 Sam. v. 23, and מְסִבַּי, Psalm cxl. 10; Ges., *Lex.*, 4, p. 577); hence the Vulg., Syr., Chald., and Auth. Vers. render it here intrans.: so Winer, Gesen., and Keil.

Vers. 12-14.—The same order of march, as on the first day, is repeated on the second and four following days.

Vers. 12.—"*Rose early*": Activity and promptitude were characteristics of Joshua.

Ver. 13.—הֹלְכִים הָלוֹךְ, (were) "*continually proceeding*": The participle has here the same construction with the infin. absol. as the finite verb (§ 131, 3, Rem. 3). וְתָקְעוּ, the finite verb frequently succeeds in Hebrew to the participle (§ 134, Rem. 2). Gesenius, indeed (in § 131, 3, *b*), says that this is an instance of the finite verb being put instead of the infin. (תָּקוֹעַ, ver. 9); but rather it here corresponds with וְתָקְעוּ in ver. 8. In the last clause the Qᵉri הָלוֹךְ need not be read for the Kᵉthibh הֹלֵךְ, for the latter, as expressive of continuance, differs little from the former, and frequently the infin. absol. and the participle are interchanged, see, *e.g.*, Gen. xxvi. 13, Judges iv. 24, 2 Sam. xvi. 5, where an infin. absol. is followed by a participle instead of by another infin. absol.

Vers. 15-19 (*The Seventh Day's Proceedings, and Joshua's Final Commands respecting Jericho*).—Ver. 15.—"*On the seventh day*": According to Jewish writers, the *Sabbath day*. To the objection of Marcion, that thus the Sabbath was violated, Tertullian replies that the work here commanded was not a human but a Divine work (Tertul., *c. Marcion.*, iv., 12). בַּעֲלוֹת, the Qᵉri is כַּעֲלוֹת, "*about the time that* (the morn) *arose*": On the distinction between בְּ and כְּ see iii. 3. כַּמִּשְׁפָּט הַזֶּה, lit., "*according to this rule*," *i.e.*, "in the same prescribed manner" (cf. Lev. v. 10, ix. 16). "*Seven times*": As Jericho was of considerable size, and an interval of rest was probably required after each circuit, the seven circuits may not have been finished till the close of the

Sabbath, and thus the slaughter, which followed, may not have taken place on that day.

Ver. 16.—" *When the priests blew* " (Auth. Vers.) : The word " *when* " is not in the original. Keil more correctly renders " *the priests had blown the trumpets, then Joshua said,*" etc.

Ver. 17.—חֵרֶם, once חֶרֶם (Zech. xiv. 11), " *a thing devoted* " : Sept. ἀνάθεμα, from חָרַם, to shut up, and hence, to devote, to consecrate, and to exterminate (Ges., *Lex.*; see Levit. xxvii. 21, 28, 29). Jericho, as being the first city captured in Canaan, was to be devoted with all its inhabitants (except Rachabh and her household) and property to destruction, in vindication of the Divine justice in the punishment of the wicked, and as a kind of firstfruits to the Lord, in acknowledgment of His gift of the land, and of His help in its conquest. In the case of the other Canaanitish cities the inhabitants only were to be destroyed, but the cattle and other possessions became the booty of the conquerors (Josh. viii. 26-7), whereas in Jericho nothing was to be preserved (ver. 21), except the silver and gold, etc. (ver. 19), which, being indestructible, were to be brought into the treasury of the Lord (cf. Joseph., *Antiq.*, v., 1, 5). הֶחְבִּאָתָה: Hiph. 3 p. f. s., with ה parag., which is perhaps emphatic, " *she carefully concealed,*" written in ver. 25, הֶחְבִּיאָה, but the form here is borrowed from verbs לה (see § 75, Rem. vi., 21, a). Another reason for her preservation was the oath of the spies (ii. 14).

Ver. 18.—" *But only be ye on your guard against the devoted thing, lest ye devote a thing to God, and take of the thing devoted* " : פֶּן־תַּחֲרִימוּ has not, according to the Auth. Vers., a reflex sense, "*lest ye make yourselves accursed*," nor, as Kimchi and Drusius say, is the ו before לְקַחְתֶּם explanatory of the foregoing verb, *e.g.*, "*that is, lest ye take;*" but Joshua here warns the Israelites not to appropriate to themselves what they had previously devoted to God (cf. Deut. xiii. 17). Among the ancient Gauls and Germans there were similar enactments with regard to what had been devoted to their deities (see Cæsar's *Bell. Gall.*, vi., 17 ; Tacit., *Annal.*, xiii., 57). In the last clause, עֲכַרְתֶּם may contain an allusion to Achan (vii. 25), or may be used by the author undesignedly, since the same verb in the same sense occurs in Gen. xxxiv. 30.

Ver. 19.—אוֹצַר: Accus. loci. (§ 118, 1, a). The reference is to the treasury in the Tabernacle (cf. ver. 24 and Numb. xxxi. 54).

Vers. 20-25 (*Execution of the above-mentioned Commands of Joshua*).—Ver. 20.—וַיָּרַע הָעָם, "*and so the people shouted*": Hiph. imperf. apoc. of רוּעַ, to make a loud noise : ן (see § 49, 2). It might seem from the words which next follow, viz., "*and they blew*," etc., that the shouting preceded the blowing of the trumpets, but the next clause shows that such was not the case. As Joshua, in ver. 16, had mentioned shouting only, this, as Keil conjectures, may explain the order of the words here. On the remainder of this verse see note ver. 5.

Vers. 21.—וַיַּחֲרִימוּ . . . לְפִי חָרֶב, "*and they utterly destroyed* (devoted) *with the edge of the sword*" (cf. Deut. xiii. 16, where the same expression is used synonymously with הִכָּה לְפִי חָרֶב). לְ is here used of the instrument (see Ges., *Lex.*); it is a particle which properly denotes relation in the widest sense, and is most commonly = "*as to*," "*with respect to*," the precise relation being left to be determined by the context. The wholesale extermination of the inhabitants of Jericho was justified by their enormous wickedness, the time given them for repentance, and the necessity of making them a warning to others, and to the Israelites in particular, of the awful consequences of sin. That many innocent children were involved in the destruction shows that the guilt of parents may be visited in this life on their offspring, though doubtless all who die in infancy are objects of the Divine mercy, being delivered from sin and its consequences, and made partakers of eternal happiness.

Vers. 22.—אָמַר is used here as a pluperfect (Rosenm. and Keil), for it is hardly likely that this order was given only when the carnage had begun, and not when the commands of Joshua were issued (ver. 17, etc.) "*Go ye . . . house*": Hence it appears that that portion of the wall, against which the house of Rachabh had been built, had not fallen with the rest; a clear proof of the Divine interposition in her favour. "*As ye swore unto her*" (see ii. 14).

Ver. 23.—נְעָרִים: Not, as Kimchi, "*servants*," though נַעַר, like puer, sometimes means a servant, but "*young men*," as in A. V., Sept. δύο νεανίσκοι, Vulg. juvenes (cf. Gen. xxii. 3, xxxiv. 19, xxxvii. 2; Judges viii. 20). "*Her brothers*": But including sisters, who are mentioned ii. 13. אֶת־כָּל־ . . . לָהּ, "*all who belonged to her*," i.e., all her household, not all her goods, of which no more could have been removed than each person could carry (cf. ii. 13).

6

"*All her families*" (Hebrew), *i.e.*, all her relatives by blood or marriage. "*And they left them* (lit., made them to rest) *outside the camp,*" etc. Till they had been proselytized to the Jewish religion, they could not be admitted to the camp, which was hallowed by the ark, the seat of God's presence.

Ver. 24.—"*And they burnt*" (see note, ver. 17): Rachabh's house was no doubt consumed also, and, therefore, when "travellers of the middle ages pretend that they found the house still standing, we must set this down as one of the many delusions which were kept alive for centuries by pious superstition in the Holy Land" (Keil). "*The house of Jehovah,*" *i.e.*, the Tabernacle (cf. 2 Sam. xii. 20; Psalm v. 8): The term בַּיִת is also used of a tent, or movable dwelling, in Gen. xxvii. 15.

Ver. 25.—"*And she dwelt . . . unto this day*": Hence it seems that she was alive when this history was written, and the fact that she dwelt in Israel implies that she had embraced the Hebrew religion.

Ver. 26 (*Curse on the Rebuilder of Jericho*).— "*And Joshua adjured* (them)," *i.e.*, "he solemnly charged them" (cf. 1 Kings xxii. 16), or "made to swear" (cf. Gen. xxiv. 3, and the Greek ἐξορκίζω, Matt. xxvi. 63). אָרוּר, "*cursed*" (cf. the curse of Agamemnon on Ilium, Strabo, xiii., ch. 1, § 42; and of Scipio on Carthage, Appian, lib. i., cap. 20). "*Before Jehovah,*" *i.e.*, Jehovah Himself being the judge, and inflicting the punishment. "*Who riseth up and buildeth,*" *i.e.*, who shall attempt to build (cf. Neh. ii. 18, "*Let us rise up and build,*" *i.e.*, let us begin or attempt to build). Knobel, Kitto (*Encyc. of Lib. Lit.*), and others, understand בָּנָה here in its ordinary sense, "to build;" but it rather denotes "to fortify," for it has that meaning in 2 Chron. xiv., where, after it is said that Asa built fenced cities in Judah (ver. 6), it is added that he said unto Judah, "*Let us build these cities*" (*i.e.*, let us fortify these cities which have been already built), and make about them walls and towers, etc.; so in 1 Kings xv. 22, "*Asa built*" (*i.e.*, fortified) *with them Geba of Benjamin and Mizpeh.*" It is clear, too, that before Hiel, in the reign of Asa, incurred this curse (1 Kings xvi. 34), Jericho had been rebuilt (see Josh. xviii. 21; Judges iii. 13; 2 Sam. x. 5), and it is not stated that it had been rebuilt on a different site from that of the ancient town. Further, the expression "*to set up the gates*" is such as could be appropriately employed in reference only to the fortification of the town. בִּבְכֹרוֹ, "*In his first-born*": The prep. ב denotes the price in exchange for which a thing is procured (Ges., *Lex.*, B., 9). Keil and many others suppose that the rebuilder of the city was threatened with the loss of all his children, beginning from the eldest to the youngest, but Josephus (*Antiq.*, v., i., 8), Theodoret, Knobel, and Bishop Wordsworth limit it to the death of the eldest and youngest. Certainly, there is no express mention made of any other children, either here or in 1 Kings xvi. 34, where the fulfilment of the curse is mentioned. Perhaps the rhythmical form in which the curse is expressed may have been designed to fix it in the memory of the people (Bishop Wordsworth).

Ver. 27 (*Joshua's Renown*).—"*Jehovah was with Joshua*" (cf. the promise, i. 5, 9). שֵׁמַע, "*report,*" and hence "*fame,*" occurs again in ix. 9; Jer. vi. 24;

Esther ix. 4, only; in the Pentateuch the form used is שָׁכֵם (see Gen. xxix. 13; Exod. xxiii. 1; Numb. xiv. 15; Deut. ii. 25).

Note that the overthrow of Jericho cannot be accounted for from *natural* causes, but was undoubtedly brought about by Divine interposition. Not only is such interposition clearly indicated throughout the narrative, but was obviously *necessary*, because the Israelites, being a nomad people, and unacquainted with the art of besieging cities, could not have taken a place so strong as Jericho without supernatural aid. The city also, by its position, was the key of the eastern pass to Canaan, and, therefore, its miraculous conquest at the outset of the invasion was calculated to render the Israelites confident that God was on their side, and would be with them throughout their enterprise, while, at the same time, it struck their enemies with dismay. Further, its overthrow was *prophetical* and *typical*, for the vision of the seven trumpets in the Apocalypse (Rev. viii. 2, etc.), corresponds to the narrative of the siege and capture of Jericho. Christ, our Divine Joshua, now enables His people to overcome the world by faith (1 John v. 4), but at His second coming He will "*descend from heaven with a shout, with the voice of the archangel and the trump of God*" (1 Thess. iv. 16), and then will take place the final judgment of all His enemies. Till, however, the *full* time (denoted often in Scripture by the perfect number seven) for the execution of God's final purposes arrives, the overthrow of Satan's empire is being carried on by means which, to the eye of sense, appear inadequate to the purpose. Such a means is the preaching of the Gospel, which was "*to the Jews a stumbling-block and to the Greeks foolishness,*" but which was, and still is, "*the power of God unto salvation to every one who believeth.*" Ministers in themselves are mere "*earthen vessels*" (2 Cor. iv. 7), but God magnifies His own power in the use of them, for their weapons are "*not carnal, but mighty through God to the pulling down of strongholds.*"

CHAPTER VII.

Achan's Theft and Punishment.

Ver. 1 (*The Crime of Achan*).—יִמְעֲלוּ מַעַל: For the cognate accus. see § 138, 1, Rem. i., and cf. ἁμαρτάνοντα ἁμαρτίαν (1 John v. 16). מָעַל, prim., "to cover" (Ges., *Lex.*), whence מְעִיל, "an upper garment;" then "to act covertly," and hence "falsely, treacherously" (Lev. v. 15), as here, construed with בְּ of the thing, and in xxii. 16, with בְּ of the person. בַּחֵרֶם, "*in that which had been devoted to the Lord.*" The sin, therefore, was sacrilege. בְּנֵי יִשׂ׳: The sin of Achan is here imputed to *all* the Israelites, because the whole nation was in covenant with God (see ver. 11), and, therefore, the sin of one among them brought pollution upon the whole as a body. The Sept., after rendering "the children of Israel committed a transgression," adds, by way of explanation, καὶ ἐνοσφίσαντο ἀπὸ τοῦ ἀναθέματος, "*and purloined part of the accursed thing,*" words similar to those used respecting the sacrilege of Ananias, ἐνοσφίσατο ἀπὸ τῆς τιμῆς (Acts v. 1). עַל, so in xxii. 20, but עָכָר, in 1 Chron.

ii. 7 (probably as a play upon the word עָכַר, to trouble, cf. ver. 25, below), and so in the Vat. Sept. (*passim*); Josephus, Ἄχαρος (*Antiq.*, lib. v., c. 1, § 10). Zabhdî, called Zimri (1 Chron. ii. 6). Zerach, the twin-brother of Perez, sons of Judah by Tamar (Gen. xxxviii. 29, 30). Thus Achan was the fourth in descent from Judah, but, as in other cases, so here, some generations have been omitted, perhaps between Zerach and Zabhdî. It is probable from the character of his ancestry that he had not been religiously brought up. On מָטֶּה, see iii. 12. "*And the anger of Jehovah*," etc.: Inasmuch as the whole nation was contaminated by the sin of Achan, it justly incurred Jehovah's displeasure.

Vers. 2-5 (*The Defeat before 'Ay*).—Ver. 2.— '*Ay*,[1] always written (with the article) in Hebrew הָעַי (§ 109, 3), except in Jer. xlix. 3, where a different town belonging to the Ammonites is referred to; Sept., Γαί, but Ἀγγαί in Gen. xii. 8, written עַיָּת, Isa. x. 28, and עַיָּא in Chaldee, Neh. xi. 31: These two latter names being probably variations only of the name 'Ay here mentioned. עַי means "*a heap of ruins*," according to Gesen. (*Lex.*), but according to Rosenm. is here עַי, *cumulus*, and refers to its situation on a hill. The opinion of Dean Stanley that Haai (the ruins) may have been a later name to indicate the fall of the city (*Sin. and Pal.*, p. 203) is irreconcilable with the fact that in the time of Abraham the city was so called (Gen. xii. 8). Its site, though known in the time of Eusebius (Onom.

---

[1] According to the Jewish pronunciation the "yodh" here retains its consonant power (*Gr.*, § 8, 5).

'Αγγαί), has long been the subject of conjecture. Dean Stanley places it at the head of *Wady Harith*; Krafft, Strauss, Ritter, and Keil identify its ruins with those of *Medinet Gai*, five miles east of Bethel, and between *Wady Farah* and *Wady es Suweinit*. Probably, however, Van de Velde is correct in supposing that the true site is *Tell-el-Hajar*, the Mount of Stones, about forty-five minutes south-east of Bethel (cf. Clark's *Bib. Atlas*, Plate X.). This site answers in every way to the requirements of the Scripture account of the conquest of 'Ay, (see V. de Velde's narrative, ii., 278—282, and *Pal. Fund Reports*, 1881, p. 36). עַי, "*near*," cf. Gen. xxv. 11 (Ges., *Lex.*). *Bĕth-'Aven* (house of vanity), on the northern border of Benjamin, xviii. 12, and east of Bethel, lying between it and Michmash (1 Sam. xiii. 5). The name was afterwards transferred by the Prophet Hosea to Bethel, to denote that, though once the house of God, it had become a house of idols (Hos. iv. 15, v. 8, x. 5). Bĕth-'Êl (house of God), anciently called Lûz (=almond-tree), Gen. xxviii. 19; Judges i. 23, but by anticipation Bethel (Gen. xii. 8), one of the cities assigned to Benjamin (Josh. xviii. 13), and situated on its northern boundary, but afterwards taken by Ephraim (Judges i. 22-26), and made one of the two principal seats of Jeroboam's idolatry. It lay in the direct thoroughfare of Palestine, whence the expressions "the highway that goeth up to Bethel" (Judges xx. 31), "the highway that goeth up from Bethel to Shechem" (Judges xxi. 19). No place (with the single exception of Shechem) comprises a longer series of remarkable scenes of sacred history (*Sin.*

and Pal., p. 217). It is probably the same as the modern *Beitân* or *Beitîn*, twelve miles north of Jerusalem, on the road from the latter to Sichem (Nablus). (Robinson's *Palestine*, ii., p. 126). עֲלֵה implies an ascent to the city from the plains of Jericho. The valley of the Jordan is 3,000 feet below the mountains of Judæa (Stanley's *Sin. and Pal.*, p. 283), and Bethel lay 2,890 feet above the sea (*Great Pal. Map*).

Ver 3.—וְיַכּוּ, "*and let them smite,*" *i.e.*, let them take by assault (Ges., *Lex.*, on נָכָה, Sept. ἐκπολιορκησάτωσαν (cf. 2 Kings iii. 19; 1 Chron. xx. 1) עָיְתָה אַל־תְּיַגַּע seems to have a pregnant sense, viz., *weary not by leading thither.*" כִּי, "*for they*" (*i.e.* the inhabitants of 'Ay) "are few;" it appears from viii. 25 that the total population of 'Ay was about twelve thousand; hence three thousand men might have been supposed quite sufficient for its conquest.

Ver. 4.—"*And they fled before the men of 'Ay*": The Sept. has ἔφυγον ἀπὸ προσώπ ιυ, κ.τ.λ., as though it had read מִפְּנֵי; and thus their rendering might imply that the Israelites fled at the very sight of their enemies: such a supposition, however, is unnecessary; there may have been an engagement, and what caused the defeat of the Israelites was not the prowess of the men of 'Ay, but the anger of God on account of the sin of Achan; see the warning which had been given (Deut. xxiii. 9). Hence we may learn how the sin of even *one* individual may bring down calamity upon a whole people (cf. the consequence of Saul's sin in breaking his covenant with the Gibeonites, 2 Sam. xxi. 1, and of David's sin in numbering the people, 2 Sam. xxiv. 10-15);

and be, therefore, the more careful individually to avoid its commission, and to deter others from it.

Ver. 5.—עַד־הַשְּׁבָרִים: Some take the noun as an appellative, thus Gesenius (see שֶׁבֶר, *Lex.*, 3, p. 803), "*even to destruction*," as in Prov. xvi. 18; Isa. i. 28; Lam. ii. 11, iii. 47; Sept. (Alex.), συνέτριψαν αὐτούς, perhaps from a different reading; Keil, "*as far as the stone quarries*," for שֶׁבֶר means lit. "a breaking." But perhaps the word has reference to the deep fissures in the ground in that particular locality; thus Dean Stanley (*Sin. and Pal.*, ch. iv., p. 202) understands by it the breakings or fissures at the opening of the passes. "*In the going down*," or "*declivity*," viz., that into the Jordan valley. With the expression "*the hearts melted*" cf. ii. 11; here it is rendered more emphatic by the simile in the last clause.

Vers. 6-9 (*Joshua's Prayer*).—Ver. 6.—"*Rent his clothes*." שִׂמְלָה properly denotes the ordinary outer garment, but is here used in the plural, as in Gen. xxxvii. 34, for clothes generally. Rending of the clothes was designed to be a symbol of rending of the heart (Joel ii. 13). "*And fell upon his face*" (cf. Numb. xx. 6). "*Before the ark*," i.e., before the Tabernacle, in which the ark was, and with his face towards the ark. "*Until the eventide*": And, therefore, we may infer that they fasted during the whole time (see 2 Sam. i. 12). "*The Elders*": The term is applied to the heads of tribes, families, and households. They were the representatives of the people of Israel, and seem from the earliest period to have formed a political council or senate (Exod. iii. 16, iv. 29). "*And put*" (lit. made to ascend) "*dust*" (cf. Job ii. 12; 1 Sam. iv. 12; 2 Sam. i. 2). So *Achilles*, when he heard of the death of Patroclus, *Il.*, Σ, 22, etc., and *Latinus*, when he grieved for the death of his queen (*Æneid*, xii., 609-611, "*it scissa veste Latinus, etc.*").

Ver. 7.—יְהוָה, so pointed, because it follows אֲדֹנָי but to be pronounced Elohim (see Keil on Gen. ii. 4). הֶעֱבַרְתָּ is an unusual form for הֶעֱבַרְתָּ (§ 63, Rem. 4), cf. הַעֲלֹה, for הַעֲלֵה, Hab. i. 15. The infin. absol. הַעֲבִיר, with the unusual *i* in the last syllable, is here put for emphasis after the finite verb (§ 131, 3 Rem., 1), "*Why hast thou at all brought over*" (Auth. Vers.), or, "*Why hast thou in so wonderful a manner brought us over.*" "*The Emorite*," iii. 10. וַנֵּשֶׁב ... וְלוּ, "*And would that we had been content to remain*": Sept., καὶ εἰ κατεμεί- ναμεν, κ.τ.λ., where εἰ = εἴθε, utinam (see for the construction, § 142, 3, *a*); the primary meaning of הוֹאִיל is "*he willed*," or "let himself be pleased," Hiph. of יָאַל, to will, to wish (Ges., *in Thess.*); cf. Keil on Exod. ii. 21).

Ver. 8.—בִּי, a particle of entreaty, "*Pray,*" contracted from בְּעִי, prayer, rt. בָּעָה, to ask; always joined with אֲדֹנָי or אֲדֹנִי (Gen. xliii. 20, xliv. 18; Exod. iv. 10, 13). "*What shall I say after that Israel hath turned the neck before his enemies?*" חָפַךְ עֹרֶף or פָּנָה עֹרֶף (ver. 12) corresponds to our expression, "to turn the back," *i.e.*, to flee.

Ver. 9.—"*All the inhabitants of the land*": Here probably the Philistines, who were not of Canaanitish race (Gen. x. 14), but had established themselves in place of the Avvim, whom they had exterminated (Deut. ii. 23). סָבַב, followed by עַל, means "to surround in a hostile manner" (cf. Gen. xix. 4. "*And what wilt Thou do to* (*i.e.*, with regard to) *Thy Great Name?*" *i.e.*, how wilt Thou preserve it from being dishonoured among the heathen, who will impute the destruction of Israel to a want of faithfulness, or power, on Thy part to fulfil to them Thy promises? See a similar plea urged by Moses (Exod. xxxii. 12; Numb. xiv. 13; Deut. ix. 28). The (··) in the last syllable of תַּעֲשֵׂה is regarded by Gesenius as an Aramaism (see § 75, Rem. v., 17). Maurer considers such forms as instances of a constructive state in verbs, analogous to that of nouns ending in הָ֭, which in construction become הֵ֭ (§ 89, 2, c). Joshua's piety was shown by this his concern for the Divine glory, but, at the same time, the despondency and unbelief, which his complaint and expostulation evinced, are not to be excused, for he should have called to mind God's past mercies, and have relied upon His gracious promises. But here we see how impartially Holy Scripture records the failings of good men.

Vers. 10-15 (*Jehovah's Answer and Directions to Joshua*).—Ver. 10.—לְךָ (in pause for לְךָ, § 103, 2, *a*) gives greater intensity to the verb. זֶה, "*thus*" (cf. Gen. xxv. 22). This reproof on the part of God indicated that the time spent in fruitless lamentation should be employed in earnest reformation.

Ver. 11.—"*Israel hath sinned*," see on ver. 1. גַּם, "*also;*" the repetition of this word before each clause of the indictment is intended to put their guilt in the strongest light. "*They have transgressed my covenant*," *i.e.*, the covenant mentioned in Exod. xix. 8, xxiv. 7, in which they had pledged themselves to obey all the commands of God (cf. Josh. i. 16-18).

Some, as Drusius, think that the reference is to the command given with respect to Jericho (vi. 18-19), and render וְגַם in the next clause "*for even*" (cf. Auth. Vers.), but the rendering "*and also*" marks their disobedience with regard to Jericho as one particular item of their general breach of the covenant. (See above in this note.) מִן־הַחֵרֶם, "*of the ban*," or "*devoted thing*," of which they had been expressly charged not to take (vi. 18-19). וְגַם כִּחֲשׁוּ, "*and have also lied*": Though no denial of the theft is recorded, yet perhaps Joshua, after the destruction of Jericho, may have inquired whether the silver and gold, etc., had been brought into the treasury of the Lord, and all else destroyed, and may have been assured that it had; or, if no inquiry had been made, the verb may here denote concealment of what ought to have been confessed with penitence (Keil after Schmidt). "*Among their own stuff*" (A.V.), or "*house furniture*": This was the climax of their offence, viz., the appropriation to their own use of what had been consecrated to God and stolen from Him.

Ver. 12.—וְלֹא יָכְלוּ, "*Therefore the sons of Israel cannot stand*," etc. ו often means "therefore" at the beginning of a sentence, when the reason is contained in what preceded: see Ges., *Lex.* (5), p. 235. עֹרֶף יִפְנוּ, "*they turn the neck*" (cf. ver. 8). כִּי . . . לְחֵרֶם, "*for they have become a devoted thing*," *i.e.*, have fallen under the ban (cf. vi. 18). "*Neither will I be with you any more, unless ye shall destroy*," etc. (cf. St. Paul's address to his Corinthian converts, 1 Cor. v. 6, 7, 13; 2 Cor. vi. 17, 18).

Ver. 13.—קֻם, "*arise*": Not implying, as in ver. 10,

that Joshua was still lying on the ground, but inviting him to activity. "*Sanctify the people*," *i.e.*, command them to sanctify, or to purify themselves (cf. iii. 5). "*Thou canst not stand*," etc. ; so in our spiritual conflicts one hidden, unrepented, sin may lead to our discomfiture.

Ver. 14.—וְנִקְרַבְתֶּם, "*then ye shall approach*," or lit., "*ye shall be brought near*": The same word in Niphal occurs again in Exod. xxii. 7 only, where it denotes, as here, an *involuntary* approach, and is followed by אֶל־אֱלֹהִים, "to God," *i.e.*, to the place where judgment was given in God's Name. "*Which Jehovah shall take*": As לָכַד is used of taking by lot in 1 Sam. x. 20, xiv. 42, so probably here; thus Josephus, after recording this command of God, says that Joshua κατὰ φυλὴν ἐκλήρου (*Antiq.*, lib. v., cap. i., § 14). The Hebrew word for "*lot*" is גּוֹרָל, a stone, or pebble, which, having a name inscribed on it, was cast into an urn, whence the expression, "*the lot came up*" (Josh. xviii. 11) and "*came out*" (xix. 1). From Prov. xvi. 33 it appears that the lot was thought to be under the Divine direction. It was used on many occasions among the Jews, as, *e.g.*, in the apportionment of land (Numb. xxvi. 55; Josh. xiv. 2 [see note], xviii. 10; Acts xiii. 19); the appointment of persons to offices and duties (1 Sam. x. 20, 21; Acts i. 24-26; cf. Herod., iii., 128, vi., 109); the division of spoil or captives (Joel iii. 3; Nahum iii. 10; Matt. xxvii. 35; cf. Xenophon, *Cyroped.*, iv., 5, 55; Thucyd., iii., 50); in the settlement of doubtful questions (Prov. xvi. 33, xviii. 18); in the detection of guilty persons, as here of Achan, of Jonathan (1 Sam. xiv. 41, 42), of Jonah (Jonah i. 7), כִּי,

"*families*": From יָפַח, to spread out; each tribe was divided into families, and each family into houses, and each house into persons (Keil). In Judges vi. 15, a "*thousand*" is used as = "mishpach" (cf. 1 Sam. x. 19, 21), because the number of the heads, or chiefs, of the families in a tribe would, on the average, amount to that number. (See Keil on Exod. xviii. 25; Numb. i. 16).

Ver. 15.—הַנִּלְכָּד בַּחֵרֶם, "*he who is taken in* (with) *the ban*," *i.e.*, he, on whom the lot falls, and who is thus proved to have stolen what was devoted to God. יִשָּׂרֵף: The Niph. future is here used as an impers. active, and followed by the object of the action in the accus. (§ 143, 1, *a*). As it appears from ver. 25 that Achan was stoned, the burning can refer to his dead body only. The severity of the penalty was increased by this treatment of the body after death. "*He hath transgressed the covenant of Jehovah*" (see ver. 11): By his sacrilege he had brought himself under the ban, ver. 12, vi. 18, and was justly doomed, like Jericho, to destruction. "*Folly*," not only of the mind, but of the heart; so in Gen. xxxiv. 7; Judges xx. 6; 2 Sam. xiii. 12. The expression "wrought folly" is not found in the later books.

Vers. 16-26 (*The Detection of Achan, his Confession, and Punishment*).—Ver. 17.—"*The family of Judah*": For the sing. "*mishpachath*," seven MSS. (see De Rossi in Append. *Varr. Lect.*, vol. iv., p. 227) read "*mishpᵉchoth*," and are followed by the Sept. and Vulg. Gesenius and Winer say that it is here used loosely for שֵׁבֶט, but rather, according to Schmidt and Keil, it denotes collectively, or distributively, *all* the families of Judah.

לִגְבָרִים, "*man by man*": Some MSS. have לַבָּתִּים, which reading is followed by the Aldine edition of the Sept., and by the Vulg., also by Dathe, Maurer, Rosenm., and others; but the Alex. Vers. of the Sept. has κατ' ἄνδρας, Vat. κατ' ἄνδρα, nor is there any reason to alter the reading in the Hebrew text, since לִגְבָרִים may denote, not that all individuals composing the houses, but only their *chiefs*, were present at the casting of the lot. So Keil.

Ver. 18.—"*Achan*" (see note on ver. 1). The detection of the sin of Achan strikingly displays the awful omniscience of God, and the truth of the declaration, "Evil shall *hunt* the wicked man to overthrow him" (Psalm cxl. 11).

Ver. 19.—"*My son*": Spoken, not ironically, but sincerely, and showing us that judges, while they punish offences, ought, as far as justice permits, to be merciful to the offender. "*Give glory . . . and make confession*": A form of adjuration (cf. John ix. 24), calling on a man to tell the truth. The confession of Achan would tend to the glory of God's Omniscience, Truth, and Holiness. תּוֹדָה, "*confession*" (Ges., *Lex.*), or *praise* (Keil), cf. Ezra x. 11; but as the latter meaning has been already expressed by the word כָּבוֹד, the former seems preferable, and the confession would be virtually a giving of praise to God.

Ver. 20.—אָמְנָה, "*truly*": Adverb of affirmation (§ 150, 3, *c.*; cf. Gen. xx. 12). By his confession, which was full and explicit, without any attempt at excuse, Achan seems to have been truly penitent, and therefore, though punished in this life, may have been rendered happy in the next (see Prov. xxviii. 13).

Ver. 21.—וָאֵרֶא, "*and I saw*": The vowels belong to the apoc. form in the Qᵉri, but with "Vav" consec. the full form without apocope frequently occurs in verbs לה, especially in the first person (see § 75, Rem. i., 3, c, second par.). Note that the loosely connected sentences, "thus and thus have I done; *and* I saw . . . *and* I coveted," etc., exhibit the simplicity of the Hebrew style (see Ges., *Lex.* on the letter ו, p. 233), and well express the disturbed state of Achan's mind. "*A goodly robe* (or cloak) *of Shinar*" (see Gen. x. 10, xi. 2). אַדֶּר, from אָדַר, to be wide, a garment worn by kings on state occasions (Jonah iii. 6), also by prophets (1 Kings xix. 13; 2 Kings ii. 13, 14). Shinar was the plain in which Babylon was situated (Gen. x. 10, xi. 2). The Sept. renders the term in Isa. xi. 11 by Βαβυλωνία, and in Zech. v. 11 by γῆ Βαβυλῶνος; and so here Aquila, and the Chald., Syr., and Arab. Versions render אַדֶּר שִׁנְעָר, "a Babylonish cloak." These cloaks were not hairy like that mentioned in Zech. xiii. 4, but smooth, and embroidered with pictures of men and animals (Pliny, *Hist. Nat.*, lib. viii., ch. 48); Sept. ψιλὴν ποικίλην; Vulg. "pallium-coccineum." As Jericho lay in the route from Babylon to the ports of the Mediterranean, it is not surprising that articles of commerce from that city, or at least from the district around (for it cannot be proved that the garment was undoubtedly Babylonish) should have been found in it. "*Two hundred shekels of silver*": = £25 in English money, if the shekel is valued at 2s. 6d. The reference is to *uncoined* money, as there is no mention of coined money in Scripture before the Babylonish captivity. "*A tongue of gold*": Probably a golden ornament shaped like a tongue. The name "*lingula*" was given by the Romans to a spoon (Pliny, *N. H.*, xxi., 49), and to an oblong dagger formed in the shape of a tongue (Gellius, *Noct. Attic.*, x., 25). Gesenius (*Lex.*) thinks that here a bar of gold, resembling a tongue, is meant; Vulg., "regula aurea." "*Fifty shekels in respect to its weight*": *i.e.*, = about 25 ounces, at the rate of about half an ounce avoirdupois, or 220 English grains, to the shekel. "*And I coveted and took them*": He first saw, and next coveted, and next took (cf. the several steps in the sin of Eve, Gen. iii. 6). טָמַנְתִּי, not merely "hid" (A. V.), but "*buried,*" as in Gen. xxxv. 4; Exod. ii. 12. Josephus (*Antiq.*, v., c. 1, § 10) says that Achan dug a deep hole, or ditch, in his tent, and put there the Babylonish garment and the wedge of gold, supposing that he should not only be concealed from his fellow-soldiers, but from God Himself also. הָאָהֳלִי: The article prefixed to a noun with a suffix is contrary to the rule (§ 110, 2); it may, however, be regarded as either = a demonstrative pronoun, "*that* my tent" (cf. הַחֵצִי, viii. 33, § 110, 2, Rem. *a*), or, according to Hengstenberg (*Christol.*, iii., p. 362), has lost its force, and become absorbed into the noun. תַּחְתֶּיהָ, "*underneath them,*" *i.e.*, the cloak of Shinar was probably put on the top, and below it the tongue of gold, and underneath that the silver. The fem. suff. is a neuter coll., and refers to all the stolen property except the silver; Sept. ὑποκάτω αὐτῶν.

Ver. 22.—הָאֹהֱלָה, "*to the tent,*" ־ָה, loc. (§ 90, 2, *a*).

Ver. 23.—וַיַּצִּקֻם, "*and they placed them*": Sept. κ' ἔθηκαν αὐτά. יצק means to pour out, and so the

Hiphil form הוֹצִיק (see 2 Kings iv. 5); but הָצִיק has nearly the same meaning as הָצִיג (Ges., *Lex.*, p. 361), and signifies here and in 2 Sam. xv. 24, "*to place,*" or "*to set.*" "*Before Jehovah,*" *i.e.*, before the Tabernacle, where was the Ark, the seat of the Divine Presence (cf. vi. 8).

Ver. 24.—"*The son of Serach,*" *i.e.*, the great grandson of Serach (see ver. 1). "*His sons and his daughters*": Because in Deut. xxiv. 16 it is forbidden that children should be put to death for the sin of their parents, Schulz, Hess, and others, have thought that Achan's family were merely obliged to be spectators of his punishment, that they might take warning therefrom; it is probable, however, that they were privy to his guilt, since the stolen goods had been hidden in the midst of the tent, and the fact that the crime of Achan had brought himself and family and property under the ban, would justly involve all in the same fate (see ver. 15). Moreover, it is a principle of God's government, to regard children as represented in their parents, and parents in their children; see the case of Canaan, the son of Ham (Gen. ix. 25), and the death of the firstborn of the Egyptians (Exod. xii.), and confer the declaration of Jeremiah (Jer. xxxii. 18). וְאֶת־שׁוֹרוֹ: This and the two accusatives which follow are used coll. (§ 108, 1). וְאֵת כָּל ... לוֹ, "*and all its furniture.*" The following words, "*and all Israel with him,*" are to be joined with וַיִּקַּח יְהוֹשֻׁעַ, at the beginning of the verse. The reference is to all Israel as acting by their chiefs and representatives. "*The valley of Achor*" (*i.e.*, of trouble). עֵמֶק is always translated "*valley*" by A. V., rt. עָמַק, to be deep, but used rather of lateral extension than depression, like βαθέη αὐλή (*Il.*, v., 142), and the expression deep, as opposed to shallow, house; thus the word is not applied to ravines, but to the long broad sweeps sometimes found between parallel ranges of hills. Such is the valley of Jezreel, between Gilboa and Little Hermon (Dean Stanley, *S. and P.*, Append., p. 481). The valley of Achor lay to the south or south-west of Jericho, and was on the north border of Judah (xv. 7), and from the camp of the Israelites at Gilgal there were probably ridges to be ascended before the valley could be reached, hence the use of the word יַעֲלוּ here. The name "Achor" is, like "Gilgal" in iv. 19, used proleptically, or by anticipation (see ver. 26).

Ver. 25.—וּמֶה, "*Why hast thou troubled us?*" (Auth. Vers.), or "*What trouble hast thou brought upon us?*" So Ahab was the troubler of Israel (1 Kings xviii. 18). "*And all Israel stoned him.*" רָגַם, prop. "to pile" (Gesen.), "to overwhelm with stones" (Syr. and Arab.); frequently in this latter sense in the Pentateuch; here followed by two accus. (cf. Levit. xxiv. 23), once with omission of אֶבֶן (Levit. xxiv. 14). Achan only is referred to because the principal offender, but that all the rest suffered the like punishment is evident from the occurrence of אֹתָם in vers. 24, 25. Stoning was the ordinary mode of execution among the Jews (Exod. xvii. 4; Deut. xiii. 10; Luke xx. 6; John x. 31; Acts xiv. 5). "*And they burned them*" (*i.e.*, after they were dead). The Sept. omits this. Burning alive does not occur anywhere among the punishments inflicted by the Jewish law, says Keil after Michaelis (*Mos. R.*, v., § 235), in which case, however, Levit. xx. 14, xxi. 9 cannot be understood without qualification. וַיִּסְקְלוּ (omitted by the Vulg., as well as by Sept.), "*and they pelted them with stones*": סָקַל, to pelt (Lee), "to overwhelm with stones," rt. שָׁקַל, to be heavy (Ges., *Lex.*). Michaelis thinks that stoning of the ashes of the dead is meant; Knobel, that the clause has been inserted to prevent any misunderstanding of the preceding אֹתוֹ; Keil, that the allusion is to the heaping of a pile of stones on the dead bodies. If this latter meaning is here adopted, we must regard the first clause of ver. 26 as intended to give only a fuller description of the same fact. The punishment thus inflicted for Achan's sin, though terrible, was not too severe, for by that sin he had robbed God, and endangered the safety of the whole nation.[1] He had also committed it shortly after his renewal of his covenant with God by circumcision and the eating of the Passover, and after the recent proof of God's power and love to Israel in the overthrow of Jericho. From his history we may learn especially (1) the deceitfulness of sin, inasmuch as it never affords the gratifications expected from it; (2) the certainty of its exposure, because nothing can escape the all-seeing eye of God; (3) the awful retribution which often overtakes it in this life, and will certainly do so in the next, if not averted by repentance, confession, and faith in Christ; (4) its injuriousness to others as well as to ourselves. "One sinner destroyeth much good" (Eccles. ix. 18).

---

[1] See note on ver. 1. There is an analogy between Achan's sin and that of Ananias and Sapphira, and the severity of the punishment in both cases, occurring at the outset of a new career, was a salutary warning to future generations (cf. Numb. xv. 32-36; 2 Sam. vi. 6-12).

Ver. 26.—גַּל, "a rude cairn," or "pile of stones" (אֲבָנִים is generally added, as here) roughly rolled together (Dean Stanley, *Sin. and Pal.*, p. 119), from גלל, to roll; it was intended to be a memorial of the punishment (cf. viii. 29; 2 Sam. xviii. 17). A like custom prevailed among the Romans (Propert., iv., 5, 75), as still among the Arabs. It was not always a mark of dishonour (Burkhardt, *Beduinen*, p. 81). "*Unto this day*" (cf. iv. 9, קָרָא, indeterm. 3rd pers., = passive, § 137, 3, *a*). "*Achor*" (see ver. 24). The only other places in which the name is found are xv. 7; Hos. ii. 17 (Heb.); Isa. lxv. 8, 10.[1]

CHAPTER VIII.

VERS. 1-29.—*The Conquest of 'Ay*.

Ver. 1.—"*Fear not . . . dismayed*" (cf. i. 9; Deut. i. 21, xxxi. 8). "*All the people of war*": Vulg. "*omnem multitudinem pugnatorum;*" as, however, out of all the fighting men of Reuben, Gad, and the half-tribe of Manasseh, who were commanded to cross over Jordan before their brethren (i. 14), the actual number sent was only 40,000 (iv. 13); so here the term *all* may imply not every man capable of bearing arms, but the army generally, as compared

---

[1] Understood spiritually, every Achor (trouble) becomes "a door of hope," when it is sanctified by repentance and faith. Thus, in Achan's case, we may trust that his confession, if sincere, was followed by pardon, and by happiness in a future life (see note on ver. 20).

with the detachment which had been previously sent. "*Go up*": 'Ay stood on higher ground than Jericho, but עָלָה is also used of the advance of an army against a fortified place, because such a place was regarded as a height to be scaled (Keil). "*I have given*" (see note vi. 2).

Ver. 2.—*Only the . . . spoil for a prey*" (see note on vi. 17). עֹרֵב, used coll., "*liers in wait*," from עָרַב, to weave, and hence "nectere insidias." "*From behind it*," *i.e.*, on its western side, see אָחוֹר, Isa. ix. 11 (12 Auth. Vers.); Job xxiii. 8. On the sanction given by God to the employment of stratagem in war, Calvin (as quoted by Keil) remarks, "If war is lawful at all, it is indisputably right to avail oneself of those arts by which victory is usually obtained. It is, of course, understood that neither must treaties be violated, nor faith broken in any other way."

Ver. 3.—"*Thirty thousand*": There is difficulty in reconciling this number with the number five thousand in ver. 12. Some, as Ewald, Maurer, and Knobel, unwarrantably assume that vers. 12, 13 have been inserted from another narrative by a later editor, who omitted to harmonize them with ver. 3. Others (Abarbanel, Clericus, etc.) suppose that there were two distinct companies of liers-in-wait, an opinion irreconcilable with vers. 9, 12, where the spot in which each was posted is described as being *between Bethel and 'Ay*, and *on the west of 'Ay*. True, Abarbanel conjectures that, though both ambushes were on the same side of the city, the smaller was set nearer to it, and was only intended to skirmish with the enemy when they came out of the city, while the larger captured the city itself; but in the account of the execution of Joshua's order (vers. 12, 13, 14, 19) there is nothing to support this view. הָאֹרֵב, in ver. 19, clearly seems to indicate that there was one ambush only. Nor is the difficulty solved by supposing, with Bishops Patrick and Wordsworth, that the 5,000 men were sent as a reinforcement to the 30,000, for so large a force as 30,000, or 35,000, could hardly have eluded observation while lying in ambuscade near to, and between, two hostile cities, apparently for two nights and an intervening day (vers. 3, 9, 10, 13). Others, as Masius, Rosenmüller, and Calvin, conclude that the number 30,000 refers to the entire army sent against 'Ay, and the number 5,000 to those placed in ambush. But thus the words "*sent them*," in ver. 3, must denote by synecdoche, "sent *some* of them," a meaning rather forced, and though the expressions "*the people*" (ver. 10) and "*all Israel*" (ver. 15) need not include everyone capable of bearing arms (see note, ver. 1), yet they would seem to imply a much larger number than 30,000. On the whole, therefore, the solution of Keil is, perhaps, the most satisfactory, viz., that for "thirty thousand" in ver. 3 should be read "five thousand," the letter ל (30) having, by the mistake of a copyist, been substituted for ה (5). That there is sometimes an inaccuracy in the figures of the historical books is evident on a comparison of those in the earlier with those in the later books (see Keil and Del., *Comm.*, p. 86).

Ver. 4.—וּרְאוּ, "*see*" (or "take heed") "*ye who are about to lie in ambush for the city . . . that ye go not very far*," etc. רְאוּ should be construed with the words אַל־תַּרְחִיקוּ (Rosenm.). נְכֹנִים, "*prepared*" (cf. Exod. xix. 11, 15), *i.e.*, to rise up and assault the city.

Ver. 5.—"*At the first*," viz., when the former attack was made on 'Ay (vii. 4). וְנַסְנוּ, "*then* (or "that") *we will flee*," נוס, to flee; ן with the apod.

Ver. 6.—"*And they will come out after us*": These words need not be put in a parenthesis, as in the Auth. Vers. ("for they will come out," etc.) "*Until we have drawn*," lit., have torn away, Hiph. infin. with suffix, see נָתַק. Render ן in the last clause "*and*," not "*therefore*" (Auth. Vers.).

Ver. 7.—הוֹרַשְׁתֶּם, "*ye shall occupy*," lit., ye shall make yourselves to possess" (cf. xvii. 12). נְתָנָהּ, "*will deliver it*": The perfect denotes, as in ver. 1, God's determinate purpose.

Ver. 8.—"*When ye shall have taken*": In Deut. xx. 19, תָּפַשׂ is also used of capturing a town. תַּצִּיתוּ, "*ye shall set on fire*": Hiphil imperfect of נָצַת, *i.q.*, יָצַת, (§ 71), "to set on fire," a word not found in the Pentateuch. "*According to the commandment*" (word), etc.: No express command had been given to burn the city, but it was implied in the command to treat it like Jericho (ver. 2). In the last clause, "*See*," etc., there is perhaps a covert allusion to the circumstances of Achan's disobedience.

Ver. 9.—Here, as in iv. 8, an account of the execution of the command follows on that of the command itself. הַמַּאֲרָב, "*the place of ambush*": The prefix מ denotes place (§ 84, 14). מִיָּם, "*on the west*": יָם is so called, because the Mediterranean Sea was on the west of Palestine. The exact site of the ambush cannot be ascertained; but, as between Bethel and 'Ay rise two rocky heights, it would seem that the liers-in-wait took their position behind them (Van de Velde, *Narrative*, ii., p. 280). This could not have been far from the site of Abraham's altar (Gen. xii. 8). "*In the midst of the people*," i.e., in the camp, with the rest of the army.

Ver. 10.—וַיִּפְקֹד, "*and reviewed*," Sept. ἐπεσκέψατο: Keil supposes that this had really been done before the despatch of the liers-in-wait, and that the beginning of this verse, "*And Joshua rose up*," is only a *résumé* of the beginning of ver. 3, further particulars being added; there is, however, nothing in ver. 3 which forbids the conclusion that, after Joshua had despatched the ambuscade, he proceeded, the following morning, to review the remainder of his forces, preparatory to their march with him against 'Ay. "*The elders of Israel*," i.e., not as Masius says, "military tribunes," who were called elders on account of their superior military skill, but the heads, or representatives, of the people, who attended Joshua as a council, and whose presence and authority may have been necessary to ensure a proper division of the booty (Numb. xxxi. 27).

Ver. 11.—הָעָם הַמִּלְ': For the construction see § 110, 2, c, and cf. iii. 14. כִּצְפוֹן לְעַי: Construc. state with prep., § 116, 1. The Sept. and Arab. for *north* put *east*, as though they had read מִקֶּדֶם, which, however, is not found in any of the MSS. וְהַגַּי, "*and the ravine*" (was). גַּיְא or גַּיְ, and by omission of Aleph, גַּי, means properly a ravine or gorge, generally translated φάραγξ by the Sept., but "valley" by Auth. Vers. (*passim*), rt. גָּוָה, i.q., גָּוָה, "to flow together," because water flows together there (Ges., *Lex.*); or rt.

גִּיחַ, "to break out," whence perhaps the name Gihon (Stanley's *Sin. and Pal.*, Append.). The article indicates that the author is referring to a well-known locality. Probably the allusion is to the deep and steep-sided ravine to the north of Tell-el-Hajar (Van de Velde). בֵּינֵי should probably be pointed בֵּינוֹ (cf. iii. 4).

Ver. 12.—וַיִּקַּח, "*and he took*": Masius, Cor. a Lapid., and others, render as a pluperfect; but, though the verb refers to what Joshua had already done (ver. 3), it should rather be here regarded as a kind of aorist (Keil), which in the New Testament often has the force of a pluperfect (Winer, *Gram. of New Test.*, part iii., sect. xl.). On the discrepancy between the numbers five thousand here and thirty thousand in ver. 3, see note above on that verse. לָעִיר evidently refers to 'Ay, and, therefore, need not be altered to לָעַי, to correspond to ver. 9.

Ver. 13.—Render, "*and so the people posted the whole camp.*" הָעָם may be best regarded as a noun-collec., and as the subject of the verb (§ 146, 1 ; cf. Vulg. and Chald.), for, if it was the object, as in the Syr., Arab., and A. V., having אֶת־כָּל־הַמַּחֲנֶה in apposition to it, אֶת־, the sign of the def. accus., would hardly have been omitted (Keil). "*And its ambuscade,*" rt. עָקַב, to circumvent, to defraud (Gen. xxvii. 36) ; so in Psalm xlix. 6. עֲקֵבַי is rendered "my supplanters" by Ewald, Hitzig (who refers to this passage), and Delitzsch, who quotes other like forms. The rendering of Gesen. and Winer, "*its rearguard,*" cannot be supported, as they allege, by Gen. xlix. 19. The word evidently here relates to what had been stated in ver. 12, and corresponds to אוֹרֵב, in ver. 12.

"*That night*": Not that in which the liers-in-wait had been sent out (ver. 9), but that on which Joshua and the rest of the host had arrived on the north of 'Ay. "*The valley*" (Auth. Vers.): See note on the Hebrew word in vii. 24. When Joshua went that night into the valley, he was no doubt accompanied by a chosen detachment from his main army, that thus at the early dawn he might engage the attention of the enemy, and give them no time to discover the ambush in their rear.

Ver. 14.—"*When the king of 'Ay saw*": Either with his own eyes, or by information from others. After "*saw*," the Auth. Vers. supplies "*it*," viz., Joshua and the picked body of troops with him. "*Against*": The Hebrew word always indicates the going forth to meet an enemy, see Deut. i. 44; Psalm xxxv. 3 (Dean Perowne's critical note). לַמּוֹעֵד, "*at* (or "*to*") *the place appointed*" (Ges., *Lex.*, and Keil; cf. 1 Sam. xx. 35). The reference seems to be to a spot selected for a concentrated attack. "*Before the plain*" (Auth. Vers.): See iii. 16, *i.e.*, at the entrance of the tract sloping down into the Jordan valley, and probably the same as the wilderness of Bethaven (xviii. 12).

Ver. 15.—"*And they feigned themselves to be beaten*": So Gesen. (*Lex.*) and Masius, and cf. Auth. Vers. Niphal has here the signification of Hithpael (§ 51, 2, *c*), for that the flight was designed is evident from ver. 6. "*By the way of the wilderness*" (Auth. Vers.). מִדְבָּר properly means "a pasture ground," from דָּבַר, to drive (to pasture), cf. the German *trift* from *treiben*. "The idea" (says Dean Stanley) "is that of a wide open space, with or without actual pasture;

the country of the nomads, as distinguished from that of the agricultural and settled people. With the article it is generally used for the desert of Arabia, but sometimes for the barren tracts which reach into the frontier of Palestine, as in the valley of the Jordan (Josh. viii. 15), or in the southern mountains of Judæa (Judges i. 16; Gen. xxi. 14)." —Appendix to *Sin. and Pal.* Here and in vers. 20, 24, it seems to be used for the same region as the Arabah in ver. 14.

Ver. 16.—נִתְּקוּ, lit., "were torn away," *i.e.*, were completely separated (cf. ver. 6).

Ver. 17.—לֹא אִישׁ, *i.e.*, no one of the fighting men, for it appears from ver. 24 that some persons were left in the town. "*Bethel*": This name is omitted in the Sept., but in none of the other ancient versions. Probably Bethel sent succour to 'Ay after Joshua's first attack on the latter (vii.).

Ver. 18.—נְטֵה, subaud. יָדְךָ (cf. vers. 19, 26; Exod. viii. 1). בַּכִּידוֹן, *with the javelin*, Sept. ἐν τῷ γαισῷ or "light spear," which is thrown, distinguished from חֲנִית, which was much heavier (1 Sam. xvii. 7). Such is its meaning in all the other passages where it occurs, viz., in 1 Sam. xvii. 6, 45, where, though the Vulg. renders it "clypeus," as here, and Auth. Vers. "target," and "shield," it probably denotes a javelin or spear, which was slung across the shoulders, as often the sword in like manner (see *Il.*, ii., 45); so in Jer. vi. 23, l. 42; Job xxxix. 23, xli. 29. It may have been furnished on this occasion with a flag at the extremity, and being light could have been held for some time without fatigue. Probably Joshua stood on an eminence to render the signal (the raising of which, but not the time, was doubtless preconcerted) the more visible.

Ver. 19.—יַצִּיתוּ, for יָצִיתוּ (§ 72, Rem. v., 9), from צוּת, *i.q.*, יָצַת, to set on fire.

Ver. 20.—יָדַיִם, lit., "two hands," hence metaph. "strength," as in Psalm lxxvi. 6, "None of the men of might have found their hands"; so the Vulg., Chald., Syr., Arab., Jarchi, Drusius, etc. The rendering "space" or "place" (Calvin, Masius, Clericus, Ges., *Lex.*) would require לָהֶם for בָּהֶם. וְהָעָם וגו, "*and the people, which was fleeing to the wilderness* [ver. 15], *turned back upon the pursuers*": וְ seems to have here the force of "for," cf. Ges., *Lex.* (4).

Ver. 21.—"*And Joshua*," etc.: Since it appears from ver. 26 that Joshua remained apart from his troops, holding out his spear till 'Ay had been destroyed, Masius thinks that the name Joshua may be here put for the detachment he had brought into the valley, and "all Israel" for the rest of the army, which now came to the aid of its comrades; but this supposition is unnecessary, since the mention of Joshua may merely imply that what was done was done by his orders. Vers. 21, 22 more fully explain how all escape was cut off from the men of 'Ay.

Ver. 22.—וְאֵלֶּה, "*and these*," viz., the men who had been placed in ambush (ver. 19), contrasted with the Israelites who had fled (ver. 20). לִקְרָאתָם, "*to meet them*," *i.e.*, the Israelites, who had turned round to attack the 'Ayites (ver. 21). עַד־בִּלְתִּי, "*until not*," followed here, according to Ges. (*Lex.*, p. 124, 3, *c*), by a pret., as in Numb. xxi. 35; Deut. iii. 3; Josh. x. 33; but, rather, in all these passages the verb is in the Hiph. infin., and the characteristic ה has *i* instead of a (cf. הִשְׁמִיד, xi. 14 ; הִרְגִּיעַ, Jer. l. 34; Ewald, *Lehrb.*, § 238, *d*). שָׂרִיד וּפָלִיט, "*a survivor, or one who has escaped by flight*": Masius thinks that the former word is = τὸν ζωγρηθέντα, "one who had been taken prisoner," a meaning not contained in the rt. שָׂרַד, to escape ; the Sept. correctly renders by σεσωσμένον καὶ διαπεφευγότα.

Ver. 24.—"*In the wilderness*" (see ver. 15, note): Here put in apposition to בּוֹ ... בַּמִּדְבָּר אֲשֶׁר, *i.e.*, in which the men of 'Ay had chased the Israelites (see vers. 15, 16). לְפִי, cf. vi. 21 ; the expression always denotes a great slaughter of the enemy. עַד־תֻּמָּם, lit., "*unto their finishing*," *i.e.*, wholly (Ges., *Lex.*; cf. Deut. xxxi. 24, 30). וַיָּשֻׁבוּ, "*that all Israel returned unto 'Ay.*" "*And they smote it*": viz., all the inhabitants, old men, women, and children, who had been left in the town. Cf. ver. 14 for the construction, and iv. 1 for the Pisqa in the middle of the verse.

Ver. 25.—"*All the men of 'Ay*": This expression taken in connection with the preceding מֵאִישׁ וְעַד־אִשָּׁה, shows that the number twelve thousand comprised the entire population (cf. note vii. 3). No mention is made of the Bethelites, who probably shared the fate of those 'Ayites who were slain outside the town.

Ver. 26.—The same custom of not lowering a signal till the battle was finished prevailed among other ancient nations : see Suidas in Σημεῖα (quoted by Rosenm.). Some, however, think that this act of Joshua, like that of Moses, recorded in Exod. xvii. 11, etc., carried with it a Divine efficacy, and was a means of securing victory to the Israelites (see Poole's *Annot.*).

Ver. 27.—They were allowed to take possession

of the cattle and spoil of 'Ay, because it was not
the intention of Jehovah to give to His people a
barren and empty land (see Deut. vi. 10, etc.), but in
the case of Jericho the cattle and spoil had been
offered to Jehovah as the firstfruits of the land.
"*According unto the word*," etc., see ver. 2.

Ver. 28.—"*Joshua burnt*," lit., "absorbed by fire,"
i.e., the town was totally burnt down, whereas before
(see ver. 19) it had been only set on fire. תֵּל־עוֹלָם, "*a
permanent heap*": תֵּל, from תָּלַל, to heap up, occurs
only here and in xi. 13; Deut. xiii. 16; Jer. xxx.
18, xlix. 2, and in the compound names of some
Babylonian cities (Ezek. iii. 15; Ezra ii. 59; Neh.
vii. 61). עוֹלָם, as in Deut. xv. 17; 1 Kings i. 31,
denotes a long time only, for 'Ay appears to have
been rebuilt, if not on the same site, yet near to it
(see Isa. x. 28; Ezra ii. 28; Neh. vii. 31).

Ver. 29.—"*He hanged on the tree*": The def. art.
before עֵץ denotes the tree selected for the purpose.
תָּלָה means simply "*he suspended*," and, therefore, does
not of itself authorize the rendering of the Sept.,
ἐκρέμασεν ἐπὶ ξύλου διδύμου, "he hung on a double
tree" (or wood), *i.e.*, on two transverse pieces of wood,
viz., a cross; nor that of the Targum of Jonathan,
and Arab. Vers., "*he crucified*," Hieron. "suspendit
super patibulo." Sometimes, however, the word
הוֹקַע is used (see Numb. xxv. 4), which means to
rend, tear, or dislocate, and might be applied to im-
paling on a cross. Such suspension, whether from
cross or gallows, took place *after* the penalty of death
had been inflicted, and was used to enhance the dis-
grace of the punishment (see Numb. xxv. 4; Deut.
xxi. 22, 23). Hanging, or crucifixion, was not a

mode of execution among the ancient Jews (Lightfoot, *Hor. Hebr.*, in Matt. xxvii. 31). "*Until the eventide,*" see Deut. xxi. 23. אֶל־פַּחַת, the Sept. εἰς τὸν βόθρον, may have arisen from a transposition of letters, viz., פַּחַת for פַּחַת, or from a wish to assimilate the rendering to that in 2 Sam. xviii. 17, where פַּחַת is used. גַּל, see note on vii. 26.[1]

VERS. 30-35.—*Erection of an Altar on Mount Ebal, and a Rehearsal of the Blessings and Curses upon Mount Gerizim and Mount Ebal.*

Though in the Vat. and Aldine copies of the Sept. this paragraph is inserted after ix. 2, and some commentators would assign it a place after xi. 3, yet

---

[1] It is not stated in this chapter whether Bethel, which had taken part with 'Ay, was at this time taken by Joshua, nor is it certain that the Bethel in xii. 16 is identical with it (see note there). "With the conquest of Ai a sure footing in the land," Geikie (*Hours with the Bible*, vol. ii., p. 408, etc.) remarks, "had been obtained, and such a dread of the invaders excited among the inhabitants as of itself made them resistless. The population of Central Palestine seems to have fled before them, for no intimation of a struggle with them is found either in Joshua or Judges. Perhaps the subdivision into small communities, incapable of prompt united action, may have aided the general demoralisation, and it is noticeable besides, that very few fortified towns are mentioned in this region. But the terrible fate of Jericho and Ai sufficiently account for a universal panic and abandonment of all, before the advancing Hebrews. . . . Some of the fugitives seem even to have emigrated to Africa, if we can trust the statement of Procopius (*De Bello Vandalico*, ii., 10) that two marble pillars were to be seen in the Numidian town Tigisis, with a Phœnician inscription:— 'We are those who fled from the face of Jesus (Joshua), the robber, the son of Nun.' Suidas states this also; giving the words as 'We are Canaanites, whom Jesus, the robber, drove out' (*s. v.* Χαναάν); and the Talmud states that the Girgasites, driven out by Joshua, wandered to Africa (*Jerus.*, Tr. Schebiit, vi., 36, 3)."

there is no proof that it does not here occupy its original and proper position. We might reasonably suppose from the terms of the command in Deut. xxvii. 4, 5, that Joshua would take the earliest opportunity of obeying that command, and such an opportunity occurred, when the conquest of 'Ay had laid open the road to Shechem, and "*the terror of the Lord*" (cf. Gen. xxxv. 5) had fallen on the inhabitants of the surrounding country. Moreover, as Hävernick has shown, the distance between 'Ay and Ebal was not more than twenty miles, or less than two days' journey (*Einleit.*, ii., 1, p. 17).

Ver. 30.—אָז, followed by an imperf. (§ 127, 4, *a;* cf. x. 12, xxii. 1; Exod. xv. 1). This particle, says Ewald (§ 136, *b*), is used in cases where the historian either wishes to introduce contemporaneous facts, which do not carry forward the main course of the history, or loses sight for the time of the strictly historical sequence, and simply takes note of the occurrence of some particular event. "*God of Israel*": The expression indicates that He only, as the true God, was to be worshipped. "*On Mount Ebal*": In the Samaritan Pentateuch "Gerizim" is read for Ebal (Deut. xxvii. 4), which reading is followed by Kennicott, Semler, Colenso, etc., but is opposed to the Hebrew MSS. and the ancient versions, and no doubt arose from a wish to give a scriptural sanction to the Samaritan worship. עֵיבָל means "void of leaves," from עָבַל (unused), in Arab., "*to strip a tree of leaves*" (Ges., *Lex.*). Dean Stanley, however, says that the present aspect of the mountain, as compared with Gerizim, is not so barren as to justify this derivation (*Sin. and Pal.*, ch. v.,

p. 237). It lies to the north of Sichem, in the tribe of Ephraim, and is about 2,700 feet in height. The true situation of Ebal and Gerizim is evident from Deut. xi. 30 (see Stanley's *Sin. and Pal.*, pp. 238-9), where it is shown that the opinion of Jerome (which had been before held by Eusebius, Procopius, and Epiphanius), that these mountains were near Jericho, cannot be sustained. As Ebal was the mount of cursing, the altar may have been erected there, rather than on Gerizim, to signify that by Christ, our true altar, the curse of the Law is removed.

Ver. 31.—The words "*as Moses .... law of Moses*" form a parenthesis, and מִזְבֵּחַ in the next clause must be joined to the preceding verse, *e.g.*, "*an altar* (I say) *of*," etc. שְׁלֵמוֹת, lit. "*sound*," *i.e.*, stones which had been unviolated by any tool, rough, unhewn. "*On which no one hath lifted up* (lit. hath shaken) [any] *iron*": See Exod. xx. 22 (25, Auth. Vers.); Deut. xxvii. 5. הֵנִיף, with indeter. nominative (§ 137, 3). The reason of this command probably was that no image or figure might be carved on the stones and afterwards worshipped. "*Burnt-offerings*": עֹלָה means "what ascends," *i.e.*, in smoke and fragrance; hence sometimes called כָּלִיל, because the *whole* victim was consumed, Sept. ὁλοκαύτωμα. Here these burnt-offerings were symbolic of the dedication of the whole nation to the service of God. "*Peace-offerings*," offered in thanksgiving (Levit. vii. 12) to God for bringing them to the Promised Land. These burnt-offerings and peace-offerings had been enjoined (Deut. xxvii. 6, 7).

Ver. 32.—-וַיִּכְתָּב־, ׳, Qamets-chatuph for ׳ before

Maqqeph, § 47, 3, Rem. 1. " *The stones,*" not of the altar (ver. 30), as Josephus (*Antiq.*, iv., 8, § 44), the Syr. Vers., Maurer, Rosenm., but the great stones mentioned in Deut. xxvii. 2, 4, and which are clearly distinct from those of the altar afterwards mentioned in ver. 5. The fact that the setting up of the former, and the plastering of them with plaster, is not recorded in the brief narrative here before us, but apparently assumed as a matter of course, it having been so expressly enjoined by Moses, probably led to the above error ; cf. John xxi., where " *the stone* " is that mentioned, not by John himself, but by the other Evangelists, and which, therefore, John deemed it sufficient to allude to as already well known. Evidently the Book of Deuteronomy had been written before the time of Joshua. מִשְׁנֵה, properly " *a duplicate or repetition of* " (cf. Deut. xvii. 18), Sept. Alex., τὸ δευτερονόμιον, Vulg. Deuteronomion. The meaning here has been much disputed. According to Cor. a Lapid. the whole of Deuteronomy was inscribed, which is very unlikely. Keil, in his earlier commentary, supposes with Vater and Hengstenberg that the *commandments* (not the exhortations by which they were enforced) from Deut. iv. to xxvi. 19, called the second Law, are here meant ; others, as Grotius and Kennicott, " *the Decalogue* " : Masius, Maurer, and Rosenm., *the curses and blessings* which had just been pronounced (so Josephus, *Antiq.*, iv., 8, § 44), which opinion Bishop Patrick, on Deut. xxvii., thinks not improbable, as in those curses and blessings several select precepts are cited, and the last of them seems to respect the whole law of Moses (Deut. xxvii. 26).

But neither of these two latter views accords with the expression "*all the words of this law*" in Deut. xxvii. 3, nor would the "*large* stones" (ver. 2) have been necessary to contain either the "Decalogue" or "the blessings and cursings." The choice, therefore, seems to lie between the view of Vater and Hengstenberg given above, and that of Michaelis (*Laws of Moses*, ii., § 60), Knobel on Deut. xxvii. 1, and of Keil on Deut. xxvii. 3, viz., that all the legal enactments (not the historical, didactic, ethnological, nor any other legislative matter) contained in the Pentateuch were inscribed,—a thing not impossible, as we know not the number of the large stones.

Ver. 33.—"*All Israel*," i.e., all the congregation above twenty years old, and not merely their representatives who are next mentioned. עֹמְדִים, (were) "*standing*": The Sept. has παρεπορεύοντο, as though it had read עֹבְרִים. "*On this side and on that of the ark*," i.e., the ark was between them in the valley, near to Shechem. "*Priests and Levites*," viz., those of the Levites who were priests, for the rest of the tribe are mentioned in Deut. xxvii. 12 as among the six tribes who stood on Mount Gerizim. "*As well the stranger*," i.e., the proselyte (cf. ver. 35). "*As the native*" : The term אֶזְרָח denotes primarily, according to Gesenius, "a native tree," from זָרַח, to shoot forth. אֶל־מוּל, "*over against*" (Auth. Vers.), which may be understood as meaning that six tribes stood on Mount Ebal, and six tribes on Gerizim over against Ebal ; so Poole (on Deut. xxvii. 12); but Ges. (*Lex.*) "*towards*," Sept. πλησίον, Vulg. juxta. The preposition used in Deut. xxvii. 12 is עַל upon (A. V.), which might also be translated "nigh," or "beside." It is evident that, whether they stood on the top or slopes of the mountain, half of the tribes were ranged on the side of Sichem towards Gerizim, and half on that towards Ebal. *Gerizim* was to the south of Sichem, and rather less high than Ebal. Gesenius derives it from גֵּרִזִי, "dwellers in a shorn (*i.e.*, desert) land," from גָּרַז, to cut off; perhaps the tribe subdued by David (1 Sam. xxvii. 8 ; Stanley, *Sin. and Pal.*, p. 237). The sides of both Ebal and Gerizim, as seen from the valley between, are alike bare and sterile, the only exception in favour of the latter being a small ravine coming down opposite the west end of the town, which is full of fountains and trees (Robinson's *Pal.*, iii., 96-7). Gerizim may have been chosen as the mount of blessing, because situated in the south, the sunny region, symbolical of blessing ; and Ebal, for the contrary reason, as the mount of cursing. הֶחָצִי, for the art see note on ha-Ooli, vii. 21. בָּרִאשֹׁנָה should be construed with צִוָּה, for Moses had given this command as early as Deut. xi. 29. לְבָרֵךְ : The blessing is mentioned and not the cursing, because the former concerned the whole people, and was what God chiefly designed in giving the Law : if they fell under the curse, the fault was their own.

Ver. 34.—וְאַחֲרֵי־כֵן, "*and after it had been so done,*" *i.e.*, after the altar had been erected, and the people had taken the places assigned to them. קָרָא, lit. cried out, proclaimed, and hence, " recited," or " read aloud ; " here it probably means he caused to be read by the Levitical priests. " *The blessing and the curse*": Apparently put in apposition to the preceding " *all the words of the Law;* " but whether limited to the blessings and cursings in Deut. xxvii., xxviii., depends on the extent here assigned to the term Law (see note, ver. 32).

Ver. 35.—קְהַל יִשׂ׳ differs from עֲדַת יִשׂ׳, which meant the congregation represented by its elders (see Keil, Exod. xii. 3, 21). Here are included not only men but women, etc. If this vast multitude was assembled on the lower slopes of Ebal and Gerizim, they probably heard without difficulty the reading of the Law, especially as in a clear atmosphere, like that of Palestine, sound travels far.[1]

With vers. 33, 34 of this chapter cf. Luke vi. 20-26, where the blessing and curse are set over against one another.

CHAPTER IX.

Vers. 1 and 2 are introductory to chapters ix., x., xi. The war, which had hitherto been limited to attacks on single cities, was now to be waged by the Israelites against their enemies in combination, first in the south, secondly in the north of Canaan.

---

[1] In Tristram's *Land of Israel*, p. 152, it is said, "A single voice might be heard by many thousands, shut in and conveyed up and down by the enclosing hills. In the early morning we could not only see from Gerizim a man driving his ass down a path on Mount Ebal, but could hear every word he uttered, as he urged it; and in order to test the matter more certainly, on a subsequent occasion two of our party stationed themselves on opposite sides of the valley, and with perfect ease recited the commandments antiphonally."

VERS. 1-2.—*The First League of the Canaanites against Israel.*

This included the inhabitants of the land to the utmost western and northern borders, though, owing to subsequent events, detailed in this chapter, it became limited at first to a confederacy of five kings in Southern Canaan.

Vers. 1.—כְּשָׁמֹעַ, the object, which is omitted, may be easily supplied, viz., what Joshua had done to Jericho and 'Ay. בְּעֵבֶר הַיְ, here applied to the west of Jordan, as in v. 1, but with the omission of יָמָּה. בָּהָר, "*in the hill country*," cf. Numb. xiii. 17; Deut. i. 7; not limited to the mountains of Judah, but embracing the hill country of southern and central Canaan. It commenced a few miles below Hebron, and extended to the plain of Jezreel, going out in a north-westerly direction to the headland of Carmel. בַּשְּׁפֵלָה, "*in the plain*" or "*low country*," from שָׁפֵל, to be low, always found with the definite article as the designation of the maritime plain of Philistia, except in Josh. xi. 16 ("the valley of the same") where it seems to be used of the tract of Sharon. חוֹף, "*coast*" or "*shore*," from חָפַף, to rub off, to wash off. It is used in poetry only, with the exception of this place and Deut. i. 7 (see Gen. xlix. 13; Judges v. 17; Jer. xlvii. 7; Ezek. xxv. 16). "*Over against*" (or towards) *Lebanon.*" The Sept. and the Vulg. suppose an omission of the copulative וְ, and the former renders καὶ οἱ πρὸς τῷ Ἀντιλιβάνῳ, the latter " hi quoque, qui habitabant juxta Libanum ; " but the words in the Hebrew are only added to define the line of the sea coast more accurately, and the reference is to the coast of North Galilee and Phœnicia. "*The Hittite*" (see note, iii. 10): The Girgashites mentioned in this latter passage are here omitted, perhaps because a very small tribe. The name, however, is found in many copies of the Sept.

Ver. 2.—פֶּה־אֶחָד, "*with one mouth*," or "*voice*," *i.e.*, with one accord (cf. 1 Kings xxii. 13; 2 Chron. xviii. 12), adverb. accus. (§ 118, 3).

VERS. 3-15.—*The Craft of the Gibeonites by which they obtain a Separate Peace with Israel.*

Ver. 3.—גִּבְעוֹן, rt. גָּבַע, to be high, situated, according to its name, on a hill, and forty stadia from Jerusalem (Josephus, *Antiq.*, vii., 11, 7), fifty stadia, according to his *Bell. Jud.*, ii., 119. Eusebius says that in his time it still went under its old name, and was four miles west from Bethel. It was a city of the Hivites (ver. 7), though said, in 2 Sam. xxi. 2, to be of the "remnant of the Amorites," because the Amorites, being a principal nation of Canaan, these denote the Canaanites in general (cf. Deut. i. 7). It is described in x. 2 as a *great* city, because the head of the powerful Hivite league, and the key of the pass of Bethhoron, and, though not under royal government, equal in rank to one of the royal cities, celebrated for its strength, and the wisdom of its inhabitants (ix. 4, x. 2). Its government under the Hittites was republican, whence the expression "*the inhabitants of Gibeon*" (ix. 3), and "*our elders*," and "*all the inhabitants of our country*" (ver. 11). In league with it, and under the same government, were four other cities (ver. 17). It was afterwards assigned to the tribe of Benjamin (xviii. 25), and to the priests (xxi. 17); hard by it was the "*great high place*" (1 Kings iii. 4, ix. 2 ; 2 Chron. i. 3, 13), whither the Tabernacle after the destruction of Nob by Saul was brought (1 Chron. xxi. 29, 30), and which "high place" is probably identical with the lofty height of *Nebi Samuel,* towering immediately over *El-Jib*,[1] the modern name of Gibeon (Stanley, *Sin. and Pal.*, ch. iv., pp. 215-16).

Ver. 4.—גַּם, "*also*" (not translated in the Auth. Vers.) is emphatic, and refers to what Joshua had done (ver. 3), for, though Jericho was not taken by stratagem, as 'Ay had been, yet the Gibeonites may have imputed its capture to surprise, and resolved, therefore, themselves to deal craftily ; Sept. καὶ ἐποίησαν καί γε αὐτοὶ μετὰ πανουργίας. יִצְטַיָּרוּ, Hithp. (ת transposed and changed into ט, § 54, 2, *a*), from צִיר, not elsewhere used as a verb, " to go round in a circle," whence צִיר, a hinge, or, as in Arabic, "to go," whence צִיר, a messenger (Ges., *Lex.*), and, as Hithpael, sometimes implies simulation (§ 54, 3), hence the A. V., "*made as if they had been ambassadors,*" or rather (as they actually were ambassadors, and only feigned that they had come from a distant land), "*made themselves ambassadors,*" *i.e.*, acted as such ; Keil, " *set out as ambassadors.*" The ancient versions appear to have read יִצְטַיָּדוּ, " *they furnished themselves with victuals,*" denom. from צֵידָה, "*provision for a journey,*" which rendering Gesenius (*Lex.*) and others prefer: it is, however, unnecessary here, and may have arisen from the occurrence of the same word in

---

[1] Jib in Arabic is merely a contraction of the Hebrew Gibeon (Kitto's *Cyclop.*).

ver. 12. בָּלִים, "*worn out*" or "*decayed*," from בָּלָה, to fall away. The sacks were used to carry provisions and baggage, because inns being then unknown, travellers took with them what things they needed. נֹאד for נֵאד, a skin in which water is brought, *i.q.*, חֵמֶת in Gen. xxi. 14, 15, 19 (rt. נָאַד [unused], Arabic, to give forth water), noun masc. with fem. term. in the plur., but retaining the gender of the sing. (see § 87, 4); hence here נאדות is followed by three adjectives in the masc. "*Torn and bound together*": The latter word in Hebrew, from צָרַר, "to bind together," has reference to the mode of mending shoes by tying the rents together, which was generally adopted when there was not time to put in a patch.

Ver. 5.—נְעָלוֹת, a form used here only (Ges., *Lex.*); on נַעַל, see v. 15. מְטֻלָּאת, Pual intens., "*strongly patched up*," Symm. ἐπιβλήματα ἔχοντα, Sept. καταπεπελματωμένα, "patched in the soles," from πέλμα, a sole: "*clouted*" (Auth. Vers.), which also here means "patched," being derived from the Anglo-Saxon "clut," a clout or rag; not "nailed," from the French "clou," a nail. שְׂלָמוֹת, by transp. for שְׂמָלוֹת Sept. ἱμάτια, were outer garments, and sometimes the term is used for clothes in general, as in Gen. xxxv. 2; Exod. iii. 22, etc. Travellers who were poor were obliged to perform much of their journey on foot, even though they had asses for their baggage, and this would account for the worn condition of the shoes and clothes of these Gibeonites. נִקֻּדִים, "*marked with points (or little spots)*," used of sheep and goats, Ges. xxx. 32, etc., rt. נָקַד, to prick or mark with points. Some, as Kimchi, think that the term refers to spots of mould, Sept. ἄρτος εὐρωτιῶν καὶ βεβρωμένος, "bread, mouldy and corrupt;" Theod., ἄρτοι βεβρωμένοι: others, as Keil, "*crumbled;*" Aquila, ἄρτος ἐψαθυρωμένος; Vulg., "panes in frusta comminuti;" so Gesen. (*Lex.*). The Auth. Vers. "*dry and mouldy,*" well conveys the sense. Kitto remarks that the bread commonly used in the East is calculated to last only for the day on which it is baked; and in a day or two more it becomes exceedingly hard and unfit for use. But besides this sort of bread there is another, which will keep a considerable time, though it ultimately becomes hard and mouldy, and the use of this latter sort is almost exclusively confined to travellers. "It is a kind of biscuit, usually made in the shape of large rings, nearly an inch thick, and four or five inches in diameter. The bread is, when new, very firm, and rather crisp when broken; but not being so well prepared as our biscuits, it becomes gradually harder, and at last mouldy from the moisture, which the baking had left in it. In general, it is seldom used till previously soaked in water. The bread of the Gibeonites may have been something of this sort" (*Illust. Family Bible*).

Ver. 6.—In the Hebrew, "Gilgal" is put in appos. to "the camp." A few MSS. read הַגִּלְגָּלָה, with ה parag. Keil thinks that this is not the Gilgal near Jericho, but another between Jerusalem and Shechem, near Mount Ebal and Gerizim (see Deut. xi. 30), now known as *Jiljilia:* it seems, however, strange that, after Gilgal has always in the preceding chapters denoted the Gilgal near Jericho, it should in chapters ix., x. refer to another town, without any intimation to that effect. It is true that the Gilgal near Jericho, at the south-east corner of the land, may not have been advantageously situated for the conquest of central and northern Palestine, but the holy associations connected with it as the spot where the twelve Memorial Stones had been set up, Circumcision renewed, and the Passover kept, are strong reasons for concluding that it continued the headquarters of Joshua during the early part of the conquest (see Smith's *Dict. of the Bible*, vol. i., p. 700). אִישׁ יְיָ, used collectively as in the next verse, perhaps, however, not the same as בְּנֵי יְיָ, but here meaning the principal men of the congregation, for אִישׁ sometimes refers to eminence or rank [Psalm iv. 2 (3), xlix. 2 (3), lxii. 9 (10)]; and that this is the force of the term here may be gathered from vers. 15, 18, 19, 21. "*From a far country*," and, therefore (as they would insinuate), they stood on a different footing from the Canaanites (see Deut. xx. 11). "*Make ye a league with us*" (Auth. Ver.), כָּרַת refers to the slaying and dividing of the victims in making a covenant (Gen. xv. 10); cf. ὅρκια τέμνειν, *Il.*, B., 124, Γ., 252, and Latin *fœdus ferire*.

Ver. 7.—אִישׁ, coll., cf. ver. 6, and hence the verb is in the plur. (§ 146, 1). The suffix in בְּקִרְבִּי is also collec.—"*And how shall I make a league with you?*" The allusion is to the prohibition in Exod. xxiii. 32-3; Deut. vii. 2. Note that the Qᵉri has אֶכְרָת for the Kᵉthibh אֶכְרוֹת, because, according to the accentuation, Cholem (ō) is changed by Maqqeph into chamets-chatuph (ŏ) (see § 16 with § 27, 1).

Ver. 8.—"*We* (are) *thy servants*": Probably only an expression of obsequious courtesy, usual in the

East, for they wished not to submit themselves to Joshua, but only to make a treaty with him. מִי used in reference to the plur. (§ 122, 3). "*Whence may you have come?*" The imperfect (תָּבֹאוּ), says Maurer, is here used out of modesty and politeness (cf. Judges xvii. 9, xix. 17), whereas the perfect is used when the question is asked emphatically and sternly, as in Gen. xvi. 8, xlii. 7, "Whence have ye come?" (Heb. בָּאתֶם).

Vers. 9, 10.—לְשֵׁם, according to Masius, Junius, and Tremellius, "*unto the name,*" *i.e.*, they were come to profess it, and embrace the religion of the Israelites; but rather, "*on account of the name.*" לְ expresses the cause or object with reference to which anything has been done (Ewald, *Lehrb.*, p. 411): what is here signified by the "name" of Jehovah is explained by what follows, viz., the fame of Him and all that He did in Egypt, etc. With ver. 10 cf. ii. 10, Numb. xxi. 21, etc., 33, etc. "*Ashtaroth,*" a city of Bashan, in which Og dwelt (Deut. i. 4), called after the Assyrian goddess Ashtoreth (the Astarte of the Greeks and Romans), who was there worshipped. This city was assigned by Moses to the half-tribe of Manasseh (Josh. xiii. 29-31). Some identify it with *Ashtaroth Karnaim* (Gen. xiv. 5), but see Smith's *Dict. of the Bible*, vol. i., p. 122. The ambassadors wisely abstain from mentioning what had really alarmed them, viz., the overthrow of Jericho and 'Ay, for to have betrayed their knowledge of such recent events would have awakened suspicion.

Ver. 11.—"*Our elders, i.e.,* the leaders of our republic (see note, ver. 3).

Ver. 12.—זֶה לַחְמֵנוּ, "*this bread of ours,*" *sc.*, look at it (Keil). זֶה, without the article, and prefixed to a noun, is emphatically demonstrative [Ges., *Lex.*; cf. ver. 13; Exod. xxxii. 1; Psalm xlviii. 14 (15), lxxviii. 8 (9)]. הִצְטַיַּדְנוּ, "*we took as provision*," denom. of צֵיד, "provision for a journey." ט for ת transposed (§ 54, 2, *a*; cf. ver. 4).

Ver. 13 (cf. vers. 4, 5).—In the last clause, "*by reason of the very great length of the way*": מְאֹד has here the force of an adjective (cf. Isa. xlvii. 9).

Ver. 14.—"*And the men* (*i.e.*, the elders of Israel, vers. 18-21) *took of their provision*," either to test its quality by tasting it, or rather in token of friendship (cf. Gen. xxvi. 30, xxxi. 46). "*But inquired not at the mouth of Jehovah*," as they ought to have done, viz., by means of the Urim and Thummim of the High Priest (Numb. xxvii. 21). Not only priests, but prophets are called "the mouth of Jehovah" (see Isa. xxx. 2; Jer. xv. 19). From this neglect of the princes of Israel to consult the Urim and Thummim, Christians may learn their own duty to consult "the lively oracles of God," and thereby to try the claims of any who call themselves God's messengers (see 1 John iv. 1).

Ver. 15.—וַיַּעַשׂ לָהֶם, "*and Joshua granted to them peace*" (see Ges., *Lex.*, 2, *i*, p. 658), "*and made a covenant with them;*" לָהֶם, dat. commodi, "*in their favour.*" "*To let them live*": There may have been other articles of the covenant, but this is mentioned as the principal, and because these Gibeonites, being Canaanites, ought to have been destroyed (Deut. xx. 16, 17). The word עֵדָה, which occurs fifteen times in this book, means literally "an appointed meeting," from יָעַד, to appoint; and is generally rendered συναγωγή (Sept.), "congregation" (Auth. Vers.).

VERS. 16-27.—*The Discovery and Punishment of their Fraud.*

Ver. 16.—The sing. suffixes in אֵלָיו and בְּקִרְבּוֹ are collec., and refer to the Israelites.

Ver. 17.—" *On the third day,*" viz., after the discovery of the deception which had been practised on them. Gibeon was less than three days' journey from Gilgal, and on a subsequent occasion Joshua, by a forced march, accomplished the distance in a single night (x. 9), but now there was no necessity for hurry, and Eastern armies and caravans are proverbially slow in their movements (see Stanley's *Sin. and Pal.*, p. 219); yet had the Gilgal here mentioned been that near to Bethel (see on ver. 6), it would not have been easy to account for the time spent in the journey. Hak-Kᵉphîrah (lit. the village or hamlet, rt. כָּפַר, to cover, to shelter), situated eight or nine miles west of Gibeon, afterwards assigned, together with Gibeon and Beeroth, to Benjamin (xviii. 25, 26), now *Kefir*, two miles east of Yalo. Its inhabitants, and those of Beeroth and Kirjathjearim, are mentioned among those who returned from Babylon (Ezra ii. 25; Neh. vii. 29). "*Bᵉêrôth*," lit. "wells," from בָּאַר, to dig, to *bore*, for the wells in Palestine were deep holes bored far under the rocky surface by the art of man (*Sin. and Pal.*, p. 147), allotted to Benjamin (xviii. 25); the murderers of Ishbosheth dwelt there (2 Sam. iv. 2). It is said in the legends of Palestine to have been the place where the parents of the child Jesus discovered that He was not in their company (Luke ii. 43-45), now called *El-Bireh*, the customary resting-place at this day for caravans going northward, at the end of the first day's journey from Jerusalem (*Sin. and Pal.*, p. 215), "*Qiryathycʽ 'arîm*" (city of woods), called Baalah and Qir-yath-baal, perhaps because sacred to the worship of Baal (xv. 9, 60, xviii. 14), apportioned to the tribe of Judah (xv. 60); hither the ark was removed from Bethshemesh, and there remained twenty years (1 Sam. vi. 20, 21, vii. 2), whence it was transferred by David to the house of Obededom (2 Sam. vi. 2, 10), an event probably alluded to in Psalm cxxxii. 6. It is situated about ten miles north-west of Jerusalem (Eusebius and Jerome, *Onomas.*), and is perhaps identical with the modern *Kuriet el Enab*, the city of grapes (Grove, Art. in Smith's *Bib. Dict.*; Rob., *Bib. Res.*, ii., 334-336; Keil).

Ver. 18.—וְלֹא־הִכּוּם, "*and the Israelites smote them not*," i.e., killed them not by the sword. וַיִּלֹּנוּ, "*and all the congregation murmured*": לוּן, to tarry, to continue, and hence, in Niphal, to show oneself obstinate, to murmur, to complain, the signification of remaining and persisting being applied in a bad sense (Ges.). Elsewhere, the word in Niphal occurs in Exodus and Numbers only (see Exod. xv. 24, xiv. 2; Numb. xiv. 2, xvii. 6). The cause of the murmuring on this occasion may not have been disappointment of anticipated revenge and booty, but a fear of the Divine displeasure for sparing these Canaanites (see 1 Sam. xv. 11).

Ver. 19.—נָגַע בְּ, "*to touch*," but here "*to injure*," as in Gen. xxvi. 11; Zech. ii. 12 (8, Auth. Vers.). Some, as Masius, Munster, and Calvin, have said that the ahth of the princes was not binding, the Gibeonites having deceived them; but Bishop Sanderson (*Prælec.*,

ii. and iv.), Cor. a Lap., Keil, and others, have judged otherwise, for the oath, though illegal, was not to do a thing in itself illegal, *i.e.*, always and absolutely forbidden, such, *e.g.*, as murder. Had the oath not been kept, the Israelites would have been charged with perfidy, and the name of God have been dishonoured among the heathen. The whole question, too, is set at rest by the fact, that God prospered the arms of Israel in defence of the Gibeonites (cf. x. 8), and at a later period exacted satisfaction from the descendants of Saul, because he had violated this oath (2 Sam. xxi. 1).

Ver. 20.—הַחֲיֵה, Hiph. infin. absol., used emphatically for the finite verb in the fut., "*will let them live*" (§ 131, 4, *a*). וְלֹא, "*that wrath may not come upon us.*" "*On account of the oath*" (cf. Matt. xiv. 9, διὰ τοὺς ὅρκους).

Ver. 21.—"*Unto them*," *i.e.*, to the Israelites. "*Let them live*," emphatic imper. וַיִּהְיוּ, "*and so they became*," וְ, § 49, 2. Our Auth. Vers. renders "*but let them be*," and so Masius after the Sept.; but this would require וַיְהִי, or וְהָיוּ (§ 126, 6, *c*). The preceding sentence is called by the Hebrews מִקְרָא קָצֵב, "an abbreviated discourse." Thus Kimchi supplies after "let them live," the words "and let them become hewers of wood": so the Sept. and Arab. versions. וַיִּהְיוּ, therefore, merely describes the final issue, or result, of the deliberations of the princes; cf. 1 Kings xv. 22, where the execution of a command is related, but without previous mention of the terms of that command. "*To all the congregation*," *i.e.*, in their collective capacity as a congregation of the Lord (Numb. xxvii. 17). The Gibeonites were not reduced to domestic slavery, but were the servants of the Levites (and thus indirectly of the congregation) by discharging for them the more laborious duties of the Sanctuary. By this measure the Gibeonites were disabled from tempting the Israelites to idolatry, the danger from which was assigned as a special reason for destroying the Canaanites (Deut. vii. 2, 4). It would seem from Exod. xii. 48 that they must have been circumcised, and from Deut. xxix. 11 that they were admitted to a share in the covenant of God with His people. They were also an emblem and pledge of the reception of the Gentiles into the Church of God. Thus the curse of slavery, which fell on them as descendants of Ham (Gen. ix. 25), was turned to a blessing. לָהֶם, "*concerning them,*" *i.e.*, the Gibeonites. With this meaning of לְ, cf. Gen. xx. 13, אִמְרִי לִי, "*say concerning me.*"

Vers. 22, 23 (Joshua here announces to the Gibeonites the determination which the princes of the congregation had come to concerning them).— Ver. 23.—עֶבֶד ... וְלֹא, "*and there shall not be cut off from you a slave,*" *i.e.*, there shall not fail from you a slave, ye shall be slaves for ever (cf. 2 Sam. iii. 29 ; 1 Kings ii. 4). עֶבֶד is here used collec. for "*slaves ;*" the following וְ is explicative (§ 155, 1, *a*, 2nd par.), "*and that as woodcutters and water-drawers.*" These were the lowest class of slaves (Deut. xxix. 11) "*For the house of my God,*" *i.e.*, for the Tabernacle, and afterwards for the Temple.

Ver. 24.—"*It was certainly told*": The absolute, infin. (in the Hebrew) before the verb expresses intensity (§ 131, 3, *a*). For the (..) in the final syllable of הֻגַּד see § 53, 3, 10, and with that in the final syllable of וַיְהִי, cf. vii. 9 (note). It is evident from this verse that the motive which had actuated the Gibeonites was *fear*, not any religious feeling such as had prompted Rachabh (ii. 9, etc.).

Ver. 27.—וַיִּתְּנֵם, "*and Joshua made* (or "appointed") *them*," Sept. κατέστησεν αὐτοὺς: נָתַן sometimes = שׂוּם (Ges., *Lex.*, 3, *a*, p. 573). Some think that therefore they were from the first called *Nethinim* (*given* or *dedicated*), but this title does not appear to have been assigned to them till the reign of David (see Ezra viii. 20), who probably enrolled among them other captives taken in war. "*For the congregation*": see note on ver. 21. לְמִזְבַּח is added to define more accurately their service as a religious one. אֶל־הַמָּקוֹם, "*to the place*"; grammatically dependent on נָתַן, but not implying that Joshua sent them at once thither, but assigned them to it as soon as it should have been chosen by God. אֲשֶׁר־יִבְחָר, "*which He* (Jehovah) *should* (or shall) *choose*": The preceding words "*unto this day*" show that, when this book was written, no place had yet been definitely chosen (so Keil); but as Shiloh, where after the subjugation of Canaan the Tabernacle was set up (Josh. xviii. 1), is expressly called by God "My place, where I set My name at first" (Jer. vii. 12), there is no reason to think that the Gibeonites were not employed in their office till Solomon's Temple had been built.

CHAPTER X.

VERS. 1-27.—*The Defection of the Gibeonites causes Five Kings in their Neighbourhood to Combine against them. Joshua succours them, and gains a Great Victory over the Five Kings.*

Ver. 1.—"*Adonizedek*," lit. "lord of righteousness," cf. *Melchizedec*, "king of righteousness," probably an official title, as Pharaoh and Ptolemy of the Egyptian kings. יְרוּשָׁלַםִ: See for the etymology and orthography Ges., *Lex.*, p. 367, and Smith's *Dict. of the Bible*, p. 981. The name occurs here in the Old Testament for the first time; anciently the city was called שָׁלֵם (Gen. xiv. 18; Psalm lxxvi. 3 [2]), where some think that the first half of the compound name is dropped, for brevity's sake, as קִרְיַת for קִרְיַת הַיְעָרִים (Josh. xviii. 28). It was allotted to Benjamin (xviii. 28), but stood on the edge of the territory of Judah (xv. 8), by whom the lower part of the city was conquered after Joshua's death (Judges i. 8, with Joseph., *Antiq.*, v., 2, § 2). The upper city and the citadel remained in the hands of the Jebusites, the ancient inhabitants, who not only could not be expelled by the men of Judah and Benjamin (Josh. xv. 63; Judges i. 21), but seem to have so far gradually gained possession of the whole place, that it was called Jebus in the time of the Judges (Judges xix. 10-12); they were finally expelled in the reign of David (2 Sam. v. 6-9). Before כַּאֲשֶׁר repeat כִּי with וְ, "*and that.*" וַיְהִי, "*and were in the midst of them,*" *i.e.*, were living among them on friendly terms.

Ver. 2.—וַיִּֽירְאוּ, "*Then* (or "that") *they* (*i.e.*, Adonizedec and his subjects) *feared exceedingly.*" כִּי, "*because Gibeon was a great city,*" etc. : See note on ix. 3. The fact that so powerful a city should have been induced to make a league with Israel showed how formidable the latter people must be.

Ver. 3.—The names of the kings mentioned in this verse were probably characteristic, *e.g.*, *Hô-ham* (probably for יְהוֹהָם, "whom Jehovah drives," Ges., *Lex.*); *Pir-'am* ("the wild ass," rt. פָּרָא, to run swiftly); *Ya-phi-'a* [1] (splendid); *D^ebhîr* (the writer). Their respective cities were (1) *Hebron* (Chebh-rôn), a city of Judah (Josh. xv. 54), situated among the mountains (xx. 7), and built seven years before Zoan in Egypt (Numb. xiii. 22). The name signified *community* or *society*, from חָבַר, "to join together," and it was the earliest seat of civilisation in Palestine, where Abraham and the patriarchs had their first home and abiding settlement (Gen. xiii. 18, xxxv. 27). It was called Kirjath-arba (Gen. xxiii. 2), or "the city of Arba," from Arba, the progenitor of the giants Anakim (Josh. xxi. 11, xv. 13, 14); afterwards it came into the hands of the Chittites, and was governed by Ephron the Chittite (Gen. xxiii. 10). Many (Hengstenberg, Keil, etc.) think that Chebhron was the original name, which, while the Israelites were in Egypt, was changed into Kirjath-arba by the Anakim when they took the city, but was again restored by Caleb after its reconquest (Josh. xiv. 15), which opinion is confirmed by Gen. xiii. 18. Eusebius and Jerome (*De Loc. Heb.*, fol. 87, E.) place it

---

[1] The same name was given to a son of David (2 Sam. v. 15).

twenty-two miles south of Jerusalem. At the present day it is called by the Mahommedans *El-Khalil*, "the friend (of God)," because Abraham sojourned there. The cave of Machpelah is still there, surrounded by a mosque, and probably contains the dust of Sarah, Abraham, and Isaac, and the embalmed body or mummy of Jacob (Gen. l. 13, see Stanley's *Sin. and Pal.*, p. 102). (2) *Yarmûth* (high) from רָמָה, to be high, a town of the Sh^ephêlah, or low country, of Judah (xv. 35; Neh. xi. 29), according to the *Onomast.* ten Roman miles south-west of Jerusalem, on the road to Eleutheropolis,[1] and probably identical with the modern Yarmûk (Robin., *B. R.*, ii., 17), on a hill called Tell-Armuth, where are remains of ancient walls and cisterns. (3) *Lakhish* (obstinate, *i.e.*, hard to be captured [Ges., *Lex.*]), also in the Sh^ephêlah of Judah (xv. 39), fortified by Rehoboam (2 Chron. xi. 9), besieged and captured by Sennacherib (2 Kings xviii. 14-17, xix. 8; Layard's *Nineveh*, p. 150), reoccupied by the Jews after the captivity (Neh. xi. 30), regarded by Von Raumer, Keil, and Van de Velde, as probably identical with the *Um Lâkis*, about twenty miles south-west of Yarmûth, on the road to Gaza. (4) *'Eglôn*

---

[1] Not mentioned in the Bible. It was a town of South Palestine, at the foot of the hills of Judah, on the borders of the great Philistine plain, and about twenty-five miles from Jerusalem, on the road to Gaza. Its ancient name was Betogabra, which is first mentioned in the writings of Ptolemy in the beginning of the second century. Its new name Eleutheropolis first occurs upon coins in the reign of the Emperor Septimius Severus. A.D. 202-3. In the time of Eusebius, Bishop of Cæsarea, it was so important a place as the capital of a large province and the seat of a bishop, that he makes it in his *Onomasticon* the central point in South Palestine, from which the positions of more than twenty other towns are determined. The name in Arabic is Beit Jibrin.

(large bull-calf [Simonis]) in the Shᵉphēlah of Judah (xv. 39, xii. 12), less than three miles east of Lachish, and the same as the modern *Ajlân* (Robinson, *B. R.*, ii., 249). In the *Onomasticon* it is identified with Adullam from the Sept. reading 'Οδολλάμ here and in x. 34, but it is evident from Josh. xii. 12, 15, xv. 35, 39, that 'Eglon and Adullam were different cities.

Ver. 4.— "*Come up to me*," in a military sense, *i.e.*, with forces. There had been a previous determination among the Canaanites in general to form a league against Israel (ix. 1); but, before any active steps had been taken, the defection of Gibeon led at once to the combination against it of the five kings (ver. 3), in its immediate vicinity. The object of these latter probably was not only to punish Gibeon, and deter others from following its example, but by its capture, and that of its dependent cities, to impede the further advance of Israel. The king of Jerusalem took the lead, his being, perhaps, the principal city, and most exposed to attack, as lying between Gibeon and the camp of the Israelites at Gilgal.

Ver. 5.—(Of) "*The Emorites*," Sept. τῶν Ἰεβουσαίων. Both were mountain tribes (iii. 10, note); but the reading "Emorites" (Auth. Vers. "Amorites") is countenanced by ver. 6. As, however, Jarmûth, Lachish, and 'Eglon were in the low-country (Josh. xv. 35, 39), it appears as if the name Emorites was not always confined to those who dwelt on the mountains; cf. Judges i. 34, 35, where it would seem that, having drawn the Danites into the mountain, the Emorites themselves occupied the plain. Perhaps, however, as Keil conjectures, the name is here employed because the Emorites were the most powerful of the Canaanites.

Ver. 6.—"*Slack not*," lit. "do not let down" (cf. i. 5, note). "*And save us*," lit. "make ample room for us." Ample space is in Hebrew applied to deliverance from dangers (Ges., *Lex.*). The expressions successively employed in this clause show the urgency of the peril. אֵלֵינוּ, "*against us*": When the motion towards an object is hostile, אֶל־ has the force of "*against*" (cf. Gen. iv. 8; Judges xii. 3; Isa. ii. 4). יֹשְׁבֵי הָהָר, see note on ver. 5.

Ver. 7.—וְכָל־גִּבּוֹרֵי, "*even all the mighty men of valour*": Put in apposition to the preceding "all the people of war." וְ is explicative (§ 155, 1, *a*; cf. ix. 23). It is probable that a selection was made of the best warriors, and the rest were left to protect the camp at Gilgal. On this assistance, so promptly rendered by Joshua to the Gibeonites, Origen remarks, " Even although thou art but a hewer of wood or a drawer of water in Christ's Church, yet thou mayest expect to be attacked by her enemies, but thou mayest also hope for succour from Christ."

Ver. 8.—וַיֹּאמֶר: Some (Masius, Drusius, Rosenm.) render the imperfect here as a pluperf., but unnecessarily. God may well have renewed at such a crisis the assurance of special aid, which He had before given (viii. 1, vi. 2). בְּיָדֶיךָ, in the margin בְּיָדְךָ, and the sing. is more commonly used in this expression (see ii. 24, vi. 2, viii. 1, 18).

Ver. 9.—Cf. Stanley's *Sin. and Pal.*, iv., p. 219), " As in the battle of Marathon, everything depended on the suddenness of the blow which should break in pieces the hostile confederation. On the former occasion of Joshua's visit to Gibeon, it had been a three days' journey from Gilgal, as, according to the slow pace of Eastern armies and caravans, it might well be. But now by a forced march 'Joshua came unto them suddenly, and went up all night.'"

Ver. 10.—יְהֻמֵּם, "*threw them into confusion*," from הָמַם, *i.q.*, הוּם, "to put in motion" (Keil; cf. Exod. xiv. 24, xxiii. 27). This may have been effected by inspiring them with a sudden panic, or by terrifying them by thunder and lightning (cf. 1 Sam. vii. 10, and ver. 11 below). "*At Gibeon*": With this meaning of בְּ (viz., "*at*") cf. v. 13. דֶּרֶךְ, "*on the way which goeth up to Beth-chôrôn*" (lit. "the house of caves," in allusion to the rocky nature of the ground). Beth-choron the Upper is meant, as distinguished from Beth-choron the Nether (ver. 11). Both towns were built by Sherah, the grand-daughter of Ephraim (1 Chron. vii. 24), and were on the boundary line between Benjamin and Ephraim (Josh. xvi. 3, 5; 1 Chron. vii. 24); they were afterwards fortified by Solomon (2 Chron. viii. 5). Beth-choron the Upper was about four miles north-west of Gibeon, and דֶּרֶךְ מַעֲלֵה denotes the hilly road which led from Gibeon to it. The modern name is *Beit-ur el Foka* (the upper), as *Beit-ur el Tahta* (the lower) is that of Beth-choron the Nether (Stanley, *Sin. and Pal.*, p. 208; Grove, *Bib. Dict.*, i., 201). "*'Azêqah*" (a field dug over, broken up), from עָזַק, to dig or to till the ground (Ges.). It lay to the north of the plain of Judah, and near Beth-choron; but its site is not now discernible (Grove); it is mentioned along with Adullam and Socoh, towns of Judah (Josh. xv. 35), and as near

Socoh (1 Sam. xvii. 1). It was fortified by Rehoboam (2 Chron. xi. 9); besieged by Nebuchadnezzar (Jer. xxxiv. 7), and inhabited after the return from the captivity (Neh. xi. 30). "*Maqqêdah*" (probably "place of shepherds" [Ges. *Lex.*]), its site unknown. Eusebius (*Onomast.*) says that it was eight miles east of Eleutheropolis, where east, says Keil, seems to be an error for west. Probably it stood where the mountains sink into the plain, for in xv. 41 it is mentioned as in the Sh^ephêlah, or maritime plain, of Judah (Stanley, *Sin. and Pal.*, p. 211). It undoubtedly lay to the south of Beth-choron the Nether, as the defeated Canaanites were fleeing to the south in order to take refuge in their fortified cities (ver. 19).[1]

Ver. 11.—בְּמוֹרַד, "*in the descent of Bêth-chôrôn*," *i.e.*, as they were descending the pass between Beth-choron the Upper and Beth-choron the Nether. The first stage of the flight of the Canaanites had been in the long ascent from Gibeon to Beth-choron the Upper (ver. 10). The second stage was when having outstripped their pursuers, and crossed the

---

[1] Captain Warren, R.E., in 1871, proposed the village of El Moghâr (the caves) as the probable site of Maqqedah. "This position," says he, "might well have been chosen for a royal city. It is situated on the north side of a narrow *tajo*, which the valley of Sorek has scooped through the sandstone hills. Immediately south is Kutrak (Gederoth); to the west Dejan (Beth-Dagon); north-east, Akir (Ekron); and about three miles further north-east, Nianeh (Naamah) (see Josh. xv. 41). It is about seven miles south-west of Ramleh, in the position, or nearly so, where the writer of the article 'Makkedah' in Sm th's *Biblical Dictionary* proposes it may be found." (*Recent Explorations in Bible Lands*, Paper read at Church Congress, 1875.) This view has been more recently confirmed by the surveyors of the Pal. Explor. Fund (*Report*, January 1881).

high ridge of Beth-choron the Upper, they were in full flight down the descent to Beth-choron the Nether (Stanley's *Sin. and Pal.*, ch. iv.). This pass was rocky and rough, and was the scene not only of this victory of Joshua, but that of Judas Maccabæus over the Syrians, under Seron (1 Macc. iii. 13, etc.), and, still later, of the destruction of the army of Cestius Gallus by the Jews (Josephus, *Bel. Jud.*, ii., 19, § § 8, 9). As the main road to the sea coast from Jerusalem and the Jordan valley lay through this pass, both Beth-choron the Upper and Nether were strongly fortified by Solomon (2 Chron. viii. 5). "*Great stones,*" explained in the next clause to be hail-stones, Sept. λίθους χαλάζης. Cf. Exod. ix. 19, 25; Job xxxviii. 22, 23; Psalm xviii. 13, 14, where hail is represented as employed by God against His enemies. Though terrific storms occasionally burst over the hills in Palestine, yet this storm was evidently *miraculous*, like that in Exod. ix. 24; 1 Sam. vii. 10, for the stones were of unusual size, and appear to have slain the Canaanites, but not the Israelites. It must have served to convince the Israelites, on the one hand, that God fought for them, and their enemies, on the other, that a greater than human power was the cause of their discomfiture.[1]

---

[1] The student of ecclesiastical history need hardly be reminded of the story of the thundering legion, in answer to whose prayers a great storm was sent to aid Marcus Aurelius in his victory over the Guadi, A.D. 174 (Euseb., *Hist.*, v., 5). This particular wonder is, however, now given up, even by those Protestants who insist on the perpetuity of miraculous powers in the Church. (P. Smith's *Anct. Hist.*, vol. iii., ch. 39, p. 520.)

Vers. 12-15.—The thread of the narrative is here broken off, and not resumed till ver. 16. Some regard the passage (vers. 12-15) as an interpolation by a late reviser of this book, who took it from some older historical narrative, in which was contained the quotation from the Book of Yashar. But for this opinion there is no good authority. It is based on the questionable hypothesis that the Book of Joshua is in part derived from older documents, such as those of the Elohist and Jehovist. Nor can we, consistently with any just conception of the inspiration of the writer of our book, suppose that he would have left wholly unnoticed the remarkable incident recorded in the Book of Yashar, whatever may be the explanation given of that incident. Most probably, therefore, vers. 12-15 is a parenthesis from our author's own hand, in which he inserted the above mentioned quotation, in order to convey a more vivid impression of the event which he wished to record, than if he had simply related it in his own historical narrative.

It is doubtful where the quotation begins and ends, but reasons are given in the following notes for regarding it as commencing with the word "Sun" in the latter half of ver. 12, and terminating with the first half of ver. 13; all that follows the formula of quotation to the end of ver. 14 being taken as a comment of the author of our book, and ver. 15 as probably misplaced from ver. 43 by the error of some ancient transcriber.

Ver. 12.—אָז, "*then*," Sept. τότε; Vulg. tunc; followed by the imperf. in a past sense (§ 127, 4, *a*); cf. viii. 30, where Keil remarks that there is not the least foundation for the assertion of some critics, adduced in support of their fragmentary hypothesis, that every paragraph commencing with אָז and followed by an imperfect, is either a fragment or an interpolation. יְדַבֵּר, "*spake*," *i.e.*, in prayer, as seems implied by ver. 14. Joshua would not have presumed to give the command which follows, unless he had first prayed to the Lord, and believed that his prayer had been answered (cf. 1 Kings xvii. 1 with James v. 16-18)[1]. The Chald. renders by יְשַׁבַּח, "*decantavit*," but when דִּבֶּר has this sense, it is followed by שִׁיר, as in Judges v. 12. תֵּת לִפְנֵי, "*to give into the power of*," cf. Deut. ii. 31, 33, 36; Judges xi. 9. לְעֵינֵי יִשְׂ׳, "*before the eyes of Israel*," *i.e.*, "in their presence," "coram iis" (Vulg.), so that they were witnesses of his words (cf. Numb. xx. 8; Deut. xxxi. 7). שֶׁמֶשׁ, a word which has reference to the *light* of the sun, as חַמָּה and חֶרֶס have to its heat. The absence of the article, which is usually found with the vocative in prose (§ 109, 3, Rem. 2), indicates poetry; so יָרֵחַ[2] in the next clause (cf. the use of אָרִין, Job xvi. 18); hence it is probable that our author begins his quotation from the Book of Yashar (see ver. 13 below) at the word "shemesh" (see Lowth's *Prælec.*, vol. ii., lect. 23, p. 152). בְּגִבְעוֹן, "*at*" or "*on*" (*i.e.*, over) *Gibeon.*" דֹּם, Qal. imper. of דָּמַם, properly "to be dumb with astonishment," then "to be silent," then

---

[1] Other remarkable instances of the importance and efficacy of prayer are Gen. xx. 17; 2 Kings xix. 2, etc.; Acts xii. 5, 11.
[2] This word is masc., whereas לְבָנָה, another name for the moon, is fem. Both names are derived from colour, meaning respectively the yellow (or pale) and the white, and thus were silent protests against the heathen notion that the moon was a personal female deity.

"to rest," "to be still," "to wait" (cf. 1 Sam. xiv. 9 and the synonymous use of הֶחֱרִישׁ, in Gen. xxxiv. 5; Exod. xiv. 14). It is here not unfitly rendered by our Authorised Version "*stand still*" (Sept. στήτω), because עֲמָד in ver. 13 is parallel to it, as in 1 Sam. xiv. 9. "*And thou moon*": This direct address to the moon implies that it was at the time visible; cf. Stanley's *Sin. and Pal.*, p. 210, "In front, over the western vale of Ajalon, was the faint figure of the crescent moon visible above the hailstorm, which was fast driving up from the sea in the valley below." The time of day was probably about noon (cf. ver. 13, "in the midst of heaven,") not, as Cor. a Lap., Clericus, and others, late in the afternoon, for then the sun would have appeared to Joshua not in the east, but sinking below the horizon in the west. Fay remarks that "the joint apparition of the sun and moon is not very unusual; on the contrary, it may be witnessed in a clear sky at any time, during the moon's first quarter, in the afternoon, and during the last quarter, in the forenoon, and, indeed, from what is kindly communicated to me by the astronomer Mädler, may be seen in the much clearer southern heavens early in the afternoon, during the moon's first quarter, and until late in the forenoon during her third." אַיָּלוֹן (place of deer or gazelles, from אַיָּל, a stag). The valley is identified by Robinson (*Bib. Res.*, ii., 253, iii., 145) with the modern Merj. Ibn Omeir, and described by him as a broad and beautiful valley (now a valley of cornfields), running in a westerly direction from the mountains towards the great western plain (see also Stanley's *Sin. and Pal.*, p. 207). The town has been identified with the village Yâlo, situated on a hill skirting the south of the valley. After the conquest it was allotted to the tribe of Dan (xix. 42), but from it the Emorites could not be expelled (Judges i. 35); was assigned with its suburbs to the Levites (xxi. 24; 1 Chron. vi. 54, [69]). Saul and Jonathan defeated the Philistines near it (1 Sam. xiv. 31). It was fortified by Rehoboam after the revolt of the ten tribes (2 Chron. xi. 10), and captured by the Philistines in the reign of Ahaz (2 Chron. xxviii. 18).

Ver. 13.—גוֹי. *i.e.*, the people of Israel (cf. iii. 17), more usually designated by עַם; thus the Chaldee here renders by עַמָּא יִשְׂרָאֵל; the omission of the article is a sign of poetry. אֹיְבָיו, accusative, of those from whom vengeance is sought to be taken, but the verb is usually used with the prep. מִן or לְ (see Ges., *Lex.*). הֲלֹא, *nonne?* = הֲנֵה (§ 153, 2, Rem.; see 2 Sam. i. 18). עַל, "upon," for in writing the letters were inscribed upon a tablet or parchment. סֵפֶר הַיָּשָׁר, quoted here and in 2 Sam. i. 18 only, lit. "*the book of the upright one*" (cf. margin of Auth. Vers., "book of the upright;" Aldine and Complut. edition of Sept. ἐπὶ βιβλίου τοῦ εὐθοῦς, Vulg. "in libro justorum;" but the Peshito Syr. "*the book of hymns*," reading הַשִּׁיר for הַיָּשָׁר).[1] "Yashar," from יָשַׁר, to be upright, was probably a poetical appellation of Israel as the covenant people of God, cf. "Jeshurun" in Deut. xxxii. 15, and see Numb. xxiii. 10, 21; Psalm cxi. 1, whence, and from

---

[1] Lowth (*Prælec*, lec. 23, note 10) adopts this view, and says, "I suppose the Book of Jashar to have been some collection of sacred songs, composed at different times and on different occasions, and to have had this title, because the book itself, and most of the songs, began in general with this word 'veyashar.'"

David's elegy over Saul and Jonathan in 2 Sam. i. 18, it has been inferred that the Book of Yashar was a collection of odes in praise of certain heroes of the Theocracy, with historical notices of their achievements interwoven, and that the collection was formed by degrees, so that the quotation of it here is neither a proof that the passage has been interpolated by a *later* hand, nor that the work was composed at a very late period (Keil). The formula of quotation "*Is not this written?*" is not found elsewhere in the middle of a verse, but always either at its beginning (Numb. xxi. 14, 27), or at its close (2 Kings xv. 21, xx. 20, etc.); and hence some (as Maurer, Fay, Kamphausen) are of opinion that the quotation itself terminates in the first half of ver. 13. This view seems also confirmed by the absence in vers. 13^b-14 of the parallelism in 12^b-13, and in its being simply stated as a matter of fact that the sun stood still, without any mention being made of the moon, and then the whole account being closed with the prosaic remark in ver. 15. On the other hand, Keil, Hengstenberg, and others, think that the whole passage, vers. 12-15, is taken from the Book of Yashar; but on that supposition we must conclude that that book was not entirely written in poetry, for ver. 15 is certainly prose, and of vers. 13^b-14 more can hardly be said than that they are written in a somewhat elevated style, such as is often used in prose itself. בַּחֲצִי הַשָּׁמַיִם, not "*in the hemisphere*," *i.e.*, in the upper heavens, those visible to the spectator, those above the horizon (Cor. a Lap., Rosenm., Calmet (*Frag.*, No. 154), but "*in the midst* (or *half*) *of heaven*" (cf. Stanley's *Sin. and Pal.*, p. 210, note 5). "The emphatic expression (ver. 13), not simply "*in the midst,*" but "*in the bisection of the heavens,*" seems intended to indicate noonday. "*And hasted not,*" אוּץ, " to hasten," in xvii. 15, "to be narrow, to be strait," a word used in poetry, but also in prose (see Exod. v. 13, and [in Hiphil] Gen. xix. 15). כְּיוֹם תָּמִים, not, as Clericus, "*when the day had passed,*" nor, as Rosenm., "*as is the case in a perfect day;*" but "*about a whole day,*" i.e., about twelve hours, the time between sunrise and sunset, cf. שָׁנָה תְמִימָה, "a whole year" (Lev. xxv. 30), and for the particle כְּ in the sense of "about," see Ges., *Lex.* (A) (3), p. 378.

Ver. 14.—"*And there was not like that day before and after it, that Jehovah hearkened to the voice of a man,*" etc. The Vulg. for "that day" has "tam longa dies," for which there is no authority in the Hebrew, which here gives prominence only to the fact that the wonder (ver. 13) was effected by Jehovah at the request of a man.[1] In the last clause כִּי assigns a reason why the prayer of Joshua was heard. God had before given a promise that He would deliver these enemies into Joshua's hand (ver. 8). "*Jehovah fought,*" cf. Exod. xiv. 14 ; and the title "*man of war*" given to Jehovah in Exod. xv. 3. The לְ before יִשְׂרָאֵל denotes a dat. commodi (cf. 1 Sam. xxii. 15, לְיָשִׁאל).

Ver. 15.—It is evident from ver. 43 that this verse is not suitably placed here, and hence some MSS., and the Vat. and Alex. editions of the Sept., omit it, though it is found in the Complut. and Aldine edition.

---

[1] In Hezekiah's case the retrogression of the shadow on the sun-dial was given to him as a sign, and not as an answer to his prayer (2 Kings xx. 9-11).

Masius, Drusius, and Cor. a Lapid. attempt to preserve the connection with the remainder of the chapter by rendering וַיָּשָׁב " *and* (Joshua) *proposed to return ;* " but this sense would rather have been expressed by וַיְחֶל לָשׁוּב. Either, therefore, ver. 15 may have been intended to be merely a finish off to the preceding narrative, after which the history is resumed from ver. 11,[1] or some ancient transcriber, misled by the similar endings of vers. 14, 42, may have transposed ver. 43, and inserted it here. So Ilgen, Rosenm., and others.

As to the remarkable event recorded in the above passage (vers. 12-14), it cannot be accounted for from natural causes, nor satisfactorily explained as a mere poetical description, meaning nothing more than that the day was made to seem to Joshua and the Israelites longer than it really was.[2] The repeated assertion that the sun stood still, and the emphatic declaration in ver. 14 concerning the unusual character of the event, are at variance with any such supposition. Yet we are not required to believe in an actual interruption of the course of the sun,[3] for it is well known that Scripture speaks of celestial phenomena not scientifically, but according to their appearance, as we say in popular language " the sun rises," or " the sun sets," because it seems to do so. All, therefore, implied by a stoppage of

---

[1] See Bishop Wordsworth *in loc.*, who remarks that this practice of finishing off a subject, and of afterwards returning to a point in the narrative, is common to both Testaments.

[2] Such is the view of Keil and Hengstenberg, and was that of the learned Jew Maimonides (*More Nevo*, ii., c. 53). So Herder, *Heb. Poesie*, vol. i., p. 237.

[3] This literal interpretation is the most ancient.

the sun might be either that the revolution of the earth on its axis was for a time interrupted (an event which God could have so ordered by His power and wisdom as to prevent any disastrous consequences to the system of the universe), or that, in some way unknown to us, God may have so interfered with the phenomena of light, as to have prolonged the daylight without interrupting the course of the heavenly bodies.[1]

Allusions to this miracle are probably made in Isa. xxviii. 21, "He" (the Lord) "shall be wroth as in the valley of Gibeon;" and in Hab. iii. 11, "The sun and moon stood still in their habitation."[2] There are also, as in the case of the Deluge, many ancient *traditions and fables*, which possibly have a

---

[1] If, as some think (see Calmet's *Frag.*, No. 154), "*shemesh*" and "*chammah*" are distinguished by denoting, the one the light, the other the orb or substance of the sun, God may, on this occasion, have continued the solar light, while He permitted the solar orb to set. Professor Young (*Science and Scripture*), in illustration of the manner in which the miracle was possibly wrought, remarks that "light is not merely an emanation of luminous particles, any more than sound is an emanation of sonorous particles from a sonorous body: in each case a *medium* of conveyance is necessary; and that the vehicle of light is luminiferous ether. Suppose now a void had been introduced above the scene of Joshua's operations, then, if the vibrations essential to light in the lower region had not been suffered to cease, the light would have continued to be supplied without any abatement of intensity. Such a temporary separation of the upper and lower portions of the luminous ethereal fluid would have been analogous to the temporary separation of the two portions of aqueous fluid in the miraculous passage of the Red Sea. And as the water was held in suspense in both portions in the one miracle, so might the light be held in suspense in the two portions in the other."

[2] זְבֻלָה, "in (their) habitation;" where the הָ֑ denotes a general direction only to the place where an object is (cf. שָׁמָּה, "there," Jer. xviii. 2, oftener "thither," § 90, 2, b).

reference to it ; such as the *Chinese* tradition that the sun did not set for ten days (perhaps a mistake or exaggeration for *hours*) in the reign of the seventh Emperor Yao, who is conjectured to have lived about A.M. 2554, and, therefore, to have been nearly contemporary with the date of the miracle. (Martin, *Sinic. Hist.*, l. 1., p. 25) ; and the *Egyptian* tradition, which may refer both to this and the miracle in the time of Hezekiah (2 Kings xx.), viz., that the sun had twice risen where it usually sets, and set where it usually rises (Herod., ii., 142). The fable also of Phaeton (Hesiod, *Theog.*, 985 ; Ovid, *Met.*, i., fab. 17, l. 2), and the poetical imagery in *Il.*, ii., 4, where Agamemnon prays that the sun may not go down till he has sacked Troy (cf. *Il.*, xviii., 232, etc. ; *Odyss.*, xxiii., 241, etc. ; Callim., *Hymn to Diana*), may contain allusion to the same event. The absence, however, of any positive testimony to it by Pagan writers has been accounted for on the supposition that no Pagan records are so ancient as this miracle, and that, like the darkness over the land of Egypt, it may have been strictly local (see *Comment.* of Keil and Delitz., p. 111, and Bp. Wordsworth *in loc.*). Sufficient reasons why God should have permitted the occurrence of so stupendous an event are, that thus He put the highest honour on Joshua as His servant, and gave the greatest encouragement to His people Israel in their warfare against their enemies. Also He signally rebuked the idolatry of the Canaanites, who were worshippers of the sun and moon, by showing that those objects of their adoration were wholly subservient to His will, and, therefore, powerless to aid them. Lastly, by this miracle He may have prefigured the glorious victory which Christ, our true Joshua, will hereafter achieve over His and His people's, enemies, when by a not less exercise of omnipotence the sun will be " turned into darkness and the moon into blood before the great and terrible day of the Lord."

Ver. 16.—The narrative is here resumed from ver. 11. בַּמְּעָרָה, "*in the cave*" (rt. עוּר, to excavate) : The article denotes a cave which was well known (§ 109). The hills in Palestine were chiefly of limestone, and, therefore, abounded in caves, which were frequently used as places of refuge (Stanley's *Sin. and Pal.*, p. 150) ; cf. the mention of the cave of Adullam in the history of David (1 Sam. xxii. 1 ; 2 Sam. xxiii. 13 ; 1 Chron. xi. 15). בְּמִקְדָה : The prep., being the same as that before בְּעָרָה, denotes that the town and cave were close together. All efforts to discover it have hitherto proved in vain. Captain Warren, R.E. (see note on ver. 10 above), remarks, " It is quite possible that the cave itself may have remained closed to this day, the tradition hanging to the spot, and the Hebrew name, *the Cave*, being changed to the Arabic name, *the Caves* (El-Moghâr)." (*Recent Explorations in Bible Lands*).

Ver. 17.—נֶחְבָּאִים for נֶחְבְּאִים, cf. נִמְצָאִים for נִמְצְאִים, 1 Sam. xiii. 15 ; Esther i. 5 ; from the singulars, נִמְצָא, נֶחְבָּא, the vowel (ָ) in the last syllable being borrowed from verbs לה (§ 75, vi., 21, *a*).

Ver. 18.—פִּי : So the entrance to a cave is termed "*os*" by Tacitus (*Annal.*, lib. iv., cap. 59). וְהַפְקִידוּ עָלֶיהָ, "*and appoint ye as guardians over it*," cf. Gen. xxxix. 5 ; Numb. i. 50 ; Isa. lxii. 10.

Ver. 19.—וְאַתֶּם, emphatic, "*but as for you*." עָמַד

here means to stand still or stop, as in 1 Sam.
xx. 38; Numb. ix. 8. The Piel זִנֵּב found here and
in Deut. xxv. 18 only, is a denominative from זָנָב, a
tail, and means properly "to injure the tail," and
hence " to rout the rear-guard of an army" (§ 52, 2, c),
Sept. καὶ καταλάβετε τὴν οὐραγίαν αὐτῶν, Chald.
and Syr. "assequimeni eos," but more exactly the
Vulg. "et extremos quosque fugientium cædite."

Ver. 20.—עַד־תֻּמָּם, see viii. 24. In the last clause
וְ before הַשְּׂרִידִים introduces the apodosis according to
our Auth. Vers., Jerome, and Michaelis, but it might
equally well be rendered "and" (e.g., "and the sur-
vivors had fled from them, and had entered into fortified cities"), the apod. beginning at ver. 21, "*that
all the people returned.*"

Ver. 21.—It appears from the first clause that
Joshua remained at Maqqedah with the guards who
kept watch over the cave, while the rest of his forces
pursued the enemy; hence, at the beginning of
ver. 20, he is mentioned, only because his soldiers
acted by his authority. בְּשָׁלוֹם, "*in safety*," cf. Gen.
xxviii. 21; Judges viii. 9. לֹא־חָרַץ, "*sharpened not*"
(Ges., *Lex.*); the verb is either in the indeterminate
3rd pers. (§ 137, 3); or אִישׁ must be understood, or
perhaps כֶּלֶב (see Exod. xi. 7, where the same proverb
[though nowhere else in the Bible] occurs; also
Judith xi. 19, καὶ οὐ γρύξει κύων τῇ γλώσσῃ αὐτοῦ
ἀπέναντί σου). לְאִישׁ is put in apposition to לִבְנֵי יִשׂ׳,
but Houbigant and Maurer think the לְ before אִישׁ
arose from the error of a transcriber, and, if so, אִישׁ
would be the nominative; Vulg. "nullusque contra
filios Israel mutire ausus est."

Vers. 22-28. What is here recorded doubtless took

place on the day after the return from the pursuit of the enemy.

Ver. 24.—כָּל־אִישׁ, i.e., all the soldiers in the camp. קָצִין,¹ lit. a judge, from קָצָה, to decide, and hence a military leader or commander (cf. Judges xi. 6). הֶהָלְכוּא; הֶ for the rel. (§ 109, 2nd par.); the א, after Arabic orthography, is paragogic, or superfluous (§ 44, 2, Rem. 4; cf. Isa. xxviii. 12, אָבוּא for אָבוּ, and נָשִׂיא for נָשִׂי, Psalm cxxxix. 20). In the imperfect the form occurs only in יִשָּׂיא (Jer. x. 5). "*Put your feet on the necks*," etc., an act symbolic of complete subjection, but not one of haughty contempt and insolence, as when Sapor I., King of Persia, set his foot on the neck of the Emperor Valerian. David says in Psalm xviii. 41 (Heb.), "Thou hast given me the neck of mine enemies." The same symbol is used to denote Christ's dominion over His enemies (Psalm cx. 1; Heb. i. 13; 1 Cor. xv. 25). We may hence learn, says Origen, to tread under foot our carnal lusts and appetites, which are Christ's enemies and ours (*Homil.*, 11 and 12). Joshua's object on this occasion was also to encourage the Israelites (see next verse).

Ver. 25.—"*Fear not*," etc. For the greater encouragement of Israel Joshua quotes the very words of Jehovah (see i. 9, viii. 1). Thus in our Christian warfare the victories which we have already gained through God should animate us to rely on His further help, till all our spiritual enemies are subdued. לָחַם here governs an accus., as in Psalm cix. 3;

---

¹ A word, like many others in this book, not found in the Pentateuch.

1 Kings xx. 25, xxii. 31. It is found elsewhere with the prep. בְּ, or עַל (Neh. iv. 8), or עִם (2 Kings xiii. 12), or אֶל (Jer. i. 19), or לְ (Exod. xiv. 14, 25).

Ver. 26.—"*Hanged them,*" see viii. 29 (note). עֵצִים, "*trees,*" from עָצַם, to be firm (cf. Acts x. 39). "*Until the evening,*" cf. Deut. xxi. 23.

Ver. 27.—הַשֶּׁ... לְעֵת, *i.e.*, on the evening of the day after that on which the soldiers of Joshua had returned from the pursuit of the enemy (see note, ver. 22). "*Until this very day,*" *i.e.*, up to the self-same day on which the author wrote this history.[1] On עֶצֶם see § 124, 2, Rem. 3.

VERS. 28-43.—*Conquest of Southern Canaan.*

Ver. 28.—בַּיּוֹם הַהוּא, "*on that day,*" *i.e.*, the day when the five kings were executed, and were still hanging on trees or crosses (ver. 26); hence לָכַד, not וַיִּלְכֹּד, is used. The capture, though it took place before the evening of that day (ver. 27), is described here on account of its connection with the subsequent events (Keil). לְפִי חֶרֶב (cf. vi. 21, viii. 24). הֶחֱרִם (see ii. 10). אוֹתָם, "*them,*" *i.e.*, the king and the inhabitants

---

[1] Keil, indeed, remarks that the formula עַד עֶצֶם הַיּוֹם הַזֶּה is not elsewhere used to denote that a thing had continued till the author's own day, but to call attention to the fact that the day referred to is the very same day about which the author is writing and no other (see v. 11; Gen. vii. 13, xvii. 23; Exod. xii. 17, 41, etc.). If, therefore, עֶצֶם (he says) has any meaning at all here, the whole clause must be connected with the one preceding, and rendered as a relative clause: "*Where they* (the kings) *had hidden themselves, and they* (the Israelites) *had placed large stones at the mouth of the cave until that very day* (on which the kings were fetched out and executed.)" The demonstrative pronoun "*that*" would, however, be rather expressed by הַהוּא than הַזֶּה (see § 122, 1, Rem.). Thus in iv. 9, vi. 25, vii. 26, viii. 29, עַד הַיּוֹם הַזֶּה means "to *this* day."

of the city. Many MSS. read אותה, and the pronoun is omitted altogether in the Sept., Vulg., and Syriac. כָּל־נֶפֶשׁ refers to human beings only, as כָּל־נְשָׁמָה in ver. 40, xi. 14; Deut. xx. 16, where it appears from the following verse (ver. 17) to refer to the inhabitants of Canaan. "*As he had done to the king of Jericho*": Nothing is said in vi. 21, etc., as to the manner of the death of the King of Jericho, but it is supposed from viii. 2, 29 that he was slain, and then hung on a cross, or gallows.

Ver. 29.—"*All Israel*," *i.e.*, all the men selected for this war. "*Libhnah*" (whiteness), a Canaanite capital (xii. 15), in the south part of the maritime lowland of Judah (xv. 42); afterwards assigned to the priests (xxi. 13). It revolted from King Joram, "because he had forsaken the Lord God of his fathers" (2 Kings viii. 22; 2 Chron. xxi. 10). Sennacherib, King of Assyria, warred in person against it (2 Kings xix. 8), but he is not said to have taken it. On account of the meaning of the name Dean Stanley identifies it with the Blanchegarde of the Crusaders, a hill on the eastern border of the plain of Philistia, opposite Ascalon (*Sin. and Pal.*, pp. 207, 257, 258); but Van de Velde places it at Arâk el Menshiyeh, a hill about four miles west of Beitjibrîn (Eleutheropolis). It is described by Eusebius and Jerome in the *Onomasticon* as a village of the district of Eleutheropolis. For the prep. עִם before לְבִנָה some MSS. read עַל, which is more commonly used with נִלְחַם, in relation to sieges (cf. ver. 36); in ver. 31 בְּ is used.

Ver. 31.—"*Lachish*," see ver. 3.

Ver. 32.—"*On the second day*," *i.e.*, from that on

which the siege began. No mention is made of the king, because he had before been put to death (ver. 23, etc.).

Ver. 33.—עָלָה see note viii. 1. "*Gezer*" (a place cut off), written often with the pause accent גָּֽזֶר and twice, where it occurs, translated Gazer by our Auth. Ver., viz., in 2 Sam. v. 25; 1 Chron. xiv. 16, but elsewhere (even when the first vowel in the Hebrew is lengthened to ־) translated Gezer (see, *e.g.*, Josh. xvi. 3, 10; Judges i. 29; 1 Kings ix. 15, etc). There was a town of this name[1] on the south-west border of Ephraim, between lower Beth-choron and the Mediterranean (Josh. xvi. 3), and which was assigned to the Kohathite Levites (xxi. 21; 1 Chron. vi. 67). According to Conder (*Handbook*, p. 412) now Tell Jezer, a large ruin. This town was, however, at least forty miles from Lachish (Um Lakis), and hence Masius and others think that there may have been another town of this name near Lachish,—an opinion which receives some countenance from Josh. xii. 12, where Gezer is mentioned in connection with Chebhron, Lachish, 'Eghlon, and D'bhir. If, however, the town on the border of Ephraim is meant, it probably was not captured at this time,[2] but Joshua, having signally defeated its troops and slain its king (xii. 12), proceeded with his conquests of the other towns in the south. עַד־בִּלְתִּי, see note on viii. 22.

---

[1] In the time of Jerome it was a small town, called Gazara.
[2] In xvi. 10, and Judges i. 29, we read that the Ephraimites did not expel the inhabitants, but put them under tribute, and in the time of Solomon the King of Egypt took and burnt the town, and slew the Canaanites who dwelt there; afterwards he gave the place to his daughter, the wife of Solomon, who rebuilt it (1 Kings ix. 16).

Vers. 34, 35.—'Egh-lôn (ver. 3); its king was one of the five whom Joshua had put to death (ver. 23, etc.). הֶחֱרִים, cf. ver. 28.

Vers. 36, 37.—*Chebh-rôn* (ver. 3): Its mountainous situation is indicated by עָלָה. "*The king thereof*": Probably the successor of the one whose death is recorded ver. 23, etc. Ver. 37.—"*All the cities thereof*," *i.e.*, certain towns which were subject to it. "*He left none remaining*": Yet we afterwards read in xi. 21, 22 of Joshua's destroying the Anakim in the mountains of Chebh-ron and D°bhir; and again (in Judges i. 10-13) of their extermination by Caleb; and hence some, as Maurer, have thought that the account here is interpolated, and not strictly historical. We may suppose, however, that on this occasion the Chittite inhabitants of Chebh-ron were destroyed, but the Anakim retained their strongholds in the mountains near the city, and, though afterwards expelled by Joshua and partially destroyed (xi. 21, 22), yet those who fled to the cities of the Philistines (xi. 22) reoccupied Chebh-ron and D°bhir, probably while Joshua was engaged in the conquest of North Palestine, and were only finally repulsed by Caleb (Josh. xiv. 12, xv. 13-17, compared with Judges i. 10, etc). Masius remarks that Joshua in this war only overran the country, and did not stay to place garrisons in the captured towns, nor to expel the enemy from every lurking-place, but left the complete conquest to the Israelites after they should have apportioned the land and settled in it.

Vers. 38, 39.—וַיָּשָׁב, "*and Joshua turned*," *i.e.*, changed the direction of his march. *D°bhi-rah* (the

ה־, here is not local, cf. ver. 39), but elsewhere D^ebhir (דְּבִר, and in Judges and Chron. דְּבִיר), translated by Jerome "oracle," from דִּבֵּר, to speak; but, according to Gesenius, "the hinder part," and hence the inmost recess of a temple, rt. דָּבַר, to be behind; formerly called Qiryath-sepher (Sept. πόλις γραμμάτων; Josh. xv. 15), and Qiryath-sannah (xv. 49), perhaps "city of palm-branches," but, according to Bochart, "city of law, or sacred learning," and thus it would seem that this city was the seat of ancient Canaanitish learning. It was situated in the highlands of Judah (xv. 49), but its site is not yet determined. "*All the cities thereof,*" *i.e.*, the towns of which it was the centre or metropolis (cf. ver. 37). "*Utterly destroyed,*" see note on ver. 37.

Vers. 40-43 (*Summary of the Conquest of Southern Canaan*).—Ver. 40.—"*Smote the whole land,*" *i.e.*, the whole of Southern Canaan from Gibeon. הָהָר, *i.e.*, the mountainous district of Judah and South Canaan generally (see ix. 1). הַנֶּגֶב, "*the Neghebh,*" or south country, from נָגַב, to be dry, the least fertile portion of the land of Canaan. Its boundaries were from Qa-dhesh, or from Mount Chalaq (xi. 17; Clark's *Bib. Atlas*), to within a few miles of Chebh-ron, and from the Dead Sea westward to the Mediterranean (cf. Josh. xv. 21-32). הַשְּׁפֵלָה, see ix. 1. הָאֲשֵׁדוֹת, "*the slopes,*" *i.e.*, undulating ground between the foot of the hills and the lowland, *i.q.*, ὑπώρειαι (*Il.*, Υ., v. 218): so it might be rendered in Deut. iii. 17, iv. 49, lit. "the pouring forth of streams," and hence, the ravines by which streams pour down from the mountains into the plains, rt. אָשַׁד, to pour forth. The Sept., Vulg., and Syr. regard the word as a proper name, but the

Chald. renders it מַיְפַּךְ מֵרָכִתָא, "a pouring forth from a height;" it occurs only in this book and the Pentateuch. כָּל־הַנְּשָׁמָה, lit. "every breath," and hence, by metonymy, that which has breath, *i.q.*, כָּל־הַנֶּפֶשׁ (vers. 32, 35, 37), but restricted here, as there, to human beings (see xi. 11, 14, and note on viii. 27). "*As Jehovah . . . commanded,*" see Numb. xxxiii. 51, etc.; Deut. vii. 1, etc., xx. 16.[1]

Ver. 41.—"*Qa-dhesh-Barnéa*": It is mentioned sometimes as being in the wilderness of Paran (Numb. xiii. 26, and at others as in the wilderness of Zin, because the name Zin was given to the north part of the great wilderness of Paran in which Qa-dhesh lay. We read also of "*the wilderness of Qa-dhesh*" (Psalm xxix. 8), because the name of the city was extended to the district around it. If Qa-dhesh is derived from קָדֵשׁ, to be holy, the word

---

[1] "If, on the one hand, the character of the religion of the Canaanites be remembered, and, on the other, the Divine purpose to develop among the Israelites a pure and lofty Theocracy, through which, hereafter, the highest manifestation of the kingdom of God on earth was to be made known among men, the apparent difficulty in accepting the policy commanded to Joshua disappears. The heathenism of Palestine and Syria was so foul and degrading in every sense, that there is no State, even at this time, which would not put it down, if necessary, by the severest penalties. Its spread to Rome was bewailed 1,500 years later by the satirists of the day as a calamity marking the utter decay of the times (Juv., *Sat.*, iii., 62). It was imperative, therefore, that the land in which the Chosen People were to be educated in the true religion, so as to become the disseminators of its doctrines through the world, should be cleared of whatever would so certainly neutralise the gracious plans of the Almighty. Nor is it wonderful that no other means of securing this great end presented itself to the Hebrew legislator or reformer, in the presence of such hideous immorality and corruption, than the rooting it out with the edge of the sword." (Dr. Geikie, *Hours with the Bible*, vol. ii., pp. 396, 397.)

perhaps denotes a religious centre, but no satisfactory explanation has been given of the term "Barnea." The Sept., in Numb. xxxiv. 4, renders it Κάδης τοῦ Βαρνή, which may imply that Barnea was regarded as a man's name, but elsewhere it has Κάδης Βαρνή. Fürst suggests בן־נוע, "son of wandering," a Bedouin, but in the Pentateuch, where the word Barnea first occurs, בַּר is never used for "son." Others derive it from בַּר, a country or land (cf. Job xxxix. 4), and נוע, to be shaken, supposing it to have allusion to a volcanic convulsion in that neighbourhood. Keil thinks that Barnea was the ancient name, but that it was called by anticipation Qa-dhesh in Gen. xiv. 7, xvi. 14, xx. 1; Numb. xiii. 26 and xx. 1, in reference to that judgment (Numb. xiv.) by which the Lord would sanctify Himself on Moses and Aaron, because they would not sanctify Him before the people. It is evident from a comparison of Numb. xiii. 26 with Numb. xxxii. 8, that Qa-dhesh and Qa-dhesh-Barnea must denote one and the same place; and that Meribah Kadesh is also the same as Qa-dhesh-Barnea is clear on comparing Ezek. xlvii. 19, xlviii. 28, with Numb. xxxiv. 4; Josh. xv. 3; Deut. xxxii. 51. Dean Stanley endeavours to identify Qa-dhesh-Barnea with Petra, but that city lies far too much to the south, to be described as on the frontier of Judah, and is not "in the uttermost part of the border of Edom" (Numb. xx. 16), but rather in the centre of Edom. Most probably, therefore, the site of Qa-dhesh-Barnea is correctly identified by Robinson (ii., 175) with the modern *Ain el-Weibeh*, which lies in the Arabah, about ten miles north of the spot where Mount Hor touches on that valley, and which is nearly opposite the *Wady Ghuwein*, which affords an access practicable for an army through the mountainous country of Edom to the north-west, and which might be fitly described as the "*king's highway*" (Numb. xx. 17). So Bishop Wordsworth, Porter, and others. The *Ain-Kudes* argued for by Messrs. Rowlands and Williams (*Holy City*, i, 463, etc)., and which is more than seventy miles to westward, in a direct line from Mount Hor, and sixty from the nearest spur of Mount Seir, does not satisfy the requirements of the Scripture history, which speaks of Qa-dhesh as "*a city in the uttermost part of the border of Edom*" (Numb. xx. 16), and Edom did not, at that time, extend to the west beyond the Arabah (Dean Stanley, *Sin. and Pal.*, p. 194, note; Clarke's *Bib. Atlas*, p. 26). Moreover, the course from Mount Sinai to a city so far west would not have been by the way of Mount Seir (Deut. i. 2), but, rather, by way of Shur. Gaza, a maritime city of Philistia, only an hour's journey from the Mediterranean (Robinson, ii., 174), Heb. "*Azzah*," " strong," Sept. and New Testament (Acts viii. 26) Γάζα, the limit of the land of Canaan on the south-west (Gen. x. 19), and on the direct route between Egypt[1] and Syria. It was allotted to Judah (xv. 47), and taken by it (Judges i. 18), but soon recovered by the Philistines (Judges iii. 3), and always mentioned afterwards as a Philistine city

---

[1] All the conquests of the Egyptians in the land of Palestine appear, according to their monuments, to have been confined to the maritime plain of Philistia, though they may have passed through the country and exacted tributes. Thotmes III., of the eighteenth dynasty, is recorded to have captured Gaza. (See Philip Smith's *Anct. Hist.*, vol. i., ch. vii., p. 117.)

(Judges xvi. 1, etc.; 1 Sam. vi. 17; 2 Kings xviii. 8). It was chiefly celebrated in profane history for its memorable siege by Alexander the Great, who, after its capture, treated the living body of Batis, its governor, with the same indignity as Achilles the corpse of Hector (Plutarch, *Alexand.*, 25; Q. Curt., iv. 6). Jonathan Maccabæus (1 Macc. xi. 61) destroyed its suburbs; Simon Maccabæus (1 Macc. xiii. 43), after great efforts, captured the city itself. Alexander Jannæus, B.C. 96, dismantled it (Joseph., *Antiq.*, xiii., 12, 3), but it was soon afterwards restored by Gabinius (Joseph., xiv., 5, 3), and was one of the cities given by Augustus to Herod (*Antiq.*, xv., 7, 3), after whose death it was united to the province of Syria (*Antiq.*, xvii., 11, 4); now *Guzzah*, a flourishing town, but on a different site from the ancient Gaza, against which the threatenings in Amos i. 6, 7; Zeph. ii. 4; Zech. ix. 5, were fully accomplished. "*All the country of Goshen*": Of course, not the Goshen in Egypt, but a district perhaps named after a city so called in the south part of Judah (xv. 51), or from the Goshen in Egypt, which it may have resembled in fertility.[1] The words "*from Goshen even unto Gibeon*" describe the extent of the conquered country from south to north on the eastern side.

Ver. 42.—"*At one time*," *i.e.*, in one campaign, which must have lasted a considerable time (xi. 18). "*For Jehovah . . . fought*," etc.: This is added to account for the marvellous rapidity of the conquest.

Ver. 43.—See note at the beginning of ver. 15.

---

[1] Hitzig derives the word from the Persian "gauzen," a cow (*Geschichte*, etc., p. 60).

CHAPTER XI.

VERS. 1-15.—*Defeat of the Second League formed against the Israelites.*[1]

Ver. 1.—כִּשְׁמֹעַ : The object of the verb is omitted, viz., those deeds recorded in the previous chapter (cf. ix. 1). "*Ya-bhîn*" (lit. "he will understand," and hence "wise," "intelligent"), a title of the kings of Cha-tsôr (Judges iv. 2; cf. x. 1 [note]). *Cha-tsôr* (lit. "a fortified place"), the principal city of North Canaan (ver. 10), situated north-west of the Lake Merom, on elevated ground (see ver. 13), overlooking the lake (Joseph., *Antiq.*, v., 5, 1), and apparently between Ramah and Kedesh (Josh. xix. 36-7 with 2 Kings xv. 29), afterwards allotted to Naphtali (xix. 36). Josephus calls it Ἄσωρος, Eusebius Ἀσώρ. It is mentioned in Egyptian inscriptions of an early date, was taken by Tothmosis III., and was again a flourishing place under Ramasis II. (Chabas, *Voyage d'un Egypt.*, p. 183). Being on the north frontier it was fortified by Solomon (1 Kings ix. 15), and its

---

[1] This is generally called the northern league, but it was not strictly limited to the north, as is evident from ver. 3. Dean Stanley remarks, "Round Jabin were assembled the heads of all the tribes who had not yet fallen under Joshua's sword. As the British chiefs were driven to the Land's End before the advance of the Saxon, so at this Land's End of Palestine were gathered for this last struggle, not only the kings of the north in the immediate neighbourhood, but from the desert valley of the Jordan, south of the Sea of Galilee, from the maritime plain of Philistia, from the heights above Sharon, and from the still unconquered Jebus, to the Hivite who dwelt in the valley of Baalbec under Hermon." (*Sin. and Pal.*, chap. xi.)

inhabitants were carried away captive by Tiglath-Pileser (2 Kings xv. 29). Once more we find evident reference to it in 1 Macc. xi. 67, where the words "plain of Nasor," the scene of Jonathan's victory over the Syrians, ought to be written "plain of Asor," *i.e.*, Chatsôr, the "N" having been erroneously prefixed from the preceding Greek word πεδίον. Now, possibly, *Tell Kuraibeh* (Robinson, *Bibl. Res.*, iii., 365). "*Ma-dhôn*": Only mentioned again in xii. 19, probably in North Canaan, and to the west of Lake Merom (Knobel), or possibly represented by the ruin Madin, west of the Sea of Galilee. (Conder's *Handbook*, p. 425). "*Shim-rôn*" (watch): Unknown, perhaps the same as Shimron-Meron in xii. 20, afterwards assigned to Zebulun (xix. 15). Some place it on Lake Merom, but the territory of Zebulun never reached so far north. It may possibly be identical, according to the Talmud, with the Simmias of Josephus (*Vita*, § 24), now Simunîyah, a village a few miles west of Nazareth, for it appears from xix. 15 to have been near to Bethlehem, in Zebulun. "*Akh-shaph*" (enchantment, rt. כָּשַׁף, unused in Qal., but meaning in Piel "to use enchantment" (Ges., *Lex.*; cf. xii. 20): Perhaps the present Kesâf, nearly halfway between Tyre and Banias, assigned to Asher (xix. 25, note).

Ver. 2.—מִצָּפוֹן בָּהָר, "*northwards in the mountains*": Construc. state before a prep. (§ 116, 1). The mountains stretching through Naphtali seem to be meant (cf. xx. 7). "*In the Arabah to the south of Kinn^{a}rôth*" (Heb.), *i.e.*, in the plain or Ghôr (iii. 16) to the south of the lake afterwards called Gennesaret. Kinn^{a}rôth is either the town called

Chinnereth (A. V.; xix. 35), which may have given its name to the lake, or the lake itself, so called perhaps from the oval, harp-like form (כִּנּוֹר, a harp) of its basin (Stanley, *Sin. and Pal.*, p. 373), or from כָּנַע, to be low, depressed; but, according to G. Grove, the name was probably an old Canaanitish word, adopted into the Israelitish language. St. Luke only calls the lake "*Gennesaret*" (v. 1); St. Matthew and St. Mark "*the Sea of Galilee*" (Matt. iv. 18, xv. 29; Mark i. 16, vii. 31); St. John "*the Sea of Tiberias*" (vi. 1, xxi. 1), from the city Tiberias; now *Bahr Tubarîyeh*, remarkable for its deep depression, being seven hundred feet below the level of the ocean (Rob., *Pal.*, i., 613; Stanley, *Sin. and Pal.*, 370); its length is thirteen geographical miles, and its breadth six miles. שְׁפֵלָה (see ix. 1): Here the north part of that plain, extending as far as Joppa; it included the fertile valley of Sharon. בְּנָפוֹת דּוֹר, "*in the highlands of Dor*": נָפָה, *i.q.*, נוּף, a height. The Sept. joins Naphoth with Dor, and renders as a proper name, *e.g.*, Νεφεδδώρ (cf. Jerome, *Onom.*, "*Dornapheth*"). The town Dor was on the coast of the Mediterranean, below Carmel, and about nine Roman miles north of Cæsarea, and was the extreme boundary of North Canaan toward the west; a royal city (xii. 23), which gave its name to the district around it (xii. 23; 1 Kings iv. 11). It was in the territory of Asher, but was assigned to Manasseh (xvii. 11), by whom its Canaanite inhabitants were not driven out (Judges i. 27); afterwards it was taken possession of by the Ephraimites. Solomon made it the residence of one of his twelve purveyors (1 Kings iv. 11). In the time of the Maccabees it was a fortified town (1 Macc. xv. 11), and so under the Romans (Joseph., *Antiq.*, xiv., 5, § 3). Pliny (*H. N.*, v., 17) and Stephen Byzan. (*s.v.* Δῶρος), speak of it as a Phœnician settlement, and most probably the Phœnicians may have selected the spot on account of the *Murex trunculus* with which its rocks abounded, and which furnished the famous Tyrian dye. In early Christian times it was an episcopal see of the province of Palestine Prima, but in the fourth century the city was already ruined and deserted (Jerome in *Epitaph. Paulæ*). The modern name is *Tantûra*, or *Dandora* (Ritter, *Geogr. of Pal.*, iv., 27-8 ; Reland, *Palest.*, p. 738, etc.).

Ver. 3.—"[And to] *the K'naanite . . . and the Y'bhûsite in the mountains*," see on iii. 10. The "*P'rizzites*" probably inhabited the hills above the plain of Sharon (Stanley, *Sin. and Pal.*, Append., § 87). Subau. "he sent" from ver. 1. "*And to the Chivvite under Chermôn*" : This latter tribe was thus distinguished from the Chivvites in Gibeon, who made peace with Joshua (ix. 15). Chermôn means in Arabic a "lofty prominent peak," the "nose" of a mountain (Ges., *Lex.*). It formed the southern extremity of Antilibanus, and the northern boundary of Palestine on the east of Jordan. It was called by the Sidonians שִׂרְיוֹן, from שָׂרָה, to glitter, and by the Amorites שְׂנִיר, from נָמַר, to clatter, both nouns meaning "*breastplate*," and referring to its glittering, snowclad summit (Deut. iii. 9 ; Cant. iv. 8 ; Ezek. xxvii. 5) ; also שִׂיאֹן, "the upraised" (Deut. iv. 48) ; it was about 9,500 feet high,[1] and

---

[1] According to Porter 10,000 feet (see Art. "Hermon" in Dr. Smith's *Dict. of Bible*).

visible from most parts of Palestine. The modern name is *Jebel esh-Sheikh* (with its south-eastern arm Jebel Heisch), "the chief mountain," or "mountain of the old white-headed man" (Stanley, *Sin. and Pal.*, ch. xii., p. 403-4), also "*Jebel eth Thelj*," "the snowy mountain." It has been well called the Mont Blanc of Palestine (*Sin. and Pal.*, p. 403). The plural הֶרְמוֹנִים (Psalm xlii. 7 [6]) may refer to the whole range of its snowy heights, or to its three summits, which are about a quarter of a mile from each other, and not much different in elevation (Porter's *Five Years in Damascus*, vol. i.) "*In the land of Mitspah*"[1]: Nowhere else mentioned in the Bible, but no doubt identical with "the valley of Mitspeh" (ver. 8), a plain stretching from the foot of Hermon south-westwards towards the Bahr el Hûleh (Lake Merom).

In this valley or plain is a hill called *el-Mutalleh*, "the look out," or "the look down," commanding a fine view over the Lake Hûleh and the surrounding district (Rob., *Bibl. Res.*, iii., 373). The name Mits-peh, or Mits-pah, is given in Scripture to many places (see Ges., *Lex.*).

Ver. 4.—"*And they went out*": יֵצְאוּ is often used of going forth to war (see Numb. xxi. 23 ; 1 Sam. viii. 20; Job xxxix. 21), with an ellipsis of לַמִּלְחָמָה, which is supplied in viii. 14. "*Their hosts*," lit. their camps (cf. Exod. xiv. 24 ; Judges iv. 16). "*As the sand*," etc. : A frequent simile in Hebrew (except in

---

[1] The ו in the last syllable is changed into ר by the pause accent (§ 29, 4). As the word in the Hebrew has the article before it, the literal rendering is " in the land of the watch-tower " (or eminence).

the later books of the Old Testament) to denote a large number (see Gen. xxii. 17, xxxii. 12 [13]; Judges vii. 12), and used in Rev. xx. 8 of the vast forces of Gog and Magog. "*Upon the brink* (lit. lip) *of the sea*": The same imagery is applied to a river (xii. 2, xiii. 9, 16). "*With* (lit. and) *horses and chariots*": סוּס and רֶכֶב are here used collectively. Josephus says that the confederate forces amounted to 300,000 foot, 10,000 cavalry, and 20,000 war chariots (*Antiq.*, v., 1, § 18). The chariots, here mentioned for the first time, are described in xvii. 16 as chariots of iron, *i.e.*, strengthened and tipped with iron, as those of the Egyptians (Exod. xiv. 7), but not, as some suppose, armed with scythes; this latter kind having been first introduced by Cyrus (see Xen., *Cyrop.*, vi., c. 1, § 27, 30). The later Jabin had nine hundred chariots of iron.

Ver. 5.—וַיִּוָּעֲדוּ, "*and they assembled themselves together by appointment*": Niph. imperf. of יָעַד, to appoint (cf. Psalm xlviii. 4 [5]); the kings were assembled (נוֹעֲדוּ), so the Chald. Vers.; or "*they agreed together*," sc., concerning the war and place of battle (Keil). "*Merom*," lit. "a high place," from רוּם, to be high. "*The waters of Merom*" are generally taken to mean the Lake Merom, the High Lake, as contrasted with the lower "Lake of Gennesareth," and the still lower "Lake of Asphaltitis." It is supposed identical with the Lake Semechonîtis (Joseph., *Antiq.*, v., 5, 1; *Bel. Jud.*, iii., 10, 7, iv. 1, 1), which may perhaps be derived from the Arabic Samak, "high" (Stanley's *Sin. and Pal.*, xi., p. 391, note 1), now the *Bahr el Hûleh* of the modern Arabs, which may derive its name from the depressed plain *Ard el Hûleh*, in which it lies, and which extends about fifteen miles between the hills of Galilee on the west, and the slopes of Hermon on the east. The lake is nearly triangular in form, and the Jordan, which flows through it, makes its exit at the apex. Josephus calls it thirty furlongs in breadth, and sixty in length (*Bel. Jud.*, iv., 1). The tableland on the south-west shore of the lake is wider than that on the south-east, and, therefore, it is probable that Jabin and his allies encamped in that quarter. There is, however, some uncertainty as to the locality, for Merom is not elsewhere found in Scripture, nor is it mentioned by Josephus, who says that the confederate kings encamped near Beroth, a city of Upper Galilee, not far from Kedes, and makes no mention of water (*Antiq.*, v., 1, § 18). Eusebius, also, in the *Onomasticon*, gives the name as "Merran," which he states to be a village twelve miles distant from Sebaste (Samaria), and near Dothaim (see Smith's *Bib. Dict.*, vol. ii., p. 332). Again, Keil, after Knobel, would identify Merom with Meirôm, or Meirûm, a celebrated place of pilgrimage among the Jews, because Hillel and other noted rabbis are said to be buried there (Rob., *Pal.*, iii., p. 333), about two hours' journey north-west of Szafed, upon a rocky mountain, at the foot of which there is a spring that forms a small brook, which flows away through the valley below Szafed, and is said to reach the Lake of Tiberias in the neighbourhood of Bethsaida. It is doubtful, however, whether this locality was suitable, like the level shores of the Lake Merom, for the numerous chariots and horses of Jabin. Dean Stanley adopts the more generally received view that this latter is the spot intended (*Sin. and Pal.*, ch. xi.)

Ver. 6.—"*Be not afraid,*" etc., cf. viii. 1, x. 8. "*To-morrow about this time*": Hence it seems that Joshua, with his wonted expedition (cf. x. 9), had set out from Gilgal, and was within a day's march of the enemy. אָנֹכִי, emphatic. נֹתֵן, lit. "(am) *giving*," represents the execution of God's purpose as already begun. חֲלָלִים, lit. pierced through, mortally wounded, and hence "*slain*" (cf. Deut. xxi. 1, 2, 3). תְּעַקֵּר, "*thou shalt hough,*" i.e., shalt sever the houghs, or tendons, of the hind feet, and thus cause incurable lameness; Piel of עָקַר, to root out (cf. Gen. xlix. 6, "houghed oxen" [marg. reading]; 2 Sam. viii. 4); but, as a rule, the arteries were not cut so as to cause the animal to bleed to death (Keil, note on Gen. xlix. 6). It is remarkable[1] that in the Bible we have not hitherto met with the horse except in Egypt. In the war with the Amalekites (Exod. xvii.), and with the Midianites, an Arab tribe (Numb. xxxi.), no mention is made of horses, nor in the war with Sihon and Og on the east side of Jordan, nor in that with the kings in the south of Palestine. Probably, therefore, the Egyptians out of policy may not at this time have exported horses to those Asiatic countries adjacent to them, and hence the cavalry of the northern Canaanitish kings may have been derived from Armenia, a country perhaps then famous for its traffic in horses, as undoubtedly it was at a later period (see Ezek. xxvii. 14). Horses, at this time, seem to have been used only for war, but were for-

---

[1] Compare note of Dr. Kitto in the *Pictorial Bible.*

bidden to the Israelites (Deut. xvii. 16), who in their wars were to rely on God, rather than on creature might (see Psalm xx. 7 [8]), and had they not houghed the horses might have been tempted to reserve them for their own use.

Ver. 7.—"*And they fell upon them*": נָפַל is also used of a hostile attack in Job i. 15. The Sept. here adds ἐν τῇ ὀρεινῇ, which may imply that Joshua fell upon them in the mountain slopes of the plain, before they could rally on the level ground (Stanley, *Sin. and Pal.*, xi., p. 392).

Ver. 8.—"*Chased them*," *i.e.*, as they fled in two directions, some towards the north-west, others towards the north-east. "*Great Tsî-dhôn*" (cf. xix. 28), called the Great, רַבָּה, *i.e.*, the populous, because at that time the capital of Phœnicia; allotted to Asher (xix. 28), but not conquered by it (Judges i. 31, iii. 3), now called *Saida*, situated to the west of ancient Zidon, and a port of some commerce, but insecure from the sanding up of the harbour. Since from the time of David Tyre, not Zidon, comes prominently into notice as the principal city of Phœnicia (2 Sam. v. 11; Isa. xxiii. 12; Jer. xlvii. 4; Zech. ix. 2), we have here an incidental proof of the antiquity of the Book of Joshua. *Mis-r⁰phôth-Ma-yim*, unknown. The name probably means "*burnings of waters*," from שָׂרַף, to burn, and may refer to hot springs or baths (Kimchi), or smelting factories near the waters (Ges., *Thes.*, *s.v.*). It appears from xiii. 6 that the place was closely connected with Zidon, and it may, therefore, be the same as Zarephath (Sarepta, Luke iv. 26), to which the name bears a resemblance, between Tyre and Zidon (cf. 1 Kings xvii. 9,

"*Zarephath, which belongeth to Zidon*"; cf. Article in Smith's *Bib. Dict.*, p. 384, and Conder's *Handbook*, p. 420). On the other hand, Thomson (*Land and Book*, p. 203) would identify it with a collection of springs, called *Ain-Musherifeh*, at the foot of the promontory, to which, with its steep pass, the name *Ras el Nakhura* is given, the "*scala Tyriorum*" of the Crusaders, between Tyre on the north, and Acco, or Ptolemais, on the south. Again, according to Dean Stanley (*Sin. and Pal.*, 392, note 4), its name, "the flow of waters" (a derivation found in Ges., *Lex.*, from יָרַף, to drop), is naturally applied to the exit of the Leontes from the valley of Baalbec. Both, however, of these opinions probably place it too far from Zidon. The meaning also of Misrephoth elsewhere is "burnings," not "flowings" (see Isa. xxxiii. 12, and cf. יְרֵפָה, Gen. xi. 3; Jer. xxxiv. 5). "*And unto the valley of Mitspeh eastward*," see on ver. 3. בִּקְעָה, lit. "a cleft place," from בָּקַע, to cleave, is uniformly applied to the district of Cœle-Syria (cf. xi. 17, xii. 7); hence it would seem rather to denote a large plain between mountains than a valley strictly so called, to which the word עֵמֶק more nearly corresponds (Stanley's *Sin. and Pal.*, Append., p. 484). עַד . . . הִשְׁאִיר, see viii. 22, xi. 4. The meaning is that Joshua slew all whom he overtook in the pursuit.[1]

Ver. 10.—The expression "*at that time*" being

---

[1] "The battle of the Lake of Merom," says Dean Stanley, "was to the north what the battle of Bethhoron had been to the south; more briefly told, less complete in its consequences, but, still, the decisive conflict by which the four northern tribes were established in the south of Lebanon; by which Galilee with its sacred sea, and the manifold consequences therein

indefinite, admits of the supposition that the pursuit may have lasted several days. "*And smote the king thereof*" : Jabin must, therefore, have escaped to his capital. לְפָנִים, "*of old*" (cf. Deut. ii. 10, 12).

Ver. 11 (cf. x. 28, 40).—הַחֲרֵם, "*utterly devoting* (them)," Hiph. infin. absol. (§ 53, 3, Rem. 2 ; cf. הָבֵן, iii. 17). "*And he burnt Cha-tsôr*" (Hazor), because it was the chief of the confederate cities, and was too strong to be left in his rear ; afterwards, however, it was rebuilt, by whom is unknown, and mightily oppressed the Israelites for twenty years (Judges iv. 2, 3).

Ver. 12.—הֶחֱרִים, "*he utterly devoted.*" "*As Moses,*" etc., *i.e.*, as Moses by God's direction had commanded (cf. x. 40). No charge, therefore, of undue severity can be brought against Joshua.

Ver. 13.—Render the first clause, "*only the cities which stood each on its own hill.*" The Sept. κεχωματισμένας, "fortified with mounds," does not express the meaning of the Hebrew. תֵּל is here not "agger," but "tumulus," or "collis ;" it means primarily "a heap," from תָּלַל, to heap up, and is found in the names of several Babylonish cities, situated near hills or mounds, *e.g.*, Tel-abib (Ezek. iii. 15) ; Tel-harsha, or haresha (Ezra ii. 59 ; Neh. vii. 61) ; Tel-melah (Ezra ii. 59 ; Neh. vii. 61 ; Ezek. iii. 15) ; Telassar (Isa. xxxvii. 12); whence it passed into Arabic as the

---

involved, was included within the limits of the Holy Land. The name of Joshua is preserved in a local tradition, which points out the tomb of Yusha (Joshua) near Mellahah, at its north-west extremity, still visited by the sect of the Metawileh. Also it appears in the mountain Tel Farash (Farash being an Arabic name for Joshua) on the east of the plain." (*Sin. ana Pal.*, xi., p. 393.)

common name for a hill (cf. Stanley's *Sin. and Pal.*,
p. 119). Though Canaanite cities were frequently built
on an eminence, yet not universally so; see, *e.g.*, Jericho
and 'Ay: hence, though Keil takes the contrast here
to be between Hazor and all the other cities, it is perhaps more natural to understand it as made between
cities in the plains and those on eminences. The
former could not have been so easily defended by the
Israelites as the latter, and, if left ungarrisoned, would
probably soon have been reoccupied by the enemy,
and for this reason were destroyed. The sing. תֵּל is
used with a plural suffix to denote distribution.
זוּלָתִי, properly "except me," but here י is parag., as in
Deut. i. 36, iv. 12.

Ver. 14 (cf. viii. 27, note).—"*Until they* (the
Israelites) *had destroyed them.*" With the infin. form
הִשָּׁמֵד cf. viii. 22 (note).

Ver. 15.—"*As Jehovah commanded Moses,*" etc.,
see Exod. xxxiv. 11-16; Numb. xxxiii. 52, etc.;
Deut. vii. 1, etc., xx. 16. "*So did Moses command
Joshua,*" see Deut. iii. 21. לֹא־הֵסִיר דָּבָר, lit. "*he put not
away a word,*" *i.e.*, he left nothing unperformed (cf.
ver. 12, and i. 7, 8). In this Joshua was a type of
Jesus, the Captain of our salvation, "*whose meat it
was to do His Heavenly Father's will, and to finish
His work*" (John iv. 34). Joshua's triumphant success also foreshadowed that which the Gospel ever
since the first Advent of Christ has been achieving
over the Jabins and Hazors (the wisdom and power)
of this world (1 Cor. i. 21), but which will not be
finally consummated till His second Advent.

Here terminates the account of Joshua's wars, and
what follows to the end of the chapter is a review of

the conquest of the whole land, *i.e.*, of Western Palestine.

VERS. 16-23.—*The Whole Extent of the Conquered Land from South to North.*

Ver. 16.—"*Took all that land*," see note on ver. 23. הָהָר, *the mountain, i.e.*, the hill country of South and Central Canaan, see ix. 1 (note). הַנֶּגֶב, x. 40 (note). "*All the land of Goshen*" : The same as that mentioned in x. 41 ; if not, a portion of the maritime plain of Judah (the Sh^ephêlah[1]). It seems to have lain between it and the Negeb. הָעֲרָבָה, see xi. 2. וְאֶת־הָר יִי: The reference is to the northern highland of Palestine, as opposed to the valley and the plain, and to the mountains of Judah (ver. 21) ; called "the mountain of Ephraim" (xvii. 15), a limestone range running from Kirjath-jearim, where the mountains of Judah terminate, to the plain of Jezreel. When Joshua divided the land, its summits were densely covered with wood (xvii. 15). וּשְׁפֵלָתֹה, "*and the lowland thereof*," as opposed to the highland. Dean Stanley thinks that it refers to the tract of Sharon (cf. note on ix. 1). ה–, an old form of 3rd pers. m. suffix (*Parad.*, A., p. 276 ; cf. עִירֹה, Gen. xlix. 11) ; in the margin וּשְׁפֵלָתוֹ.

Ver. 17 (*The Boundaries of the Conquered Land on the South and North*).—"*The mount Chalaq*" (Halak, Auth. Vers.), from חָלָק, to be smooth ; lit. "*the smooth* (or bare) *mountain*" : Sept. Alex. ὄρος Ἀλάκ ; Vat., Χελχά ; mentioned here and in xii. 7 only. Site uncertain. Clark (*Bible Atlas*, p. 15, notes) would

---

[1] See on ix. 1.

identify it with Jebel-el-Mukrah, sixty miles south of the Dead Sea, so that it would include the whole of the Negeb or south country; but others (Keil, Fay, etc.) think it may have been a range of white cliffs stretching obliquely across the Arabah, and up which was the ascent of the pass called Akrabbim (Numb. xxxiv. 4; Josh. xv. 3), about eight miles south of the Dead Sea, forming the south limit of the Ghôr, and the north limit of the Arabah. The view of these cliffs from the shore of the Dead Sea is very striking. They appear as a line of hills shutting in the valley, and extending up to the mountains of Seir (Porter, Art. in Smith's *Bib. Dict.* on Seir). G. Grove, however, objects that we should expect the word *Sela'*, rather than *Har*, to be used in reference to such vertical cliffs (Art. in Smith's *Bib. Dict.*, vol. i., p. 741). Again, Knobel identifies Halak with *Madurah*, or *Maderah*, an isolated hill of curious shape, rising to a height of five hundred feet, forming the point of separation between Wady-el-Fikreh (a valley running into the Ghor) and Wady-el-Marrah (a valley running into the higher level of the Arabah). But, as this hill rather lies on the west side of the Wady-el-Fikreh, it could not be said to go up to Seir. From this diversity of opinion it is evident that the south boundary of the land cannot be accurately determined. "The question, however," says Clark (*Bible Atlas*, notes, p. 15), "is of less practical importance than it would else be, owing to the unprofitable character of the Negeb." "*That goeth up to Seir*," cf. xii. 7. *Se-'îr* (Seir [A. V.], rough, wooded) was a mountainous region extending from the Dead Sea to the Elanitic Gulf. It was occupied in succession by the Horites (Gen. xiv. 6), the Esauites (Gen. xxxii. 3 [4]), and the Edomites (Deut. ii. 4). *Ba'al-Gadh* (lord of fortune), mentioned also in xii. 7, xiii. 5, and probably so called from the worship of Gad, or Fortune (Ges., *Lex.*). By reason of the mention of "the valley of Lebanon," some (Knobel, Kitto) would identify it with Baalbec, between Lebanon and Antilebanon, but there is no evidence that Joshua's conquests extended so far north, and the expression "under mount Hermon" would lead us to suppose it close to that mountain, and probably the same as the Baal-Hermon of Judges iii. 3; 1 Chron. v. 23; hence Raumer, Robinson, and Keil, perhaps rightly, regard it as the same with Panium, or Paneas (Banjas), the Cæsarea Philippi of a later time.

Ver. 18.—"*Many days*": Josephus says the war lasted five years (*Antiq.*, v., 1, 19), but the rabbis more correctly say seven, for Caleb, when sent from Kadesh-barnea to spy the land, was forty years old, after which he wandered thirty-eight years in the wilderness, and at the conclusion of the war was eighty-five years old (see xiv. 7-10). It is evident, therefore, that this and the former chapter record only the more remarkable events of the war.

Ver. 19.—הִשְׁלִימָה, not followed here by אֶת־, as in x. 1, 4, but by אֶל, "had submitted itself to by a treaty of peace" (Ges., *Lex.*).

Ver. 20.—לְחַזֵּק, "*to harden*" (cf. Exod. iv. 21; Deut. ii. 30). The meaning is not that God merely permitted their hearts to be hardened, but that He decreed that such should be the natural result of their own obstinate impenitence. לְמַעַן הַחֲ, "*in order that he* (Israel) *might execute the ban upon them.*" תְּחִנָּה, "*mercy*," from חָנַן, to be (favourably) inclined towards. כִּי, "*but.*" לְמַעַן הַשְׁמִידָם, "*that he* (Israel) *might destroy them*": Their fate is a warning to all who by persistence in sin "treasure up unto themselves wrath against the day of wrath," etc. (Rom. ii. 5, etc.).

Vers. 21, 22.—As the Anakim had been the cause of great terror to the Israelites (Numb. xiii. 21, etc.), there is here added to the foregoing narrative an especial notice of their extermination.

Ver. 21.—"*At that time*," *i.e.*, not after the conquest of the north and south was completed (Rosenm.), but in the course of the war of many days (ver. 18). "*And cut off the Anakim*," *i.e.*, as Clericus says, "he killed those who fell into his hands, the rest he expelled, but after a short time, as we learn from xv. 14, they came back again." הָעֲנָקִים, lit. the long-necked, from עֲנָק, *i.q.*, Arabic "length of neck " (and stature) (Ges., *Lex.*) The name does not seem to indicate a distinct nation or tribe, but was applied to men of extraordinary stature among the Amorites, and seems to have been borne by three families in particular (see Numb. xiii. 22 ; Josh. xiv. 15 ; Judges i. 10). מִן־הָהָר, *i.e.*, not merely from the mountains in the south of Judah (Rosenm.), where Debir and Anab lay, but all the hilly country of Palestine, explained afterwards in this verse by the expression "all the mountains of Judah," and "all the mountains of Israel." On Hebron and Debir see x. 3, 38. "'*A-nabh*" ("a place abounding in grapes ; see עֵנָב, a cluster, rt. עָנַב, to fasten together), a city in the mountain district of Judah (xv. 50), a few miles S.S.W. of Hebron, and still retaining its ancient name

(Robinson, *Pal.*, ii., 194-5). "*Destroyed them utterly with their cities*": Yet the next verse shows that a remnant of the population escaped, who seem to have afterwards returned and occupied Hebron, whence they were finally driven by Caleb (xiv. 12, etc., xv. 13, 14; see note on x. 36-7 [1]).

Ver. 22.—לֹא־נוֹתַר, followed by a plural subject (§ 147, *a*). "*In the land of the children of Israel*": Called theirs, because they afterwards took possession of it, and held it at the time when this book was written. "*Gaza*" (see x. 41); "*Gath*" (a winepress): A royal city of Philistia (xiii. 3; 1 Sam. vi. 17); the native place of Goliath (1 Sam. xvii. 4); twice fled to by David during his persecution by Saul (1 Sam. xxi. 10-15, xxvii. 2-4; Psalm lvi.); captured by David (1 Chron. xviii. 1)[2]; one of the cities fortified by Rehoboam (2 Chron. xi. 8); taken by Hazael, King of Syria, in the time of Joash (2 Kings xii. 17), and again taken by Uzziah (2 Chron. xxvi. 6). It appears to have been an inland city, on the borders of Philistia and Judah. Its site is unknown, but probably identical with the hill now called Tell es Safieh, ten miles east of Ashdod, and about ten miles south by east of Ekron (see Smith's *Bibl. Dict.*, i., p. 656). '*Ash-dôdh* ("a fortified place," or "castle," from שָׁדַד, to be strong).

---

[1] The early campaigns of Joshua may, as Ewald thinks, have borne resemblance to sudden incursions, irresistible at the time, but not reducing the country to complete subjection (Ewald's *Geschichte*, ii., 39).

[2] In the parallel passage (2 Sam. viii. 1) for "Gath and her towns" we have Methegh-ha-ammah, "the bridle of the metropolis" (Gesenius, Keil), or "the bridle of the arm," *i.e.*, the supremacy (Ewald and Bertheau); either a different reading, or an explanatory rendering.

Sept. and New Testament (Acts viii. 40), Ἄζωτος, an inland town, three miles from the Mediterranean, on an eminence, about eighteen miles north of Gaza ; allotted to Judah (xv. 47), but, if taken by it, soon recovered by the Philistines, of whose worship of Dragon it was the principal seat (1 Sam. v. 1, etc.). Like Gaza, Ashkelon, and Ekron, it was often denounced by the prophets (see Jer. xxv. 20 ; Amos i. 8, iii. 9 ; Zeph. ii. 4 ; Zech. ix. 6). As it commanded the entrance from Palestine to Egypt, it was besieged and captured by Tartar, the general of Sargon, King of Assyria, about B.C. 716, probably to frustrate the league between Hezekiah and Egypt (Isa. xx. 1) ; again, after a siege of twenty-nine years (according to Herodotus), it was taken by Psammetichus (Herod., ii., 157) about B.C. 630. Though destroyed by the Maccabees (1 Macc. x. 77-84, xi. 4), it was afterwards rebuilt by the Roman general, Gabinius (Joseph., *Antiq.*, xiv., 5, 3) B.C. 55 ; was one of the towns bequeathed by Herod the Great to Salome, his sister (Joseph., *Antiq.*, xvii., 8, § 1). In Christian times it became an episcopal city, and its bishop was present at the Council of Nice. Now *Esdûd*, a small and poor Moslem village (Ritter, *Pal.*, iii., 220, etc.).

Ver. 23 (*Completion of the Narrative of Joshua's Conquests*).—" *Took the whole land* " (cf. ver. 16, xii. 7, 8, etc.) : The statement was true in a general sense ; Joshua had overrun the whole land, and broken the power of the Canaanites, and it only remained for the children of Israel to follow up and complete his conquests. Hence there is no discrepancy between this assertion and xiii. 1, etc., xvii. 14, etc., xviii.

3, xxiii. 5, 12, 13. "*According to* ... *Moses*": See Exod. xxiii. 22, 27-33; Deut. vii. 12, 22-26, whence it appears that God had not promised to exterminate at once the Canaanites, but only by little and little, and had made the fulfilment of His promises conditional on the obedience of the Israelites. "*Joshua gave it for an inheritance*": So by *Jesus*, not Moses; by the *Gospel*, not the Law, we inherit the promises (Rom. xv. 8; Heb. xi. 13, 40). נַחֲלָה denotes a lasting possession, handed down from father to son (see 1 Kings xxi. 3, 4; and Numb. xxxvi. 8, where it is evidently not synonymous with יְרֻשָּׁה). "*According to their divisions by their tribes*": כְּמַחְלְקֹתָם, plur. of מַחְלֹקֶת, rt. חָלַק, to divide, here denotes the divisions of the twelve tribes into families and households; so in xii. 7, xviii. 10; it is also used of the courses or classes of the priests and Levites (1 Chron. xxiii. 6, xxiv. 1, xxvi. 1-12); and of military arrangements (1 Chron. xxvii. 1). In the last clause, שָׁקְטָה, to rest (cf. xiv. 15), is not found in the Pentateuch.

The latter half of this verse (23) is introductory to the second part of the book, which treats of the partition of the land.

CHAPTER XII.

THIS chapter is designed to be supplementary to chapters x. and xi. From chapters x. 40-42 and xi. 12-17 it is evident that Joshua must have slain more kings and conquered more cities than are named in those chapters; and, therefore, the omission is supplied in this chapter, which is thus indispensable to the completeness of the history. First, in vers. 1-6 mention is made of the kings and country conquered by Moses on the east side of Jordan; and next, in vers. 7-24, of the conquests of Joshua on the west of Jordan. The fact that the writer does not limit himself to an account of the conquests of Joshua, but mentions those also of Moses (vers. 1-6), shows that his design throughout the book is to relate the conquest of Canaan as a *proof of God's faithfulness to His covenant.*

Ver. 1.—הַשָּׁמֶשׁ ... בְּעֵבֶר, see note on i. 15. The ה in מִזְרְחָה is local (§ 90, 2, *a*). "*From the river* (torrent[1]) *Arnon*": The boundary between Moab and the Amorites (Numb. xxi. 13), afterwards between Moab and Reuben (Deut. ii. 24, 36), now the *Wady el Môjeb*, which flows into the east side of the Dead Sea. According to Gesenius (*Lex.*), אַרְנוֹן = רִמוֹן, rushing, roaring, *i.e.*, roaring stream. "*Chermôn*," see xi. 3. "*And all the plain*" (see note on Arabah, iii. 16): Here is meant that portion of the depressed plain now termed El-Ghôr, on the east side of Jordan.

Ver. 2.—*Chesh-bôn* (Heshbon, Auth. Ver.), the capital of Sihon, the King of the Amorites (see Numb. xxi. 21-26), assigned by Moses to Reuben (Josh. xiii. 15, 17), by whom it was rebuilt (Numb. xxxii. 37); afterwards it came into the possession of the Gadites, probably (says Keil) because it stood on

---

[1] The word נַחַל is derived by Dean Stanley from חָלַל, to perforate (*Sin. and Pal.*, Append., p. 496); it answers to the Arab. "Wady," or watercourse, which is sometimes an impetuous torrent, at others, a brook, a dry channel, or valley. For its distinction from נָהָר, see i. 4 (note).

the border of their inheritance ; and it was assigned to the Levites (Josh. xxi. 39). After the captivity it was retaken by the Moabites, to whom it had originally belonged (Numb. xxi. 26), and thus became included in the prophetic denunciations against Moab (Isa. xv. 4, xvi. 9 ; Jer. xlviii. 2, 45-47). At a later period, according to Josephus (*Antiq.*, xviii., 14, § 4), it was again in the possession of the Jews. It lay on the border between Gad and Reuben, midway between the Arnon and Jabbok, and nearly opposite to the entrance of the Jordan into the Dead Sea.[1] The ruins of the modern *Hesbân*, or *Hüsban*, twenty miles east of the Jordan, and, according to Von Raumer, more than a mile in circuit, are supposed to mark the site. *'Arô-'êr* (= " ruins," places of which the foundations are laid bare ; rt. עָרַר, to be bare, naked), a city on the north bank of the Arnon, assigned to the tribe of Reuben (xiii. 9, 16), of which it formed the most southerly city ; afterwards came into the possession of the Moabites (Jer. xlviii. 19); now *Arâir*, on the north edge of the ravine of the Mojeb (Clark's *Bib. Atlas*). Burckhardt, in 1852, found the ruins on the edge of a cliff overlooking the river (*Travels*, pp. 372-4). It was distinct from the Aroer before Rabbath Ammon, in the land of Gad (Josh. xiii. 25), but appears to have been occupied on the first acquisition of the territory by the Gadites, and by them to have been rebuilt or fortified (see Keil on Numb. xxxii. 34, and on Josh. xiii. 25). It is also distinct from the Aroer in the tribe of Judah (1

---

[1] According to Kiepert's map it was over 4,000 feet above the Dead Sea, and about 3,000 feet above the level of the Mediterranean.

Sam. xxx. 28). וְתוֹךְ הַנַּחַל, "*and in the midst of the torrent* (or watercourse)" (De Wette, Fay), *i.e.*, the city lay partly on, and partly in, the Arnon, on an island, now Araayr. But perhaps the words are elliptical, and more fully expressed in xiii. 9, 16 by וְהָעִיר אֲשֶׁר בְּתוֹךְ הַנַּחַל, "*and* (from) *the city which is in the midst of the torrent*" (valley, Keil). The city thus referred to is, not Aroer, but *Ar Moab* (Numb. xxi. 15, 28 ; Deut. ii. 36), near the spot where the upper Arnon (Seil Saideh) receives the tributary Nahaliel (Numb. xxi. 19), on a hill between the two torrents, where are still the ruins of an ancient city (Burckhardt's *Travels*, pp. 372-4, and Art. "Arnon" in Smith's *Bib. Dict.*) ; probably Balak went hither to meet Balaam (Numb. xxii. 36). It must not be confounded with Rabbath-Moab, which lay ten or fifteen miles south of the Arnon. See Hengstenberg (*Geschichte Bileams*, pp. 234, etc.) and also Ritter, in opposition to Reland and many modern scholars who identify the two. "*Half-Gilead*,"[1] *i.e.*, a mountainous district south of the Jabbok. The other half-Gilead belonged to Og, and the Jabbok was the division between them (see note on ver. 5, and cf. Deut. iii. 12, 13). As is usual with geographical names in Palestine, Gilead (Heb. Gil-'adh) describes the physical aspect of the country, and means "hard, rocky region," contrasted with Bashan, "a level, fertile tract." The name גַּלְעֵד, "heap of witness" (Gen. xxxi. 47), may, by a change of vowels, have been formed from this word. The "*Jabbok*" (Yab-bôq,

---

[1] Lit. "half of *the* Gilead," for, as the name of a place, the word in Hebrew generally has the article (cf. xiii. 25, 31, xvii. 1, xxii. 9, see *Gr.*, § 109, 3).

either from בָּקַק, to pour forth, to gush forth, or from
אָבַק, in Niph., to wrestle (Ges.; Gen. xxxii. 24), rises
in the plateau east of Gilead, and, after receiving
some tributary streams, of which one comes from
Rabbath-Ammon, the capital of the Ammonites (2
Sam. xi.), falls into the Jordan, forty-five miles north
of the Arnon, about half way between the Sea of Galilee and the Dead Sea (Porter, Art. in Smith's *Bib.
Dict.*). It was crossed by Jacob on his road from
Haran (Gen. xxxii. 22 [23]), and is now called *Wady
Zurka*, *i.e.*, blue torrent. "*The border of the children of
Ammon*": Popularly so called, both here and in Deut.
iii. 16, because the children of Ammon had held the
whole territory between the Arnon and Jabbok, till
dispossessed of it by the Amorites (Emorites), and
still continued to claim it (Judges xi. 12-22). Others,
however (as Keil), think that the border here meant
is the Nahr Ammon, called the Upper Jabbok, on
the banks of which stands Rabbath Ammon, and
which, according to them, is the source of the Lower
Jabbok. In its course northward and westward,
between Rabbah and Gadara, it formed the boundary
between the Ammonites and the territory which had
been wrested from them by the Amorites.

Ver. 3.—Render, "*And* (he reigned over) *the
Arabah*," etc.: *i.e.*, the kingdom of Sihon comprised
the whole of the Arabah or Ghôr between the Lake
of Tiberias and the Dead Sea. כִּנְרוֹת, see xi. 2.
"*Beth-jeshimoth*" (house of the wastes; Heb. Bêth-
ha¹-yᵉshi-môth), in the deserts of Moab, at the end of

---

¹ הַ is here written for הַ, the dagesh forte being omitted
(§ 20, 3, *b*).

the Dead Sea (Numb. xxxiii. 48, 49); allotted to Reuben (Josh. xiii. 20), but afterwards in the possession of Moab (Ezek. xxv. 9). *"Ashdoth-Pisgah"* (Heb. 'Ash-dôth-hap-Pis-gah), not known, used here and in xiii. 20; Deut. iii. 17, as a proper name, but in Deut. iv. 49 translated " *Springs of Pisgah.*" As to the meaning of Ashdoth (lit. " pourings out," from אָשַׁד, unused, "to pour out," see note on x. 40) opinions differ, but whether translated springs, or slopes, or roots, it probably denotes some peculiar feature of the country, at the north-east border of the desert, by the Dead Sea. *"Pisgah"*[1] ("a part" or "fragment," rt. פָּסַג [unused], Chald. to cut up, divide), is unknown, but generally supposed to be a ridge of the Abarim mountains, westward from Heshbon, the most celebrated peak of which was Mount Nebo (see Numb. xxi. 20, xxxiii. 47, xxvii. 12; Deut. xxxii. 49). The name seems to have been transferred under its Arabic form Feshkhah to the opposite headland, on the west of the Dead Sea.

Ver. 4.—גְּבוּל, here, as often, = the space included within certain borders, *i.e.,* "*territory;*" the accus. after וַיִּירְשׁוּ, which is understood from ver. 1. Og (Heb. 'Ogh, long-necked, gigantic (Ges., *Lex.*), an Amoritish king (Deut. iii. 8, iv. 47, xxxi. 4; Josh. ix. 10), whence it seems that the Rephaim (giants), from whom he was descended, were not, as Bertheau, Ewald, and Lengerke say, aboriginal inhabitants of Palestine, but a tribe or branch of the Amorites or Canaanites, remarkable for their gigantic height (cf. note on xi. 21). So Keil, "In the very earliest

---

[1] The word is always used in Hebrew with the article, "*the* Pisgah" (§ 109, 3).

times they [*i.e.*, the Rephidim] had obtained possession of Palestine on the east of Jordan, but at a later period they were dispossessed and overthrown by the Moabites and Ammonites (see Deut. ii. 20-1). Subsequently, however, the Amorites, having been reinforced by their kinsmen from West Canaan, again obtained the upper hand, and under Sihon and Og founded two powerful kingdoms, which were subdued by the Israelites under Moses." "*Ashtaroth,*" ix. 10 (note), probably now *Tell-Ashterah,* "rising to a height of from 50 to 100 ft. above the plain, in which ruins lie scattered. At the foot of the hill are ancient wall-foundations and copious springs" (Von Raumer, p. 243). "*Edrei*" ('Edh-rĕ-'i, "strong," from אֶדְרָע, Chald., *i.q.*, דְּרָע, "an arm," with א prosthetic), a capital city of Bashan, situated on a rocky promontory at the south-west corner of Argob, and on the northern edge of the Hauran, or "Burnt Country," where Og was defeated and slain by the Israelites (Numb. xxi. 33-35; Deut. iii. 1-3), still called *Edr'a* (Porter, *Damascus,* p. 271, etc.). Others, following the doubtful testimony of Eusebius (*Onom.*), place it a few miles further south, at the modern Der'a ; but for reasons against this site see Smith's *Bible Dict.*, vol. i., p. 492.[1]

Ver. 5. *The Limits of Og's Territory.*—*Salcah* (Sal-khah),[2] cf. Deut. iii. 10, afterwards the limit of

---

[1] "Og's capital was in ordinary circumstances almost unassailable, since it was, strange to say, built in a hollow, artificially scooped out of the top of a hill, which the deep gorge of the Hieromax isolates from the country round. Its streets may still be seen running in all directions beneath the present town of Adraha." (Geikie's *Hours with the Bible*, vol. ii., p. 360.)

[2] The ב being without daghesh, the word is here put for סַלְכָה (Ges., *Lex.*).

the possessions of the Gadites (1 Chron. v. 11), situated on the south-east border of Bashan, now *Sâlkhad* (Porter, *Five Years in Damascus*), a town with eight-hundred houses, and a castle of basaltic rock, commanding an extensive view over the plain of the great Euphrates desert. "*And over all Bashan*," extending from Gilead to Hermon, and from the Jordan valley to Salcah, and embracing the four (later) provinces of Gaulanitis, Auranitis, Trachonitis, and Batanæa. The present Ard-el-Bathanyeh represents the last mentioned province. Bashan was famous for its oak forests (Isa. ii. 13; Ezek. xxvii. 6) and fat bulls and rams (Deut. xxxii. 14; Amos. iv. 1; Psalm xxii. 12 [13]). "*The Geshurites*," a people north-west (so Keil, Rosenm., and Gesen., *Thes.*, i., 308) of Bashan, between that land and Aram, and on the east side of the Upper Jordan, near Hermon. Geshur means *a bridge*, and a bridge is now found in that region, where the Jordan is crossed (Ges., *Lex.*). But Porter places them on the north-east corner of Bashan, adjoining the province of Argob, and the kingdom of Aram. David married a daughter of Talmai, King of Geshur, and by her was the father of Absolom (2 Sam. iii. 3); and to Geshur Absolom fled after the murder of his brother Amnon (2 Sam. xiii. 37). "*The Maachathites*," mentioned along with the Geshurites (Deut. iii. 14), with whom they seem to have been closely allied (for the daughter of Talmai was named Maachah), and dwelling probably on the east of Geshur, and south of Damascus (Keil). They took part with the Ammonites against David (2 Sam. x. 6). "*And half-Gilead*," cf. ver. 2: Before חֲצִי is either repeated עַד־גְּבוּל, or the preposition בְּ is understood, *i.e.*, he ruled over the half-Gilead, the other half of which was in the dominions of Sihon, the Jabbok being the line of separation between the two. That section, over which Og reigned, lies between the Jabbok and the Hieromax, and is now called Jebel Ajlûn, while that to the south of the Jabbok forms the modern province of Belka. The northern section is most thickly timbered, the southern most fertile, and the Arabs have a proverb, "Thou canst not find a country like the Belka" (Tristram, *Land of Israel*). Sihon is represented by Josephus as the friend and ally of Og (*Antiq.*, iv., 5, § 3).

Ver. 6.—הִכָּם, "*smote them*" (see Numb. xxi. 21, etc.) וַיַּכֻּם: Two MSS. have וַיַּכֵּם, but the fem. suffix הָ‍ָ evidently refers to the land on the east side of Jordan. The actual possession of this was given by Joshua according to Moses's directions (Josh. xxii. 1-6, with Numb. xxxii. 28).

VERS. 7-24.—*A Summary of the Kings and Country conquered by Joshua on the West Side of the Jordan.*[1]

Ver. 7.—"*From Baal-gad*," etc., see note xi. 17. "*And Joshua gave it to the tribes of Israel*," etc., cf. xi. 23. This similarity of statement is inconsistent with the view of Hasse, Bertholdt, and others, who

---

[1] Though as many as thirty-one kings are mentioned, yet this is not surprising when we consider that in the earliest times sovereignties often comprised no more than a single town and a small surrounding district. Thus in the vale of Sodom were five kings, one for each town (Gen. xiv.). To the siege of Troy a vast number of petty kings were sent from Greece and

regard the following list as not authentic, but an heterogeneous fragment.

Ver. 8.—"*In the mountainous district . . . in the Arabah,*" see xi. 2 (note). בָּאֲשֵׁדוֹת, x. 40. מִדְבָּר, viii. 15. יֻתַּהִ, etc., ix. 1, iii. 10. Here, and in ix. 1, xi. 3, the Girgashites are omitted. Nothing is known of them beyond their name. Von Raumer thinks that they settled as colonists on the west side of the Jordan (see xxiv. 11). In Gen. x. 16 the Girgasite is mentioned as the fifth son of Canaan. Perhaps the race became wholly extinct or absorbed in other tribes.

Ver. 9.—"*Jericho,*" vi. 1. "*'Ay,*" vii. 2, viii. 1, etc.

Vers. 10-18. This list refers to those who were conquered by Joshua in Southern Palestine, either in the battle of Bethhoron (x. 1, etc.), or in the campaign immediately following it.

Ver. 10.—Cf. x. 1, 3,

Ver. 11.—Cf. x. 3.

Ver. 12.—Cf. x. 3. "*King of Gezer,*" x. 33.

Ver. 13.—"*King of Debir,*" see x. 39. "*King of Geder*" (Gedher): The town has not been before mentioned, and is thought by some to be the same as Gedor (xv. 58), which lay between Hebron and Bethlehem, *i.q.*, the modern Jedûr (Rob., *Bibl. Res.*, ii., 13), or identical with Gederah (xv. 36), in the lowlands of Judah (Keil); but perhaps from its being named along with Debir, Hormah, and Arad, it lay

---

her islands. Cæsar tells us that in the county of Kent, in Britain, were four kings; also the Silures, Brigantes, and other small tribes, had each their own king. Gaul, Spain, and Germany were in like manner subdivided into a vast number of little states or kingdoms. Often one such little state has absorbed others into itself, or foreign invaders have united several of them into one large kingdom.

more to the south, and was the same as the Gedor mentioned in connection with the Simeonites, 1 Chron. iv. 39 (Grove).

Ver. 14.—"*Hormah*" (Chôr-mah, "a devoting" or "ban," a place laid waste, Ges.) ; anc. called Zephath (the watch-tower), Judges i. 17, though called by anticipation Hormah in Numb. xiv. 45. The name was changed to Hormah for the reason given in Numb. xxi. 3. It stood in the south of Palestine, in the territory of Judah (Josh. xv. 30), and was allotted to Simeon (xix. 4). Perhaps at, or near, the pass *Es Sufa* (Rob., *Bib. Res.*, ii., 181).[1] "*Arad*" ('A-radh ; Numb. xxi. 1-3 ; Judges i. 16, 17), a royal city, near the wilderness of Kadesh, on a small hill, now called *Tell-'Arâd* (Rob., *Bib. Res.*, ii., 101, 201), twenty Roman miles south of Hebron (Euseb., *Onom.*), described as a barren-looking eminence, rising above the country around.

Ver. 15.—"*Libnah*," see x. 29. "*Adullam*" ('A-dhullam, "the justice of the people," Ges., *Lex.*). This town was evidently in the lowland (cf. Gen. xxxviii. 1, "Judah *went down*," etc.), between Jarmuth and Sokoh (Josh. xv. 35). Sept. 'Οδολλάμ, and so called in 2 Macc. xii. 38 ; fortified by Rehoboam (2 Chron. xi. 7) ; occupied by the Jews after the return from Babylon (Neh. xi. 30). Near it was the celebrated

---

[1] See Art. in Smith's *Bib. Dict.*, vol. i., p. 826. "It was the great point from which the roads across the desert, after having been all united, again diverge towards Gaza and Hebron, and its site is still marked by the ruins of a square tower of hewn stones, with a large heap of stones adjoining, on the top of a hill, which rises a thousand feet above the wady on the edge of which it stands." (Dr. Geikie, *Hours with the Bible*, vol. ii., p. 331.)

cave (1 Sam. xxii. 1; 2 Sam. xxiii. 13; see Stanley's *Sin. and Pal.*, p. 258, note 8), though monastic tradition places it near the modern Khureitân, not far from Bethlehem, a position which does not satisfy the requirements of the sacred narrative. More recently the site of the town has been identified by M. Clermont Ganneau with ruins on a height, overlooking the valley of Elah (1 Sam. xvii. 19), called *Aid-el-Ma*. Here "the surveyors" (employed by the Palestine Exploration Fund) "found a cave close to the ruins of the ancient town, a cave sufficiently large to have been the habitation of David, while his band were garrisoning the hold or fortress." (*Quarterly Statement of Pal. Explor. Fund*, January, 1881, p. 44.)

Ver. 16.—"*Makkedah*," cf. x. 10, 28. "*Bethel*," see vii. 2, viii. 17; but, as it is mentioned here along with Makkedah, which was in Judah, Grove thinks that it is identical with the Bethel in 1 Sam. xxx. 27, which was in the south of Judah, and apparently corresponds to the Bethul of xix. 4, and the Chesil of xv. 30. (See Smith's *Bibl. Dict.*, vol. i., p. 199.)

Ver. 17.—"*Tappuah*" (Tap-pû-ach, a place fruitful in apples, תפוח, an apple), not to be confounded, as by Rosenmüller, with that mentioned in xvi. 8, which was on the boundary of Ephraim and Manasseh, and identical with En-tappuah (xvii. 7), but situated in the lowland of Judah, apparently in the same district as Adullam and Jarmuth (xv. 34), about twelve miles west of Jerusalem (Grove), and now called Teffûh. Like Bethel in ver. 16, the towns in this verse and ver. 18 are not mentioned among those taken after the battle of Beth-horon (x. 28-39), yet they may have been in league with the others against Israel. "*Hepher*" (Chê-pher, a digging, a well, from חָפַר, to *dig*), unknown, but probably the town after which was named the land of Hepher (1 Kings iv. 10), near Socoh, in Judah (xv. 35); quite distinct from Gath-Hepher in Zebulun (xix. 13).

Ver. 18.—"*Aphek*" ("'A-phêq, strength), a name given in Scripture to many strong places, not all necessarily towns, but perhaps only encampments, as that mentioned in 1 Sam. iv. 1, xxix. 1; but here probably identical with Aphekah (xv. 53), a town in the mountains of Judah, near Hebron. "*Lasharon*" (Lash-Sha-rôn): Vulg. "Sharon," a town which gave its name to the plain so called (ל being taken as a sign of the genitive), but which lies too much to the north. The Chald. and Arab. Vers. regard the ל as part of the noun, and there seems, says Grove (Art. in Smith's *Bib. Dict.*), no reason why the construction in this particular place should differ from the rest in the list. By the Sept. (Alex. and Vat.) the word is omitted. Site unknown.

Vers. 19-24. The towns here mentioned were connected with the northern confederacy (xi. 1, etc.).

Ver. 19.—"*Madon*," see xi. 1. "*Hazor*," xi. 1, 11, 13.

Ver. 20.—Cf. xi. 1.

Ver. 21.—"*Taanach*" (Ta-'a-nakh, sandy soil, Ges., *Lex.*), a town in the tribe of Issachar, but assigned to the half-tribe of Manasseh (xvii. 11; 1 Chron. vii. 29), which did not drive out the native inhabitants (Judges i. 27); afterwards bestowed on the Kohathite Levites (Josh. xxi. 25), the scene of Barak's victory (Judges v. 19). Its name is preserved in the modern *Ta'annûk*, near Lejjûn (Grove), a small village, near to some ruins in the plain of Esdraelon. "*Megiddo*" (M^eghid-dô), generally associated with the preceding city (xvii. 11; Judges i. 27, v. 19; 1 Kings iv. 12). Here Ahaziah died (2 Kings ix. 27), and Josiah was fatally wounded in battle against Pharaoh Necho (2 Kings xxiii. 29). Now probably *el-Lejjûn*, the Roman "Legio" (Rob., *Bibl. Res.*, i. 316, 328; Van de Velde, *Memoir*, p. 333).

Ver. 22.—"*Kedesh*" (Qe-dhesh, sanctuary), in Issachar, and, according to the list in 1 Chron. vi. 72, allotted to the Gershonite Levites, but in the parallel list (Josh. xxi. 28) called Kishon. Being mentioned along with Megiddo and Jokneam, it seems more probably to have been this city in Issachar than that of the same name in Naphtali (xix. 37), with which it is identified by Keil and others. "*Jokneam*" (Yoq-n^e'am, "possessed by the people," Ges., *Lex.*), in Zebulon (xix. 11), near Carmel; assigned to the Merarite Levites (xxi. 34); probably the modern *Tell Kaimôn*, at the foot of the east end of Carmel (Rob., *Bib. Res.*, p. 114, 115), and commanding the main pass from Phœnicia to Egypt. Traces of this modern name are found in Cyamon, Κυάμων (Judith vii. 3). "*Carmel*" (hak-Karmel, "the fruitful field,"[1] or "garden"), a mountainous range, on the northern border of the tribe of Asher (xix. 26), the highest summit of which is nearly 1,750 ft. above the sea. It was probably regarded by the ancient Canaanites as sacred, and the

---

[1] This word in Hebrew commonly has the article, which is here involved in the prefix. prep. בְּ (§ 102, 2, *b*), "on, or in, the Carmel."

Israelites may have early established there an altar of the Lord (see 1 Kings xviii. 30). Tacitus (*Hist.* ii., ch. 78) says that Vespasian came thither to consult the oracle of the god Carmel (the god having the same name as the mountain itself), who had neither image nor temple; "ara tantum et reverentia." In modern times the mountain became celebrated for the convent of Barefooted Carmelite Friars, built on its west headland by St. Louis. This convent was used as a hospital by Napoleon I. when he besieged Acre, was destroyed by the Arabs after his retreat, and rebuilt in 1833. Carmel is now called *Jebel Mar Elias*, in memory of the great deeds of Elijah, and the same name Mar Elias is usually given to the convent, though dedicated to the Virgin Mary. See Smith's *Bib. Dict.*, p. 279; Stanley's *Sin. and Pal.*, p. 352.

Ver. 23.—"*Dor*," xi. 2. דוֹר לִנְפַת, "*in*," or "*pertaining to, the highlands of Dor*," see note on xi. 2. "*King of the nations of Gilgal*" (Auth. Vers.), or "*king of the Go-yim at Gilgal*" (Keil): גּוֹיִם being taken as a proper name, referring to an aboriginal tribe. It may, perhaps, denote an aggregate of mixed and nomadic tribes, to whom Gilgal was a centre and capital, cf. the phrase "*Galilee of the nations*" (Isa. ix. 1; Matt. iv. 15). Gilgal (which cannot be the Gilgal near Jericho) is supposed by Keil and others to be the same as Galgulis, six miles north of Kefr Saba, the ancient Antipatris (Euseb. and Jerome, *Onom.*), on the main road from Egypt and Phœnicia, in the plain of Sharon, and still to be seen in the modern village of *Jiljuleh*, or Jiljulieh, now almost a ruin (see Robin., *Bib. Res.*, p. 136). It is distinguished by Keil from the village of Jiljilia (see ix. 6), supposed to be the site of the Gilgal from which Elijah and Elisha went down to Bethel (2 Kings ii. 1, 2). Over the plains of Sharon the nomadic Goyim may have spread themselves.

Ver. 24.—"*Tir-tsah*" ("pleasantness," from רָצָה, to be delighted), in the tribe of Ephraim (Clark's *Bib. Atlas*); afterwards the capital of the ten tribes, till the time of Omri (1 Kings xiv. 17, xv. 33, xvi. 8-18, 24), alluded to for its beauty (Cant. vi. 4); the scene of Menahem's conspiracy against Shallum (2 Kings xv. 14, 16); probably the modern *Tellûzah*, an elevated and beautiful place, three miles north of Nablûs (Shechem). See Robinson's *Later Bib. Res.*, p. 303; Van de Velde, *Syr. and Pal.*, iii., 334.

The specification of *each* king by himself singly in this chapter, says Bishop Wordsworth, and the summing-up of *all* collectively, may be designed to remind the reader of Holy Scripture that each individual particularly, and especially each individual in a place of eminence and responsibility, will be judged by the Divine Joshua; as He Himself says, "Behold, I come quickly, and My reward is with Me, to give to *every man* according as his work shall be" (Rev. xxii. 12); and that this judgment will be universal.

SECOND PART.

THE DIVISION OF THE LAND OF CANAAN.[1]
(CHAPTERS XIII.—XXIV.)

CHAPTER XIII.

VERS. 1-7.—*God's Command to Joshua to Distribute the Land of Canaan on the West Side of Jordan by Lot among the nine and a half Tribes; and an Enumeration of the still Unconquered Districts.*

Ver. 1.—וגו זָקֵן, (*was*) *old* (and) *far gone in years*": Cf. Gen. xviii. 11, xxiv. 1; 1 Kings i. 1; Luke i. 6, 18; יָמִים = "years" or "time of life" (Ges., *Lex.*, p. 342). The expression denotes great age in its several stages even up to the near approach of death (xxiii. 1). It never seems used in Scripture of any but holy persons; the days of the wicked are consumed in vanity (Psalm lxxviii. 33); Bishop Wordsworth. הַרְבֵּה־מְאֹד, used adverb. (§ 131, 2). לְרִשְׁתָּהּ, " to take possession of it"; see on the word יָרַשׁ, Ges.,

---

[1] We are expressly told concerning seven of the tribes that this division was made according to previously prepared records (see xviii. 8, 9), and it is probable that such was the case also in reference to the other tribes on the west of Jordan. Topographical surveys of the land may have been made as soon as it had been overrun by the armies of Joshua. Otherwise, as Knobel remarks, a single Hebrew writer would hardly have had so accurate a knowledge of the land as the author of this book displays, especially in regard to the boundaries.

Lex. (1). For an explanation of the assertion in the last clause of this verse see note on xi. 23.

Ver. 2.—This verse to the first half of ver. 6 is parenthetical, and mentions the districts still unconquered in the south and north. After הַגִּשָׁאֶרֶת supply לְרִשְׁתָּהּ. "*Borders*" (Auth. Vers.), lit. circles, from גָּלַל, to roll; Vulg. Galilea; but Sept. correctly ὅρια. The reference seems to be to carefully marked out districts around the five principal towns of the Philistines.[1] "*And all Geshuri*": A district in the desert between Arabia and Philistia (1 Sam. xxvii. 8), distinct from the country of the Geshurites mentioned in ver. 13, xii. 5.

Ver. 3.—"*From the Sihor*" (Shî-chôr, black, turbid, rt. שָׁחַר, to be black): Though the Nile is so called (Isa. xxxiii. 3; Jer. ii. 18; cf. Virg., *Georg.*, iv., 291, "viridem Ægyptum nigra fecundat arena"), yet here the name probably refers to the נַחַל מִצְרַיִם (Numb. xxxiv. 5), on the south border of Philistia, the 'Ρινοκορούρα of the Greeks, and the modern *Wady el Arish*. In Josh. xix. 26 the same name Shichor is given to a border stream of Asher. The Nile, which flows through the middle of Egypt, could not be correctly described as "before Egypt." "*Ekron*" ('Eqrôn, "eradication," from עָקַר, to root out; cf. Zeph. ii. 4), Ἀκκαρών, Sept.; Accaron, Vulg.; the most northern town of Philistia, assigned first to the tribe of Judah (xv. 11, 45), secondly to Dan (xix. 43); after the death of Joshua conquered by Judah (Judges i. 18), but soon recovered by the Philistines (1 Sam. v. 10), and though reconquered by Samuel (1 Sam.

---

[1] No portion of the territory of the Philistines was conquered in the lifetime of Joshua, nor after his death was any permanent conquest effected (Judges iii. 3).

vii. 14), yet afterwards spoken of as a Philistine city
(1 Sam. xvii. 52 ; 2 Kings i. 2, 16; Jer. xxv. 20 ;
Amos i. 8, etc.). It was the last place to which the
ark was carried before its return to Israel (1 Sam.
v. 10), and was the seat of the worship of Beelzebub,
the fly-god (2 Kings i. 2, etc.). Now *Akir*, a small
mud village, five miles south-west of Ramleh (Rob.,
Bib. Res., ii., 227-9.). צָפוֹנָה, *northward*, Sept. ἐξ
εὐωνύμων, because "the north" is on the left of one
looking towards the east. "(Which) *is counted to the
Canaanite*" (Auth. Vers.) : The relative, as here, is
often omitted (§ 123, 3), or "it," *i.e.*, the whole district from Sichor to Ekron, "shall be counted," etc.
The rendering of Keil, "To the Canaanite is reckoned
(the territory of the) five lords of the Philistines," dis-
regards the athnach under הֵחָשֵׁב. Though the Philistines were not a Canaanitish, but a foreign race (Gen.
x. 14; Deut. ii. 23), yet their land having originally
belonged to Canaan, is here reckoned part of it.
סַרְנֵי, lit. "*axles* (of)," the term being used metaphorically of princes, as hinges of the state (cf. cardinal,
from cardo, a hinge). It is applied only to the five
princes of the Philistines (cf. Judges iii. 3, xvi. 5, etc. ;
1 Sam. v. 8, etc.), and is interchanged with שָׂרִים
(1 Sam. xxix. 6, compared with vers. 4, 9). In
Arabic a cognate term is used of a prince and commander of an army. "*The Gazathites*" (the 'Az-za-
thite, see x. 41) : The Hebrew gentilic being in the
singular may agree with סֶרֶן understood (cf. Sept. τῷ
Γαζαίῳ, κ.τ.λ.) ; or it may be here used collectively,
as in Auth. Vers. and Vulg. "*The Ashdothites*" (the
'Ash-dô-dhite), xi. 22. "*The Eshkalonites*" ('Esh-
qᵉlô-nite) : The gentile noun in Hebrew occurs here

only. Ashkelon[1] lay on the seacoast between Ashdod and Gaza; it is not named among the Philistine towns assigned to Judah (xv. 45-47; though mentioned by Josephus, *Antiq.*, v., 1, § 22), but was conquered by that tribe (Judges i. 18), yet soon regained its independence (Judges xiv. 19; 1 Sam. vi. 17). Herod the Great was born there (Euseb., *H. E.*, i, 6). It was remarkable (like Gaza, Ashdod, and Ekron) for the extreme beauty and profusion of the gardens surrounding it, and for the temple of the Syrian Venus with its sacred doves (Diod. Sic., ii., 4). It became a bishop's see in the fourth century, was unsuccessfully besieged by the crusaders in 1100 A.D., and again in 1148 A.D. Baldwin III. captured it in 1157, but it was retaken by Saladin in 1187, and burnt by him in 1191. Richard I. of England obtained possession the same year, and restored the fortifications in 1192. "Within the walls and towers now standing he held his court" (Stanley's *Sin. and Pal.*, p. 257). Sultan Bibars destroyed its fortifications, and filled up its harbour in 1270. The ruins of massive walls and towers attest its former strength, and it still bears the name Askulân. "*The Gittites*" (Gittite or Gathite), see xi. 22. "*The Avites*" ('Av-vim, "those who inhabit desert places," from עָוָה, "overturning," Ges.), probably a remnant of those who had been exterminated by the Caphtorim (Deut. ii. 23). Some (Ewald and Lengerke) think that they were aborigines of Palestine, but, more probably, they were Canaanites, for the border of the latter extended into Gaza (Gen. x. 19).

---

[1] This word is always so pointed in the Hebrew (see Ges., *Lex.*).

Ver. 4.—כְּתֵימָן: According to the arrangement of the Masoretic text the portion of Canaan here meant must be that to the south of Gaza, viz., the country of King Arad (Numb. xxi. 1), bordering on the deserts of Paran, Zin, Kadesh, etc.; but as the districts named in the rest of the verse belong to North Canaan, and not to the quarter mentioned in vers. 2 and 3, it is better, with the Sept., Vulg., and Syr., to join כְּתֵימָן with the preceding verse, *e.g.*, "*the Avvim from* (or *on*) *the south,*" *i.e.*, on the south of Philistia between Gaza and the district of Shur. So Keil. "*All the land of the Canaanites,*" *i.e.*, all the district here referred to, viz., that along the coast of Phœnicia. "*Mearah,*" rendered "cave" in x. 18, and so here by Keil and others after the Chald., Syr., and Arab. Versions, and supposed by some to be the same as Mugr Jezzin (the cave of Jezzin), between Tyre and Zidon; but it seems unlikely that if a cave was meant, the article would have been omitted in the Hebrew. Probably, therefore, a town or village is denoted, as in Auth. Vers., though, according to Grove, there are no traces left of it. (See Art. by Grove, in Smith's *Bib. Dict.*). Lieut. Conder would identify it with Mogheiriyeh, north of Zidon. אֲשֶׁר לְ, not as in Auth. Vers., "*that is beside,*" but "*which belongs to.*" "*Unto Aphek*": The ־ה in the Heb. noun is local(*Gr.*,§ 90,2,c). '*A-phcg* (Heb.)=strength, from אפק, to hold fast, was probably the same city as that assigned to Asher (xix. 30); and, therefore different from that in xii. 18, of which that tribe could not take possession (Judges i. 31). Gesenius is probably right in identifying it with *Aphaca*, a city on the north-western slopes of Lebanon, famous for its temple of Venus, whose ruins are still called *Afka* (Rob., *Bib. Res.*, iii., 606-7) ; for though Afka is beyond the proper limits of Asher, yet so was Gebal (see next verse), and so was Kedesh beyond Judah on the south. "*To the borders of the Amorites*," *i.e.*, to the border of the land which was formerly inhabited by the Amorites, and afterwards belonged to Og, King of Bashan. Thus the words give another terminus ad quem, viz., in an easterly direction, and describe the breadth of the unconquered district (Keil).

Ver. 5.—"*The land of the Giblites*," *i.e.*, the territory belonging to the inhabitants of Gebal (mountain) in Phœnicia, on the shore of the Mediterranean, under Mount Lebanon, now called by the Arabs *Jebail*, which stands on a rising ground, near the sea to the north of Beirut. Gebal possessed a fleet in the time of Alexander the Great (*Exp. Alex.*, ii., 20), and was renowned for its temple of Adonis (Strabo, xvi., 755). The plur. גִּבְלִים is rendered by the Auth. Vers. "stone-squarers" in 1 Kings v. 18 (32 Heb.), whence it appears that the Giblites were so employed by the Tyrians ; also as "calkers" (A. V., Ezek. xxvii. 9). The Greeks called the place Βίβλος or Βύβλος, hence the Alex. Sept. Βίβλιοι (1 Kings v. 18). Here, and in other Phœnician cities, have been found huge stones like those in the foundation of Solomon's Temple (Ritter's *Geog. Pal.*, ii., 214-15).[1] "*Baal-gad*," see xi. 17, and xii. 7. "*Hermon*," xi. 3, 17. "*On the*

---

[1] The "Gebal" mentioned in Psalm lxxxiii. 7 (8), seems to have been a different place. It was probably a tract of Edom, south of the Dead Sea, and called Gabilene by Josephus, Eusebius, and Jerome.

entering into Ha-math" (Ch^amâth, "defence," or citadel, from הָמָה, "to surround with a wall") was the name of a distinguished city of Syria, on the Orontes, on the northern frontier of the Holy Land (cf. Numb. xiii. 21, xxxiv. 8 ; Judges iii. 3), the Epiphania of the Greeks (Joseph., *Antiq.*, i., 6, 2). The same name "Hamath" appears to have been given to the territory or kingdom, as well as to its capital (see 2 Chron. viii. 4, where Solomon is said to have built store-cities in Hamath), and in this wider meaning the name is probably used here (Josh. xiii. 5). The בּוֹא, or pass, was the gate of approach to Canaan from Babylon and all the north (Zech. ix. 2 ; Jer. xxxix. 5). The inhabitants of Hamath were descendants of Ham (Cham) (Gen. x. 18). For its connection with David see 2 Sam. viii. 10, and with Solomon 1 Kings iv. 21-24 ; 2 Chron. viii. 4. After the latter's death it seems to have recovered its independence, but was reconquered by Jeroboam II. (2 Kings xiv. 28); afterwards it was subjugated by the Assyrians (2 Kings xvii. 24, xviii. 34, xix. 13 ; Isa. x. 9, xi. 11), and again by the Chaldeans (Jer. xxxix. 5). It is now *Hamah*, the seat of a Greek bishop, and, according to Winer, numbers 100,000 inhabitants. (Rob., *Later Res.*, p. 568 ; Burckhardt's *Travels in Syria*, pp. 146-7 ; Stanley's *Sin. and Pal.*, pp. 406-7.)

Ver. 6.—"*Misrephoth-maim*," cf. xi. 8 (note). "*All the Sidonians*": Put here for the Phœnicians generally (cf. Judges iii. 3 ; Homer, *Il.*, vi., 298). אָנֹכִי, emphatic. אוֹרִישֵׁם, "*I will dispossess them*" (see iii. 10, note): The pron. suff. shows that the first sentence of the verse is put absolutely (§ 145, 2). The words "*only assign it*," to the end of the verse are connected with the end of verse 1 (see note at the beginning of verse 2). רַק, "*only*," i.e., though thou hast not yet conquered it. "*Assign thou it by lot*," lit. "cause it to fall," i.e., assign it by lot. There is an ellipsis of גּוֹרָל (cf. xxiii. 4 ; Ezek. xlvii. 22), by which the verb is followed in Psalm xxii. 19 ; Prov. i. 14 ; Isa. xxxiv. 17. "*As I have commanded*," etc., see i. 6.

Ver. 7.—This command to apportion the land among the nine and a half tribes before they had completely subdued it, was, as Calvin remarks, a pledge on the part of God that He would put them in possession of it, if they were obedient to His will. It was a trial of Joshua's faith. Before חֲצִי is an ellipsis of the foregoing prep. לְ (cf. the Heb. in i. 12), and for the construction of the two following nouns see note on iii. 14, viii. 11.

Vers. 8-32.—From the mention of the inheritance of the nine and a half tribes on the west of Jordan a transition is made to the inheritance of the two and a half tribes on the east. These latter were regarded by some ancient expositors (Origen, *Hom.* 3 ; and Theodoret, *Qu.* 16) as representative of the ancient Jewish Church, to which the promises were made, but which did not receive their accomplishment till Christ came, and, therefore, had no advantage in this respect over the Christian Church (cf. note on xi. 23).

Ver. 8.—עִמּוֹ, "*with it*," i.e., with the half tribe of Manasseh, but that half which had received its inheritance on the east of Jordan ; hence the Arab. Vers. paraphrases "Nam dimidia tribus altera Manasse," etc. The words "as Moses the servant of

Jehovah gave them" are not a tautological repetition of the clause "which Moses gave them," but imply that the arrangements which had been made in general terms by Moses were now to be exactly carried out by Joshua. For the fact alluded to see Numb. xxxii. 33; Deut. iii. 13.

Vers. 9-13.—A general description is first given of the borders of the territory beyond Jordan, and afterwards the cities assigned to each tribe are enumerated (vers. 15-31).

Ver. 9.—" *From Aroer, which is upon the bank* (lit. lip or edge) *of the watercourse of Arnon, and* (from) *the city*," etc., see xii. 2 (note). " *And all the plain* " (Auth. Vers.) : מִישׁוֹר, from יָשַׁר, to be straight, even, level, is used with the article for the upland downs or table land east of Jordan (cf. vers. 16, 17, 21; xx. 8), apparently in contradistinction to the rocky soil and more broken ground on the west, though in later times this distinction was probably lost, and plains on the west of the Jordan were so called. (Stanley's *Sin. and Pal.*, Append. § 6, note 1). The term is here applied to the southern portion of the territory of the Amorites, which was assigned to the tribe of Reuben (Deut. iii. 10, iv. 43; Josh. xx. 8; Jer. xlviii. 21), what is now the *Belka*, or pasture ground, of the modern Arabs. The portion of it from Medeba to Dibon is called (in Numb. xxi. 20) after its former inhabitants "the field of Moab," and (in Numb. xxiii. 14) "the field of the watchmen" (צֹפִים, Keil). "*Medeba*" (Mê-dhᵉbhâ', "waters of rest," rt. דָּבָא [unused], to rest), a town assigned to the Reubenites (ver. 16), but formerly belonging to Moab, from whom it was taken by the Amorites (Numb.

xxi. 29, 30); afterwards recovered by the Moabites (Isa. xv. 2); before it Joab defeated the Ammonites (1 Chron. xix. 7). It lay four or five miles southeast of Heshbon, on a round hill, on which there are still ruins called Mâdeba (Burckhardt's *Syr.*, p. 625). "*Dibon*" (Dî-bhôn, "pining," rt. דוּב, *i.q.*, דָּאַב, to pine away, Ges., *Lex.*), a Moabitish city, about four miles north of the Arnon, conquered by the Israelites (Numb. xxi. 30); assigned by Moses to the Reubenites (ver. 17), but apparently at first occupied by the Gadites, by whom it was rebuilt (Numb. xxxii. 34), and from whom it may have been called Dibon-Gad (Numb. xxxiii. 45, 46); afterwards recaptured by the Moabites (Isa. xv. 2; Jer. xlviii. 24). It is mentioned by Eusebius and Jerome, in the *Onomas.*, under the names Dabon or Debon, and as a very large village beyond the Arnon. Its extensive ruins, still called *Dhîbân*, were seen by Seetzen and Burckhardt, and here the Moabite stone was discovered by the Rev. T. Klein in 1868.

Ver. 10.—See xii. 2; Numb. xxi. 25.

Ver. 11.—"(The) *Gilead*" (hag-Gil-'adh), *i.e.*, the whole of the territory so called on both sides of the Jabbok (xii. 2, 5). For the remainder also of the verse see note on xii. 5.

Ver. 12.—See xii. 4. The form מַמְלְכוּת at the beginning of the verse (cf. vers. 21, 27, 30, 31) is not found in the Pentateuch, but מַמְלֶכֶת (Numb. xxxii. 33; Deut. iii. 4, 10); one proof that the Book of Joshua, though resembling the Pentateuch in style and phraseology, yet has its own distinctive features.

Ver. 13.—Here we have the first notice of that want of faith and perseverance which was afterwards the cause of so much disaster to the Israelites (see Books of Judges and of 1 Samuel). "*But the Geshurites . . . until this day*" (see note on xii. 5): Even in the time of David they appear to have been independent (2 Sam. iii. 3, x. 6, 8).

Ver. 14.—With what is here said of the portion of Levi cf. ver. 33, xiv. 3, 4. אִשֵּׁי, plural construc. of אִשֶּׁה,[1] a sacrifice, so called from the fire by which it was burned (אֵשׁ), used primarily of sacrifices burnt in honour of God, but, in a wider sense, of all kinds of sacrifices, even of those not burned (Lev. xxiv. 7, 9); thus here it includes tithes and firstfruits (Lev. xxvii. 30-32, compared with Numb. xviii. 21-32); and is rendered in the Chald. קוּרְבָּנַיָא, and by Jerome "sacrificia et victimæ." הוא, "*that* (is)" (§ 121, 2, with § 147, *d*, note *). "*As He said*," etc., see Numb. xviii. 20; Deut. x. 8, 9, xviii. 2.

VERS. 15-23.—*Inheritance of the Tribe of Reuben.*

Their territory was the most southern of the allotments of the trans-Jordanic tribes, and adjoined the country of Moab, to which it had formerly belonged before its conquest by the Amorites (see Numb. xxi. 26, etc.). The latter, however, did not wholly extirpate the Moabites, who, dwelling at first as a subject race among the Reubenites, seem to have gradually recovered their old supremacy in the land.

Ver. 15.—After יִתֵּן supply נַחֲלָה. On the distinction between מַטֶּה and שֵׁבֶט see note on iii. 12. "*Reuben*" (Reʾû-bhen, "see a son"), Gen. xxix. 32

---

[1] The word is used in only one other place besides the Pentateuch, viz., in 1 Sam. ii. 28, and is there copied from it (Keil).

Ver. 16.—Cf. ver. 9. The Chald., Sept., Syr., and Arab. read עָר for עַל, which is probably an emendation on account of the כִּי before עָרוֹעֵר (Maurer). *Medeba*, see ver. 9.

Ver. 17.—"*Heshbon*," xii. 2. בַּמֵּייִשׁוּר, cf. ver. 9 (note). "*Dibon*," ver. 9. "*Bamoth-baal*," lit. "the high-places of Baal," more briefly written "Bamoth" (Numb. xxi. 19; Isa. xv. 2), the spot whence Balaam saw the outskirts of the camp of Israel (Numb. xxii. 41), and probably in the vicinity of the Arnon (cf. *Onomast.*, s. v. Bamoth). "*Beth-baal-meon*," called "*Baal-meon*" (place of habitation, Numb. xxxii. 38), and, in a contracted form, "*Beon*" (Numb. xxxii. 3). The Moabites seem, at a later period, to have gained possession of it, and to have called it Beth-meon (Jer. xlviii. 23) or Baal-meon (Ezek. xxv. 9). Now probably *Myûn*, nearly two miles south-east of Heshbon (Burckhardt, ii., 624).

Ver. 18.—"*Jahaza*" (Ya-h͡tsah, "a place trampled down," perhaps "a threshing-floor," rt. יָהַץ, unused, Arab. "to trample"), written Jahaz Isa. xv. 4; Jer. xlviii. 34, where it is mentioned among the cities of Moab, having been retaken by it. Close to it Sihon was defeated by Moses and slain (Numb. xxi. 23-4; Deut. ii. 32, 33); it was assigned by the Reubenites to the Merarite Levites (xxi. 36 [not in the Hebrew text]; 1 Chron. vi. 78 [63 Heb.]). Its site unknown, though Eusebius (*Onom.*, Ἰεσσά) says it lay between Medeba and Dibon (Smith's *Bib. Dict.*, vol. i., p. 915). "*Kedemoth*" (Qᵉdhê-môth, "easternmost parts"), a town in the neighbourhood of Jahaza, now unknown. From the adjacent wilderness (midhbar), to which the town seems to have given its name, Moses sent am-

bassadors to Sihon (Deut. ii. 26). It was given by
the Reubenites to the Merarite Levites (xxi. 37 [not
in the Heb. text]; 1 Chron. vi. 79 [64 Heb.]).
"*Mepha'ath*" (beauty, from יָפַע, to shine [the full
form of the Heb. word is מֵיפָעַת, 1 Chron. vii. 64]),
in the district of the plain (mishor, ver. 17), assigned
to the Levites (xxi. 37 [not in the Heb. text];
1 Chron. vi. 79 [64]), apparently retaken by the
Moabites (Jer. xlviii. 21), mentioned by Eusebius
and Jerome (*Onom.*, s. v., Μηφάθ) as a Roman
military post for keeping the inhabitants of the desert
in check. Site unknown.

Ver. 19.—"*Kirjathaim*" (Qir-ya-tha-yim, "double
city"), first mentioned in Gen. xiv. 5 as in possession
of the Emim. In the time of Eusebius it was called
Karias, and he describes it as a village of Christians,
ten miles west of Medeba (*Onomast.*, Καριαθιείμ), but
Burckhardt places it three miles south of Heshbon, in
the ruins known as Et-Teym, half an hour west of
Medeba; so Keil. In Numb. xxxii. 37, 38, it is
mentioned as between Elealeh and Nebo, and said
to have been built (*i.e.*, rebuilt or fortified) by the
Reubenites, but appears to have been retaken at a
later period by the Moabites (Jer. xlviii. 23; Ezek.
xxv. 9). It is possibly *Kureiyat*, close to *Jebel attarus*
(Grove). "*Sibmah*" (Sibh-mah, "coolness" or "sweet
smell," rt. שָׂבַם [unused], Arab., to be cold, or *i.q.*, בָּשַׂם,
to be sweet-scented), see Numb. xxxii. 38; afterwards
famous among the cities of Moab for its vines (Isa.
xvi. 8; Jer. xlviii. 32). Its name is perhaps traceable in the ruins *es-Sameh*, four miles east of Heshbon;
but according to Jerome (Comment. on Isa. xvi. 8)
it was only five hundred paces from the latter city.

"*Zareth-shahar*" (Tse-reth-hash-sha-char, "the splendour of the dawn"), mentioned here only. "*On a mount of the valley*": The valley may be that of the Jordan (ver. 27), or of Shittim, on the side of the Dead Sea (Numb. xxxiii. 49). Seetzen (*Reisen*, ii., 369) would identify the town with a place called *Sara*, or *Zara*, at the mouth of the Wady Zerka Main, about a mile from the edge of the Dead Sea. It is probable from the name that it stood upon a sunny hill (Keil and Rosenm.).

Ver. 20.—"*Beth-peor*" (house of Peor, an "opening," Numb. xxiii. 28), a place where Baal was worshipped (Numb. xxv. 3, 18). According to Eusebius it was six miles above Libias or Beth-haran, on the east of Jordan, opposite Jericho (Euseb., *Onomast.*), near the burial-place of Moses (Deut. xxxiv. 6), but not known. On the two last-mentioned names in this verse see xii. 3.

Ver. 21.—"*And all the cities of the plain*" (tableland), *i.e.*, all those which had not yet been mentioned in ver. 17. "*All the kingdom of Sihon*" (Sî-chôn), etc., *i.e.*, so far as it extended over the plain, for the northern portion of this kingdom was allotted to the Gadites (ver. 27). "*Whom Moses slew and the chieftains of Midian*": In Numb. xxxi. 8 these chieftains are called מַלְכֵי מִדְיָן, *i.e.*, petty kings or rulers. "*Dukes of Sihon*" (A. V.), duces (Vulg.), so Syr., but נְסִיכִים means "*princes*" in Psalm lxxxiii. 11 (12); Ezek. xxxii. 30; Micah v. 4, and is so rendered here by Gesenius (*Lex.*) and Rosenm., from נָסַךְ, to anoint, though the authority given by Gesenius (*Lex.*, 3) for this meaning of the verb, viz., Psalm ii. 6, is unsupported by other examples. Hence Keil renders "*vassals of Sihon*," from נָסַךְ in the sense of "to pour melted metal into a mould," and then metaphorically "to mould or enfeoff any one with power," a meaning, which though supported by Gusset (*Lex.*) and Hengstenberg (*Psalms*, i., p. 35), is rather forced. More usually נָסַךְ means "to pour out a libation" (Exod. xxx. 9; Hosea ix. 4), and hence, perhaps, here "to dedicate or appoint with a libation." In any case tributary princes are denoted. יֹשְׁבֵי, "*dwellers in the land*," *i.e.*, as tributaries to Sihon.

Ver. 22.—"*Balaam*" (Bil-'am, perhaps derived, as by Simonis, from בְּלִי and עַם, "the destruction of the people;" or from בָּלַע, to devour, with a formative syllable attached, and meaning "destroyer" or "glutton"). "*Beor*," written "Bosor" (2 Peter ii. 15), an Aramaic form of the word which St. Peter may have learnt in Babylon.[1] Balaam's residence was Pethor (Numb. xxii. 5), in Mesopotamia (Deut. xxiii. 4). הַקּוֹסֵם, "*the soothsayer*" (from קָסַם, to divine[2]), always denotes a false prophet; see Isa. iii. 2, where he is distinguished from the true prophet. Yet there is no sufficient reason for concluding with Philo, Josephus, Origen, S. Augustine, Cor. a Lap., and others, that Balaam was a prophet of the devil, who was compelled by God to bless where he wished to curse; but rather that he possessed a knowledge of the true God, and the gift of prophesying, but under the influence of ambition, pride, and covetousness, perverted both to unrighteous purposes. אֶל־חֲלָלֵיהֶם, "*among*" (A.V.), or

---

[1] Or Βοσόρ is a Galilean mode of writing בְּעוֹר, the ע being pronounced *s* (Vitringa, *Observ. Sacrae*, vol. i., p. 936).
[2] The original meaning seems to be "to divide," or "to partition out" (Ges., *Lex.*).

"*in addition to, their slain.*" Ges. says אֶל sometimes has the meaning of adding or superadding, as in Levit. xviii. 18 (*Lex.*, 6). In the parallel place (Numb. xxxi. 8) there is עַל; so in the Targum.

Ver. 23 (*The Boundary of the Portion of Reuben at its North-West Extremity*).—"*And the border of the sons of Reuben was the Jordan, and the border thereof.*" גְּבוּל at the end of the clause and in ver. 27 = גְּבוּלָה, Chald. תְּחוּמָיהּ; Keil regards it as explanatory, and gives to the conjunction וְ before it the force of "*or rather,*" *i.e.*, the actual boundary was not the river, but the land immediately adjoining it. "*And their villages,*" lit. "enclosures," rt. חָצַר, to surround, Sept. ἐπαύλιδες, farm premises (Keil), enclosed by a fence, but not by a wall (cf. Lev. xxv. 31, and see Stanley's *Sin. and Pal.*, Append., § 83 [1]). The plural feminine suffix הֶן refers to עָרִים, which, though masculine in termination, comes from a feminine noun. Some MSS. read חַצְרֵיהֶם, as in ver. 28, where the masculine suffix is used, as often, for the feminine, in the 3rd person (cf. iv. 8).

The recently discovered Moabite stone proves that most of the cities assigned by Joshua to the Reubenites were either wholly, or in part, wrested from them by the Moabites, with whom they probably became gradually much intermixed (see Schottmann, *Die Siegesäule Mesa's*, p. 36, etc.). The prediction "Thou shalt not excel" (Gen. xlix. 4)

---

[1] He remarks that topographically *Cha-tser* means a village, generally a Bedouin village (Gen. xxv. 16; Sept. σκηνή), such as are formed of tent-cloths, spread over stone walls, the latter often remaining long after the tribes which they sheltered, and the tents which they supported, have vanished away.

was remarkably fulfilled in this tribe, as no individual in it is mentioned as having attained to eminence. It degenerated into a tribe of shepherds (Judges v. 15, 16), became alienated from its western brethren, and at length lapsed into idolatry (1 Chron. v. 25).

VERS. 24-28.—*Inheritance of the Tribe of Gad* ("a troop," Gen. xlix. 19; cf. xxx. 11).

This tribe was of a fierce, warlike character (Deut. xxxiii. 20; 1 Chron. v. 18-22; xii. 8, etc.).

Ver. 25.—"*And their border was Jazer* (Ya'-zêr = "which Jehovah aids"), a town taken from the Amorites (Numb. xxi. 32), rebuilt by the children of Gad (Numb. xxxii. 35), described by Eusebius (*Onomast.*) as ten miles west from Philadelphia (Rabbath-Ammân), and fifteen from Heshbon; identical, as Keil and Van de Velde, after Seetzen, conjecture, with the ruins of *Sîr* or *es Sîr*, consisting of a castle, and a large walled pool, the latter probably the remains of the מֵי יַעְזֵר (Jer. xlviii. 32). It was assigned to the Merarite Levites (Josh. xxi. 37 [39]; 1 Chron. vi. 66 [81]), but belonged after the exile to the Moabites (Isa. xvi. 8; Jer. xlviii. 32); taken by Judas Maccabæus (1 Macc. v. 8). "*All the cities of Gilead,*" *i.e.*, the southern half of Gilead, included in the territory of Sihon, for the northern half came within the territory of Bashan, and was assigned to the half-tribe of Manasseh. "*And half the land of the children of Ammon,*" *i.e.*, that portion of the land between the Arnon and the Jabbok, which Sihon had wrested from them, and which the Israelites, when they conquered Sihon, took for their own; but the land which the Ammonites possessed in the time of Moses the Israelites had been forbidden to attack (Deut. ii. 19). "*Unto Aroer, which is before Rabbah.*" "*Aroer*" ('A-rô-êr, naked; rt. עָרָה, to be bare), distinct from the city of the same name on the Arnon (xii. 2, xiii. 9, 16), in the territory of Reuben. It is mentioned again in Judges xi. 33; 2 Sam. xxiv. 5, only; site unknown, but Keil thinks it was on the north-east of Rabbah, in the Wady Nahr Ammân, where Kalat Zerka Gadda is marked upon Kiepert's map. *Rabbah* (Great),[1] the chief city of the Ammonites, called "*Rabbath* of the sons of Ammon" (Deut. iii. 11; 2 Sam. xii. 26, xvii. 27). It seems to have been divided into two parts, one (the lower town) named the city of waters or the royal city, taken by Joab (2 Sam. xii. 26, 27); the other (the upper town), containing the citadel, and taken by David (ver. 29).[2] At a later period it appears again as an Ammonitish city (Amos i. 13-15; Jer. xlix. 3; Ezek. xxx. 5); it was called Philadelphia by Ptolemy Philadelphus in the third century B.C., and by Polybius, 'Ραββατάμενα; was captured by Antiochus the Great (Polyb., v., 16), and in later times became the seat of a Christian bishop. Its extensive ruins now bear the name of *Ammân*, and are about twenty-two miles from the Jordan, on the bank of the Wady Zerka, usually identified with the Jabbok. So Abulfeda, Burckhardt, Seetzen.

---

[1] Applied to a capital city as great in size and importance. The same name, "Rabbah," was given to Ar, the capital of Moab (Euseb., *Onomast.*, "Moab").

[2] Josephus (*Antiq.*, vii., 7, § 5) says that the citadel contained only one small well of water, which would account for its speedy capture, when communication with the perennial stream in the lower town had been cut off.

Ver. 26.—"*Heshbon*," xii. 2. "*Ramath - ham-mitspeh*" ("the high-place of the watch-tower"), here only; probably the spot where Jacob and Laban erected their cairn of stones (Gen. xxxi. 43-53), and identical with Ramoth-Gilead (xx. 8 ; Deut. iv. 43) ; where also Ahab was slain (1 Kings xxii.), and Joram, his son, was wounded (2 Kings viii. 28). The site unknown, though supposed by Gesenius and Keil to be that of the modern *Szalt*, or *es-Salt*, situated, according to Porter, on a peak of Mount Gilead (Jebel Jil'ad), seven miles south of the Jabbok (Art. "Gilead," Dr. Smith's *Bib. Dict.*). *Betonim* ("pistachio nuts," so called from being flat on one side, and bellying out on the other, rt. בָּטַן, to be empty, hollow ; Gen. xliii. 11), called *Bothnia* by Jerome in the *Onomasticon;* site unknown. "*Mahanaim* (Ma-chªna-yim, "double camp," or "two hosts"), see Gen. xxxii. 2, north of the Jabbok (Keil ; Clark's *Bib. Atlas*), on the border of Manasseh, but in the tribe of Gad ; assigned to the Merarite Levites (xxi. 38). Here Ishbosheth was crowned (2 Sam. ii. 8, 9), and hither David fled from Absalom (2 Sam. xvii. 24) ; mentioned also as one of Solomon's twelve provision cities (1 Kings iv. 14). Now probably *Mahneh* (Robinson, Grove). "*Unto the border of Debir*": There were two other places of the same name, one in the mountainous part of Judah (x. 39, xv. 49) ; the other between Jerusalem and Jericho (xv. 7). The ל here before the name is taken as a sign of the genitive by all the versions, but is unusual in the Book of Joshua ; hence Hitzig considers it the error of a copyist, who doubled the ל at the end of the preceding word ; Keil would make it part of the word, and reads "Lidhbir." Reland (*Pal.*, 734), J. D. Michaelis, and Knobel would point the word Lo-dhebar, and identify it with the town of the same name (2 Sam. ix. 4, xvii. 27), whence provisions were brought to David at Mahanaim. Whichever conjecture is adopted, the site is unknown; but if the rt. of the word is דָּבַר, to lead to pasture, the town probably lay in the grazing country, on the high downs east of Jordan.

Ver. 27.—בָּעֵמֶק, "*in the valley*," i.e., the valley of the Jordan, or the Arabah, which was along the east side of the river from the Wady Heshbon, above the Dead Sea, to the Sea of Galilee, and formed part of the kingdom of Sihon (xii. 3). "*Beth-aram*" (Beth-haram, "house of the height"), written Beth-Haran (Numb. xxxii. 36), now Beit-haran; in Aramaic, Beth-rametha; at the foot of Mount Peor, and near the entrance of the Jordan into the Dead Sea; it afterwards was called Betharamptha, and was rebuilt by Herod Antipas, and named by him *Julias*, or, according to Eusebius, *Livias*, in honour of the wife of Augustus (Josephus, *Antiq.*, xviii., 2, § 1; *Bel. Jud.*, iv., 7, § 6), now *er-Rameh*. "*Beth-nimrah*" (house of sweet waters, cf. Isa. xv. 6), called Nimrah, Numb. xxxii. 3, five miles north of Libias (Beth-Haran), according to Eusebius and Jerome (*Onomast.*). Perhaps identical with a ruined city called *Nimrin*, south of Szalt (ver. 26), which Burckhardt mentions (*Syria*, p. 355) as situated near the point where the Wady Shoaib joins the Jordan (Kitto, *Encyclo. of Bib. Lit.*); Grove says it may possibly be Beth-abara (Smith's *Bib. Dict.*, i., p. 204). "*Succoth*" (Suk-kôth, "booths"), rt. סָבַךְ, to weave (Gen. xxxiii. 17). Site unknown.

Jerome says, "Sochoth is to this day a city beyond Jordan in Scythopolis" (Qu. Heb. on Gen. xxxiii. 17). Burckhardt (note to p. 345 [July 2nd]) speaks of the ruins of Sukkot, near where he crossed the river Jordan, and which were evidently on the east of Jordan, and entirely distinct from the Sâkût discovered by Dr. Robinson (*Bib. Res.*, iii., 309, etc.), and by Van de Velde (*Syr. and Pal.*, ii., 343), on the west of the Jordan. The place is mentioned in connection with the exploits of Gideon, and was evidently on the east of Jordan (Judges viii. 4, 5, 13-17); so in Psalm lx. 6 (8) it represents the east of Jordan, as Shechem does the west. "*Zaphon*" (Tsâ-phôn, "north"), near the south end of the Sea of Chinnereth. Site unknown. "*The rest of the kingdom*": The southern portion of that kingdom had been assigned to the Reubenites (ver. 21). On הַיַּרְדֵּן וּגְבוּל, see ver. 23. "*Sea of Chinnereth*," cf. xi. 2.

Ver. 28.—"*And their villages*," cf. ver. 23 (note).

VERS. 29-31.—*Inheritance of the Half-Tribe of Manasseh* (Heb. M^enash-sheh, "causing to forget," Gen. xli. 51).

Ver. 29.—After וַיִּתֵּן, subau. נַחֲלָה, as in ver. 24' וַיְהִי, "*and* (it, viz., the possession assigned them) *was*.' This half-tribe of Manasseh were descendants of Machir, son of Manasseh, and their territory on the east of Jordan was assigned to them probably on account of their valour (see xvii. 1), not, as Aben Ezra thinks, because they solicited it, for no such request on their part is recorded in Numb. xxxii. 33-42.

Ver. 30.—"*Mahanaim*," see ver. 26; it was on their southern border. "*All the kingdom of Og*," comprehending not only the province of Bashan, but Argob and the northern portion of Gilead (cf. Deut. iii. 13). חַוֹּת denotes not "towns" (Auth. Vers.), but "*tent-villages*," properly places where one lives and dwells, from חָיָה, life. The Bedouins of the present day use the same word for their own villages (Stanley's *Sin. and Pal.*, Append., § 84). "*Jair*" (Yâ-'îr, "whom He [God] enlightens"), was descended on the father's side from Judah, on the mother's from Manasseh (1 Chron. ii. 21, 22). He was the conqueror of Argob (Deut. iii. 14). "*Threescore cities*" (cf. Deut. iii. 4); perhaps, though at first villages, they afterwards grew into cities. In 1 Chron. ii. 22 Jair is said to have had three-and-twenty cities (עָרִים) in Gilead (cf. Numb. xxxii. 41), which would seem in 1 Kings iv. 13 to be distinguished from these sixty cities in Argob.

Ver. 31.—"*Half Gilead*," (lit. "half of the Gilead," cf. xii. 2), viz., the northern half, see ver. 25. *Ashtaroth and Edrei*, see xii. 4. לִבְנֵי "(belonged) *to the children*, etc. (even) *to the half of the children of Machir*," for the other half received their inheritance on the west of Jordan (xviii. 2, etc.). The name Machir here supersedes that of Manasseh used in ver. 29, a token of the power which the descendants of Machir had attained.

Ver. 32.—אֵלֶּה, "*these*," not, as the Sept. οὗτοι, referring to the persons to whom the possessions were assigned, but to the possessions themselves; Vulg. "hanc possessionem," which is confirmed by xiv. 1, xix. 51. "*The plains of Moab*" (Auth. Vers.), rather "*the dry regions of Moab,*" the sunk district in the tropical depths of the Jordan valley, where the Israelites had their encampment (Numb. xxxiii. 49), and which took its name from that of the great valley itself (Arabah) : see Art. "Moab," Smith's *Bib. Dict.*, ii., p. 392. בְּעֵבֶר וגו (lit. "*beyond the Jordan—Jericho,*" *i.e.*, on the other side of that part of Jordan which skirted the territory of Jericho ; Vulg. "trans Jordanem contra Jericho ;" Revis. Vers. "beyond Jordan at Jericho ;" the same form of expression occurs in xvi. 1, xx. 8 ; also in Numb. xxii. 1, xxvi. 3, 63, xxxiii. 48, 50. These trans-Jordanic tribes were eventually carried into captivity by Pul and Tiglath-pileser, and placed in the districts on and about the river Khabûr, in the upper part of Mesopotamia (1 Chron. v. 26).

Ver. 33.—A repetition of ver. 14, and omitted by the Sept.

CHAPTER XIV.

Commencement of the Account of the Distribution of the cis-Jordanic Canaan among the Nine Tribes and the Half-Tribe of Manasseh, which terminates at xix. 51. (*Vers.* 1-5 *are introductory.*)

Ver. 1.—וְאֵלֶּה, see xiii. 32. The account, however, of the distribution does not begin till the fifteenth chapter. נָחֲלוּ, "*distributed for a possession,*" followed by an accus. of person and of thing (§ 139, 1). The distribution, according to the command in Numb. xxxiv. 16-29, was to be made by the high priest Eleazar and by Joshua. *Eleazar*[1] ('El-'a-zar, "whom God helps") is named here, and in xvii. 4, xix. 51, xxi. 1; Numb. xxxiv. 17, *before* Joshua, perhaps, as the representative of the Divine government over Israel; so in Numb. xxvii. 18-21 Joshua is directed to act in accordance with his direction.[2] "*And the heads* (of the houses) *of the fathers of the tribes of the sons of Israel.*" בֵּת. which is here omitted after רָאשֵׁי, is supplied in Exod. vi. 14; Numb. vii. 2; 1 Chron. v. 24, vii. 2, 7, 40, ix. 13. Except in the first book of Chronicles, where probably it is borrowed from an ancient source, the phrase does not occur except in the Pentateuch and Joshua. לְ is used before בְּנֵי to prevent the repetition of the construc. state (cf. xix. 51; Ges., *Gr.*, § 115, 2, *b*). Each tribe had its own prince (Numb. xxxiv. 18).

Ver. 2.—"*By lot* (was) *their inheritance*" (Auth. Vers.), but גּוֹרַל being in the construc. form, Vatablus, Keil, and Rosenm. properly connect the words with נַחֲלוּ in the preceding verse, and render "by the lot of their inheritance," *i.e.*, by casting lots for the apportionment of their inheritance. בְּיַד, "*through*" (by means of), where יַד loses its force as a noun (Ges., *Lex.*, p. 330): More commonly it is used with שָׁלַח (see Exod. iv. 13), and cf. the use of ἀποστελλω with διά (Rev. i. 1). For the command referred to see Numb. xxvi. 52-6, xxxiii. 54, xxxiv. 13. לְתִשְׁעַת הַמַּטּוֹת,

---

[1] He was Aaron's third son (Exod. vi. 23, 25), and succeeded his father in the high priesthood (Numb. xx. 26-28; Deut. x. 6.). His death is recorded in Josh. xxiv. 33.

[2] On the other hand, Moses is named before Aaron, except where priority of age is indicated, as in Exod. vi. 20, 26; Numb. iii. 1.

not, as in the Sept., governed by צִוָּה, but by נִחֲלוּ in ver. 1, "*which they distributed for inheritance to,*" etc.: In Numb. xxxiv. 13 the same words לְתִשְׁעַת הַמַּ׳ are preceded by לֵאמֹר, and so here in some MSS. and editions, though probably it is an interpolation of a later date. On the distribution of the land by lot see Numb. xxvi. 53, etc. Calvin and Clericus remark that the lot determined the *position* only of the inheritances, but left their exact dimensions to be afterwards settled according to the size of the tribes to which they fell; see, *e.g.*, the alteration made in the extent of Judah's territory (ch. xix. 1-9). How the lots were drawn is nowhere stated. There may have been two urns containing, the one, descriptions of the several inheritances, and the other, the names of the nine and a-half tribes; and the drawing from each may have been simultaneous; or the prince of each tribe may have drawn in turn from the one urn containing the descriptions of the inheritances. The reason of this decision by lot was not only to prevent jealousies and disputes between one tribe and another (Prov. xviii. 18), but that each tribe might be satisfied that its inheritance had been assigned to it by God Himself (Prov. xvi. 33). It may be also remarked that the accordance in many particulars between the prophecies of Jacob and Moses respecting the inheritance of the tribes of Israel (Gen. xlviii., xlix.; Deut. xxxiii.), and the distribution of the territory recorded in the Book of Joshua, is a proof of the inspiration of those prophecies. Among heathen nations a like custom prevailed in the division of territory among conquerors or colonists (see Herod., v., 77; vi., 100; Thucyd., iii., 50;

Cic., *Epist. ad Div.*, xi., 20, "sorte agros legionibus assignare ").

Vers. 3-4.—Ver. 3 gives a reason why the land was to be apportioned among nine and a-half tribes only, viz., because two and a-half tribes had received their inheritance, on the other side of Jordan, but, inasmuch as the tribe of Levi received no share of territory, ver. 4 declares that the number nine and a-half was made up by the division of the tribe of Joseph into two tribes, viz., Manasseh and Ephraim.

Ver. 4.—וְלֹא־נָתְנוּ: The ן is not here = "therefore" (Auth. Ver.), but = *and*, or with לֹא = *neither*. "*Cities to dwell in*": Cf. Numb. xxxv. 3, where Keil remarks that the Levites had not the whole of the cities as their own property, but as many houses in them as their necessities required, which houses could be redeemed (Lev. xxv. 32-33), if sold at any time, and reverted to them without compensation in the year of Jubilee, even if not redeemed before; but any portion of the towns, which was not taken possession of by them, together with the fields and villages, continued the property of those tribes to which they had been assigned by lot (see also his note on xxi. 12). "*And their suburbs*" (Auth. Vers., Luther, and Vulg. "suburbana"), rather, "*their pasture grounds*," *i.e.*, the districts around their cities in which their cattle might graze, from גָּרַשׁ, to drive, to drive out. For their extent see Numb. xxxv. 4-5. With the m. suff. הֶם referring to עָרִים cf. xiii. 23 (note). "*For their cattle and for their (other) possessions*": The latter word (Heb. קִנְיָן used here coll.) is rendered by the Vulg. "pecora" (lesser cattle), Sept. κτήνη, as by Chald.

Vers., but by the Syr. and Arab. "possessions," from קָנָה, to possess (cf. Gen. xxxiv. 23; Numb. xxxv. 3, where רְכוּשׁ, "substance," is used for it, as here by A. V.). The Levites had no territorial inheritance, like the rest of the tribes, in order that their influence on the nation at large might be increased.

Ver. 5.—"*As Jehovah—Moses*," cf. ver. 2. "*And they portioned out* (divided, A. V.) *the land.*" This is a general statement relating to the distribution of the land, for we learn from chapter xviii., etc., that not all the nine and a-half tribes received at once their inheritance.

VERS. 6-15.—*Before the Casting of the Lots an Inheritance is assigned to Caleb.*

Ver. 6.—"*And the children* (sons) *of Judah,*" doubtless not all the tribe, but the principal men, especially Caleb's relatives, whom he took with him as able to testify to the integrity of his conduct. "*In* ("*in the,*" § 109, 3] *Gilgal,*" i.e., the Gilgal near Jericho (ix. 6, note). "*Caleb*" (Ka-lebh),[1] "*son of Jephunneh*"[2]: A prince of Judah, and one of those appointed to portion out Canaan (Numb. xxxiv. 19). Keil thinks that he was the same as the Caleb in 1 Chron. ii. 18, a descendant of (בֶּן) Hezron, the son of Pharaz, and grandson of Judah. The house

---

[1] Perhaps "dog," *i.q.* כֶּלֶב, from כָּלַב (unused), to bark (Ges.), and the name may indicate fidelity, courage, vigilance; or "seizing vehemently," from כָּלַב (Fürst), hence "bold, impetuous."
[2] "*Jephun-neh*" (perhaps meaning "for whom a way is prepared," see Pual of פָּנָה, Ges., *Lex.*), neither his father nor ancestors are named.

of Caleb may have been incorporated into the house of Hezron; but doubtless the genealogy in 1 Chron. ii., iv. is involved in much obscurity. "*The Kenezite*" (the Qᵉniz-zite, hunter, rt. קנז, to hunt), cf. Numb. xxxii. 12. The term may imply that Caleb was a descendant of Kenez; and as that was a name borne by the dukes of Edom (Gen. xxxvi. 15, 42; 1 Chron. i. 53), and as in the genealogy of the family of Caleb (1 Chron. i., ii., iv.) there occur also other Edomitish names, *e.g.*, Shobal (1 Chron. ii. 50, 52; cf. Gen. xxxvi. 20-23); Korah (1 Chron. ii. 43; Gen. xxxvi. 5, 16); Ithran (1 Chron. i. 41; Gen. xxxvi. 26); Elah (1 Chron. iv. 15; Gen. xxxvi. 41); it has been surmised that the family of Caleb was of Edomite extraction, and incorporated as proselytes into the family of Judah (see Smith's *Bibl. Dict.*, Art. "Caleb," vol. i., p. 242). On the other hand, as Esau and Judah were alike of Israelitish descent, the same names might possibly be found among the descendants of both. אִישׁ הָא, "*the man of God*" = נָבִיא (cf. 1 Kings xiii. 1, 18), and so rendered here in the Chald.; the same title is given to Moses in Deut. xxxiii., 1; Ezra iii. 2, and in the inscription of Psalm xc. עַל אֹדוֹתַי, lit. "*about my and your affairs*,"[1] *i.e.*, "concerning me and thee" (Auth. Vers., Sept., and Vulg.). For the promise referred to see Numb. xiv. 24, 30. The express mention of Joshua refutes the assertion of Knobel here that he was not one of the spies. "*Kadesh-barnea*," x. 41.

Ver. 7.—וָאָשִׁב "*and I brought back*," followed by an accusative both of person and thing (cf. xxii.

---

[1] Properly "turnings," from אדר, to bend, to turn.

32.) עִם־לְבָבִי, "*in* (lit. "with") *my heart*," *i.e.*, according to the best of my convictions, without fear of man, or regard to any one's favour. The rendering of the Sept., κατὰ τὸν νοῦν αὐτοῦ, "according to his mind," *i.e.*, the mind or wish of Moses, though supported by one MS. of Kennicott, and approved by Clericus, is rightly rejected by Maurer as containing a most improbable statement.

Ver. 8.—"*My brethren*," *i.e.*, the rest of the spies, of course with the exception of Joshua, to whom he was speaking. הִמְסִיו, an Aramaism for הִמַסּוּ (§ 75, v. 17), from מָסָה, *i.q.* מָסַס, to melt (cf. ii. 11).[1] כִּלֵּאתִי אַחֲרֵי, construc. prægnans (§ 141), subaud. לָלֶכֶת after the verb, "*I fully followed*," lit. "fulfilled to follow" (cf. Numb. xxxii. 11, 12 ; Deut. i. 36).

Ver. 9.—"*Moses sware*": Keil thinks that, as we do not elsewhere read of this oath of Moses, it is here for the first time recorded ; but more probably the oath of God, as made known through Moses, is referred to (see Numb. xiv. 23, 24, 30; Deut. i. 34-36, in which latter verse [ver. 36] a like expression to that in this occurs, viz., "*the land that he hath trod upon*," in allusion, evidently, to the territory around Hebron). On אִם־לֹא, to denote strong affirmation, see § 155, 2, *f*, 2nd par.

Ver. 10.—"*Jehovah hath kept me alive*": Caleb's piety appears in his thus attributing his preservation not to his own care, or strength of constitution, but to the kind providence of Jehovah. "*Forty-and-five years*": These are dated from the autumn of the

---

[1] According to Ewald (*Lehrb.*, § 142, *a*), הִמְסִיו is really the regular and earliest form, which the Hebrew lost, but the Chaldee retained.

second year after the exodus. The Israelites wandered thirty-eight years in the wilderness after that date, and were occupied seven years in subduing Canaan (xi. 18, note), which seven years are here reckoned in their wanderings, as they had not during them any fixed settlements. אֲשֶׁר הָלַךְ, "*during which Israel walked*": On אֲשֶׁר in this sense see Ewald, *Lehrb.*, § 321, c.; it refers to the forty-five years.

Ver. 11.—עוֹדֶנִּי, "*I am yet*" (§ 100, 5). בְּיוֹם ... מֹשֶׁה, "*in the day that Moses sent me*," infin. constructive, with subject and object, the latter being unusually placed after the infin. (§ 133, 3, Rem.). כְּהִי: Being followed by a monosyllable, its accent is retracted (§ 29, 3, *b*). צֵאת וָבוֹא: Used to express the performance of active duty (cf. Numb. xxvii. 17; Deut. xxxi. 2; 1 Kings iii. 7). Caleb, like Moses (Deut. xxxiv. 7), was made, on account of his fidelity, an especial exception to the infirmities incident to old age (Psalm xc. 10).

Ver. 12.—תְּנָה for תֵּן, imper. with ה parag. (§ 66, 1). "*This mountain*, *i.e.*, the mountainous country around Hebron (xi. 2, xx. 7). "*Whereof Jehovah spake in that day*": We may, therefore, conclude that Jehovah's promise in Numb. xiv., Deut. i., to give Caleb an inheritance in Canaan had special reference to Hebron. "*For thou didst hear in that day*" (viz., what Jehovah spake): The second כִּי is not = "*that*" (ὅτι) or "*how*" (Auth. Vers.), but is co-ordinate (Keil), and gives a farther reason why the mountain should be given to him, "for (because) the Anakim are there" . . . (cf. the Sept. and Vulg.). Joshua himself had been one of the spies (Numb. xiii. 8), and, therefore, did not learn merely by report that there were Anakim in Hebron. אוּלַי, "*perhaps*," but here expressing hope and desire, as in Gen. xvi. 2; Amos v. 15. אוֹתִי for אִתִּי, "*with me*" (§ 103, 1, Rem. 1), subau. יִהְיֶה. וְהוֹרַשְׁתִּים, "*and I drive* (or root) *them out*": The perfect here expresses assurance (§ 126, 4). How this declaration of Caleb is reconcilable with xi. 21, 22, see note there. His address (vers. 6-12), while removed alike from false modesty and self-presumption, blends gratitude with firm confidence in God.

Ver. 13.—"*And Joshua blessed him*," *i.e.*, invoked a blessing upon him, prayed God to prosper him. "*Hebron*" (x. 3), not only the city so called, but the neighbourhood; the city was afterwards appointed a city of refuge (xx. 7), and assigned to the Levites (xxi. 11).

Ver. 14.—The expressions "Kenezite" and "God of Israel" have been thought to indicate that Caleb was a foreigner and a proselyte (see note on ver. 6).

Ver. 15.—"*Before*" (לְפָנִים), *i.e.*, prior to the date at which this book was written, but not necessarily from the time of the city's origin. "*Kirjath-arba*" (Qir-yath-'Ar-ba', "city of Arba"), see note on x. 3. אַרְבַּע, "hero of Baal" (Fürst), for אַרְבַּעַל; like אֲרִיאֵל, "the lion (*i.e.*, hero) of God;" or, according to Ges. (*Lex.*), perhaps "homo quadratus." הָאָדָם הַגָּדוֹל, "*the greatest man*," perhaps in size and strength, as well as authority and renown. The adjective with the art. has here the force of a superlative (§ 119, 2), and אָדָם = אִישׁ, which is more properly used of an individual (cf. Eccles. vii. 28). The strange rendering of Jerome "*Adamus maximus ibi inter Enakim situs est*" is based on a Jewish tradition in the Beresh-Rabba, that Kirjath-arba means "city of the four," because Adam, Abraham, Isaac, and Jacob were buried there. "*And the land had rest,*" etc. (cf. xi. 23): The Canaanites were so far subdued as to be unable to offer an effectual opposition to the partition of the land, of which the author commences an account in the following chapter.

CHAPTERS XV.—XVII.

The Lots belonging to Judah and Joseph.

THE account of the distribution, which was interrupted at the end of xiv. 1-5, is here resumed, and it is in accordance with the preference given by Jacob in his prophetic blessing (Gen. xlix.) to Judah and Joseph, that their descendants first received their share of the conquered territory (xv.-xvii.). How, says Kitto, the lot was taken at the first division we do not know, but it was probably the same in principle as in the mode followed with respect to the remaining seven tribes (xviii.). We may, therefore, conclude that, when this first conquered portion of the land had been surveyed and found sufficient to furnish three cantons, *all the tribes* cast lots for them, and they fell to Judah, Ephraim, and the half-tribe of Manasseh. The difference was, that at the first division the question was not only what lot should be had, but whether *any* should at present be obtained by a particular tribe; at the second division the former question was only to be determined, there being then as many lots as there were tribes unprovided for (*Illust. Bible*).

CHAPTER XV.

The Inheritance of the Tribe of Judah ("praised," Gen. xlix. 8 ; see יָדָה). *Its General Boundaries* (1-12). *Renewed Mention of Caleb's Inheritance, because included in that of Judah* (13-20). *A List of the Towns of Judah* (21-63).

Ver. 1. (*The General Position of Judah's Territory*). —וַיְהִי וגו׳, "*and there was the lot to the tribe of the sons of Judah according to their families, toward the frontier of Edom, toward the desert of Zin southward, on the extreme south.*" In xvi. 1, xix. 1, יְהִי is expressed by יָצָא, "*there came out.*" "*By* (according to) *their families,*" see vii. 14. "*Edom*" ran parallel with the desert of Zin on the east, and "*Zin*" (not to be confounded with "Sin") was the north-east part of the great desert of Paran. מִקְצֵה תֵימָן, lit. "*from the extremity of the south*," *i.e.,* on the extreme south ; see on מִן Ges., *Lex.* (3), c., p. 483.

Vers. 2-4. *The Southern Boundary*,—corresponding generally with that of Canaan (Numb. xxxiv. 3-5), and including what was afterwards the territory of Simeon (xix.).

Ver. 2.—מִן־הַלְּ, "*from the bay* (tongue) *which looketh* (turneth) *southward*" (Auth. Vers.), *i.e.*, from that southern point of the Dead Sea which now terminates in a salt marsh (cf. Isa. xi. 15, "tongue of the Egyptian Sea").

Ver. 3.—"*And it went out to the south side to* (of) *Maaleh-Acrabbim*" : On the composition of the particles לְ, מִן, אֶל, see § 154, 2, *b.* "*Ma-'a-leh 'Aq-rab* bîm," "the ascent of 'Aq-rabbim," the "*scorpion pass*,"[1] between the south end of the Dead Sea and Zin, perhaps the steep pass *Nakb es Safâh* (Pass of the Bare Rock), by which the final step is made from the desert to the level of the actual land of Palestine (Grove, Smith's *Bib. Dict.*, i., p. 42). "*And passed along* (went across) *to Zin*": ה local (cf. Numb. xxxiv. 4). "*Qa-dhêsh-Bar-nê-'a*," see x. 41 (note). "*Chets-rôn*" (from חָצַר, to enclose), perhaps a collection of nomad-hamlets, הַצְרִים, Deut. ii. 23; site unknown. אַדָּרָה, "*to 'Addar*" (rt. אָדַר, to be wide), perhaps one of the nomad hamlets above referred to, for in the parallel passage (Numb. xxxiv. 4) this and the foregoing word are joined. It is possibly identical with the modern *Ain-el Kudeirât*, on the north side of the ridge, between Canaan and the desert (Robinson, i., p. 280). וְנָסַב, "*and turned itself*," Niph. of סָבַב. "*Towards haq-Qar-qa-'a*" (with art. and ה loc.), lit. "the low-lying flat," ἔδαφος (Symm.), not mentioned in Numb. xxxiv. 4, nor elsewhere in Scripture, but Eusebius (*Onomast.*) speaks of Ἀκαρκὰς, and calls it a village. The Sept. has κατὰ δυσμὰς Κάδης, and may have read יָמָּה קָדֵשׁ.

Ver. 4.—"*Toward 'Ats-môn*" (robust, rt. עָצַם, to be strong; see Numb. xxxiv. 5): Its site unknown, though the later Jewish Targum would identify it with Kesam, the modern Kasaimeh, a group of springs at a short distance to the west of Ain-el Kudeirât. Grove (*Bib. Dict.*) thinks it may possibly be another form of the word Heshmon (xv. 27). Eusebius and Jerome

---

[1] עַקְרָב, a scorpion. It is found in great numbers in the Jordan valley below Jericho (Von Raumer, p. 103).

mention it in the *Onomast.*, but evidently it was not actually known to them. "*The torrent* (water-course) *of Egypt*," *i.e.*, the Wady el Arish, on the confines of Egypt and Palestine, which empties itself into the Mediterranean. "*And the goings out of the boundary were to the sea*": ם׳ here means the Mediterranean. For the sing. הָיָה, with a plural noun, see § 147, *a*, and cf. xi. 22. The last words of the verse, "*this shall be your southern boundary*," refer to Numb. xxxiv. 2-5, and show that the southern boundary of Judah was also that of the land promised to the Israelites.

Ver. 5 *a* (*The Eastern Boundary*).—This was the whole length of the Salt Sea to the end (*i.e.*, the mouth) of the Jordan. קְצֵה, "the extreme edge or end," from קָצָה, "to cut off the end," here denoting the point of junction with the Dead Sea.

Ver. 5 *b*-11 (*The Northern Boundary*).—"*And the boundary of the side northwards* (was) *from the tongue of the* (salt) *sea from the extremity* (*i.e.*, the mouth) *of Jordan.*" The northern boundary of Judah corresponded with the southern boundary of Benjamin, traced in the opposite direction (xviii. 15-19).

Ver. 6.—"*Bêth-chŏgh-lah*," "house of partridge" (Ges.): Jerome (*Onomast.*) identifies it with the threshing floor of Atad, between the Jordan and Jericho, the ruins of which are probably still to be seen at or near a magnificent spring called *Ain-Hajla* and *Kusr-Hajla* (Grove). It stood on the border of Benjamin, as well as of Judah, and was assigned to the former (xviii. 21). "*Bêth-hā-'ă-rā-bhāh*" (house of the desert plain): Doubtless so called because it lay in the wilderness (midh-bar) of Judah (ver. 61). In xviii. 18

it is simply called Arabah, and in xviii. 22 is reckoned a Benjamite city. It probably stood on the border between the two tribes; now *Kaffr Hajla*. " *The stone of Bôhan*": Perhaps erected to commemorate some exploit by a Reubenite leader in the wars of Joshua (cf. 1 Sam. vii. 12); it was on the border of Benjamin as well as of Judah (xviii. 17), and apparently on the slope of a hill, but the site unknown.

Ver. 7.—"*To D^ebhir*": Not the town mentioned in vers. 15, 49, x. 38, nor that in Gad (xiii. 26), but perhaps to be sought in the Wady Dabir, about half way between Jericho and Jerusalem (Keil). " *Valley of 'A-khôr*," vii. 24. " *And northward turning toward* (the) *Gilgal*": According to Keil, Gilgal is here the same as Geliloth in xviii. 17; but others, as Knobel, identify it with the Gilgal in iv. 19. The name Geliloth (says Grove) never occurs again in this locality, and it, therefore, seems probable that Gilgal is the right reading. Many glimpses of the Jordan valley are obtained through the hills in the latter part of the descent from Olivet to Jericho, along which the boundary in question appears to have run; and it is very possible that from the ascent of Adhummim, Gilgal appeared through one of these gaps in the distance, over against the spectator, and thus furnished a point by which to indicate the direction of the line at that part " (Art. in Smith's *Bib. Dic.*, vol. i., p. 661). " *Which* (is) *over against the ascent of 'Adhummîm*": Probably the Pass of Jericho, leading up from the Jordan valley to Jerusalem. According to Jerome (*Onom.*) " A-dhum-mim " (red places) alludes to the blood shed there by robbers, or according to Stanley (*Sin. and Pal.*, 424, note 4) to the red colour of the hair of some Arab tribe which infested the pass (cf. Sept. ἀνάβασις πύρρων). Here was the scene of the parable of the good Samaritan (Stanley, *Sin. and Pal.*, 424; Trench *On Par.*, p. 307-8); and the defence of travellers through this pass led to the establishment of the Order of the Templars, A.D. 1118 (Wilke's *Hist.*, p. 9). Keil supposes that the name refers to the red colour of the rocks, but Dean Stanley says, "There are no red rocks, as some have fancied, in order to make out a derivation. The whole pass is white limestone" (*Sin. and Pal.*, p. 424, note 4). "*On the south side of the watercourse*": Now the gorge of the *Wady Kelt* (Robinson, *Bib. Res.*, i., p. 558). "'*Ên-she-mesh*" (fountain of the sun): About a mile below Bethany, on the road to Jericho, now perhaps *Ain-Haud* or *Ain-Chôt*, "the well of the apostles." The aspect of Ain-Haud is such that the rays of the sun are on it the whole day (Grove). '*Ên-rôghel*, "fountain of the fuller," rt. רָגַל, to tread : Probably now "the fountain of the Virgin," near the walls of Jerusalem, which supplies the pool of Siloam (Dr. Bonar's *Land of Promise*, App. v.). Here Jonathan and Ahimaaz concealed themselves after the rebellion of Absalom, in order to gain news for David (2 Sam. xvii. 17), and near it Adonijah held his feast (1 Kings i. 9). Keil, after Robinson and others, identifies it with the well of Job or Nehemiah, at the south-east corner of Jerusalem, where the valleys of Hinnom and Kedron unite ; but see forcible reasons against this view in the work of Dr. Bonar, above referred to, quoted by Grove (Art. *Bib. Dic.*, i., p. 558).

Ver. 8.—"*And the border went up into the ravine of the son of Hinnom*": This ravine[1] is first mentioned here, and next in xviii. 16; written "ravine of the sons of Hinnom" (2 Kings xxiii. 10; Jer. xix. 2, etc.), and "ravine of Hinnom" (Neh. xi. 30). It surrounded Jerusalem on the south and west. Stanley supposes that it derived its name from Hinnom, an ancient hero who encamped in it (*Sin. and Pal.*, p. 172); but Hitzig and Böttcher regard Hinnom as an appellative = "moaning," "wailing," in allusion to the cries of the innocent victims there offered to Moloch, and to the drums beaten to drown those cries. Tophet, at the south-east of the ravine, was the scene of those sacrifices (2 Chron. xxviii. 3, xxxiii. 6), and was defiled by Josiah (2 Kings xxiii. 10). The later Jews applied the name to the place of torment, hence γέεννα (גֵּי הִנֹּם, Matt. v. 22).[2] "*To the side* (lit. shoulder) *of the Jebusite on the south*": The Gentile noun יְבוּסִי is either put ellip. for עִיר הַיְבוּסִי (Judges xix. 11), or the name of the tribe is mentioned instead of the city. The word occurs again in xviii. 16, 28, where it is rendered, "Jebusi" in the Auth. Vers. "*And the border went up to the summit of the mountain, which* (lieth) *before the ravine of Hinnom westward, which* (is) *at the end of the valley of Rephaim northward*": הַר here denotes, not one particular mountain, but a rocky ridge curving westward on the left side of the road to Joppa (Keil; cf. Robinson, *Bib. Res.*, i., 219). On

---

[1] גַּי, see note, viii. 1.
[2] Compare Milton's *Paradise Lost*, i., 39, 2 ver., "First, Moloch, horrid king, etc.," to ver. 405.

עֵמֶק see note vii. 24. This valley, or valley-plain, of Rephaim was on the west of Jerusalem, and extended as far south as Bethlehem (Joseph., *Antiq.*, vii., c. 12, § 4), but at its northern extremity was separated from the ravine of Hinnom by a mountain ridge. It was famous for the victories of David over the Philistines (2 Sam. v. 18, 22, xxiii. 13). The Rephaim were an ancient and gigantic tribe (Gen. xiv. 5).

Ver. 9.—תָּאַר, "*was marked out*," or "*was described*" (Ges., *Lex.*), cogn. to הוּר, to go round, whence תֹּאַר, form, outline. מַעְיָן, lit. "a place watered by springs," but here=עַיִן, a fountain (cf. Gen. vii. 11, viii. 2). "*The waters of Nephtôach*" ("opening," rt. פָּתַח, to open), a spring mentioned here and in xviii. 15 only; now probably *Ain-Lifta*, in a short valley which runs into the east side of the great Wady Beit Hanina two and a half miles north-west of Jerusalem (Van de Velde, *Memoir*). The name *Lifta* is not less suitable to this identification than its situation, since "N" and "L" frequently take the place of each other, and the rest of the word is almost entirely unchanged (Art. by Grove in Dr. Smith's *Bib. Dict.*).[1] "*Mount Ephron*," not mentioned elsewhere; probably the range of hills on the west side of the Wady Beit Hanina (traditional valley of the Terebinth), opposite Lifta, which stands on the east side (Grove). "*Baalah, which* (is) *Kirjath-jearim*" (Auth. Vers.). See note on ix. 17. It seems that Baalah (mistress) was the

---

[1] According, however, to Lieut. Conder's proposed alteration of the boundary line of Judah, Nephtoach is made identical with the spring '*Aîn*, the Talmudic Etam, near the pools of Solomon, south of Bethlehem (Map, sheet xvii).

early or Canaanitish name (cf. xviii. 28, "Jebusi, which (is) Jerusalem ").

Ver. 10.—וְנָסַב, cf. ver. 3. "*Mount Sê-'îr* (hairy, rough) ;" not that in Edom (xi. 17, xii. 7, xxiv. 4), but a shaggy or rugged mountain ridge running south-west of Kirjath-jearim. The name may have been derived from an ancient incursion of the Edomites into these parts. "*Mount Y^e'a-rîm*"[1] (mount of forests) : Possibly the ridge separating Wady Ghuzab from Wady Ismail (Grove). "*K^esa-lôn*" (" firm confidence," Ges.; or rather, from כֶּסֶל, in reference to the "loins" of the mountain), a town apparently on the shoulder (side) of mount Yearîm, probably *Kesla*, eight miles west of Jerusalem (Grove, Bib. Dic.). "*Bêth-shemesh*" (house of the sun), called "'Ir-shemesh" xix. 41, when it had afterwards been assigned to Dan, on whose border it stood ; one of the cities allotted to the priests (xxi. 16). For its further history see 1 Sam. vi. 9, etc. ; 1 Kings iv. 9 ; 2 Kings xiv. 11 ; 2 Chron. xxviii. 18 ; now called *Ain-Shems*, on the north-west slopes of the mountains of Judah, "a low plateau at the junction of two fine plains" (Rob., iii., 152), about two miles from the great Philistine plain, and seven from Ekron (ii., 224-6). "*Timnah*" ("a part assigned," rt. מָנָה, to divide, Ges., unless the word rather refers to some natural feature of the country, Grove), written also Timnathah (xix. 43) and Timnath ; assigned to Dan (xix. 43), and thence Samson fetched his wife (Judges xiv. 1), probably distinct from the Timnath in Gen.

---

[1] יַעַר means a wood of some extent, a forest, as distinguished from חֹרֶשׁ, a thicket.

xxxviii. 12, which may have been identical with the Timnah in Josh. xv. 57, in the mountains of Judah; now perhaps *Tibneh*, at the mouth of Wady Surar two miles west of Ain-Shems (Beth-shemesh) (Rob., *Pal.*, i., p. 344; Grove).

Ver. 11.—Here the border follows a north-western course. "*'Eq-rôn*," see on xiii. 3. "*Shik-k^erôn*" (drunkenness, from שָׁכַר, to drink to the full), on the north-west border of Judah, probably between 'Eqron (Akir) and Yabhneel (Yebna), see Smith's *Bib. Dic.*, iii., p. 1273), or perhaps the modern Sugheir, about three miles south of Yabhneel (Tobler and Knobel). Because the word in Hebrew means drunkenness, Simonis (*Onomast. V.T.*, p. 348, coll. p. 209) conjectured that the locality abounded with vines. "*Mount Ba'alah*": Mentioned here only; the name must have been given to one of the ranges near the coast, in the vicinity of Yebna. "*Yabh-n^e-'êl*" ("may God cause to be built"), called Yabneh in 2 Chron. xxvi. 6, where Uzziah is said to have taken it from the Philistines, and to have destroyed its fortifications; also Jamnia in 1 Macc. iv. 15, v. 58, etc., and in Joseph., *Antiq.*, v., 1, § 22, xii. 8, § 6. Once famous as a school of Jewish learning, and the seat of the sanhedrim after the fall of Jerusalem (Philo, *Op.*, ii., p. 575); now *Yebna*, or, more accurately, *Ibna* (Grove), about two miles from the coast, and eleven miles south of Joppa. Its ruins stand on the edge of the Nahr Rubin, along which ran the boundary line between Judah and Benjamin towards the coast (Robinson, *Bib. Res.*, ii., 227, Another town of the same name is mentioned in xix. 33.

Ver. 12.—"*And the west border* (was) *to* (or *at*) *the great sea* (*i.e.* the Mediterranean) *and the adjoining territory* (thereof)." On וּגְבוּל in the last clause see xiii. 23.

VERS. 13-20.—*Inheritance of Caleb.*

This narrative, though involving a repetition of xiv. 6-15, is properly inserted here, because Caleb's inheritance was included in the territory assigned by lot to Judah, and it was fit that it should be mentioned before the enumeration of the cities of Judah (ver. 21, etc.) commenced. As we meet with the same narrative, almost *verbatim*, in Judges i. 10-15, among the events described in that chapter as happening after the death of Joshua (ver. 1), it may have been either inserted here from the Book of Judges by a later hand, perhaps by Ezra, according to Bishop Patrick, or, according to Keil, both accounts may have been drawn from one common source. Caleb's delay in taking possession of his inheritance till after Joshua's death might be explained by his disinterestedness in preferring the public service to his own private interests; cf. a like unselfishness on Joshua's part (xix. 50, note).

Ver. 13.—"*He gave*": The nominative is not expressed in the Hebrew, and is either, therefore, "Joshua," or the verb is used impers. (§ 137, 3). "*A portion among* (in the midst of) *the children of Judah*": The expressions here used may imply that Caleb was a foreigner by birth, and became a proselyte (see note on xiv. 6). "*According to the commandment,*" etc.: Though that commandment is nowhere expressly recorded, it is consistent with the promise referred to in xiv. 9. "*Arba*," see xiv. 15. "*The father of Anak*," *i.e.*, the progenitor of the Anakim (see note on xi. 21).

Ver. 14.—וַיֹּרֶשׁ, Hiph. imperf. apoc. (§ 49, 2, *b*). "*And drove out*," see note on הוֹרִישׁ, iii. 10. "*Shéshay*,"[1] etc. : Probably names, not of individuals, but of three principal families of Anakim, a supposition which seems confirmed by the mention of their names here after the first mention of them in Numb. xiii. 22. At the end of the verse, יְלִידֵי הָעֲ is added as a still further definition of בְּנֵי הָעֲ, to prevent us from thinking of the actual sons of Anak.

Ver. 15.—*D͗-bhîr*, see x. 38.

Ver. 16.—וְנָתַתִּי, "*then will I give*": וְ = "*then*" in the apod., after a condit. protasis (cf. Judges iv. 8 ; Psalm lxxviii. 34 ; § 155, 1 (*d*). The perfect denotes the certain fulfilment of the promise (§ 126, 4), Sept. δώσω ; Vulg. "dabo." "'*Akh-sâh*" (an anklet or ring, worn as an ornament by women round their ankles (cf. Isa. iii. 18), mentioned also in 1 Chron. ii. 49, as Caleb's daughter, though the genealogy of Caleb in that chapter is very obscure. Cf. with Caleb's promise here that of Saul in 1 Sam. xvii. 25, xviii. 17, and that of Creon, King of Thebes, who promised his sister Jocaste in marriage to him who should destroy the Sphinx (Hygin., *Fab.* lxvii).

Ver. 17.—"*'Oth-nî-'êl*" (lion of God). "*The son of Kenaz, the brother of Caleb*": The Hebrew accent Tiphcha, after קְנַז shows that in the opinion of the Masorites the word "brother" here refers to

---

[1] The according to § 8, 5, retains its consonant power (cf. vii. 2).

Othniel; cf. the Vulg., "Othniel, filius Cenaz, frater Caleb junior;" but the Sept., Arab., and Syr. regard it as referring to Kenaz, though in Judges i. 13, iii. 9, the Sept. agrees with the other view. According to the canon of Rabbi Moses ben Nachman on Numb. x. 29, designations of this nature generally refer to the principal foregoing word; thus in Isa. xxxvii. 2 (Heb.) "*prophet*" refers not to Amon, but Isaiah (cf. Jer. xxviii. 1). "*Son of Kenaz*," probably = Kenizzite in xiv. 6. The Jewish law did not expressly prohibit marriage with a niece (see Lev. xviii. 12, xx. 19, and cf. Talmud "Jebamoth," 62a, 63b).

Ver. 18.—בְּבוֹאָהּ, "*on her entering*," into the house of Othniel to be his wife. וַתְּסִיתֵהוּ, "*then she urged him*," Hiph. of סות or סית, not used in Qal., perhaps "to be excited," whence in Hiph. "to excite." Knobel thinks that by שָׂדֶה the land belonging to Debir is meant, but that would naturally be assigned along with it, whereas the allusion is to some piece of land in the neighbourhood of Debir, plentifully supplied with water. וַתִּצְנַח, "*and she lept*" or "sprung down quickly." The dismounting was a mark of respect (cf. Gen. xxiv. 64; 1 Sam. xxv. 23). צָנַח occurs here and in Judges i. 14, iv. 21 only, in which latter place it is used of a nail, and is rendered by Gesenius "went down" (into the earth). It is hardly connected, says Keil, with צָנַע, to be lowly or humble (Ges.), but rather means primarily, according to Fürst, "to press or force oneself away," being connected with זָנַק =, in Piel, "to leap forth." Thus it corresponds here with תִּפֹּל in Gen. xxiv. 64. The Sept. καὶ ἐβόησεν ἐκ τοῦ ὄνου, and the Vulg. "suspiravitque ut sedebat in asino," may have arisen from a different reading, viz., הָיְצָק. "*What wouldest thou*" (Auth. Vers.), lit. "what is to thee?" As nothing is said about Othniel's making the request which Achsah had urged him to make,[1] we may suppose that, because he hesitated, she had determined herself to accost her father.

Ver. 19.—בְּרָכָה, "*a blessing*," Sept. εὐλογίαν (cf. 2 Cor. ix. 5), a gift expressing goodwill and affection, or offered with prayers for a blessing on the recipient (cf. Gen. xxxiii. 11; 2 Kings v. 15). אֶרֶץ הַנֶּ֫, "*a land of the south country*," evidently with allusion to its aridity, for נֶגֶב comes from נָגַב, to be dry (Syr., Chald., and Sam.), cf. Psalm cxxvi. 4, where "the south" = "a dry or barren land." נְתַתָּנִי, either the accus. suff. is used briefly for the dat. (§ 121, 4), or the verb governs two accusatives (Ewald, *Lehrb.*, § 283, b). The rendering of the Sept., Chald., Syr., and Arab., "Thou hast given me into a south land," *i.e.*, sent me thither by marriage, though followed by Michaelis, Bertheau, and others, is forced, but not ungrammatical, as אֶרֶץ הַנֶּ֫גֶב may be an accus. loci. "*Give me springs of water*," *i.e.*, a piece of land with springs of water in it (Keil). גֻּלֹּת, lit. "bubblings," from גָּלַל, to tumble or roll over, perhaps in allusion to the globular form in which springs bubble up (Stanley, *Sin. and Pal.*, p. 512), used here, and in the parallel passage (Judges i. 15), only. In Cant. iv. 12 the shorter form גַּל occurs. The Alex. Sept. renders by Γωλαθ-μαΐμ, a proper name; so Fürst. "*The upper and lower springs*," cf. Bethhoron, the "Nether" and "Upper" (xvi. 3, 5). Their site was no doubt a mountain slope, which had

---

[1] Perhaps he might have feared lest he should seem to have married Achsah from self-interested motives, *i.e.*, with a view to the dowry he might get with her.

springs both on its higher and lower ground, possibly the modern *Kurmul* (Wilton's *Negeb,* p. 16; *Speaker's Comm.*).

This liberality of Caleb to his daughter, while it teaches us that parents should make suitable provision for their children, should also remind us of those words of Christ, "If ye being evil know how to give good gifts unto your children, how much more shall your Father which is in heaven give good things to them that ask Him" (Matt. vii. 11).

VERS. 21-63.—*A List of the Towns of Judah, arranged according to the Four Districts into which their Territory was Divided, viz., those in the Negeb or South Land* (vers. 21-32); *those in the Shephelah or Lowland Plain* (vers. 33-47); *those in the Hill Country* (vers. 48-60); *and those in the Wilderness* (vers. 61, 62).

Vers. 21-32 (*The Towns in the Neghebh*[1]).—The towns in this district are arranged into four groups, the names in each group being connected by the copulative "Vav." First group of nine towns (vers. 21-23).

Ver. 21.—"*And the towns from* (*i.e.,* at) *the extremity of the tribe-territory of Judah towards the border of Edom, in the region lying towards the south were* (the following)." בַּנֶּגְבָּה, can only be rendered, as above, by a circumlocution. "*Qabh-ts^e'ēl*" (God gathers), probably the same as Jekabzeel (Neh. xi. 25), the birthplace of the hero Benaiah, a slayer of lions (2 Sam. xxiii. 20; 1 Chron. xi. 22), of which the

---

[1] See note on x. 40.

Negeb was a common haunt (Wilton's *Negeb*, p. 42, etc.). "*'E-dher*" (a flock) and "*Yâ-ghûr*" (a lodging, rt. גור, to sojourn) are both unknown; the latter name is rendered in the Sept. Ἀσώρ, and is joined by Wilton with Kinah in the following verse.

Ver. 22.—"*Qî-nâh*" (perhaps "a smithy," from קין or קנן [unused], to strike upon, to forge iron), unknown. Knobel and Stanley (*Sin. and Pal.*, p. 160) would connect the name with the Kenites, who settled in the south of Arad (Judges i. 16), but this settlement probably took place after the period here referred to. "*Dî-mô-nah*," mentioned in the *Onomasticon*, but evidently unknown to Eusebius and Jerome; perhaps the same as Dî-bhôn (" pining," rt. דוב, *i.q.* to languish), a town re-inhabited by the men of Judah after the return from captivity (Neh. xi. 25); "M" and "B," letters of the same organ, are often interchanged (§ 19, 1); possibly identical with the ruins called *el-* (or *eh-*) *Dheib* (Van de Velde, *Mem.*, 252), to the north-east of Arad. "*'Adh-'â-dhâh*" (Syr. "festival"), not mentioned in the *Onomasticon* of Eusebius; perhaps Sudeid (Robinson).

Ver. 23.—"*Qe-dhesh*" (sanctuary), possibly the same as Qâ-dhesh-Bar-nê-'a (ver. 3, Keil). "*Châ-tsôr*" ("enclosed"), mentioned nowhere else, and unknown (Rob., ii., 34, note). Another of the same name in Naphtali (xi. 1). The Vat. Sept. joins it with the following word, and the Alex. MSS. omit it altogether. "*Yith-nân*" ("strong place," rt. יתן, to be firm, stable), probably on the borders of the desert, if not actually in it, but no trace of it yet discovered. The word is joined by the Alex. MSS. of the Sept. with Ziph in the next verse.

Ver. 24, 25 (*Second Group of Five or Six Towns*).
—Ver. 24.—"*Zîph*" (perhaps "refining-place," rt. זוף,
in Arab. "to become liquid"), omitted in the Vat.
Sept., and, therefore, thought by Wilton (*Negeb*, 85) to
be an interpolation, but found in the Alex. and Peshito
(Zib); perhaps now *Kuseifeh* (Knobel; Rob., *Pal.*, ii.,
191, 195), south-west of Arad. "*Te-lem*" (oppression,
rt. טָלַם, to oppress), unknown. Kimchi, Raumer, and
others, would identify it with Telaim ("young lambs,"
rt. טָלָה, to be fresh [unused], 1 Sam. xv. 4), though this
latter word could have been more easily corrupted
into the former than *vice versâ*. Possibly now *el-
Kuseir*, a spot in the Negeb, occupied by the Arab
tribe Dhullâm (Wilton, *Negeb*, p. 85-9). "*Be'alôth*"
(ladies, mistresses), probably the same as Baalath-
Beer, the Ramath of the south, assigned to the
Simeonites (xix. 8), and called simply Baal (1 Chron.
iv. 33), and South Ramoth (1 Sam. xxx. 27).
Knobel and Wilton (*Negeb*, pp. 91, 92) would identify
it with the modern *Kurnub*.

Ver. 25.—"*Châ-tsôr-ch^a-dhat-tah*" (New Chatsor),
probably so called to distinguish it from the Chatsor
in ver. 23. The conjunctive accent under Chatsor in
the Hebrew text, and the absence of the copulative
ו, authorise this rendering; Vulg. "Asor nova"; but
omitted by Sept. Some identify it with el-Hu-
dhairah on the south of Jebel Khulil (Rob., *Bib. Res.*,
i., p. 151; Keil). *Q^erî-yôth* (cities, hamlets): This
word has in the Hebrew a great distinctive accent,
which is some authority for its being regarded by our
Auth. Vers. as the name of a separate city; but,
on the other hand, there is no copulative "Vav"
between it and the following word, and with this

latter it is connected by the Sept. (αἱ πόλεις Ἀσερών), the Syr., and by Reland, Maurer, Keil, and others; the proper rendering, therefore, probably is, "*Q'ri-yôth-Chets-rôn, which is Cha-tsôr.*" The latter name, meaning "an enclosure," or "hamlet," may have been the original name, which, when the place was taken by the Anakim and fortified, was changed to Q^eri-yôth, and afterwards by the tribe of Judah to Q^eri-yôth-Chets-rôn, in honour of their ancestor, Chets-rôn (Gen. xlvi. 12; Ruth iv. 18). Possibly now *el-Kuryetein*, south of Hebron (Rob., *Bib. Res.*, ii., 101; Wilton, *Negeb*, pp. 100-106). The name Ἰσκαριώτης (Matt. x. 4) is thought by some to mean אִישׁ קְרִיּוֹת.

Vers. 26-28 (*Third Group of Nine Towns*).— Ver. 26.—"*A-mâm*" (gathering-place), in the south of Judah, but quite unknown. "*Sh^emâ'*" (fame, repute): Probably the same as Sheba, in xix. 2 (where, as here, it precedes Moladah), the labials "M" and "B" being often interchanged (cf. ver. 22). Mô-la-dhah (birth), a town afterwards given to the tribe of Simeon (xix. 2; 1 Chron. iv. 28), inhabited after the captivity by the children of Judah (Neh. xi. 26), and perhaps identical with Malatha, mentioned by Josephus as an Idumæan fortress (*Antiq.*, xviii., 6, 2). Now probably the ruins of *el-Milh*, seventeen or eighteen Roman miles south of Hebron (Rob., *Bib. Res.*, ii., 201-2; Wilton, p. 109, etc.).

Ver. 27.—"*Ch^atsar-Gaddah*" (village of good fortune). Some think that Jurrah, near Moladah (el-Milh), is the modern site. "*Chesh-môn*" (fatness, fat soil, rt. חָשַׁם, to be fat), possibly identical with Atsmon, one of the landmarks of the southern boundary of Judah (Numb. xxxiv. 4 ; Grove), or with Chashmonah (Numb. xxxiii. 29), lying beyond the natural frontier of the Holy Land in the extreme north of the wilderness. "*Bêth-pa-let*" (*pā* in pause for *pĕ* ; "house of escape"), mentioned with Moladah in Neh. xi. 26 as still inhabited by Judæans.

Ver. 28.—"*Cheₐtsar-shû-'al*" (fox, or jackal, village[1]), given up to Simeon (xix. 3), and after the captivity inhabited by the children of Judah (Neh. xi. 27). Perhaps "*Saweh*," in Van de Velde's *Map* (1858), may mark the site, and be a corruption of the original name (Grove). "*Beʾêr-she-bhaʿ*" (well of the oath ;[2] see Gen. xxi. 14, 31, xxii. 19), mentioned in Judges xx. 1 ; 2 Sam. xvii. 11, as on the southern frontier of Palestine ; given to the Simeonites (xix. 2), but in 1 Kings xix. 3 said to belong to Judah, the Simeonites being at that time absorbed into Judah ; after the captivity still inhabited (Neh. xi. 27). It was in the Wady es Seba, a wide watercourse, twelve miles south of Hebron, where there are still relics of an ancient town, called *Bir-es-Seba*, with two deep wells (Rob., *Bib. Res.*, i., p. 204 ; Wilton, p. 141) ; said by Jerome to have been extant in his day (Qu. ad Gen., xxi. 31). "*Biz-yô-thʿyah*" (contempt of Jehovah), site unknown.

---

[1] Doubtless so called because those animals abounded in the neighbourhood.

[2] Or, "well of seven," the compact between Abraham and Abimelech having been ratified by the setting apart of seven ewe lambs (Gen. xxi. 28).

[3] So Gesenius (*Lex.*), who seems to regard the final syllable יָה as = יָהּ; so in the forms דְּרִידָה (2 Sam. xii. 25); מַאְפֵּלְיָה (Jer. ii. 31) ; חֲנַנְיָה, עֲנָתֹתִיָּה (1 Chron. viii. 24); יַעֲרֵשְׁיָה (ver. 27). Perhaps, however, יָ in these instances merely intensifies the form of the word.

Vers. 29-32 (*Fourth Group of Thirteen Towns in the West Portion of the Negeb*).—Ver. 29.—" *Ba-'a-lah,*" afterwards assigned to the Simeonites (xix. 3, where it is called Balah, but Bilhah 1 Chron. iv. 29); identified by Knobel, Wilton, and others, with the present *Deir-el-Belah*, near Gaza. "*'I-yîm*" (ruinous heaps, rt. עָוָה, to overturn), not known; the same name was given to a city of the Moabites (Numb. xxxiii. 45). "*'A-tsem*" (firmness, strength), in pause for 'E-tsem (1 Chron. iv. 29); afterwards assigned to the Simeonites (xix. 3; 1 Chron. iv. 29). Wilton (*Negeb*, p. 156, etc.) somewhat arbitrarily connects this word with the foregoing, and traces the compound name Ije-Azem in the modern *el-Aujeh*, a spot covered with ruins, near the Wady-el-Ain, in the country of the Azazimeh Arabs, whose name resembles Azem.

Ver. 30.—"*'El-tô-ladh*" ("whose posterity is from God"). 'El is either the Arab. article, or means "God;" written Toladh (1 Chron. iv. 29), the first part of a compound word being often omitted for brevity, cf. שָׁלֵם for יְרוּשָׁלַם (Psalm lxxvi. 3), שָׁנִים for אֲבֶל הַשָּׁנִים, but supposed by Wilton to be near the Wady-el-Thoula, in the extreme south of the Negeb, not far from the western extremity of the Jebel-el-Mukreh. He thinks that Isaac was born there, and that it was named after that great event. (*The Negeb,* p. 180.) "*K^esîl*" (fool, impious), rt. כָּסַל, to be fleshy, fat, applied in a bad sense to languor and inertness, and hence to folly (Ges., *Lex.*, 3), Sept. Βαιθήλ, and, therefore, perhaps the same as Bethul (xix. 4), and Bethuel (1 Chron. iv. 30), and identical with the Bethel of 1 Sam. xxx. 27, and, therefore, not far from Ziglag. The place may have been called K^esil (fool) by the Israelites, because it had been a seat of idolatry, perhaps of the worship of Orion (which Kᵉsîl means in Job xxxviii. 31 ; Amos v. 8), and they may have changed its name to Bethel (the house of God), as the name of the Bethel in Benjamin was changed to Beth-aven (Hosea iv. 15). Probably now *el Khulasah*, the same as the Elusa of ecclesiastical writers, about fifteen miles south-west of Beersheba (Rob., *Bib. Res.*, i., 202). Jerome, in the fourth century, states that there was here a temple of Venus Astarte, where Lucifer, the morning star, was worshipped by the Saracens (*Vit. Hilarion*, c. 25). "*Chor-mah*," see on xii. 14.

Ver. 31.—"*Tsiq-lagh*," written צִיקְלַג in 1 Chron. xii. 1, 20, perhaps from קָלַק צִי, "wilderness of destruction" (Ges.),[1] eventually assigned to Simeon (xix. 5) ; recovered by the Philistines, and given by the King of Gath to David, in whose family it permanently remained (1 Sam. xxvii. 6 ; Joseph., *Antiq.*, vi., 13, 10) ; burnt by the Amalekites (1 Sam. xxx. 1) ; after the captivity inhabited by the people of Judah (Neh. xi. 28). The site unknown, but it appears from 1 Sam. xxx. 9, 10, 21, to have been north of the brook Besor. Kiepert, in his *Map*, places it about twenty miles south-east of Beersheba, and nearly fifty from Gath, on the edge of the desert. "*Madhman-nah*" (dunghill, rt. דָּמַן, unused, Arab., to dung), not to be confounded, as in the *Onom.* (*s.v.* Mademena), with Madmena in Isa. x. 31, which was north of Jerusalem, but probably identical with Menoïs, now *el-Minyây*, on the caravan route south of Gaza. So

---

[1] Simonis derives it from יָצִיק בַּל, an outflowing of a fountain

Keil and Robinson, and Kiepert (*Map*, 1856). This, and the next place "*Sansannah*" (palm-branch), are supposed by Reland, Keil, and others, to correspond with "*Bêth-ham-mar-ka-bhôth*" (house of the chariots) and "*Ch^atsar-sûsah*" (horse village) in xix. 5, 1 Chron. iv. 31, names which indicate that the places so called were stations or depôts for horses and chariots, probably on the road between Egypt and Palestine (Stanley, *Sin. and Pal.*, p. 160), by which the eunuch of Candace was returning to Egypt when overtaken by Philip (Wilton). They are perhaps rightly identified with the modern Minyay and Wady-es-Suny, on the caravan route south of Gaza. More recently it has been supposed by Lieut. Conder that possibly Madmannah may be identical with the ruin *Umm Deimneh*, north of Beersheba (*Pal. Explor. Fund Map*, sheet xxiv.).

Ver. 32.—"*L^ebha-'ôth*," called Bêth-l^ebha-'ôth (house of lionesses, xix. 6), and Bêth-bir-'î ("house of my creation" [perhaps a corrupted form] 1 Chron. iv. 31): The word indicates that the south of Judah was the resort of lions. Site uncertain, though Lebben, the first station between Gaza and Egypt, bears a resemblance to the name. Wilton, with less likelihood, places it at el-Bey-udh, near Mesada or the Dead Sea. "*Shil-chîm*" (armed men), written by A. V. *Sharuhen*[1] (xix. 6) and Shaaraim (1 Chron. iv. 31), supposed by Van de Velde to be *Tell-Sheriah*, between Gaza and Beersheba, but by Wilton to be el-Bircin, near Wady-es-Serum, much further to the

---

[1] Heb. Sha-rú-chēn, "dwelling of grace," or "pleasant lodging-place;" for חֵן שָׁרוּת, see שָׁרָא, Chald. to loose, specially used of those who turn aside at evening to an inn and loose the burdens of their beasts; hence "to lodge" (Ges., *Lex.*).

south, and not far to the north-west of Kadesh-Barnea. It is not mentioned by Eusebius and Jerome. "*'A-yin*" (a fountain[1]), and "*Rim-môn*" (a pomegranate) occur among the cities of the Simeonites (xix. 7 ; 1 Chron. iv. 32), but without a connecting "Vav," though they are evidently reckoned as separate cities. Perhaps being close together, they afterwards became one city (cf. the modern Mezières-Charleville), for after the captivity we find the name "En-Rimmon" in Neh. xi. 29. The fertility of the situation seems indicated by the meaning of the word, viz., "Fountain of the pomegranates." Rimmon is supposed to be identical with *Um-er-Rumamim, i.e.,* "mother of pomegranates," about ten miles north of Beersheba. "*All the cities are twenty and nine.*" In the Hebrew they are thirty-six, reckoning two only in ver. 25 (see note). Of this discrepancy the best solution perhaps is that of Keil, viz., that the number nine is the error of some early copyist, who misread the Hebrew numeral letters ; see a similar error in xix. 15, 38. The Syrian version reads thirty-six. In this once populous district there is now only desolation, the waters once supplied by the rains having been allowed to go to waste.

Vers. 33-47 (*Towns in the Lowland or Shephelah*).—These are arranged in four groups, of which the first (vers. 33-36) contains fourteen towns, situated in the north-east portion of the shephelah.

---

[1] Properly, an eye, "the spring in an Eastern country being the eye of the landscape" (Stanley, *Sin. and Pal.*, p. 509). Many towns and places in Palestine are formed or compounded of this Hebrew word, as is natural from the importance of living springs in the East (*id.*).

Ver. 33.—בַּשְּׁפֵלָה, see on ix. 1; it here includes the foot-hills sloping off gradually into the lowland (x. 40). *'Esh-tā-'ôl* (perhaps "petition, request," as if infinitive Hithp. of an Arab. form from the rt. שָׁאַל [Ges.]), and *Tsŏr-'ah* (place of hornets)[1] were border-towns between Judah and Dan, and were afterwards assigned to Dan (xix. 41); the former is now perhaps *Kustul*, east of Kuriet el-Enab (Kirjath-jearim [Grove]); the latter, which was the native place of Samson (Judges xiii. 2), fortified by Rehoboam (2 Chron. xi. 10), and re-inhabited by the Jews after the captivity (Neh. xi. 9), is mentioned by Eusebius and Jerome (*Onomast.*) as ten Roman miles from Eleutheropolis, on the way to Nicopolis, and is probably now *Sûrah*, at the head of Wady Sûrah (Robinson, Grove). Between Tsorah and Eshtaol was the Danish camp (Judges xiii. 25), and the burial-place of Samson (Judges xvi. 31). "*'Ash-nah*" (strong, rt. אָשֵׁן, to be hard, strong), probably north-west of Jerusalem, but unknown. Another town of the same name is mentioned in ver. 43.

Ver. 34.—"*Za-nô-ach*" (perhaps "a marshy place" [Ges.], from זָנַח, "to have an offensive smell"), now *Zânûa*, not far from Surah towards the east, and on the side of the Wady Ismail (Grove); it was reoccupied by the people of Judah after the captivity (Neh. xi. 30). The other Zanoach on the mountains (ver. 56) is unknown. "*'Ên-gan-nîm*" (fountain of gardens), apparently the present ruin *Umm Jîna* (Lieut. Conder, *Pal. Explor. Fund*). "*Tap-pû-ach*" ("a place fruitful in apples"), not to be confounded with the Beth-Tappuach near Hebron (ver. 53), but situated on the

---
[1] The name seems to imply that hornets infested that part of the country.

lower slopes of the mountains of the north-west portion of Judah, about twelve miles west of Jerusalem (Grove). "*ha-'Ê-nam*," contract. for *ha-'Ê-na-yim* (the two fountains), probably the same as Enayim (Gen. xxxviii. 14), which was on the road from Adullam to Timnath.

Ver. 35.—"*Yarmûth*," see x. 3. "*'A-dhul-lam*," xii. 15. "*Sô-khôh*" (hedge), near to Ephesdammim, where the combat between David and Goliath took place (1 Sam. xvii. 1); fortified by Rehoboam (2 Chron. xi. 7), and taken by the Philistines in the reign of Ahaz (2 Chron. xxviii. 18). It is mentioned in the *Onomast.* under the name Soccoth, and described as two villages, an upper and lower, on the road to Jerusalem, about eight or nine miles from Eleutheropolis. Robinson (*Bib. Res.*, ii. 21) identifies it with *esh-Shuweikeh*, on the southern slope of Wady es-Sumt (probably the valley of Elah, the scene of Goliath's death), a mile south-west of Yarmuth. *'A-zê-qah*, see x. 10: Though it seems to have been to the north of the shephelah, near Beth-horon, yet Eusebius and Jerome speak of it as lying between ($\dot{\alpha}\nu\dot{\alpha}$ $\mu\acute{\epsilon}\sigma o\nu$) Eleutheropolis and Jerusalem, *i.e.*, farther south, and in the mountains of Judah; but perhaps, like Sokhoh, Apheq, etc., there was more than one place of the same name (Grove).

Ver. 36.—"*Sha-'a-ra-yim*" (two gates), mentioned in connection with the defeat of the Philistines after the death of Goliath (1 Sam. xvii. 52); it was westward of Sokhoh, and perhaps identical with Tell-Zacharia on Wady es-Sumt (Rob., *Bib. Res.*, ii., 16). "*'A-dhî-tha-yim*" (twofold ornament), unknown. "*hag-G^edhê-rah*" (the sheepcote), apparently in the east part of the shephelah, because Azeqah, Sokhoh, etc., are mentioned just before (ver. 35); perhaps the same as the Gederoth taken by the Philistines from Ahaz (2 Chron. xxviii. 18), (so Keil), and as the Gedrus of the *Onomast.*, situated ten Roman miles south of Diospolis (Lydda), and identified by Lieut. Conder with the present ruin *Jedireh* (*Pal. Explor. Fund, Map*, sheet xvi). Grove thinks that the Hebrew word here with the art. indicates a sheep-breeding locality. So the following word G^edhê-rô-tha-yim (two sheepfolds) is connected by the Sept. with the preceding, and rendered αἱ ἐπαύλεις αὐτῆς. "*Fourteen cities*": The correct number is fifteen, but the discrepancy may be explained as in ver. 32, or G^edhêrothayim may be taken as synonymous with Gederah (Kimchi, and margin of Auth. Vers.).

Vers. 37-41 (*Second Group, containing the Towns in the Middle Portion of the Shephelah*).—Ver. 37.— "*Ts^enân*," probably the same as Tsa-'a-nân (place of flocks, Micah i. 11), supposed by Knobel to be the ruins of *Chirbet-es-Senat*, a little north of Beit-jibrin (Eleutheropolis). "*Ch^adha-shah*" (new): According to the Talmud the smallest city in Judæa, having only fifty houses, perhaps the same as the *Adasa* of 1 Macc. vii. 40, 45, a day's journey from Gazera (Gezer), and thirty stadia from Bethhoron (Joseph., *Antiq.*, xii. 10, § 5), but the site unknown (Grove). "*Migh-dal-Gadh*" (tower of Gad), unknown, though perhaps *Mejdel*, two miles west of Ascalon (Grove).

Ver. 38.—"*Dil-'an*" (cucumber-field), possibly *Tina*, about three miles north of Tell-es-Safieh, in the maritime plain of Philistia, south of Ekron (Van de Velde, ii., 160). "*ham-Mits-peh*" (the lofty place) a name given to many places (see xi. 3). It stood, according to the *Onomast.*, north of Eleutheropolis, and may be identical with the present *Tell-es-Sâfiyeh*, the Blanche-garde of the crusaders (Van de Velde, Grove). "*Yoq-the'él*" ("subdued by God," for יְקַתְּהָ אֵל, from rt. קָתָה, to serve), probably near to Lakhish, but undiscovered. Possibly the ruins *Keitulaneh* in that neighbourhood (Robinson, iii., App. 126).

Ver. 39.—On *La-khîsh* and *'Egh-lôn* see x. 3; near to them was "*Bots-qath*" ("swelling ground," rt. בָּצֵק, to swell up), the birthplace of the mother of Josiah (2 Kings xxii. 1, where it is written Boscath in Auth. Vers.) ; site unknown.

Ver. 40.—"*Kab-bôn*" ("a bond," rt. כָּבַד, to bind), perhaps the ruins called *Kubeibeh*, about ten miles south of 'Eghlon, and once a strong fortification and key to the mountainous passes (Van de Velde), whence probably the name. "*Lach-mas*," Sept. Λαμᾶς, Vulg. Leheman : Thirty-two copies have לְחָמִים, and here A. V. "Lahmam." It is not mentioned in the *Onomasticon ;* perhaps now the ruined site called *el-Lahem*, discovered by Tobler (*Dritte Wanderung*, p. 129), a little south of Beit-jibrin. "*Kith-lîsh*" (probably contracted from כְּתָל = בֹּתֶל, a wall, perhaps as made of compacted clay (Cant. ii. 9), and אִישׁ (Ges., *Lex.*), not mentioned by Eusebius and Jerome, nor yet discovered by any later traveller. Possibly to be found in *Tell-Chilchis*, S.S.E. of Beit-jibrin (Van de Velde, *Res.*, ii., p. 157; Keil).

Ver. 41.—"*Gᵉdhê-rôth*" (folds), apparently not that referred to in ver. 36, but in the middle portion of the lowland (see Keil). Lieut. Conder suggests the present village *Katrah*, near Yebnah, as proposed also by Col. Warren, R.E. (*Map*, sheet xvi.). "*Běth-Daghôn*" (house of Dagon), according to Clark's *Bib. Atlas* between Joppa and Lydda; perhaps the *Beth-dedshan* visited by Tobler on his fourth journey. Another town of the same name was on the border of Asher (xix. 27). "*Na-à-mah*" (pleasant) : Probably *Na'ăneh*, south of Ramleh,[1] as proposed by Col. Warren, R.E. The situation is suitable (Lieut. Conder, R.E., *Map*, sheet xvi.). "*Maq-qè-dhah*," see on x. 10.

Vers. 42-44 (*Third Group in the South of the Shephelah*).—Ver. 42.—"*Libh-nah*," x. 29. "'*E-ther*" (abundance) and "'*A-shan*" (smoke) were afterwards given to the Simeonites (xix. 7). The former may be the same as Tochen in 1 Chron. iv. 32, and is mentioned twice by Eusebius (*Onomast.*), who also confuses it with Yattir (ver. 48). The name has not yet been certainly identified with any existing remains, but Van de Velde heard of a *Tel-Athar* in this direction (Grove, Smith's *Bib. Dict.*, vol. i.), and more recently Lieut. Conder has suggested the ruin *el'Atr*, near Beit Jibrin, on the west, as a satisfactory situation. '*Ashan* is perhaps identical with *Kor-'ashan* (1 Sam. xxx. 30), and with '*Ayin* (Josh. xxi. 16); it was one of the cities of the priests (1 Chron. vi. 59), in the south of Judah, on the border of the Negeb (Grove).

Ver. 43.—"*Yiph-tach*" (he will open), "'*Ash-nah*" (cf. ver. 33), and "*Netsîbh*" (garrison, or station) have not been discovered. In the *Onomast.* a "Neesib" is mentioned as seven or nine miles east of Eleutheropolis (Beit-jibrin), between that city and Hebron, and

---

[1] Marked in Arrowsmith's *Map of Modern Syria* (Southern) as lying to the north-east of Yebna, and south-east of Jaffa, in what was afterwards the territory of Dan.

now called Beit-Nûsib, on the Wady es Sûr. This position, however, is among the mountains, rather than in the shephelah.

Ver. 44.—"*Q'î-lah*" (fortress); probably near to the borders of the Philistines (see 1 Sam. xxiii. 1); mentioned after the captivity (Neh. iii. 17).[1] Eusebius and Jerome describe it in the *Onomast.* as existing under the name Κηλά or Ceila, the present *Kila*, about eight Roman miles to the east of Eleutheropolis, on the road to Hebron; but this position, like that of Beit-Nûsib (ver. 43) is among the mountains of Judah, and not in the shephelah, and, therefore, is properly rejected by Keil (*Comment. in loc.*). "*Akh-zîbh*" (deceit, Micah i. 14), perhaps identical with K^ezîbh (Gen. xxxviii. 5). The ruins of *Kussâbeh*, or Kesâba, a place with a fountain about five hours south-west of Beit-jibrin, may mark the site (Rob., ii., 391). "*Ma-rê-shah*" (chief city, *i.q.*, מַרְאֵיָה, "that which is at the head"), one of the cities fortified by Rehoboam (2 Chron. xi. 8); near it Asa defeated the Ethiopians (2 Chron. xiv. 9); mentioned in the Maccabean wars (1 Macc. v. 66), and by Josephus (*Antiq.*, xii., 8, § 6, xiv., 4, § 4); destroyed by the Parthians B.C. 39 (*Antiq.*, xiv., 13, § 9). In the fourth century Eusebius and Jerome (*Onomast., s.v.* "Masera") mention its ruins as lying two Roman miles from Eleutheropolis (Beit-jibrin), and which appear to correspond with the *Marash*, discovered by Robinson S.S.W. of Beit-jibrin (*Bib. Res.*, ii., 67, 68). So Tobler, Van de Velde, and Grove.

---

[1] According to Geikie (on 1 Sam. xxiii. 2) it was a town on a steep hill, overlooking the valley of Elah, or the Terebinth, a short way south of Horeth and Adullam (*Hours with the Bible*, vol. iii.).

Vers. 45-47 (*Fourth Group: The Towns on the Philistine Coast*).—Ver. 45.—"*'Eq-rôn*," see on xiii. 3. "*Her daughters*," i.e., her smaller towns, dependent on 'Eqrôn, the capital, and distinct from the חֲצֵרִים, enclosures, or pastoral villages.

Ver. 46.—וָיָמָּה, "*and westwards*." עַל־יַד, "*upon the side of*." "*'Ash-dôdh*," see xi. 22.

Ver. 47.—"*'Az-zah*," see x. 41. נַחַל־מִצְ׳, cf. ver. 4. For הַגְּבוּל should be read the Qᵉri הַגְּדוּל, which is found in the ancient versions, and in more than fifty MSS. גְּבוּל, see on xiii. 23. Note that Gath (xi. 22) and 'Eshqelôn (xiii. 3), though not named here, were included in this territory. The number of the towns is not mentioned at the end of the list, as in that of those preceding, because they were probably still in the hands of the Philistines. In fact, the district of Philistia, though assigned to Judah, was never subdued by it (see xiii. 2, note ').

Vers. 48-60 (*The Towns in the Hill Country Divided into Six Groups*).—This hill or mountain district of Judah extended from the Negeb to the broad Wady, Beit-Hanina, above Jerusalem, and was bounded on the west by the shephelah, and on the east by the wilderness of Judæa. The hills are limestone, and in the neighbourhood of Hebron rise to a level of 3,000 feet above the sea. On their tops are now ruins of ancient towns, and their sides bear traces of former vegetation. The district, however, is not so much a region of hills, as a gentle undulating table-land, cut into insulated portions by deep ravines. (See Porter's *Bib. Atlas*, and Stanley's *Sin. and Pal.*, p. 161, etc.)

Vers. 48-51 (*First Group of Eleven Towns on the*

South-West).—Ver. 48.—"*Sha-mîr*" ("a sharp point or thorn"), unknown, though perhaps preserved in the ruins of *Um Shaumerah* (Rob., iii., App., p. 115). From its mention, along with Yattir, Sokhoh, and Eshtemoth, it was probably eight or ten miles south of Hebron (Grove). There was a town of the same name on the mountains of Ephraim (Judges x. 1). *Yat-tîr* (height, rt. יָתַר, "to be over and above"), allotted to the priests (xxi. 14), and one of the towns to which David sent a present from the spoil of Ziklag (1 Sam. xxx. 37); now *Attîr*, ten miles south of Hebron (Rob., *Bib. Res.*, i., 494-5). "*Sô-khôh*" (a hedge), in the Wady-el-Khalîl, about ten miles south-west of Hebron, bearing like the other So-khoh (xv. 35) the name of *esh-Suweikeh* (Grove).

Ver. 49.—"*Dan-nah*" (lowland, rt. דָּנַן, to be low), unknown, though probably south or south-west of Hebron. The village *Idhnah* in the low hills appears a suitable position (Lieut. Conder). "*Qir-yath-sannah*," see note on D^ebhîr in x. 38.

Ver. 50.—"*'A-nabh*" (see on xi. 21), north-east of Sokhoh and south-west of Hebron. "*'Esh-t^emôh*" (obedience, rt. שָׁמַע), on the east of Sokkoh and Anabh; ceded to the priests (xxi. 14; 1 Chron. vi. 57), one of the towns to which David sent a present (1 Sam. xxx. 27), now *Es-Semua*, seven miles south of Hebron, an inhabited village with remains of walls and of an ancient castle (Rob., *Bib. Res.*, ii., 204-5). "*'A-nîm*" (fountains), the Heb. עַיִם, contraction for עֲיָנִים, now *el-Ghuwein*, the ruins of a village south of Semua (Rob., *Bib. Res.*, ii., 204).

Ver. 51.—The three towns mentioned in this verse are unknown. "*Gô-shen*": There is nothing to connect it with the Goshen mentioned in x. 41. "*Chô-lôn*" (sandy, from חֹל, sand), ceded to the priests (xxi. 15), called Hilen (Auth. Vers., 1 Chron. vi. 58). Another of the same name in Moab (Jer. xlviii. 21). "*Gi-lôh*" (exile, rt. גָּלָה, to emigrate), the birthplace of Ahithophel (2 Sam. xv. 12), and the place of his death (2 Sam. xvii. 23). Lieut. Conder thinks it may probably be the ruin *Jâla*, in the Hebron mountains (*Pal. Explor. Fund*).

Vers. 52-54 (*Second Group of Towns to the North of the Former in the Country around Hebron*).—
Ver. 52.—"*'A-râbh*" (ambush); Sept. Alex., Ἐρεόβ, and described in the *Onomast.* as a village in Daroma (*i.e.*, to the south), called Eremiththa. It has been identified by Lieut. Conder with the present ruin *er Rabîyeh* (*Pal. Explor. Fund*). "*Dû-mah*" (silence), probably *ed-Daumeh*, a ruined village, six miles south-west of Hebron (Rob., *Bib. Res.*, i., 212). "*'Esh-'an*" (support), occurs here only, site unknown. Knobel conjectures that it is a corrupt reading for Shema (1 Chron. ii. 43), because the Sept. reading is Σομά, and hence he connects it with the ruins of *Simia*, on the south of Daumeh (Keil). So Lieut. Conder: "Possibly the ruin *es Simia*, near Dumah (Dômeh), south of Hebron. The situation is satisfactory, and the site ancient."

Ver. 53.—"*Ya-nûm*" (sleep, from נוּם, to slumber): Unknown to Eusebius and Jerome (*Onomast.*); probably the village *Beni Naim*, east of Hebron (Lieut. Conder). "*Bêth-tap-pû-ach*" (house of the apple or citron), now *Teffûh*, about five miles west of Hebron, where there are olive-groves and vineyards (Rob. *Bib. Res.*, ii., 71). "*'A-phê-qah*" (strength): Probably the same as that in xii. 18; but distinct from that in xiii. 4.

Ver. 54.—"*Chum-tah*" (perhaps *i.q.* Syr. "a defence," or "a place of lizards"), unknown. "*Qiryath-'Ar-ba'*," see note on x. 3. "*Tsi-'ôr*" (smallness), unknown, for the Tsîôr mentioned by Eusebius (*Onomast.*), with which Rosenm. would identify it, was between Aelia and Eleutheropolis, and not, as this, upon the mountains, near to Hebron.

Vers. 55-57 (*Third Group of Ten Towns, East of those in the two Preceding Groups, and next to the Wilderness*).—Ver. 55.—"*Ma-'ôn*" (a dwelling), gave its name to the wilderness so called (1 Sam. xxiii. 24); was the residence of Nabal (1 Sam. xxv. 2); now *Maîn*, on a conical hill, eight or nine miles south-east of Hebron (Grove). Geikie (on 1 Sam. xxiii. 24) says that it was about five miles south of Ziph, and hid in the ravines of a hill close by, which rises in a great hump of rock, 2,887 feet above the sea (*Hours with the Bible*, vol. iii., p. 167; *Map of Palestine*, Pal. Fund Survey, sheet xxv.). "*Kar-mel*" (fruitful field), now *Kurmul*, a little to the north-west of Maîn. It is mentioned as the place where Nabal and Abigail had their possessions (1 Sam. xxv. 2), and where King Uzziah had his vineyards (2 Chron. xxvi. 10). In the time of Eusebius and Jerome it was the seat of a Roman garrison (*Onomast.*). It figures in the wars of the crusades, having been held by King Amalrick against Saladin, A.D. 1172. "*Zîph*," from זִיף (unused), probably *i.q.* זוב, to flow (Arab.), to borrow (Chald.), near to the wilderness so called, whither David fled from Saul (1 Sam. xxiii. 14, xxvi. 2, 3), fortified by Rehoboam (2 Chron. xi. 8);

now *Tell Zif*, three or four miles south-east of Hebron; it lies, says Robinson (ii., 191), on a low hill or ridge between two small wadies, which commence here and run toward the Dead Sea. Another Ziph is that in ver. 24. "*Yû-tah*" ("stretched out," from נָטָה), allotted to the priests (xxi. 16), described by Eusebius (*Onomast.*) as a very large village, eighteen Roman miles south-east of Eleutheropolis, now *Yutta*, close to Main and Kurmul (Robinson, Grove). Reland (*Pal.*, 870) would identify it with the πόλις 'Ιούδα mentioned in Luke i. 39, a city in which Zacharias resided, 'Ιούτα having perhaps been changed into 'Ιούδα, either by error of the text or for euphony's sake. But this, though possible, has not yet been confirmed by any positive evidence (Grove; see also Alford's note on Luke i. 39).

Ver. 56.—"*Yiz-r^e'El*" (God sows), the native place of Ahinoam, one of David's wives (1 Sam. xxv. 43); not to be confounded with the Yizreel in the plain of Esdraelon (xvii. 16, xix. 18), but probably lying south-east of Hebron. So the two following towns. "*Yoq-d"am*" ("burning of the people," Ges., *Lex.*; or "possessed by the people," rt. קָדָה, in Syr. to possess, Ges. in *Thes.*), the site unknown. "*Za-nô-ach*," see on ver. 34; perhaps identical with *Sanûte* or *Za'nûtah* (Rob., *Bib. Res.*, ii., 204, note), mentioned by Seetzen (*Reisen*, iii., 29) as below Senuia or Za-nu'ah, and about ten miles south-east of Hebron.

Ver. 57.—"*haq-Qa-yin*" ("the lance," Ges.; or from קֵן, a nest, in allusion to its position, Grove); site unknown; possibly the same as *Jukin*, on the south-east of Hebron (Rob., ii., p. 449). "*Gibh'ah*" (hill¹), a name which under different forms often occurs in Scripture. Here supposed by Robinson to be identical with the village of *Jebah*, on a hill in the Wady el-Musurr; but this situation would be too far to the north-west (see Keil *in loc.*). It was doubtless near to Karmel (ver. 55) and the other towns in this group. "*Tim-nah*," not that mentioned in ver. 10 (see note), but probably the same as that in Gen. xxxviii. 12. Site undiscovered.

Vers. 58, 59 (*Fourth Group, on the North of the last-mentioned*).—Ver. 58.—" *Chal-chûl* " (trembling, rt. חל), called in the *Onomast.* "Alula juxta Hebron." It still retains the same name Halhul or Hulhul, and is about four miles north of Hebron (Rob., *Later Bib. Res.*, i., 281). A tomb, said by the Jews to be that of the prophet Jonah, is to be seen among the ruins. "*Bêth-tsûr* " (house of rock²), one of the towns which Rehoboam fortified (2 Chron. xi. 7), mentioned in Neh. iii. 16, and in 1 Macc. iv. 29, 61, vi. 7, 26, 31; 2 Macc. xi. 5; according to Josephus (*Antiq.*, xiii., 5, 6) the strongest place in all Judæa; now *Beit-Sûr*, north-west of Halhûl (Rob., iii., 277), and commanding the road to Beersheba and Hebron. Near the ruins of the town is a spring, Ain edh-Dirweh, which, in the days of Jerome and later, was regarded as the

---

¹ From גבע, *i.q.* גבב, to be curved like an arch, whence גב, something gibbous. The word גבעה is never applied to a high or extended mountain, like Lebanon or Sinai, while from its root it is particularly applicable to the humped or rounded hills of Palestine (Stanley, *Sin. and Pal.*, p. 497).

² Root צור, to bind together. The leading idea of the word is strength and solidity, and it is accordingly applied to rocks, irrespective of their height, height being only in one or two cases (as Numb. xxiii. 9; Psalm lxi. 2) associated with the word (Stanley, *Sin. and Pal.*, p. 498).

scene of the baptism of the eunuch by Philip (Acts viii.), but as Beit-sûr is not near the road to Gaza, this legend is improbable. "*G^edhôr*" (hedge or wall), the home of Joelah and Zebadiah, two of David's mighty men (1 Chron. xii. 7); now probably *Jedûr*, between Bethlehem and Hebron (Rob., iii., 283; Grove).

Ver. 59.—"*Ma-'a-rath*" ("a place naked of trees," rt. עָרָה, to be bare): Eusebius and Jerome mention the name (*Onomasticon*, "Maroth"), but do not seem to have known the site. Lieut. Conder would identify it with the present village *Beit Ummar* (*Pal. Explor. Fund, Map*, sheet xxi.). Perhaps, as Grove suggests, the word may be derived from מְעָרָה, a cave, since caves are a characteristic feature of the mountainous districts of Palestine. "*Bêth-'a-nôth*" (house of response or of echo), perhaps the modern *Beit-Ainûn*, near to Hallûl and Beit-Sûr, discovered by Wolcott, and visited by Robinson (iii., 281). "*'El-t^eqôn*" (God the foundation), quite unknown. Here the Sept. inserts *a fifth group* of eleven towns,[1] which lay to the

---

[1] Viz., Θεκὼ, Ἐφραθά· αὕτη ἐστὶ Βαιθλεέμ, Φαγώρ, Αἰτὰν, Κουλὸν, Τατὰμ, Θωβὴς (or Σωρὴς, *Cod. Alex.*), Καρέμ, Γαλὲμ, Θεθὴρ (Βαιθὴρ, *Cod. Alex.*), Μανοχώ. Of these Θεκὼ, the well-known Tekoa, or Tekoah (pitching, *sc.* of tents), was the home of the wise woman who interceded with David (2 Sam. xiv. 2), and of the prophet Amos (i. 1), who is said to have been buried there. It was fortified by Rehoboam (2 Chron. xi. 6), and still inhabited after the captivity (Neh. iii. 5, 27); now *Tekuah*, on the top of a hill covered with ancient ruins, two hours to the south of Bethlehem. Ἐφραθά (fruitful), *i.q.* Bêth-le-chem (house of bread; Gen. xxxv. 19, xlviii. 7; Ruth iv. 11; Micah v. 1). Jerome and Kalisch observe that the two names have virtually the same meaning, a view which is favoured by Stanley's description of the neighbouring corn-fields (*Sin. and Pal.*, p. 164). Φαγώρ, now Faghur, a heap of ruins south-west of Bethlehem (Rob., *Later Bib. Res.*, p. 275). Αἰτὰν, written

north of the preceding group, and south of Jerusalem. This, according to Maurer, Hengstenberg, and others, was an arbitrary interpolation of the Sept. As, however, it is unlikely that the writer of the Book of Joshua should have omitted the names of the towns lying in this locality,[1] and as some of those towns are still standing or in ruins, it would seem more

---

Etam (2 Chron. xi. 6), one of the cities fortified by Rehoboam; the name is still recognisable in *Ain-Attar* between Bethlehem and Phagor (Tobler, *Dritte Wand.*, pp. 88, 89). Κουλὸν, now *Kulonich*; identified by Grove and others with Emmaus (Luke xxiv. 13), a colony of the Romans, which as such was exempted by Titus from being sold (Joseph., *Bel. Jud.*, vii. 6, § 6); four and a half miles west of Jerusalem. Ταταμ is undiscovered. Σωρῆς, upon a ridge on the south of Wady Aly, now *Saris*, ten miles east of Jerusalem. Καρέμ, now *Ain Karem*, a large flourishing village, two hours to the west of Jerusalem, with a Franciscan convent, dedicated to John the Baptist, in the middle, and a fountain (Rob., ii., p. 141; *Bib. Res.*, p. 271). Γαλίμ, a different place from the Gallim (Isa. x. 30; 1 Sam. xxv. 44) which lay north of Jerusalem, in the tribe of Benjamin. Βαιθήρ, now *Bitter*, a small, dirty village, south-west of Jerusalem, with a beautiful spring and gardens arranged in terraces on the west slope of the Wady Bitter (Rob., *Bib. Res.*, p. 266). בֶּתֶר means a "section" or "division," and is applied to a country divided by mountains and valleys (see Cant. ii. 17), and this is the character of the country about Bether (Konrad Furrer, *Wanderings through Pal.*, p. 192). Μανοχὼ, conjectured by Knobel and others to be the same as Manahath in 1 Chron. viii. 6, an identification not considered satisfactory by Grove. (See on "Manahath" in Smith's *Bib. Dict.*). It may possibly, says Lieut. Conder, be the village Mâlhah, south-west of Jerusalem, "L" being often put for "N."

[1] Keil remarks it as a circumstance worthy of consideration, and one of no little importance, that not one of the groups of cities hitherto named, embraces any part of the country between Bethzur and Gedor on the one side, and Jerusalem on the other, a space, *i.e.*, of about twelve Roman miles in length, and nearly ten in breadth. Yet, to judge from the closeness with which the whole of the range of mountains was studded in other parts with cities and villages, it is impossible that the only cities within this space should have been the three mentioned in ver. 59.

probable that the eleven names were originally in the Hebrew text, but were omitted by a transcriber, who mistook the word הַצְרֵיהֶן at the end of the missing passage ("eleven cities and their villages") for the same word at the end of ver. 59. So Clericus, Capellus, Knobel, Keil, Fay, etc. This omission must have been of very ancient date, since the Sept. is the only one of the ancient versions in which the missing passage is found.

Ver. 60 (*A Sixth Group of Two Towns and on the North-West Border of Judah*).—"*Qir-yath-Ba-'al*," see ver. 9, ix. 17. "*ha-Rab-bah*" (The Great), unknown. Possibly the ruin *Rubba*, west of Beit-Ibrîn (Lieut. Conder).

Vers. 61-62 (*The Towns in the Wilderness* [*Midh-bar*] *between the Mountains and the Dead Sea*).— This district extended to Wady Fikreh on the south, and to the region of Maon, Ziph, and Bethlehem on the west. It was the scene of David's wanderings (1 Sam. xxiii. 24; Psalm lxiii. 1), of John the Baptist's preaching (Matt. iii. 1), and perhaps of our Lord's temptation (Matt. iv.). Here there is scanty vegetation, and the limestone abounds with caverns. The small number of towns mentioned seems to show that it was not much more fertile anciently than now (Clark's *Bib. Atlas*, p. 12).

Ver. 61.—"*Bêth-ha-'a-ra-bhah*," see ver. 6. "*Mid-dîn*" (measures), probably close to the Dead Sea, but unknown. "*S'khâ-khah*" (enclosure), in the Judean desert. Possibly the ruin *Sikkeh*, east of Bethany (Lieut. Conder, *Map*, sheet xvii.). Neither of these places is mentioned by Eusebius and Jerome.

Ver. 62.—"*han-Nibh-shan*" (the soft soil), cf. Bashan, mentioned by Eusebius and Jerome under the name of Nempsan, or Nebsan (*Onomast.*), but its position not indicated, nor has it since been discovered. "*The City of Salt*," probably in the salt valley at the south end of the Dead Sea (Rob., *Bib. Res.*, ii., 109), the scene of repeated defeats of the Edomites (2 Sam. viii. 13; 2 Kings xiv. 7; 1 Chron. xviii. 12; Psalm lx. 2). "*'En-ge-dhî*" (the fountain of the wild goat), so called from the numerous ibexes, or Syrian chamois, which inhabit the cliffs in this district. "The oasis, which it forms amidst the naked limestone precipices, must be one of the most striking natural scenes in Palestine" (Stanley, *Sin. and Pal.*, p. 295). Anciently it was called *Cha-tsᵃ-tsôn-ta-mar* (the pruning of the palm; Gen. xiv. 7; 2 Chron. xx. 2), for the spot was once famous for palms (Pliny, *Nat. Hist.*, v., 17); it was one of David's retreats (1 Sam. xxiii. 29, xxiv. 1), and lay near the middle of the west shore of the Dead Sea (Ezek. xlvii. 10); the water of the fountain is sweet, and the temperature of it is 81° Fah. (Rob., ii., 210); now *Ain Jidy*.

Ver. 63.—As we do not read in this book that Joshua captured Jerusalem, but only that he slew its king (x. 18-26, xii. 10), many think that the event here referred to happened after Joshua's death, viz., when, as we read in Judges i. 8, the tribe of Judah captured and set fire to Jerusalem. It is true that the A. V. renders this latter passage "*Now the children of Judah had fought*," etc., but, as M. Henry well remarks, "the original speaks of it as a thing now done, and that seems most probable, because it is said to be done by the children of Judah in particular, not by all Israel in general, whom Joshua commanded." The expression "*could not,*" in xv. 63, may allude to the fact that the stronghold of the city lay within the territory of Benjamin, to whom Jebusi was allotted (xviii. 28). Of the Benjamites themselves it is said (Judges i. 21) that they "*did not drive out the Jebusites,*" which may intimate inertness on their part rather than inability. The concluding words of ver. 63 are important as proving that the Book of Joshua was written before the time of David (cf. 2 Sam. v. 6-9).

CHAPTERS XVI.-XVII.

Territory of the Children of Joseph, viz., of Ephraim and of the Half-Tribe of Manasseh.

THERE was one lot drawn for both, that their territories might be adjacent, as both tribes were closely related. Hence (1) the southern boundary of the whole territory is described (xvi. 1-4); (2) the limits of Ephraim in particular (xvi. 5-10); (3) the limits of Manasseh (xvii. 1-13). The inheritance of these tribes comprised the fairest portion of the land of Palestine, and Jacob's prophecy concerning them was fulfilled, "Let them grow into a multitude in the midst of the earth (land)" (Gen. xlviii. 16).

CHAPTER XVI.

VERS. 1-4.—*Southern Boundary of the Inheritance of Joseph's Sons.*

Ver. 1.—"*And there came out the lot,*" etc., *i.e.*, the lot came out of the urn; cf. xix. 1, 17, 24, etc. יֵצֵא is here = יַעַל (xviii. 11), and גּוֹרָל taken in connection with the words "from Jordan, etc.," means a portion of land received by lot (cf. Judges i. 3, and Ges., *Lex.* [2], p. 165). לִבְנֵי יוֹסֵף, "*for the sons of Joseph,*" *i.e.*, the kindred tribes of Ephraim and Manasseh. מִיַּרְדֵּן יְרִיחוֹ, "*from Jordan at Jericho,*" see on xiii. 32. לְמֵי ... מִזְרָחָה, "*at the waters of Jericho eastward*": This is added to mark more clearly the point at which the boundary commenced. The allusion is to the celebrated fountain called 'Ain-es-Sultân, healed by Elisha (2 Kings ii. 19; Stanley, *Sin. and Pal.*, p. 306). "(*To*) *the wilderness going up from Jericho into*[1] *the hill district to Bethel,*" or, as Keil, "the wilderness," is put in apposition to "lot" (*i.e.*, the land obtained by the lot), so that the sense is, "namely, the wilderness going up from Jericho," etc. For a certain distance the southern boundary was the same as the northern boundary of Benjamin. The "wilderness" meant is that of Bethaven (xviii. 12, vii. 2), which stretched between Wady Suwar and Mutyar (Van de Velde's *Map*). בֵּית־אֵל (see vii. 2) according to the Masoretic text is separated from בָּהָר, and is rendered as an accus. by the Sept., Arab., and Chald., and by our Revised Vers.

---

[1] "Through" (Rev. Vers.).

Ver. 2.—"*And it went out from Bethel to Luz*": Keil thinks that Bethel here stands for the mountainous district around Bethel, because in Gen. xxviii. 19, Luz (see on vii. 2) and Bethel are names of the same town; but perhaps it denotes "the certain place" (Gen. xxviii. 11) where Abraham had set up an altar, and which Jacob after his dream called Bethel (house of God), which name, perhaps on account of its sanctity, was afterwards given to the adjacent city Luz (see Art. "Luz" in Smith's *Bib. Dict.*). "*To the border of the Archite to 'Ataroth*": Whether the patronymic "Archite" is derived from Erech, a town in Mesopotamia (Gen. x. 10), now Edessa, and implies that a colony from thence had settled in these parts, can be only matter of conjecture; possibly some ancient indigenous tribe may be so called (Grove). The name is often given to Hushai, David's friend (2 Sam. xv. 32, xvi. 16, etc.). '*A-ta-róth*, called Ataroth-addar (crowns of greatness or largeness; ver. 5, xviii. 13), perhaps to distinguish it from the tribe of Gad (Numb. xxxii. 3, 34). Robinson identifies it with the village *Atâra*, two miles south of Bireh (Beeroth), a little to the southwest of Beitin or Bethel (*Bib. Res.*, ii., 265).

Ver. 3.—"*The Yaphletite*" (freed by the Lord), a patronymic (§ 86, 5). Our A. V. renders "Japhleti," and seems to have regarded it as a place. No trace of the name is now to be found. Grove conjectures that it may have belonged to an ancient native tribe (see on ver. 2, and cf. the names Zemaraim, Ophni, Jebusi). The "Yaphlet" in the genealogy of the tribe of Asher (1 Chron. vii. 32, 33) cannot be identified with it. "*Bêth-chô-rôn the Nether*," see on

x. 10. "*Ge-zer*" (a place cut off, a precipice), x. 33, xii. 12: Grove says that it may possibly be in or about Yasûr, between Jaffa and Ramleh. "*Towards the sea*," i.e., towards the Mediterranean.

Vers. 5-10 (*Inheritance of Ephraim*).—"'*Eph-ra-yim*" (perhaps "double land," "twin land"). This tribe took precedence of that of Manasseh, according to the prophecy (Gen. xlviii. 20). It was subsequently included in the Kingdom of Samaria.

Ver. 5.—This verse gives a concise description of the southern boundary, which had been described more fully in vers. 1-4. Only the western half of that boundary is noticed, commencing from Ataroth-addar (ver. 2). Upper Bethchoron is substituted for Bethchoron the Nether (ver. 3), the two places being near together (x. 10), and belonging to Ephraim.

Ver. 6.—"*And the border went out toward the sea* [or west] *to ham-Mikh-m'thath* (the hiding-place[1]) *on the north*": The northern border is here meant. In the remainder of the verse, and in ver. 7, its direction from a central point—perhaps the watershed which separates the waters which flow into the Mediterranean from those flowing into the Jordan—is described *eastward*, and in ver. 8 its direction *westward*. Keil thinks that perhaps the original reading of the first clause was "*towards the north the border went out to Mikhmethath*." This town was before Shechem (xvii. 7), but the site is unknown. *Ta-'a-nath-Shi-lôh* ("approach to Shiloh," rt. אָנָה, to approach, to meet), said, in the *Onomast.*, to have been ten Roman miles from Neapolis (Sichem), and between it and the Jordan;

---

[1] Rt. כָּמַה (unused), probably *i.q.* כָּתַם, to lay up.

probably the Θηυα of Ptolemy (v. 16, 5), the present *Tana, Ain Tana*, a heap of ruins south-east of Nablûs (Neapolis). "*And passed by it on the east of Ya-nô-chah* (rest)." אתו, which is omitted by the Syr., Sept., and Houbigant, refers to יָעְלָה, which is masc. in form. The ה in יָנוּחָה, according to Ges. (*Lex.*), is local, but see next verse, where it evidently forms part of the word; also here the preceding noun is in the construct. form (§ 89). Perhaps the place is identical with the present Yanûn, three or four miles further than Taanath-Shiloh towards the east (Rob., *Later Bib. Res.*, p. 297), where there are very ancient and extensive ruins (Van de Velde).

Ver. 7.—"'*A-ta-rôth*" (crowns), different from the Ataroth in vers. 2, 5, which was on the southern boundary. It is probably to be sought for in the Ghor (Keil). "*To Na-'a-rah*" (hand-maiden, damsel), נַעֲרָה with ה loc.[1]; perhaps the same as Naaran (1 Chron. vii. 28), described in the *Onomast.* as a small village of the Jews, five miles from Jericho, probably on the north-east. "*And it reached to* (lit. struck upon) *Jericho*," i.e., the northern side of the territory, for Jericho belonged to Benjamin (xviii. 21), and at this point it coincided with the southern boundary of the tribe of Joseph (cf. ver. 1) and the northern of Benjamin (xviii. 12).

Ver. 8 (*Western Half of the North Boundary*).— "*Tap-pû-ach*" (a place fruitful in apples), called En-Tappuach (xvii. 8), probably west of Sichem, and distinct from the Tappuach in xii. 17. "*To the water-course of Qa-nah*" (reed), between Joppa and Cesarea,

---

[1] Written נַעֲרָתָה in the Hebrew text.

perhaps the modern *Nahr el Kassab*, called in Kiepert's *Map* the Nahr el Falik. Stanley says that a portion of the plain of Sharon is called *Khassab* (reedy), apparently from the high reeds which grow on the banks of the rivers (*Sin. and Pal.*, p. 260). הַיָּמָּה, "*towards the sea*," *i.e.*, the Mediterranean.

Ver. 9.—"*And the cities, the places which were separately apportioned to the sons of Ephraim*": הַמִּבְדָּלוֹת, lit. "the separations," rt. בָּדַל, to separate. If the full stop at the end of the preceding verse is removed, the verb "were" need not be inserted as by our Auth. Vers. before the words "among the inheritance." The verse indicates that to the inheritance of Ephraim, as described above, were added separate cities from the territory of Manasseh, doubtless because the inheritance of Ephraim was otherwise too little for them.

Ver. 10.—"*Gezer*," see xvi. 3. "*They drove not out*," see Judges i. 29; 1 Kings ix. 16,[1] and cf. xv. 63. This was in disobedience to God's express command (Exod. xxiii. 31; Deut. vii. 2), and was justly punished by the corruption of morals, etc., arising from association with idolaters (see Hosea xii. 7, 8, iv. 17). וַיְהִי וגו, "*and was reduced to the tribute of a servant*," *i.e.*, became tributary dependents, ἐγένοντο ὑπόφοροι δοῦλοι, Sept. (cf. 1 Kings ix. 21). The derivation of מַס is uncertain; perhaps it is contracted from מֶכֶס, toll, tribute, rt. כָּסַס, to number; like מִסָּה, number, contracted from מִכְסָה (Ges., *Lex.*). In what form the tribute was rendered, whether in money, products, or service, is unknown.

---

[1] Here we have a proof that the Book of Joshua must have been written before the beginning of Solomon's reign.

CHAPTER XVII.

VERS. 1-13.—*The Portion of Manasseh.*

Ver. 1.—In the first clause there seems assigned a reason why an inheritance on both sides of the Jordan was given to Manasseh, viz., because he was the firstborn of Joseph, and as such was entitled to a double portion, this his birthright not being invalidated by the preference shown to Ephraim by Jacob (cf. Deut. xxi. 15, etc.). In the second clause reference is made to the portion which the half of this tribe had already received on the east of Jordan. לְמָכִיר is first put absol., and then resumed in the לוֹ which follows וַיְהִי (see § 145, 2); render "*to Ma-khîr, the firstborn of Manasseh, the father of Gil-'adh, to him were Gil-'adh and Bashan* (allotted), *because he was a man of war.*"[1] Ma-khîr (sold) here stands for his descendants, by whom Gil-'adh was conquered (Numb. xxxii. 39; Deut. iii. 15). The expression "father of Gil-'adh," denotes lord or possessor of

---

[1] The Manassites at that time, says Dr. Geikie, were certainly the most warlike of the tribes. Machir, Jair, and Nobah, its chiefs, were not shepherds, like the Reubenites, but valiant warriors, whose deeds are frequently recorded (Numb. xxxii. 30; Deut. iii. 13-15). These districts were the most difficult in the whole country, for they embraced the hills of Gilead, and the almost impregnable tract known as the Lejah, or "refuge," from the security which its natural fortifications afforded. But Manasseh also, like Reuben and Gad, affected by its position and its isolation, gradually fell into the wandering shepherd life, and ceased to be a power in Israel. Nor did it even remain true to its ancient faith, but, like the other tribes of the east of Jordan, gave itself up to the local idolatry (1 Chron. v. 25).—*Hours with the Bible*, vol. ii., p. 376.

Gil-'adh, for in the Hebrew Gil-'adh with the article, as here, denotes the *country* so called (cf. ver. 5, xiii. 11, 31; Numb. xxxii. 40; Deut. iii. 10, etc.); but without the article the *person* (xvii. 3; Numb. xxvi. 29, 30, xxvii. 1, xxxvi. 1; 1 Chron. vii. 17).

Ver. 2 (*List of the Families which received their Portion on the West Side of Jordan*).—וַיְהִי, subau. הַגּוֹרָל, from ver. 1. הַנּוֹתָרִים, "*which were left*," *i.e.*, who had not received their inheritance on the east of Jordan. The six families mentioned are the same as those in Numb. xxvi. 30-32, but '*Al-bhî-'e-zer*[1] (father of help) is there abbreviated to Iezer, and *Sh'-mî-dha'* (fame of wisdom) is put before Che-pher (a well or pit). בְּנֵי ... הַזְּכָרִים, *the male descendants* : The term "male" is used in antithesis to the female descendants mentioned in the next verse.

Ver. 3.—Cf. Numb. xxvi. 33, xxvii. 1. "*Ts'loph-chadh*" ("first fracture, or rupture," perhaps "first-born," cf. פֶּטֶר). Some infer, from 1 Chron. vii. 15, that he was the second son of his father Hepher. He came out of Egypt with Moses, and died in the wilderness, as did all that generation (Numb. xiv. 35, xxvii. 3). "*Mach-lah*" (according to Ges., *Lex.*, "sickness," rt. חָלָה, to be sick, or perhaps *i.q.* חֶמְלָה, gentleness, the ה and מ being transposed). "*Nô-'ah*" (motion, rt. נוּעַ). "*Chogh-lah*" (partridge, Ges., *Lex.*; cf. xv. 6). "*Mil-kah*" (counsel; מָלַךְ, in Syr. and Chald., to consult). "*Tir-tsah*" (pleasantness, rt. רָצָה). All these daughters married their cousins (Numb. xxxvi. 11).

Ver. 4.—"*Before Eleazar . . . and before Joshua*,"

---

[1] From this tribe, though one of the poorest or weakest in Manasseh, sprang Gideon, the most renowned of the judges.

cf. xiv. 1, note. "*Jehovah commanded,*" etc., see Numb. xxvii. 6, 7, xxxvi. 2.

Vers. 5, 6.—" *Ten portions* " (lit. portions measured by a line), viz., five to the male descendants of Gil-'adh, and five to the daughters of Tsᵉloph-chadh, who represented the sixth family, viz., that of Chepher (Hepher, Auth. Vers.).

VERS. 7-13.—*Boundaries and Extent of the Inheritance of Manasseh, on the Western Side of the Jordan.*

Vers. 7-10 (*The Southern Boundary coinciding with the Northern of Ephraim*).—Ver. 7.—" *'A-sher* " (fortunate, happy), not the tribe so called, but a town at the east end of the southern boundary, now *Yasîr* or *Teyasîr*, about fourteen miles from Nâblus (Shechem), on the road to Beisân (Bethshean). "*ham-Mikh-mᵉthah*," see on xvi. 6. "*Shᵉchem*" (shoulder, or ridge[1]), see Gen. xii. 6 (where in the Auth. Vers. it is written Sichem); xxxiii. 18, between Ebal and Gerizim; allotted to Ephraim (Josh. xx. 7), but assigned to the Levites, and made a city of refuge (xxi. 20, 21); the capital of Jeroboam (1 Kings xii. 25), afterwards that of Samaria; generally supposed to be the Sychar of John iv. 5, but see Smith's *Dict. of the Bible*, Art. "Sychar." It derived its name Shechem either from its situation on a ridge, or from Shechem, the son of Hamor. It is now *Nablûs* (Neapolis).[2] אֶל־הַיָּמִין, " *to*

---

[1] Or rather "back," the town "Shechem" being, as it were, on the back of Gerizim (Stanley's *Sin. and Pal.,* Append., p. 496).
[2] Founded by Vespasian, after the ruin of the older Shechem, which probably lay further eastward, and, therefore, nearer to

the right," *i.e.*, to the south (cf. 1 Sam. xxiii. 19, 24). "*'En-Tap-puach*," see xvi. 8.

Ver. 8.—אֶל־גְּבוּל, "*at*" or "*upon the border*": It seems that Tappuach was one of the separate towns referred to in xvi. 9 as assigned to Ephraim.

Ver. 9.—"*The water-course of Qanah*," see xvi. 8. נֶגְבָּה, "*to the south of the water-course.*" "*These cities belonged to Ephraim among the cities of Manasseh*": The cities meant must be those which lay to the south of the water-course, and are identical with the separate cities alluded to in xvi. 9. "*But the border* [or territory] *of Manasseh was on the north of the water-course*," *i.e.*, Manasseh possessed all the territory and cities lying north of the Qanah, as is explained in the next verse. For the construction of יְהִי with תֹּצְאֹתָיו in the last clause, see on xv. 4.

Ver. 10.—"*To the south* (of the water-course of Qanah, the land belonged) *to Ephraim, and to the north to Manasseh, and the sea was his boundary; and they touched upon Asher on the north, and upon Issachar on the east*": The subject of יִפְגְּעוּן may be either the borders of Manasseh (Clericus), or the two tribes of Manasseh and Ephraim, regarded as together representing the inheritance of Joseph (Masius). The north and east boundary may have

---

the opening of the valley. The situation is thus described by Dean Stanley: "A valley, green with grass, grey with olives, gardens sloping down on each side, fresh springs rushing down in all directions; at the end a white town embosomed in all this verdure, lodged between two high mountains, which extend on each side of the valley—that on the south, Gerizim, that on the north, Ebal—this is the aspect of Nablous, the most beautiful, perhaps it might be said the only very beautiful, spot in Central Palestine" (*Sin. and Pal.*, v., p. 233-4)

been described in this general manner, because they had not yet been accurately defined.

Ver. 11.—"*Běth-shě'an*" (house of rest), in Issachar, about four miles west of the Jordan, in the Ghôr, and twelve miles south of the Sea of Galilee. To its walls were fastened the bodies of Saul and of his sons (1 Sam. xxxi. 10, 12 ; 2 Sam. xxi. 12). After the exile it was called *Scythopolis* (Judith iii. 10 ; 2 Macc. xii. 29) ; in Christian times it was the see of a bishop, who is mentioned as present at the Councils of Nice and Constantinople ; now *Beisân* (Grove ; cf. Stanley's *Sin. and Pal.*, p. 346). בְּנֵי, see on xv. 45. "*Yibh-lĕ'am*" (" devouring the people," Ges., *Lex.*), called *Bil-'am* (non-populus, perhaps, *i.q.* "a foreigner") 1 Chron. vi. 55 (70), a Levitical town (xxi. 25), near Megiddo (2 Kings ix. 27). It was probably in Issachar (Grove), and near Jenin, where the village *Jelama* now stands (Rob., *Bib. Res.*, ii., 319). וְאֶת ... דאר : the change of construct. to the accus. may be explained by regarding לְ יְהִי as = " received " or " had," and the author, when he wrote the words, may have had in his mind what he expresses in ver. 12, viz., that the Manassites could not expel the Canaanites from those towns. "*Dôr*" (circle, habitation), see on xi. 2. "*Ēn-dôr*" (spring of Dor), the scene of Sisera's overthrow by Barak (Psalm lxxxiii. 10), of Saul's visit to the witch (1 Sam. xxviii. 7). Eusebius (*Onom.*) describes it as a large village, four miles to the south of Tabor, now *Endûr*, a considerable, but now deserted, village (Grove). On "*Taanakh*" and "*M'ghiddo*" see xii. 21 ; both were in the valley of Jezreel. שְׁלֹשׁ הַנָּפֶת, "*the three heights*" : נֶפֶת is used coll., *i.q.* נוּף, see xi. 2. It is probable that this was an elevated district, comprising the three last mentioned towns, cf. the names Tripolis, Decapolis, etc.[1] Perhaps all the six towns mentioned in this verse may have been assigned to Manasseh in compensation for those which it had given up to Ephraim (xvi. 9).

Vers. 12, 13.—Cf. xv. 63, xvi. 10. In Judges i. 27-8 Endor is not mentioned, probably because it was included in the district of Dor. In ver. 12 the term "cities" is used by hypallage for the inhabitants of the cities. וַיּוֹאֶל, see on vii. 7; here it seems to imply consent to, or acquiescence in, the proposals made to them (cf. Exod .ii. 21; Judges xvii. 11). The Manassites, not being strong enough to dispossess them, may have proposed to them that they should live peaceably in the land, to which proposal they agreed. In ver. 13 the וְ before יִתְּנוּ is not only consec., but marks the apod. (§ 155, 1, *a*). לָמַס, see xvi. 10; Judges i. 28, 33. For the construc. of the infin. absol. הוֹרֵשׁ, with the finite verb, see § 131, 3, *a*.

VERS. 14-18.—*Complaint of the Children of Joseph respecting the Territory allotted to them.*

Ver. 14.—לִי, "*to me*," *i.e.*, to the tribe of Ephraim and the half-tribe of Manasseh, regarded collectively as one tribe (cf. xvi. 1; Psalm lxxvii. 16 [Heb.], lxxviii. 67; Amos vi. 6). גּוֹרָל, a portion assigned by casting a lot; חֶבֶל, a portion assigned by measure-

---

[1] "The word (נֶפֶת) would appear," says Stanley, "to be a local word applied to the plains at the foot of Carmel, much as Ciccar and Geliloth were to the Jordan valley; and probably Cinneroth to the district on the shores of the Sea of Galilee" (*Sin and Pal.*, Append., p. 494).

ment; here the two terms are used together for emphasis. עַם רָב, "*a numerous people*": According to the second census made in the time of Moses (Numb. xxvi.) the tribe of Ephraim numbered 32,500 (ver. 37), that of Manasseh 52,700 (ver. 34); therefore the tribe of Ephraim and that of half Manasseh would together be fewer in number than the tribes of Judah, Dan, Issachar, and Zebulon respectively. The territory assigned to them was fifty-five miles from east to west, by seventy from north to south, and comprised the most fruitful portion of the land of Canaan (Stanley, *Sin. and Pal.*, p. 229-30). Hence the complaint here made was groundless, and arose from their arrogance and selfishness, other instances of which we have in Judges viii. 1, xii. 1; 2 Sam. xix. 41; 2 Chron. xxviii. 9, etc.[1] עַד־אֲשֶׁר refers to gradation, "*so far as;*" עַד־כֹּה, to time, "*hitherto*" (cf. Exod. vii. 16).

Ver. 15.—Joshua was himself an Ephramite (1 Chron. vii. 27), but here in his reply he shows his impartiality. רַב is used, perhaps ironically, and = "great" or "mighty." הַיַּעַר, "*the forest,*" implying

---

[1] Bishop Wordsworth sees in their character "an example of that self-idolising and self-aggrandising spirit in nations and in churches, which seek to extend themselves by colonisation and conquest, and even by missionary enterprise, not so much that they may gain kingdoms for Christ, and win subjects to Him, but in order that they may have vassals and tributaries to themselves." "It may be worthy of consideration," says he, "whether the sacred writer in this history does not read a solemn warning to such nations as England, which publicly and privately derives an immense revenue from her two hundred millions of subjects in India, and yet has done little hitherto to bring them into subjection to Christ, from Whom all nations receive their power, and on Whom all their happiness depends (Matt. xxviii. 18)."

dense growth or an abundance of trees, from יָעַר to abound. The "forest" is evidently here distinguished from Mount Ephraim itself, and was probably a mountainous (see ver. 18, where it is called הָר), woody region, lying to the north-west and north-east of Mount Ephraim, yet being an offshoot from it. Such would be the range which runs along the northern border of Manasseh, and connects the mountains of Gilboa and Carmel, and which belonged to the Perizzites and the Rephaim, and is still well wooded (see Rob., *Bib. Res.*, ii., 455 ; Tristram, *Land of Israel*, 422). וּבֵרֵאתָ. "*and cut out room for thee there*" (Ges.), Piel Perf. for imper. (§ 126, 6, *c*), from בָּרָא, to cut. "*The Perizzites*," iii. 10. "*The Rephaim*," xii. 4. אֵין from אוּן, to be narrow, but used in a different sense in x. 13. "*Mount 'Eph-ra-yim*" (double fruitfulness, Gen. xli. 52) ; הָר is frequently used of a mountainous district (cf. xi. 16). It extended from the great plain of Esdraelon (Jezreel) on the north to as far south as Ramah and Bethel (Judges iv. 5), places but a few miles north of Jerusalem, in the tribe of Benjamin. In structure the district is limestone, rounded hills separated by valleys, with streams of running water, and continuous tracts of vegetation (see Stanley's *Sin. and Pal.*, p. 229).

Ver. 16.—לֹא־יִמָּצֵא, "*will not suffice*" (Sept., Chald., and Syr., followed by Keil), Niph. imperf. (cf. Zech. x. 10) ; and, in Qal. (Numb. xi. 22 ; Judges xxi. 14). "*In the land of the valley*," including the valley of the Jordan near Bethshean, and the broad valley of Jezreel. "*Chariots of iron*," see on xi. 4 : They are mentioned here by the descendants of Joseph as a reason why they could not take possession of the plains. "*The valley of Yiz-r^e'El*" (God sows), called in Greek the plain of Esdraelon or Esdrelon (Judith i. 8, iii. 9, iv. 6), reaching in its fullest extent from the Mediterranean north of Carmel to the Jordan. But the valley of *Yiz-r^e'El* proper ran from the town of Yizr^e'El (the modern *Zenin*), in Issachar, between the mountains of Gilboa and the range of Little Hermon (Chermon) to the Jordan eastward. This valley, the natural "battle-field of Palestine" (Stanley, *Sin. and Pal.*, p. 331), was the scene of the victory of Barak (Judges v.) and of Gideon (Judges vii. 1, 8, etc.), and of the overthrow of Saul and Jonathan (1 Sam. xxxi. 3, 8).

Vers. 17-18 (*Joshua repeats his previous declaration* [ver. 15], *intimating, apparently with some degree of irony, that if they had only sufficient courage, they could easily enlarge their territory*).—Ver. 17.— יִהְיֶה ... אֶחָד, "*there will not be to thee one lot only.*"

Ver. 18.[1]—"*For a mountainous district will be thine, for it is a forest, and thou wilt clear it.*" הַר means, not Mount Ephraim, which they already possessed, but the woody mountainous district referred to in ver. 15. הוֹצְאֹתָיו, "*its outgoings, i.e.*, the fields and plains bordering on it (Keil). "*Although*[2] (כִּי) *they have iron chariots, although they are strong*": From this reply of Joshua to the complaint of the children of Joseph we may learn that whatever

---

[1] "This verse," says Dr. Geikie, "seems to connect the destruction of the forests of Western Palestine with the Israelite invasion. But the loss of the trees has destroyed the water supply, to the permanent injury of the country" (*Hours with the Bible*, vol. ii., p. 432, note 2).

[2] See Ges., *Lex* (6, *e*), p. 393.

blessings God places within our reach, we must use our own best efforts to secure them, though in dependence on His promised help.

CHAPTER XVIII.

THIS chapter records the setting up of the Tabernacle at Shiloh (ver. 1) ; the survey of the remainder of the land (vers. 2-10) ; and the inheritance of Benjamin (vers. 11-28).

Ver. 1.—" *The whole congregation,*" see עֵדָה, ix. 15. " *Shî-lôh* " (" place of rest," rt. שָׁלָה, to be secure), written here and in ver. 8, שִׁלֹה, but שִׁלָה in 1 Kings ii. 27 ; שִׁילוֹ, Judges xxi. 21 ; שִׁלוֹ, Judges xxi. 19).[1] Hitherto the Tabernacle had been at Gilgal, but now that the tribe of Ephraim was settled, it was removed to Shiloh, probably by God's express command (see Deut. xii. 11), because Shiloh being in a central and secluded spot may have been more suitable than any other site.[2] Josephus (*Antiq.*, v., 1, 19) gives another reason, viz., the beauty of the situation, which is not corroborated by modern

---

[1] The same name written שִׁילֹה is given in Gen. xlix. 10 to the Messiah, Who is our Peace.

[2] " The most hallowed spot of that vicinity, Bethel, which might else have been more naturally chosen, was at that time still in the hands of the Canaanites (Judges i. 23-27), and thus left to choose the encampment of the Sacred Tent, not by old associations, but according to the dictates of convenience, the conquerors fixed on this retired spot in the heart of the country, where the allotment of the territory could be most conveniently made, north, south, east, and west, to the different tribes " (*Sin. and Pal.*, ch. v.).

travellers.[1] It lay north of Bethel, on the east side of the road going up to Shechem, *i.e.*, Nablous (see Judges xxi. 19); now called in Arabic "*Seilûn*" (Robinson's *Pal.*, iii., 85-89). Here the Tabernacle remained till the death of Eli (1 Sam. iv.); it was then removed to Nob (1 Sam. xxi. 2 [Heb.]), and afterwards to Gibeon (1 Kings iii. 4). In the reign of Jeroboam I., Shiloh was the residence of the prophet Ahijah (1 Kings xiv. 2); but it gradually declined, having been rejected by God (Psalm lxxviii. 60; Jeremiah vii. 12, xxvi. 6), and is mentioned in Scripture for the last time in Jer. xli. 5. Its real site was from the time of Jerome to the year 1838 completely forgotten, and its name transferred to the commanding height of Gibeon (Stanley, *Sin. and Pal.*, chap. iv., p. 216, and v., p. 232). אֶת־אֹהֶל מוֹעֵד, "*the tabernacle of the assembly*," so called either because God there met with Moses (Exod. xxv. 22), or because before it the assemblies of the people were held (Ges., *Lex.*). The word מוֹעֵד is derived from יָעַד, to appoint, and in Niph. to meet by appointment (Ges.). Perhaps the rendering "tent of meeting or of appointment," *i.e.*, the appointed meeting-place between God and man, would best express the meaning. "*And the land was subdued*," etc., cf. xi. 23, xiv. 15. Hence the occasion was favourable for the further allotment of the land.

---

[1] Thus Dean Stanley remarks that Shiloh is utterly featureless, and in this respect forms a striking contrast to the sacred localities of Delphi, Lebadea, and the Styx (*Sin. and Pal.*, v., p. 232).

VERS. 2-10.—*Survey of the Land which had yet to be apportioned.*

Ver. 2.—אֲשֶׁר לֹא חָלְקוּ וגו׳, "*whose inheritance they had not* (yet) *portioned out.*" חָלַק means "to divide," especially by lot (Ges., *Lex.*; cf. xiv. 5, xxii. 8), used here with an indeter. nominative (§ 137, 3).

Ver. 3.—אַתֶּם, "*ye*," emphatic, as contrasting the conduct of the tribes addressed with that of those who had already taken possession of their inheritances The Part. מִתְרַפִּים is not only reflexive but intensive; "*how long do ye show yourselves so remiss?*" (see Ewald's *Gr.*, § 243). This remissness may have arisen from their preference of a nomad to a settled life, and their unwillingness to wage an exterminating war against the Canaanites. No less is it our own duty, as Christians, to be up and doing, sparing no pains to make our calling and election sure (2 Peter i. 10), and to bring others to the saving knowledge of the truth (Matt. xxviii. 19).

Ver. 4.—"*Set for yourselves three men for each tribe,*" *i.e.*, for each of the seven remaining tribes: Josephus, therefore, wrongly states the total number sent to have been ten, viz., one for each of the seven tribes, and three surveyors (*Antiq.*, v., 1, 21). הָבוּ, imper. of יָהַב, to give, but here to set or appoint, as in Deut. i. 13; Vulg. "eligite." וְיִכְתְּבוּ, "*and let them describe*": The כָּתַב means, not "to measure," but "to write," as in a book (see ver. 9), to give a general account of the land which yet remained to be divided, its situation, characteristics, number of cities, etc., without delineating the exact boundaries of each district.[1] לְפִי נַחֲלָתָם, "*according to their inheritance,*" i.e., not, as Rosenm., according to the size of the inheritance of each tribe (for this could only be determined after the lots had been drawn), but according to the number of the inheritances into which the land was to be divided, viz., seven for the seven remaining tribes. This general survey might have been easily made without rousing the jealousy and opposition of the Canaanites.

Ver. 5.—וְהִתְחַלְּקוּ, "*and divide ye for yourselves,*" Hithp. imper. (§ 54, 3, c). The remainder of the verse declares that this division was not to include the territory already assigned to the tribes of Judah and Joseph. יַעֲמֹד, "*shall stand*" (i.e., remain) "*on his border.*"

Ver. 6.—"*Before Jehovah our God,*" i.e., before the Tabernacle where Jehovah manifested His presence (cf. xix. 51). Thus greater sanctity and validity was given to the lot.

Ver. 7.—With the assertion in the first clause cf. xiii. 14, 33, xiv. 3, 4. "*Priesthood*" is put by meton. for its emoluments. The sing. suffix in נַחֲלָתוֹ is used coll.

---

[1] So William the Conqueror, in A.D. 1081, appointed commissioners to make him an exact account of all the landed property of his kingdom. "This monument, called Doomsday Book, the most valuable piece of antiquity possessed by any nation, is still preserved in the Exchequer, and though only some extracts of it have hitherto been published, it serves to illustrate to us in many particulars the ancient state of England. The great Alfred had finished a like survey of the kingdom in his time, which was long kept at Winchester, and which probably served as a model to William in this undertaking" (Hume, vol. i., chap. iv., p. 295).

Vers. 8-9 (*Execution of the Command*).—Ver. 8.— לִכְתֹּב is dependent on הַהֹלְכִים, "*who went to describe*."

Ver. 9.—לְעָרִים, "*according to* (its) *cities*," see on ver. 4. The assertion of Josephus (*Antiq.*, v., 1, 21) that seven months were occupied in this survey seems to be arbitrary.

Ver. 10.—"*Cast lots*," see on xiv. 2; and on מַחְלְקֹת see xi. 23. The portions allotted were unequal, but were adapted to the circumstances and requirements of those to whom they were assigned, even as in the heavenly Canaan all the children of God will be fully blessed, but each according to his capacity (see Matt. xxv. 21-23; 1 Cor. xv. 41).

VERS. 11-28.—*Inheritance of Benjamin.*

Vers. 11-20. (*Its Boundaries*).—Ver. 11.—"*The lot . . . came up,*" *i.e.*, out of the urn (cf. Lev. xvi. 9). גְּבוּל גּוֹרָלָם, "*the border of their lot*" (*i.e.*, of the territory assigned to them by lot), "*between the children of Judah . . . of Joseph.*" By God's overruling providence the tribe of Benjamin was thus placed close to its kindred, the house of Joseph, and close to the tribe of Judah, with which, at a later period, it was to be brought into very intimate alliance (1 Kings xii. 21). The territory of no other tribe, except perhaps Manasseh, contained such important passes into the adjacent plains, nor such conspicuous heights, whether for defence or as high-places of worship (see Stanley's *Sin. and Pal.*, pp. 200-1).

Vers. 12-13 (*The Northern Boundary*).—This coincided with the southern boundary of Ephraim, as far as Lower Bethhoron.

Ver. 12.—"*And there was for them the border on the side northwards from the Jordan.*" On the construction of לִפְאַת צָפוֹנָה, see § 90, 2, *a*. פֵּאָה = פֶּה, "mouth," from פָּאָה, to blow, then "side," or "quarter," like "ora" from "os" (cf. vers. 14, 15). "*And the border went up to the side* (lit. shoulder) *of Jericho on the north,*" *i.e.*, it included Jericho within the territory of Benjamin. בָּהָר, "*into the mountains,*" see note on ii. 16, and cf. עָלָה, followed by בְּ in Psalm xxiv. 3; Cant. vii. 9 (Heb.). מִדְבָּרָה: According to the pointing, the following word "Beth-aven," stands in apposition, and denotes not the town, but the wilderness so called; *e.g.*, "*towards the wilderness, Beth-aven.*" But some emended MSS. and Kimchi read מִדְבַּרָה, the construc. form of מִדְבָּר, with the addition of הָ loc. (see § 90, 2, *a*, and cf. Ges., *Lehrgeb.*, p. 633), "*towards the wilderness of Beth-aven,*" cf. 1 Kings xix. 15, מִדְבַּרָה דַּמֶּשֶׂק, "*to the wilderness of Damascus.*" On Beth-aven see vii. 2.

Ver. 13 (see on xvi. 2, 3).—אֶל־כֶּתֶף לוּזָה, "*to the side* (shoulder) *of Luzah*": Here the הָ in Luzah, which in the former part of the verse is local (§ 90, 2) forms the termination of the word; so in the Samar. Vers., the Sept., Vulg., and Eusebius; cf. Timnath, Timnathah (xv. 10), Riblah, Riblathah (see note *a*, on Art. "Luz" in Smith's *Bib. Dict.*). Though Bethel, according to the boundary here given, was in Ephraim, it appears from ver. 22 to have been assigned to Benjamin. וְיָרַד, "*and descended,*" *i.e.*, went southward.

Ver. 14 (*The Western Border*).—וְתָאַר, see xv. 9. וְנָסַב נֶגֶב, "*and turned on the west side towards the south*": On Kirjath-baal and Kirjath-jearim see ix. 17, xv. 9.

Here, therefore, the border of Benjamin touched that of Judah. פְּאַת־יָם, "*the west quarter*," or side towards the sea (cf. vers. 12, 15). פֵּאָה comes from פָּאָה, to blow, and hence means a quarter of the heavens from which the wind blows.

Vers. 15-19 (*The South Boundary*).—This commencing from the city of Kirjath-jearim coincided with the north boundary of Judah (xv. 5-9), but was measured in the opposite direction, viz., from west to east.

Ver. 15.—"*And the south quarter* (was) *from the extremity of Kirjath-jearim*," etc. יָמָּה, "*on the west*": הָ֔ is here taken in a weaker sense than that of 'towards" (see § 90, 2, *b*). "*Neph-tô-ach*," see on xv. 9.

Ver. 16.—כֶּתֶף הַיְבוּסִי, see on xv. 8. '*Ên-rôgel*, xv. 7.

Ver. 17.—On 'Ên-shemesh and Geli-lôth, see xv. 7. "*Stone of Bôhan*," xv. 6.

Ver. 18.—הָעֲרָבָה, "*the desert plain*," i.e., of the Jordan, see iii. 16. In the Auth. Vers. it is rendered "Arabah," and appears to be identical with the Beth-haarabhah in xv. 6.

Ver. 19.—"*Beth-chŏgh-lâh*," xv. 6. צָפוֹנָה, "*towards the north*," i.e., the boundary line, though taking an eastern direction, somewhat turned towards the north תּוֹצְאוֹתָיו הַגְּבוּל, according to this reading הַגְּבוּל is put in appos. to the suffix of the governing noun, "*the outgoings of it, viz., of the border*" (§ 121, 6, Rem. 3).

Ver. 20 (*The Eastern Boundary*).—אֹתוֹ, "*it*," referring to מַטֶּה.

Vers. 21-28 (*The Towns of Benjamin*).—These are divided into two groups, one in the eastern portion of the tribe, containing twelve towns; the other in the western, containing fourteen towns.

Vers. 21-24 (*The Eastern Towns*).—Ver. 21.— "*Y⁴rî-chô*," see on ii. 1. "*Bêth-chŏgh-lāh*," xv. 6. And "'*Emcq-Q⁴tsîts*" (the latter word, if Hebrew, is derivable from קָצַץ, to cut off, and may possibly be connected with the general circumcision, which took place at Gilgal in the same neighbourhood [Grove]), mentioned here only in the Old Testament; the name is recognisable in the *Wady el Kaziz*, on the road from Jerusalem to Jericho. Possibly the Beth-Basi of 1 Macc. ix. 62, 64 (Grove, Index to Clark's *Bib. Atlas*).

Ver. 22.—"*Bêth-haarabhah*," xv. 6. "*Ts⁴ma-ra-yim*" (two cuttings off, or precipices), perhaps in the valley of the Jordan, and identical with the modern *es-Sumrah* (Van de Velde's *Map*), about four miles north of Jericho. Earlier writers, however, suppose it stood on Mount Tsemarayim, in Ephraim,[1] where Abijah besieged Jeroboam (2 Chron. xiii. 4). The name in either case may have been derived from the ancient tribe of the Tsemarites (Gen. x. 18). *Bethel*, vii. 2.

Ver. 23.—"*ha-'Av-vîm*" (the ruins), perhaps built by, or called after, the Avvites (see on xiii. 3); unknown, but Knobel would identify it with 'Ay, which stood near Bethel (vii. 2, xii. 9), and means a heap of ruins or stones; cf. עַי (Neh. xi. 31), עִית

---

[1] "The narrow territory of Benjamin soon melts into the hills which reach to the plain of Esdraelon, and which, from the great tribe which there had its chief seat, are known by the name of 'the Mountains of Ephraim'" (Stanley, *Sin. and Pal.*, p. 229). Cf. note on Ha-Ramah, ver. 25.

(Isa. x. 28 ; Ges., *Lex.*). "*hăp-Pā-rāh*" (the heifer or cow) : This name may have reference to pasture-land (cf. Eleph in ver. 28), and the mention of the "herd" in 1 Sam. xi. 5. Josephus says that the smallness of the tribe of Benjamin was compensated by the excellence of the land (*Antiq.*, v., 1). "*Parah*" is said by Jerome (*Onomast.*, "Aphra") to be five miles east of Bethel. Perhaps identical with *Fârah* (Robinson, Van de Velde), half-way between Jerusalem and Jericho. "'*Oph-rah*" (a fawn), different from the Ophrah in Judges vi. 11, which belonged to the tribe of Manasseh, but probably the same as the Ophrah in the land of Shual (1 Sam. xiii. 17), and which was called Ephrain (2 Chron. xiii. 19), and Ἐφραΐμ, whither our Lord went before His last Passover (John xi. 54) ; conjectured by Robinson (*Bib. Res.*, i., 447) to be the same as *et Taiyibeh*, a small village on a hill, four miles N.N.E. of Bethel (so Dean Stanley, *Sin. and Pal.*, p. 213).

Ver. 24.—"*K*ᵉ*phar-ha-'Am-môuay*" (hamlet[1] of the Ammonites), read in the Qᵉri and by the Chaldee כ' הָעַמּוֹנָה ; unknown, but somewhere at the head of the passes which lead up from the Jordan valley to the table-land of Benjamin. The name seems commemorative of an incursion of the Ammonites. "*ha-'Oph-nî*," also unknown, but perhaps so called after the Ophnites, a non-Israelitish tribe, mentioned here only. Grove would identify it with the *Gophna* of Josephus (*Bel. Jud.*, iii., 3, § 5), and with the present *Jifna*, two and a half miles north-west of Bethel. "*Gā-bhă*'" (in pause for Gĕ-bhă', a hill),

---

[1] Rt. כָּפַר, to cover, see כְּפִירָה, ix. 17, and cf. Lat. *tectum*.

identical with the Geba in 1 Sam. xiii. 15, 16; 2 Kings xxiii. 8; Zech. xiv. 10, distinguished from Gibeah of Saul (Isa x. 29). It was assigned to the Levites (xxi. 17); fortified by Asa (1 Kings xv. 22); inhabited after the captivity (Neh. vii. 30); now *Jeba*, on a hill opposite to Michmash, about eight miles north of Jerusalem (Robinson, *Bib. Res.*, i., 440).

Vers. 25-28 (*Second Group of Fourteen Cities, in the West Part of Benjamin*).—Ver. 25.—" *Gibh-'ôn*," see ix. 3. "*hā-Rā-māh*" (the lofty), near to Ge-bha and Gibh-'on (Isa. x. 29), conjectured by Keil to be the same as the Ramah of Samuel (1 Sam. i. 19, ii. 11, xxv. 1), but this latter was in Ephraim, and was also called Ramathaim Zophim (1 Sam. i. 1). Perhaps, however, the name Ephraim at this early period may have been extended over the mountainous region of Benjamin, which was in close alliance with and in dependence on it (see Art. by Grove in Smith's *Bib. Dict.*, vol. ii., p. 998). Now *er-Râm*, about five English or six Roman miles north of Jerusalem, described by Robinson as a wretched village on a hill, but with remains of columns, squared stones, etc., all indicating a former importance (*Bib. Res.*, i., 576).[1] "*B'ê-rôth*" (wells), see on ix. 17.

Ver. 26.—"*ham-Mits-peh*" (the watch-tower), different from the Mitspeh in xv. 38; it was the place where Samuel judged Israel (1 Sam. vii. 5, the Maspha of 1 Macc. iii. 46), and where Saul was elected king

---

[1] "*Er-Ram*, marked by the village and green patch on its summit, the most conspicuous object from a distance in the approach to Jerusalem from the south, is certainly *Ramah of Benjamin*" (Stanley, *Sin. and Pal.*, p. 213).

(1 Sam. x. 17); it was fortified by Asa against inroads from the north (1 Kings xv. 22); and was at a later period the residence of the Chaldean governor Gedaliah (2 Kings xxv. 23, 25; Jer. xl. 6). Now *Neby Samwil* (prophet Samuel), about five miles north-west of Jerusalem, and one mile south of Gibeon. "*hak-Kᵉphî-rah*" (the hamlet), ix. 17. "*ham-Mô-tsah*" ("the going out," "the spring-head;" Stanley, *Sin. and Pal.*, App., § 52), probably identical with *Kulônich*, four miles west of Jerusalem, and the *Emmaus*[1] of the New Testament (Grove, Index to Clark's *Bib. Atlas*). A ruin called *Beit Mizzeh*, west of Jerusalem, and near Kulônich, may, according to Lieut. Conder, indicate the site (*Map*, sheet xvii.).

Ver. 27.—"*Re-qem*" ("flower-garden," properly "variegated," rt. רָקַם, to adorn with colours) perhaps *Ain-Karim*, west of Jerusalem (Grove). "*Yir-pᵉÊl*" ("God heals"), probably, according to Lieut. Conder, the village Râfât, north of Jerusalem. The name, he says, is derived from a similar root, and the situation is satisfactory (*Pal. Explor. Fund*, sheet xvii.). "*Tar-'a-lah*" (perhaps *i.q.* תַּרְעֵלָה, reeling, or trembling, from רָעַל, to tremble), only, like the two foregoing towns, mentioned here, but unrecognised. The genealogy in 1 Chron. ii. 43, 44, may indicate that it was founded by a colony from Hebron.

Ver. 28.—"*Tsē-la'*" (rib, side), the burial-place and probably the residence of Kish and Saul (2 Sam. xxi. 14). Site unknown. "*ha-'Eleph*" ("the ox,"

---

[1] Porter, however, considers that the site of Emmaus still remains to be discovered (see Art. on "Emmaus" in Smith's *Bib. Dict.*, p. 549).

probably implying that the inhabitants were a pastoral people). The Alex. Sept. joins it with the preceding word, *e.g.*, Σηλαλέφ (ox-rib), but in the Heb. the ו may have been dropped by a transcriber, otherwise the number of towns would not be fourteen, as stated in this verse, though such a miscalculation might be the error of a copyist (cf. xv. 32, 36). Lieut. Conder would identify it with the present village *Lifta*, west of Jerusalem. The situation agrees with the boundary of Judah (*Pal. Explor. Fund*, 1881). וְהַיְבוּסִי, see on xv. 8. "*The same* (is) *Jerusalem*": By comparing Josh. xv. 7, 8 with xviii. 16, 17, it seems that the boundary between Judah and Benjamin (the north boundary of the former, and the south of the latter) ran at the foot of the hill on which the city stands, and, therefore, that the city itself was in Benjamin; but any one crossing the narrow ravine of Hinnom set foot on the territory of Judah. It was doubtless this position of Jerusalem, the city where the true God was worshipped, which especially contributed at a later period to a close union between these two tribes. "*Gibh-'ath*[1]" (hill), probably the same as the Gibh-'ah of Benjamin (Judges xix. 12, 14), and of Saul (1 Sam. x. 26, xi. 4; see on ver. 24), and supposed to have stood on *Tuleil-el-Phul*, south-west of Geba, and north of Jerusalem (Robinson, *Bib. Res.*, ii., 114; Van de Velde, Strauss, Keil). "(And) *Qiryath*" (city), perhaps *Kertch*, west of Jerusalem (Scholtz, *Reise*, p. 161), if Qir-yath, as Keil supposes, be a different town from Qiryath-yearim;

---

[1] For the derivation see note [1], xv. 57.

but though this latter is reckoned among the towns of Judah (xv. 60, xviii. 14), yet being on the confines of Benjamin (xviii. 14, 15), it might have been conceded to that tribe. This view (says Grove) is confirmed by Qiryath's being in the construc. state, and by the not improbable supposition that יָעָרִים, being followed by עָרִים, might have been overlooked by an early copyist. The Sept. has Ἰαρίμ, Qiryath being omitted, and three Kennicott MSS. read יְעָרִים for עָרִים. Some, however, join this word to the foregoing, and render "hill of Qiryath," but on this view we must suppose the number of the towns at the end of the verse to have been incorrectly stated (see above on ha-Eleph).

CHAPTER XIX.

VER. 1-9.—*The Inheritance of Simeon* (Shim-'ôn, "hearing with acceptance," Gen. xxix. 33).

JACOB'S prediction that this tribe should be dispersed in Israel (Gen. xlix. 7) was partly fulfilled in its portion being allotted to it within the limits of Judah (ver. 9). Its towns formed two groups: (1) those in the south-land of Judah (2-6); (2) those partly in the south-land, partly in the lowlands of Judah (ver. 7). To all these towns were added their dependent villages (ver. 8).

Ver. 1.—וַיֵּצֵא הַגּ׳, cf. xviii. 11. בְּתוֹךְ, not, as usually, "in the midst," but "within" (cf. Auth.Vers.).

Vers. 2-6 (*First Group*).—For all the towns mentioned in this group see on xv. 26-32, and cf. 1 Chron. iv. 28-32.

Ver. 2.—"*Beer-Sheba*," see on xv. 28. It would seem that having been hallowed by the altars of Abraham and Isaac (Gen. xxi. 33 ; xxvi. 23-25) it was a religious centre both to Judah and Simeon. "*She-bha'*" (Shema in xv. 26) is omitted in 1 Chron. iv. 28, perhaps through the oversight of a copyist, who may have been misled by the termination of the preceding word. It is found in all the ancient versions. "*Moladhah*," xv. 26.

Ver. 3.—Cf. xv. 28, 29.

Ver. 4.—"*B^ethûl*," written B^ethû-'Ēl (dweller in God) 1 Chron. iv. 30, and for which is found K^esil in Josh. xv. 30 (see note). "*Chormah*," see xii. 14.

Ver. 5.—See on xv. 31.

Ver. 6.—See on xv. 32. "*Thirteen cities*" : The number is fourteen, as in the Syriac Vers., unless She-bha' is omitted. A copyist may have confounded the Hebrew letters for "fourteen" with those for "thirteen" (see note on xv. 32).

Ver. 7 (*Second Group*).—'*A-yin* and *Rimmôn*, inaccurately here written Remmon (A.V.), were in the south country of Judah (see xv. 32). "'*Ether* and '*Ashan*" were in the valley (xv. 42). "*Four Towns*": In the parallel list in 1 Chron. iv. 32, the number is five, viz., Etam, Ayin, Rimmon, Tochen, and Ashan, where, according to Grove, Tochen is substituted for Ether (Smith's *Bib. Dict.*, i., p. 558).

Ver. 8.—"*All the villages*," for הָצֵר see on xiii. 23. "*Ba-'a-lath-B^e 'êr*" (having a well), called here Ramath-ne-ghebh (height of the south) ; see on Bealoth

xv. 24. It was apparently the extreme southern limit of the territory assigned to Simeon.

Ver. 9.—הֶבֶל, xvii. 14. רַב מֵהֶם, "*too large for them*" (§ 119, 1). The reason why so small a territory was assigned to the tribe of Simeon was that it had greatly diminished since the census in Numb. i. 23 (see Numb. xxvi. 14). This decrease was no doubt partly owing to the mortality consequent on the sin at Baal-peor, in which sin the Simeonites had taken a leading part (Numb. xxv.).[1]

VERS. 10-16.—*Inheritance of Z^ebhû-lun* ("habitation," Gen. xxx. 20), *and its Boundaries.*

This tribe is omitted in the lists of 1 Chron. Its territory, which embraced one of the choicest portions of the land, extended from the Sea of Galilee on the east, to the river Kishon on the west, and was bounded on the south by Issachar, and on the north by Asher and Naphtali. It afterwards formed a portion of Lower Galilee, and contained the towns Tiberias, Cana, and Nazareth (cf. Matt. iv. 13, 15).

Ver. 10.—"*Sa-rîdh*" (a fissure, rt. שָׂרַד, to make an incision), not known to Eusebius and Jerome (*Onom.*), but must have been on the south boundary, forming a landmark, whence the border was drawn to the west (ver. 11) and the east (ver. 12). Knobel, who derives the word as above, thinks it meant a gully about three miles south-east of Nazareth; more

---

[1] A brief sketch of the history of this tribe at a later period is given in 1 Chron. iv. 39-43 (cf. Stanley's *Sin. and Pal.*, p. 161).

probably, however, it was a town so called from the gully or wady near which it stood. The Sept. reads Σεδδούκ (Vat. MS.); and the original (says Lieut. Conder) may be thought to have been Sadid, in which case *Tell-Shadûd* occupies a very probable position for the site (*Map*, sheet viii.).

Ver. 11.—לְיָמָּה, "*towards the sea*," *i.e.*, westward. Though the border, according to Gen. xlix. 13, compared with Joseph., *Antiq.*, v., 1, § 22, reached to the Mediterranean, yet it seems from this ver. 11 that it stopped short at Carmel. וּמַרְעֲלָה, "*even to Mar-'a-lah*" ("place of trembling," rt. רָעַל, to tremble, perhaps so named from an earthquake); site uncertain. The word עָלָה led Keil to infer that it was somewhere on Carmel. According to Lieut. Conder it would occupy the position of the present village Malûl, "L" and "R" being easily convertible (*Pal. Explor. Fund*, *Map*, sheet viii.). וּפָגַע בְּ (cf. xvi. 7, xvii. 10), the same verb is also followed by אֶל in the next clause. "*Dab-ba-sheth*" in pause for Dab-be-sheth (a camel's hump, Isa. xxx. 6, rt. דָּבַשׁ, to be soft, round, Ges., *Thes.*), perhaps so called because it stood on the heights of Carmel. הַנַּחַל, "*the water-course*," etc., probably the Kishon. "*Yoq-nᵉ'am*," see xii. 22.

Ver. 12 (*Eastward Direction of the Border*).— "*Sa-rîdh*" as being a central point (see ver. 10) is here repeated. "*Kis-lôth-Ta-bhôr*" (loins or flanks[1] of Tabor), apparently a place on the side of Tabor,

---

[1] It is common in the Hebrew Scriptures to personify the features of a country (cf. כָּתֵף, shoulder, xv. 8; אָזְנוֹת, ears of, xix. 34; שְׁכֶם, back, xx. 7).

and possibly the same as הַכְּסֻלּוֹת in ver. 18 (Masius and others), and the vicus Chasalus of the *Onom.*, i.e., the present *village of Ik-sâl*, two and a half miles west of Tabor (Grove). "*Da-bĕ'rath*" ("pasture" or "sheepwalk," mentioned in xxi. 28; 1 Chron. vi. 57, as being in the tribe of Issachar, and as assigned to the Gershonite Levites; now probably the village *Deburich* at the western foot of Tabor (Robinson, *Bib. Res.*, ii., 350, 351). "*Ya-phî-a'*" ("shining," from יפע to shine, perhaps because seen from a distance): It must have been east of Deburich, though the site is unknown; Yâfa, with which Robinson and Grove would identify it, lies to the west of that village.

Ver. 13.—Render "*And from thence it passed toward the East, toward the rising of the sun, to Gath-chêpher*" ("wine-press of the well"); ה- loc.; the birthplace of Jonah[1] (2 Kings xiv. 25), now *el Meshhad* (Rob., *Bib. Res.*, ii., 350), where the prophet's tomb is still shown, about four miles north of Nazareth, on the road to Tiberias. "*To Eth-qa-tsîn*" ("time of the judge," עִתָּה = עֵת, with ה loc.). Site unknown. "*And went out to Rimmon which reacheth to Neah*": הַמְּתֹאָר, which is made part of the prop. name in Auth. Vers.,[2] Sept., and Vulg., is prop. the Pual. Part. with art. from תָּאַר, "to be marked out or drawn" (cf. xv. 9). "*Rimmon*" (pomegranate), allotted to the Merarite Levites (1 Chron. vi. 62, Heb.), probably now *Rummanch* in the plain of el-Buttauf, six miles north of Nazareth (Rob., *Bib. Res.*, iii., 110; Von Raum., p. 138). "*Nê-'ah*" ("shaking" [Ges.,

---

[1] The Pharisees, therefore, were mistaken in supposing that no prophet came out of Galilee (John vii. 52).
[2] "Remnon-methoar."

Lex.], rt. גָעַשׁ, to shake), unknown, but probably somewhere to the north of Rimmon (Grove).

Ver. 14 (*The Northern Boundary*).—" *And the border compassed it* (*i.e.*, Neah) *on the north to Channa-thôn.*" חַנָּ ("gracious," or "pleasant"), is probably the same as *Cana of Galilee*, the native place of Nathanael and scene of Christ's first miracle (John ii. 1, 11, iv. 46, xxi. 2); now *Kâna el Jelîl* (Keil). "*And its goings out were the ravine of Yiph-tach-'Êl*" ("God opens": On גַּי, not "valley" (Auth. Vers.), but "ravine" or "glen" (see viii. 11). Yiph-tach-'El is thought by Robinson to be identical with the Roman *Jotapata*, which Josephus long defended against Vespasian (Joseph., *Bel. Jud.*, iii., 7, 7); now *Jefât*, in the mountains of Galilee, half way between the Bay of Acre and the Lake of Gennesaret. Thus the ravine of Yiph-tach-El, at which Zebulon bordered on Asher, would correspond to the *Wady Abilên*, which commences in the hills near Jefât (Rob., *Later Bib. Res.*, p. 103, *f*), though "Wady" more accurately denotes a נַחַל than a גַּי (Stanley, *Sin. and Pal.*, Append., § 2, 38).

Ver. 15.—From a description of the boundary lines the narrative here passes abruptly to an enumeration of the towns of Zebulon. The וְ at the beginning of the verse not being followed, as in xviii. 21, xv. 21, by הֶעָרִים with the substantive verb, it is probable that the text is here imperfect; see also the concluding portion of this note. "*Qat-tath*" (small), and "*Na-h^alal*" (probably pasture, see Isa. vii. 19, from נָהַל, to lead, cf. מִדְבָּר from דָּבַר), are perhaps the same as Qit-rôn and Na-h^alôl in Judges i. 30, but their sites are unknown. In the Talmud (Megilla, 6, *a*)

Qit-rôn is identified with Zippori, *i.e.*, Sepphoris, now *Seffûrieh*. Na-h^alal, in some copies written Mahalal, was a Levitical town (xxi. 35); according to the Jerusalem Talmud (Megillah, i., 1) called in post-biblical times Mahlul, which has been identified by Schwarz with the modern *Malul* in the plain of Esdraelon, four miles west of Nazareth. So Van de Velde (*Memoir*, p. 335), Grove (Index to Clark's *Bib. Atlas*, and Art. in Smith's *Bib. Dict.*). "*Shim-rôn*," see xi. 1. "*Yidh-'a-lah*" (that which God has shown, Ges., *Lex.*), supposed by Van de Velde to be *Jeda* or *Jeida* on the west of the village Semuniyeh, but Schwarz (p. 172), probably on the authority of the Talmudical books, gives the name as Yidalah or Chirii, and would identify it with the village *Kellah el-Chiré*, about three miles south of Beit-lahm (Grove). "*Bêth-le-chem*" (house of bread), probably the residence of Ibzan (Judges xii. 8), now the miserable village of *Beit-lahm*, six miles west of Nazareth (Rob., *Bib. Res.*, iii., p. 113). The town of the same name in the south is often distinguished from it by the addition of the word *Judah* (Judges xvii. 8, 9, xix. 18; Ruth i. 1), and *Ephratah* (Micah v. 2). "*Twelve towns and their villages*": As five towns only are mentioned in this verse, and those in vers. 10-14 were border places, some of them not belonging to Zebulon, and as Kartah and Dimnah, though towns of Zebulon (xxi. 34, 35), and also Nazareth, are entirely omitted, the opinion of Michaelis, Keil, and others, is probably correct, viz., that there is a gap in the text here, as in xv. 59, xxi. 36.

VERS. 17-23.—*Inheritance of Yis-sas-khar* ("he brings wages," יִשָּׂא שָׂכָר, Gen. xxx. 18).

His allotment was bounded on the north by Zebulon, on the east by Jordan, on the west by Manasseh and Asher, on the south by Manasseh, and contained the rich and noble plain of Esdraelon or Jezreel. Like the territory of Zebulun, it afterwards formed part of Lower Galilee.[1] In vers. 18-23 a list is given of the principal towns instead of a delineation of the boundaries of the tribe; but these latter may be easily traced from those of the surrounding tribes.

Ver. 18.—"*And their border was toward Yiz-r*ᵉ*'El,*" *i.e.,* extended to and beyond it. " *Yiz-rᵉ'El*" (God sows), a town in the plain so called (xvii. 16), described in the *Onomast.* as situated between Scythopolis and Legio; now *Zerin*, a poor and small village, standing on a hill commanding a splendid and extensive view (Rob., iii., 161); it formed part of the kingdom of Ishbbosheth (2 Sam. ii. 8, 9), and was noted as the principal residence of Ahab (1 Kings xviii. 45, 46, xxi. 1). "*Kᵉsul-lôth*" ("loins," the town being perhaps on the slopes of a mountain), see on ver. 12. " *Shû-nêm,*" contrac. from שְׁנַיִם (two resting-places), where the Philistines encamped before the battle of Gilboa (1 Sam. xxviii. 4); the native place

---

[1] In this province our Redeemer spent the greatest portion of the time He sojourned here on earth, and hence was called a Galilean. Here He appointed His apostles to meet Him after His resurrection (Matt. xxviii. 7, 16), and of this same country most, if not all, of the apostles were natives, and, therefore, were called by the angels "men of Galilee" (Acts i. 11).

of Abishag (1 Kings i. 3), and celebrated in connection with Elisha (2 Kings iv. 8, viii. 1, etc.) ; now *Solam* or *Sulem*, a village on the south-west slope of the range of Jebel ed-Dûhy, commonly called from tradition "Little Hermon" (*Sin. and Pal.*, p. 336, note 2), three miles north of Jezreel (Rob., *Bib. Res.*, ii., 324).

Ver. 19.—"*Cheplia ra-yîm*" (two wells), perhaps the Chepher mentioned in xii. 17, but according to the *Onom.* (*s.v.* "Aphraim"), *villa Affarœa*, six miles north of Legio (el-Lejjûn), and identified by Knobel with the village *el Alfulch*, west of Shunem, and five miles north-east of Lejjun (Keil). Lieut. Conder would identify it with the ancient ruined site *el Farriyeh* (*Pal. Explor. Fund*). "*Shî-'ôn*" ("overturning," see rt. שוא, Ges., *Lex.*), undiscovered, but, according to Eusebius and Jerome (*Onomast.*), "villa juxta montem Thabor," possibly *Chirbet Schi'in*, one and a half miles north-west of Deburieh (Grove, Art. in Smith's *Bib. Dict.*). "*'A-na-ch^arath*" ("a narrow way," rt. אנה, *i.q.* צנח, to be narrow), identified by Lieut. Conder with the village *en Na'ûrah*," "in correct relative position to other towns of Issachar" (*Pal. Explor. Fund*).

Ver. 20.—"*ha-Rab-bîth*" (the great place), perhaps *Arab-boneh*, south of Gilboa (Rob., iii., p. 157); but Lieut. Conder proposes the present village Râba, south-east of the plain of Esdraelon, as a suitable position (*Pal. Explor. Fund, Map*, sheet xii.). "*Qish-yôn*" (hardness, rt. קשה, to be hard, and, therefore, according to Ges., *Thes.*, 1211, 1243, not to be connected with the river Kishon, "winding," rt. קוש, to be bent), allotted to Gershonite Levites (xxi. 28), but unknown; for it Kedesh is substituted in 1 Chron. vi. 72 (57 Heb.). '*E-bhets*[1] (white, shining, rt. בץ, to be white), mentioned here only; possibly (says Grove) a corruption of Thebez, now Tûbâs, not far from Engannim, and Shunaim; but, according to Lieut. Conder, probably the present ruin *el Beida*, at the north end of the plain of Esdraelon. The Arabic exactly corresponds to the Hebrew, with the same meaning, "white" (*Pal. Explor. Fund*).

Ver. 21.—"*Re-meth*" (height), called Ramoth in 1 Chron. vi. 58 (73 A.V.), and Yarmûth in ch. xxi. 29, where it is named as a Levit. city. These may be different names of the same town. "'*Ên-gan-nîm*" (fountain of gardens), also allotted to the Levites (xxi. 29), called '*A-nêm* (1 Chron. vi. 58, 73 A.V.), probably the same as the Γιναία of Josephus (*Bel. Jud.*, iii., 3, 4), and now *Jenin*, in the midst of gardens and orchards, on the southern side of the plain of Jezreel (Rob. and Keil). It is evidently, says Stanley, identical with *Bethgan* (Sept.; 2 Kings ix. 27), translated "the garden-house" in Eng. Vers. (*Sin. and Pal.*, p. 349, note 2). "'*Ên-chad-dah*" (fountain of sharpness, *i.e.*, of speed), on the border of Issachar, near Engannim. Van de Velde would identify it with *Ain-Haud*, on the west side of Carmel, and about two miles from the sea; but this, says Grove, is surely out of the limits of the tribe of Issachar, and rather in Asher or Manasseh. According to Lieut. Conder, it is probably the present ruin *Kefr Adân*, south-west of the plain

---

[1] Written in the Hebrew text אֶבֶץ, the first syllable in pause for א.

of Esdraelon. "*Bêth-pats-tsets*" (house of dispersion), unknown.

Ver. 22.—"*And the border reached to*" (lit. struck upon), cf. xvi. 7. "*Ta-bhôr*" (either "a stone-quarry" or "a lofty place" [Ges., *Lex.*], a town built on the mount so called, on which considerable ruins were found by Robinson (*Bib. Res.*, ii., 352, etc.). In 1 Chron. vi. 77 (A.V.) it is said to be in the tribe of Zebulun, and to have been assigned to the Levites, but it is not mentioned as a Levite town in Josh. xxi. Being on the borders of both tribes, it may possibly have been regarded as belonging to both (Keil). "And *Sha-ch*^{a}*tsû-mah*," for which the Q^{e}ri reads *Sha-ch*^{a}*tsî-mah*, "lofty places"[1] rt. יָנְצִי, "to raise oneself up" (Ges., *Lex.*), a town unknown, but apparently between Tabor and the Jordan. "*Bêth-she-mesh*" (house of the sun), to be distinguished from the one in Judah (xv. 10), and in Naphtali (v. 38); perhaps (as Knobel and Keil conjecture) the present ruined village of *Bessum* (Rob., *Bib. Res.*, ii., 369) ; or, according to the later researches of Lieut. Conder, the ruined site 'Ain esh Shemsîyeh, in the Jordan valley. "*Sixteen towns*," a number which would not be correct, unless Tabor was reckoned as belonging to Issachar.

VERS. 24-31.—*Inheritance of 'A-shēr* (fortunate or happy).

The territory of this tribe contained some of the richest soil in all Palestine (Stanley, *Sin. and Pal.*, p. 265), and in its fruitfulness fulfilled the predictions of Jacob (Gen. xlix. 20) and of Moses (Deut. xxxiii.

---

[1] The *ah* is properly local, and denotes motion, "to Shachatsim" (Grove).

24); it had also mines of iron and copper (Deut. xxxiii. 25, and cf. the note on Misrephoth-maim, xi. 8). It extended from Zidon to the south of Dor (see on xi. 2), on the confines of Manasseh, and was bordered by Zebulon and Issachar on the south-east, and by Naphtali on the north-east. Here it is described principally by an enumeration of its towns, and the description begins in the neighbourhood of Accho (Ptolemais), on the Mediterranean coast, which, though not included among the towns here named, is mentioned in Judges i. 31 as belonging to Asher. From this central point the description proceeds first towards the south (vers. 26, 27), and then towards the north (vers. 28-30). The position of many of the towns is unknown.

Ver. 25.—"*Chel-qath*" (portion), a town allotted to the Gershonite Levites (xxi. 31), called Chû-qôq (1 Chron. vi. 60, Heb.; 77, A. V.), perhaps by an error in copying, or because it had both names, but not to be confounded with the Chuq-qoq on the boundary of Naphtali (xix. 34); conjectured by Schwarz to be the village *Yerka*, about eight miles north-east of Accho (Akka; Van de Velde's *Map*). "*Ch^alî*" (a necklace, from הָלָה, to be polished), perhaps *Julis*, between Yerka and Accho (Knobel). "*Be-ten*" (perhaps "valley," *i.q.* κοιλάς. By Eusebius (*Onomast.*, Βατναί) called Βεβετὰν, a village, eight Roman miles east of Accho (Ptolemais). This seems to indicate the village *el Baneh* (Lieut. Conder, *Pal. Explor. Fund*). "*Akh-shaph*," see xi. 1. Knobel would identify it with Accho (Ptolemais), with which, however, it has nothing in common but the letter כ; possibly, says Grove, it may be Kesâf, nearly midway between Tyre and Banias, but he thinks the position too inland, and suggests *Khaifa* at the foot of Carmel, the Sept. rendering Κεάφ perhaps exhibiting the name in the process of change from the ancient to the modern form (see Art. on "Asher," note *a*, in Smith's *Bib. Dict.*). Lieut. Conder, however, would identify it with the present village *el Yasîf*, north-east of Acre. "It is often mentioned in Egyptian records, and the proposed site agrees both with these and with the biblical indications of situation" (*Map*, iii.).

Ver. 26.—"'*Al-lam-me-lekh*" (the king's oak): The name has been preserved in *Nahr el Malek*, or *Malik*, which falls into the Kishon near Haifa (Rob., *Bib. Res.*, iii., 113). "'*Am-'adh*" (eternal people), apparently (says Lieut. Conder) the ruin *el-'Amûd*, north of Acre (*Pal. Explor. Fund Map*, sheet iii.). "*Mish-'al*" (prayer), a Levite town (xxi. 30), written "Mashal" (1 Chron. vi. 59 [74]). According to the *Onomast.* (*s.v.* "Masan"), it was on the coast, near to Carmel, as seems indicated also in the remainder of the verse. Probably, says Lieut. Conder, the ruin *Maisleh*, near Acre (*Map*, sheet iii.). "*Kar-mel*," see on xii. 22. "*Shî-chôr-libh-nath*" (black-white), though taken for two separate places by the Sept., Vulg., and Syr., yet is more generally regarded as a river. According to Masius, Michaelis, and Stanley (*Sin. and Pal.*, p. 505), it is identical with the Belus, or glass river (so called from the glass there made from the sand), in the neighbourhood of Acre, but as this situation is too far removed from the southern boundary of Asher, more probably the reference is to the *Nahr-Zerka* (blue river), which flows into the Mediterranean about eight miles south of Dor (see on xi. 2), at the southern extremity of Asher. The epithet "blue" might correspond to "black and white." As Shichor is a name given to the Nile (Isa. xxiii. 3 ; Jer. ii. 18), its use here may have a reference to the ancient commerce of Phœnicia with Egypt.

Ver. 27.—In this verse the southern boundary is traced from the Nahr-Zerka eastward.—"*Beth-Da-ghôn*" (house of Dagon) : The site is uncertain, but Lieut. Conder would identify it with the present ruin *Tell D'aûk*, " in correct relative position near the mouth of the river Belus" (*Pal. Explor. Fund*). The name seems to signify that it was a Philistine colony; there was another town of the same name in Judah (xv. 41). "*Z^ebhû-lun*" (habitation), not a town, as Rosenm. says, but the tribe so called, which formed one of the boundaries of Asher (cf. xvii. 10, xix. 34). "*Yiph-tach-'Êl*," see on ver. 14. "*Beth-ha-'ê-meg*" (house of the valley), according to Robinson (iii., 103, 107, 108), '*Amkah*, about eight miles to the north-east of Akka (Acre), but if his identification of Jefât with Yiph-tach-El be correct, the site of Beth-ha-e-meq must be sought for farther south than Amkah (Grove). "*N^e'î-Êl*" (perhaps *i.q.* נְעִיאֵל נְעִיאֵל, perhaps "treasure of God," Ges., *Lex.*), possibly *Mî-'ar*, a village on a lofty mountain brow, between Jefât and Kabul. The change of "N" into "M," and of "L" into "R," is frequent, and Mi-'ar retains the Ayin of Neiel (Grove, Smith's *Bib. Dict.*). "*Ka-bhûl*," probably identical with the κώμη Χαβωλώ of Josephus (*Vit.*, § 43), now Kabûl, about ten miles south-east of Acre (Rob., *Later Bib. Res.*, iii., p. 88), and on the borders of Galilee. It was probably in the neighbourhood of

20

the district called "the land of Cabul" (1 Kings ix. 13). In the Hebrew the term Cabul has no certain meaning, but in the Phœnician tongue it means "displeasing" (Joseph., *Antiq.*, viii., 5, § 3).

Vers. 28-30 (*The Northern District of Asher*).— Ver. 28.—"*'Ebh-rôn*" (passage-ford), unknown, but apparently near Zidon. Fourteen MSS. read "Abdon," which occurs in xxi. 30; 1 Chron. vi. 59 (74), and possibly ר may have been written by mistake for ד. But, on the other hand, all the ancient versions accord with the Masoretic text in reading Ebh-ron, except the Vat. Sept., which has 'Ελβών. Since some towns, viz., Akko, Achlabh, and Chelbah, are omitted in this list (see Judges i. 31), perhaps by the error of a copyist, Abdon may also have fallen out. "*R^{e}chôbh*" (wide space), evidently near Zidon, but the site undiscovered. Another town of the same name is mentioned in ver. 30, and both are different from the R^{e}chobh in Numb. xiii. 21, which was probably near Tell el Kady (Laish or Dan) and Banias (cf. Judges xviii. 28; see Smith's *Dict. of the Bible*). "*Chammôn*" (warm or sunny), apparently not far from Zidon. Schultz would identify it with the modern village of *Hamul*, near the coast, about ten miles below Tyre, but both etymology and site are doubtful (Grove). Lieut. Conder suggests the ruin *Hima*, south-east of Tyre, a situation which appears to him satisfactory. "*Qa-nah*" (reed), perhaps *Ain-Kana*, eight miles south-east of Saida (Zidon; Van de Velde's *Map*). "*Great Tsî-dhôn*," see xi. 8. It does not appear that the Asherites were ever able to expel the inhabitants of any of the Phœnician towns, or to render them tributary (see Judges i. 31, 32). The character of the tribe was the reverse of warlike (Stanley, *Sin. and Pal.*, p. 265), for thus in the war against Sisera, while Zebulun and Naphtali "hazarded their lives unto the death," Asher "abode in his breaches," *i.e.*, in his creeks and harbours (Judges v. 17, 18).

Ver. 29.—"*And the border turned to ha-Ramah*": The Vulg. reads "Horma," but the other ancient versions agree with the Masoretic text, hence ה denotes the article which is prefixed to the name by way of distinction. Probably the Ramah is meant which is marked in Arrowsmith's *Bib. Atlas* as lying on the coast between Zidon and Tyre, about three miles east of Tyre, according to Van de Velde's *Map* (see also Grove, Art. "Ramah" [4], Smith's *Bib. Dict.*). With less probability Robinson places it more than ten miles south-east of Tyre (*Bib. Res.*, iii., 64). "*To the fortified city of Tsôr*" (lit. "to the city, the fortress of Tsôr") : Tsôr ("rock," *i.q.* צור), Greek Τύρος, "Tyre," is here mentioned in the Bible for the first time, and the allusion, according to Keil, is not to the insular but the inland city. Justin (xi., 10) records a tradition of the inhabitants that there was a city on the mainland before there was one on the island. Tsôr would, indeed, more properly apply to a city built upon a rocky island than to one on a fertile plain ; but if the island formed part of the territory of the inland city, the latter might have taken its name from it. It is now called Sûr. "*And the border turned to Chôsah, and the outgoings thereof were at the sea from the district towards Akh-zîbh.*" "*Chô-sah*" (a refuge), mentioned nowhere else. It is marked in Arrowsmith's *Bib. Atlas* as lying on the sea-coast below Tyre, but

Keil regards it as an inland city.[1] מֵחֶבֶל, "*from the district*," *i.e.*, by the side of it (Keil). חֶבֶל, which means lit. " land measured by a line," is here taken in the general sense of territory, as in Deut. iii. 4. The boundary, says Keil, took an inland course from the maritime cities of Zidon and Tyre to Chosah, and it was only at Akh-zibh that Asher's inheritance was bordered on the west by the sea. "'*Akh-zîbh*" (" a winter torrent," and hence " deceptive," as soon drying up, rt. כָּזַב, to lie ; from it Asher could not drive out the Canaanites, Judges i. 31) ; afterwards *Ecdippa* (Joseph., *B. J.*, i. 13, § 4 ; Plin., *Nat. Hist.*, v., 17), now *Zib*, on the coast, eight or nine miles north of Acre. Another town of the same name belonged to Judah (xv. 44).

Ver. 30.—"'*Um-mah*" (junction), unknown, though possibly *Alma* in the highlands on the coast, about five miles E.N.E. of Ras en Nakhûra (Grove).[2] "*Aphêq*," see on xiii. 4. "*Rᵉchôbh*," unknown ; see the same name in ver. 28. It is uncertain which of the two towns was assigned to the Levites (xxi. 30; 1 Chron. vi. 60 [75]) ; but probably this here mentioned was retained possession of by the Canaanites, as recorded in Judges i. 31, for there it is also mentioned along with 'A-phîq, probably *i.q.* 'Aphêq. "*Twenty and two cities*" [towns] : The number does not correspond with the list given in vers. 25-30, but perhaps there may be some omission in the text (see on ver. 28).

---

[1] According to Lieut. Conder, it is apparently the present ruin *Ozziyeh*, on the coast south of Tyre.

[2] So Lieut. Conder (*Pal. Explor. Fund, Map*, sheet iii.).

VERS. 32-39.—*The Inheritance of Naph-ta-li.*[1]

The territory of this tribe was mostly mountainous (xx. 7), but contained also the rich plains of Merj-Ayûn, and the well-watered country about Banias and Hasbeya, the springs of Jordan. Celebrated as the birthplace of Barak (Judges iv.), and the scene of Joshua's victory over the King of Hazor (xi.); bounded on the west by Asher, on the south by Zebulon and Issachar, on the east by the Sea[2] of Gennesaret and the Jordan, on the north by the ravine of the Litany, or Leontes, and the mountainous ranges of Lebanon. At a later period it was comprised in the district called Upper Galilee, where our Lord and His apostles chiefly exercised their ministry (Matt. iv. 13, 14, etc.).

Ver. 33.—In this verse the boundary is traced on the west, north, and east. "*Cheleph*" (exchange), unknown, but conjectured by Van de Velde to be identical with *Beitlif*, on the boundary between Naphtali and Asher, east of Ras Abyad, " the white promontory," and west of Kedesh. "*From the oak-forest in Tsa-'a-nan-nîm*[3] ": Here אֵלוֹן, an oak, is probably a noun of multitude (quercetum, Junius and Tremellius); in Judges iv. 11 the Hebrew word is interchanged with אֵלוֹן, which, according to Michaelis,

---

[1] Meaning "my strife," rt. פָּתַל, not used in Qal, but in Niphal, where it signifies to wrestle, to strive (see Gen. xxx. 8).

[2] This is doubtless the sea (יָם) referred to in the prophecy of Moses (Deut. xxxiii. 23), and rendered "west" in the Authorised Version.

[3] This word is written differently in Judges iv. 11, but the Q'ri of that passage adopts the form here used as more accurate.

Rosenm., Keil, and Del., means a terebinth-tree, though Gesenius (*Lex.*, p. 50) doubts this distinction. 'צע, "removings," from צעי, "to move tents," "to go forward" (Ges., *Lex.*), and hence a place where tents stand; near Kedesh Naphtali (Judges iv. 11), northwest of the Sea of Merom (Stanley, *Jewish Church*, 324, Localities, 197). Robinson found this district still wooded with oak trees (*Bib. Res.*, ii., 447). "*'A-dha-mî of the pass*"[1]: Possibly *Deir-el-Athmar* (red cloister), a place still inhabited, and deriving its name from the colour of the soil in the neighbourhood, about eight miles north-west of Baalbec (Knobel). נקב, lit. a cavern, from נקב, to excavate, and hence "a pass between mountains." But the Sept., the Jerus. Talmud, and Reland (*Pal.*, 545) separate the two words and refer them to two towns, as in the A.V., the site of neither of which is known (Clark's *Bib. Atlas*). "*Yabh-n᷄'êl*," cf. xv. 11, where the same name occurs as one of the towns of Judah, perhaps here the same as *Jamnia*, or *Jamnith*, mentioned by Josephus among the villages in Upper Galilee (*Bel. Jud.*, ii., 20, § 6). "*Lăq-qûm*" ("stopping up the way," *i.e.*, a fortified place, from an Arab. rt. "to stop up the way," Ges., *Lex.*), apparently between Yabhneel and the Jordan, but unknown. "*And its outgoings were the Jordan*": The Upper Jordan, *i.e.*, the *Nahr Hasbany*, a source of the Jordan, is meant.

Ver. 34.—In this verse the boundary line is traced on the south of Naphtali.—"*Turned westwards*," *i.e.*, from the Jordan. "*To 'Az-nôth-Ta-bhôr*" ("ears [*i.e.*

---

[1] So Keil, following the accentuation of the Hebrew text, which connects the first word with the second.

probably summits] *of Tabor*"), mentioned by Eusebius (*Onomast.*) as a village lying in the plain on the confines of Diocæsarea (probably the modern *Seffurieh;* Rob., *Bib. Res.*, ii., 337); the site is undiscovered, but may have been on the east slope of Tabor, near the Jordan. "*To Chŭq-qôq*" ("decreed portion"), mentioned by Eusebius and Jerome (*Onomast.*, "Icoc."), but unknown to them; perhaps *Yakûk*, a village on the mountains of Naphtali, about seven miles S.S.W. of Safed, and at the head of Wady el Amûd (Walcott, and Rob., *Bib. Res.*, p. 82). An ancient Jewish tradition places the tomb of Habakkuk here. "*And reached to* (struck upon) *Zebulun on the south, and reached to Asher on the west, and to Judah on the Jordan toward the sun rising*": Some (as Bachiene) have supposed that "Judah" here denotes a town on the east border of Naphtali, or a town in Issachar (Knobel), or in Asher (Fay), yet it would be strange that the mention of two tribes, Asher and Zebulun, which imply territories, should be followed immediately by that of a single town. Still less satisfactory is the conjecture of Masius that the *tribe* of Judah is meant, and that the expression, "Judah upon Jordan," signifies that Naphtali traded with Judah by means of the Jordan. If the reading in the Hebrew text is correct, the best interpretation is that of Von Raumer (*Pal.*, 405-410), which is adopted by Keil and others, viz., that "Judah here denotes the 'Havoth-Jair'" (Numb. xxxii. 41), called "Judah" here because Jair, the possessor of these villages, was a descendant of Judah on the father's side through Hezron (1 Chron. ii. 5, 21, 22). As, however, this explanation can hardly be said to clear up the difficulty of the passage, Maurer, and after him Bunsen, regards בִּיהוּדָה as a corruption for וּגְבוּלָם ("and their boundary"), referring to xvii. 10, xix. 22;[1] but Clericus simply omits it on the authority of the Vat. Alex., and Ald. MSS. of the Sept. הַיַּרְדֵּן, according to Keil, is in appos. to בִּיהוּדָה, in the sense of "Judah of the Jordan," like "Jordan of Jericho," in Numb. xxii. 1, xxvi. 3, and ought not to have been separated by the Masoretic pointing; but, according to Maurer's reading, the rendering will be, "and their border was Jordan on the east," or, omitting "Judah," "the Jordan (was) toward the sun rising," *i.e.*, formed the east border.

Vers. 35-38 (*The fortified cities of Naphtali*).— "The general character of the cities in this region is that they stand on rocky spurs or ridges, above peaceful basins, high among the hills" (Stanley's *Sin. and Pal.*, xi., p. 390).

Ver. 35.—עָרֵי מִבְ׳, "*cities of fortification.*" "*hăts-Tsĭd-dîm*" ("the sides"), wrongly read הַצָּרִים (the Tyrians) by the Vat. Sept., and צָדוֹן by the Peshito Syr., under the notion that the next name Tser was Tyre; but Tyre and Tsi-dhon were included in the allotment of Asher, and not of Naphtali (xix. 28, 29). The Jerusalem Talmud identifies it with *Kefr Chittai*, which Schwarz takes to be the present *Hattîn* at the northern foot of the well-known Kurn Hattin, or "Horns of Hattin," a few miles west of Tiberias (Grove). "*Tsêr*," probably on the south-west side of the Lake of Gennesareth, but unknown. "*Chăm-măth*" (warm baths), near Tiberias, on the west of Gennesareth, called Chammoth-Dor (xxi. 32), and

---

[1] See also Grove's Art. "Judah" in Smith's *Dict. of the Bible*, p. 1156, note *b*.

Chammon (1 Chron. vi. 61, Heb., 76, Auth. Vers.), and identical with Emmaus (Joseph., *Antiq.*, xviii., ii., 3; Stanley, *Sin. and Pal.*, p. 373, note 6). "*Răq-qăth*" (bank, shore), not known, though, according to the Talmud, occupying the site where Tiberias was afterwards built. The nearest approach to the name is *Kerak*, formerly Tarichææ, close to the embouchure of the Jordan (Grove). "*Kĭn-nĕ-rĕth*," see on xi. 2. All trace of the town is lost, but Knobel thinks that it stood in the plain of Gennesareth, on the shore of the lake, where now stands the *Khan-Manijeh*. For a glowing description of the plain see Joseph., *Bel. Jud.*, ch. x., 8.

Ver. 36.—"*'A-dhā-māh*" (red earth), unknown, but possibly *Ras el Ahmar*, i.e., red-head, on the north of Safed (Robinson, *Bib. Res.*, p. 69; Knobel). "*hā-Rā-māh*," distinct from the Ramah in ver. 29, perhaps the modern *Rameh*, between Akka (Ptolemais) and the north end of the Sea of Galilee, and about eight miles S.S.E. of Safed (Robinson, *Bib. Res.*, iii., 78). It stands on a bold spur of the Galilean Antilebanon, and is supposed by Stanley to be the "*city set upon a hill*" (Matt. v. 14; *Sin. and Pal.*, p. 429); but Grove remarks that, though the spot is distinguished by a very lofty brow, commanding one of the most extensive views in all Palestine (Rob., p. 78), and answering perfectly to the name of Ramah, yet the village of Ramah itself is on the lower slope of the hill (Smith's *Bib. Dict.*, vol. ii., p. 1000). "*Chā-tsōr*," see on xi. 1.

Ver. 37.—"*Qĕ-dhĕsh*" (sanctuary), not to be confounded with that in xii. 22 (see note). It is called Qe-dhesh-Naphtali (the home of Barak, Judges iv.

6, 10; was captured by Tiglath-Pileser (2 Kings xv. 29); now *Kades*, ten miles north of Safed, and four to the north-west of the upper part of the Sea of Merom. "*'Edh-rĕ-'î*," distinct from that in xii. 4. Apparently the present village Y'ater. The relative position is suitable, and the letters "T" and "D" often interchanged (*Pal. Explor. Fund*, 1881). "*'Ên-Chā-tsôr*" (fountain of the village of the fenced place), probably *Ain Hazur*, south of Ramah.

Ver. 38.—" *Yĭr-'ôn* " (place of terror), unknown, though possibly *Yarûn*, to the west of Lake Merom (Grove). "*Mĭgh-dăl-'Êl*" (tower of God), conjectured by some to be the same as *Magdala* (Matt. xv. 39), on the Sea of Galilee (Stanley, *Sin. and Pal.*, p. 382, note 2), and now the wretched village *el-Mejdel* (Rob., *Bib. Res.*, ii., 396, 397); but as this site would be outside the ancient limits of Naphtali, and within those of Zebulun, Grove would rather identify it with *Mujeidel* on Wady Kerkerah, near Yarûn, eight miles due east of the Ras-en-Nakurah (Scala Tyriorum). " *Chŏ-rēm* " (devoted, sacred), possibly *Hûrah*, a low tell with ruins, between Ras en Nakhurah and the Lake Merom, near Yarûm (Grove). " *Bêth-'ă-năth* " (house of response, or echo), according to Eusebius and Jerome (*Onomast.*) a village called Batanea, fifteen miles east of Cæsarea, but not discoverable. " *Bêth-shĕ-mĕsh*," distinct, of course, from that in Judah (xv. 10), and from that on the border of Issachar (ver. 22), but the site unknown. Neither from this fortress, nor from Beth-anath, could Naphtali expel the Canaanites (Judges i. 33). The total number of towns given in this verse, viz., sixteen, does not tally with the number, viz., nineteen, mentioned in the list (vers. 35-38). Probably some names are missing, for Kartan or Kirjathaim, though mentioned in xxi. 32, and in 1 Chron. vi. 61 (76), is not found in the list.

VERS. 40-48.—*Inheritance of Dhân* (judge, Gen. xxx. 6).

Dhân was own brother to Naphtali, which may be a reason for his being here mentioned after him, unless it be in anticipation of his occupying afterwards a northern position (ver. 47). His inheritance was smaller than that of any of the other tribes, but, being mainly in the sh^ephêlah, was one of the most fertile in Palestine. Here its towns only are enumerated, because its boundaries were determined by those of the neighbouring tribes of Ephraim, Judah, and Benjamin, already described. Of its towns several were taken out of Ephraim and Judah.

Ver. 41.—" *Tsŏr-'āh*" and "*'Esh-tā-'ôl*," see xv. 33. "*'Ir-shĕ-mĕsh*" (city of the sun), called also Beth-shemesh, xv. 10.

Ver. 42.—" *Shă-'ă-lăb-bîn* " ("place of foxes," cf. Ch^atsar-shual, xv. 28, and the incident recorded in Judges xv. 4), more often written Sha'albim (1 Kings iv. 9; Judges i. 35); the inhabitants seem to have been called Shaalbonites (2 Sam. xxiii. 32; 1 Chron. xi. 33); from it the Danites could not expel the Emorites (Judges i. 35). Site unknown, but may be that of *'Esalin*, lying next to Surâh, the ancient Tsor'ah (Rob., *Bib. Res.*, first edit., iii., App., 120, *b*). It is mentioned indeed by Eusebius and Jerome in the *Onomast.* (Selab), as a large village in the district of Sebaste (*i.e.*, Samaria), and then called Selaba; but there is no reason to conclude that any of the towns of the Danites were near Samaria, nor could the position here assigned to Shealbim, viz., between Irshemesh and Ajalon, be thus accounted for. (See Art. by Grove on "Shaalbim" in Smith's *Bib. Dict.*) "'*Ay-yā-lôn*," see x. 12. "*Yĭth-lāh*" (height, rt. תָּלָה, to suspend), mentioned in the *Onomast.* as 'Ιεθλάν, but without any description or indication of position. According to Knobel, the name may possibly be preserved in the Wady Atallah, west of Yâlo (Ajalon; Rob., *Bib. Res.*, pp. 143, 144); but Lieut. Conder suggests the ruin *Beit Tûl* in the low hills west of Jerusalem as a probable site.

Ver. 43.—"*'Ê-lôn*" (oak or terebinth), called 'Êlon-bêth-chānān (1 Kings iv. 9), perhaps *Ellin*, near Timnath (Knobel), mentioned by Robinson (*Pal.*, vol. iii., App., p. 120); but, according to Lieut. Conder, probably the present village *Beit Ellû* (*Pal. Explor. Fund*, 1881). "*Tĭm-nā-thāh*," xv. 10. "*'Eq-rôn*," xiii. 3.

Ver. 44.—"*'El-tᵉ-qēh*" ("to which God is fear, or object of fear," rt. קתה, unused, Arab. "to fear"), a city of the Levites, written אֶלְתְּקֵא, a Levite city (xxi. 23); apparently *Beit Likia* in the territory of Dan. In the list of the victories of Sennacherib (*Assyrian Discoveries*, pp. 302-5), the "plains of Eltekeh" are mentioned with towns of Dan. This agrees with the situation of the modern village (*Pal. Explor. Fund*, 1881). "*Gĭb-bᵉthôn*" (height), a city of the Levites (xxi. 23), held by the Philistines in the early days of the monarchy (1 Kings xv. 27, xvi. 15); probably the present village *Kibbiah*, at the foot of the hills near Lydda. "The situation agrees with the context" (*Pal. Explor. Fund*, 1881). "*Bă-'ă-lāth*," fortified by Solomon (1 Kings ix. 18 ; 2 Chron. viii. 6) ; not far from Gezer (Joseph., *Antiq.*, viii., 6, § 1). Probably the present village *Bela'în*, in a suitable position west of Bethhoron, and commanding the main road to Jerusalem (*Pal. Explor. Fund*, 1881, *Map*, sheet xiv.).

Ver. 45.—"*Yᵉhŭdh*" (praise), not mentioned by Eusebius and Jerome, perhaps identical with *el-Yehudiyeh* in the neighbourhood of Lydd (Lydda, Acts ix. 38), placed in Van de Velde's map seven miles east of Jaffa, and five north of Lydd ; see Rob., *Bib. Res.*, iii., 45). "*Bᵉnê-Bhᵉrăq*" ("sons of Berak, or of lightning," whether Danites or early settlers dispossessed by them is unknown). Scholz (*R.*, p. 256) would identify it with the present *Ibn-Abrak*, two miles from Yehudh. Eusebius and the Vulg. divide the name into two, and the former says that Βαρακαί was a village near Azotus. "*Găth-rĭm-môn*" (press of the pomegranate), according to Eusebius (*Onomast.*) twelve miles on the road from Diospolis (Lydda) to Eleutheropolis, probably near Thimnathah, afterwards given to the Kohathite Levites (xxi. 24). Site undiscovered.

Ver. 46.—"*Mê-hay-Yăr-qôn*" (the waters of paleness or greenness), unknown, but the next name may be a corrupt repetition of it (Grove). "*Hā-Răq-qôn*" (the thinness, rt. רקק, to spread out by beating, to make thin, Ges., *Lex.*). The situation of *Tell er Rakkeit* appears suitable, north of Jaffa, near the mouth of the river Aujeh. Probably the same as Mejarkon (Lieut. Conder, *Map*, sheet xiii.). "*With the border over against Yaphô*" (beauty) : Yapho was a very ancient Philistine city, thought by the ancients to be older than the Flood (Pomp. *Mela*, i. 11; Pliny, *Hist. Nat.*, v., 13); Greek Ἰόππη, the well-known port of Palestine (2 Chron. ii. 16; Ezra iii. 7; Jonah i. 3; Acts ix. 36, x. 8), often mentioned in the Books of Maccabees, annexed by Pompey to the province of Syria (Joseph., *Antiq.*, xiv. 4, § 4), but restored by Cæsar to Hyrcanus (xiv. 10, § 6). It afterwards became part of Herod's kingdom (xv. 7, 3) and that of Archelaus (xvii. 11, § 4), on whose deposition it reverted to the province of Syria. Having been destroyed by C. Cestius (Joseph., *Bel. Jud.*, ii. 18, § 10), it was subsequently rebuilt, and became infested by Jewish pirates (Strabo, xvi., 759) in consequence of which Vespasian levelled it with the ground, and erected a camp there where the citadel had been (*Bel. Jud.*, iii. 9, §§ 3, 4). It appears, however, that a new town gradually sprung up. The name of the place now is *Jaffa*, containing about four thousand inhabitants, and is celebrated for its groves and gardens (see Stanley's *Sin. and Pal.*, p. 243, note; p. 256; Thomson's *The Land and the Book*, p. 511, etc.).

Ver. 47.—"*And the border of the sons of Dan went out from them*," *i.e.*, beyond them, or beyond the inheritance allotted to them; cf. Masius, "The Danites emigrated beyond themselves, *i.e.*, beyond the inheritance in which they were first placed by the Divine lot, and set out in search of other possessions." So De Wette, Keil, and others. The fact that the Danites were unable to expel the Amorites, but were driven by them into the mountains (Judges i. 34), would account for this emigration, which, as we read in Judges xviii. 30, took place in the time of Jehonathan, the grandson of Moses (see Keil on Judges xviii. 1, 30). "*Lĕ-shĕm*" ("a kind of precious stone," Ges.) called Laish (Judges xviii. 7, 27), near the western source of the Jordan, four miles from Panium, or Cæsarea Philippi. "*And called Leshem 'Dan' after the name*," etc. (cf. Judges xviii. 29[1]) : The name Dan (judge) is preserved in that of the village " *Tell-el-Kadi* " (" mound of the judge "), which now occupies its supposed site. Here Jeroboam I. set up one of his golden calves (1 Kings xii. 29). On the question of the identity of this Dan with that in Gen. xiv. 14, see Art. by Grove in Smith's *Bib. Dict.*, pp. 386-7.

VERS. 49, 50.—*Inheritance of Joshua.*

Ver. 49.—לְהַנְחֵל, here, *i.q.* Piel, " to give to be possessed " (cf. Numb. xxxiv. 17, 18). לִגְבֻלֹו, " *according to its borders.*"

Ver. 50.—" *According to the command* (mouth) *of Jehovah* " : Though no express mention is made in the Pentateuch of this command, it is probable from

---

[1] So " Datos," or " Daton," was called " Philippi " after its conquest by Philip of Macedon ; " Byzantium " was named "Constantinople" after Constantine the Great; and "Zankle," in Sicily, had its name changed to " Messene " by the Messenians (Herod., vii., 164). The brief account in Josh. xix. 47 of a transaction afterwards more fully recorded, was added, Scott the commentator thinks, to complete the description of the inheritance at length possessed by the tribe of Dan. Probably the event occurred soon after the death of Joshua, and the addition to the narrative might, he says, have been made by Phinehas (Judges xx. 28). It is not probable that the idolatry of Micah and of the Danites would have been connived at by Joshua.

Josh. xiv. 6 that it was given at the same time as the command respecting Caleb.[1] Modesty and disinterestedness may have kept Joshua from claiming his inheritance sooner. "*Tĭm-năth-sĕ-răch*" ("a portion over and above," Ges., *Lex.*, pp. 595, 868), called in Judges ii. 9 Timnath-Cheres (portion of the sun), because, say the Rabbis, a representation of the sun was carved on Joshua's tomb in memory of the miracle of Gibeon (Josh. x. 12); though others (as Fürst, i., 442) interpret Cheres as "clay," and relating to the nature of the soil; while others again (as Ewald) consider it an error, which arose from a transposition of letters. The Vulg., Syr., Arab., and several Heb. MSS., read Serach, as in Josh. xix. 50. It is described in Josh. xxiv. 30 as being in Mount Ephraim, on the north side of the hill Gaash; thus Joshua received, like Caleb, an inheritance amid his own tribe. The site has been supposed to be where now stands *Tibneh*, six miles west of Jifneh, and about seventeen miles north of Jerusalem (Dr. Eli Smith's *Bibl. Sacra*, 1843), but for a later view see note on xxiv. 30.

Ver. 51.—*Conclusion.*—The לְ before מִשְׁמוֹת is a sign of the genitive, which is used to avoid the repetition of the construc. state (cf. xiv. 1). "*In Shiloh before the Lord*," cf. xviii. 10. פֶּתַח, an adverb accus. of place (§ 118, 1).

---

[1] Possibly, however, there is a reference here to the Urim which Joshua in Numb. xxvii. 21 is bidden to consult. That we read not in this book of his doing so on other occasions is explained by the fact that he had already received directions in those commands which God had given to Moses, whose minister he was; see, *e.g.*, i. 7, viii. 35, xi. 15.

CHAPTER XX.

Appointment of the Six Cities of Refuge.

Ver. 1.—The word וַיְדַבֵּר connecting this chapter with the preceding shows that this appointment of the cities of refuge took place immediately after the allotment of the land.

Ver. 2.—תְּנוּ לָכֶם, "*give* (*i.e.*, appoint) *for you.*" מִקְלָט, asylum or refuge, Sept. φυγαδεῖον φυγαδευτήριον καταφυγή, from קָלַט, to draw together, to contract, to draw in, and hence to receive (a fugitive to oneself), *i.q.* Chald. קְלַט. The asylums of the Greeks and Romans, and the sanctuaries of mediæval Europe, were somewhat analogous to these cities of refuge, but the main distinction was that the latter protected criminals from unmerited, the former often from merited, punishment.[1] At the same time, the restraint put upon the unintentional man-slayer by his confinement to a city of refuge sufficiently marked God's disapproval of the sin of homicide, while the exemption of him from death tempered justice with mercy. "*Whereof I spake to you,*" see Exod. xxi. 13; Numb. xxxv. 2, 6, 13; Deut. xix. 1, etc.

Ver. 3.—לָנוּס, "*that the slayer who killeth* (smiteth) *a person by mistake in ignorance may flee,*" etc., cf.

---

[1] Tacitus says that in the time of Tiberius "crebescebat Græcas per urbes licentia atque impunitas asyla statuendi; complebantur templa pessimis servitiorum; eodem subsidio obærati adversum creditores suspectique capitalium criminum receptabantur. Nec ullum satis validum imperium erat coërcendis seditionibus populi flagitia hominum, ut ceremonias Deûm, protegentis" (Tacit., *Ann.*, iii., 60).

Numb. xxxv. 15-24; Deut. xix. 4-13, where the distinction between wilful and unintentional homicide is accurately drawn. רֹצֵחַ, from רָצַח, to break or dash in pieces, to kill. בִּשְׁגָגָה, from שָׁגַג, to err, to go astray. נֶפֶשׁ, "*person*" (Ges., *Lex.*, 4, p. 560). גֹּאֵל הַדָּם, "*the avenger of blood*": גֹּאֵל, from גָּאַל, "to redeem," perhaps originally "to demand back," and hence "to extricate." As this blood revenge and redemption of an inheritance were the duty of a near relative, גֹּאֵל meant also "one near of kin" (Numb. v. 8; Levit. xxv. 25; Ruth iii. 12). The Sept. interprets by ὁ ἀγχιστεύων τὸ αἷμα, "one who by right of kindred avenges blood."[1]

Ver. 4.—"*And he shall flee to one of these cities, and shall stand at the entrance of the gate,*" etc. פֶּתַח, see xix. 51. Judges sat in the gate (Deut. xvi. 18). וְדִבֶּר אֶת־דְּבָרָיו, "*shall speak his words*," i.e., plead his cause (cf. 2 Sam. xix. 30 [Heb.]; Psalm cxxvii. 5; Jer. xii. 1). וְאָסְפוּ, "*and they shall receive him*," lit., shall gather him: The verb here implies "to receive under one's care and protection" (cf. Deut. xxii. 2; Psalm xxvii. 10). The meaning is, that, immediately on his arrival at the city, the judges should investigate his case, and if there appeared *primâ facie* grounds for believing him innocent, he should be allowed to reside in the city till the trial took place before a larger tribunal (ver. 6). "*Shall give him a place,*" etc.: According to Maimonides all the forty-eight Levitical cities had the privilege of asylum, but

---

[1] The ἀγχιστεύς, being nearest of kin, could claim the inheritance, and thus differed from the συγγενής, who had no such claim, and from οἰκεῖοι, connexions by marriage (Ammonius).

the six refuge cities were required to receive and lodge the homicide gratuitously (Calmet on Numb. xxxv.).

Ver. 5.—וְכִי, "*and if*" (or "when"), "cumque," Vulg. וְלֹא־יַסְגִּרוּ, lit., "*then they shall not shut up*," i.e., shall not deliver (cf. συγκλείω, Rom. xi. 32; Gal. iii. 22), Hiph. fut.

Ver. 6.—"*Until he shall stand* (Qal. infin. with suff.) *before the congregation.*" עֵדָה, from יָעַד, "to appoint," here means the congregation of elders or representatives of the people in a city. It seems that when the avenger of blood arrived at the city of refuge, and claimed the man-slayer, the latter was removed for trial to the congregation to which he belonged, or to the place where the deed had been committed; and if there it was decided that the deed was accidental, he was taken back to the city of refuge, where he was to remain till the death of the high-priest (so Keil). The high-priest, who was anointed with the holy oil (Numb. xxxv. 25), was a type of Christ, and his death may have been regarded as typical of that of Christ, who "through the Eternal Spirit offered Himself without spot to God" (Heb. ix. 14). This, therefore, may explain why the full expiation of the man-slayer's guilt was connected with the high-priest's death.

Ver. 7.—וַיַּקְדִּשׁוּ, "*and they consecrated*," i.e., set apart as for a holy purpose. The cities of refuge, being Levitical cities, were regarded as peculiarly the property of God. "*Qe-dhesh*," see on xix. 37. בַּגָּלִיל, lit., "*in the circuit*," Sept. ἐν τῇ Γαλιλαίᾳ; the name applies here to the small circuit of country around Qe-dhesh, in which were afterwards the twenty cities given by Solomon to Hiram (1 Kings ix. 11). At a later period Galilee embraced the whole of the northern part of Palestine. In Isa. viii. 23 (ix. 1) it is called גְּלִיל הַגּוֹיִם, on account of the many Gentiles there (cf. Matt. iv. 15). "*In Mount Naphthali*": Named nowhere else in the Bible. The mountainous district which formed the chief portion of the territory of Naphthali, answering to Mount Ephraim in the centre, and Mount Judah in the south of Palestine. This mountainous district, the modern *Belad-Besharah*, or "land of good tidings," contains some of the most beautiful scenery and fertile soil in Palestine (Porter, 363). "*Shechem*": In the centre of the land (see on xvii. 7). "*Qiryath-'Arba' which is Chebhron*," in the south (see x. 3, xiv. 15). בָּהָר, "*in the mountain district of Judah*," cf. xi. 21.

Ver. 8 (cf. Deut. iv. 41-43).—This repetition is here made to complete the narrative; so in xii. 1, etc., the account of the conquest of the land is repeated, and that of its division on the east of Jordan in xiii. 8, etc. "*Be-tser*" (cf. Deut. iv. 43), Sept. Βοσόρ, not discovered; probably the same as the Bosor of 1 Macc. v. 36. בַּמִּישׁוֹר, see xiii. 9. "*Ramoth in Gil-'adh*," identified with "Ramath-Mitzpeh" (xiii. 26). "*Gôlôn*" (Gôlân, Q^eri), cf. Deut. iv. 43: According to Eusebius (*Onomast.*) a very large village in Batanæa. It evidently gave its name to the district Gaulanitis, east of the Sea of Galilee (Joseph., *Antiq.*, viii. 2, § 3, and *Bell. Judg.*, i., 4, § 4). The word is recognised in the present *Djaulan*, mentioned by Burckhardt (*Syria*, p. 286), as giving name to a district lying east of the Lake of Tiberias.

These cities of refuge on both the sides of Jordan

were so situated that the distance from one to the next was about sixty miles. A way, or convenient road, was prepared, that they might be reached by the man-slayer with greater expedition (see Deut. xix. 3), and the Rabbis say that at the cross roads posts were erected, which pointed the way to them, and bore the inscription "Refuge, Refuge." The Gemara also notices that the cities on each side of the Jordan were nearly opposite each other, in accordance with the direction to divide the land into three parts (Deut. xix. 3 ; Reland, iii., p. 662).

Ver. 9.—עָרֵי הַמּוּעָדָה, not, as Kimchi, "urbes congregationis," *i.e.*, cities where the men-slayers were gathered together, nor, as Ges. (*Lex.*), "urbes asyli," but "cities of appointment," from יָעַד to appoint (cf. Chald., Sept., Vulg., and Arab.). "*And for the stranger,*" etc. (cf. Numb. xxxv. 15). גֵּר is translated προσήλυτος by the Sept. in both places, though in itself it denotes simply one who turns aside from his own country to abide in a foreign land.

It is generally supposed that the cities of refuge, besides being intended to be a check on the ancient custom of blood revenge, which still prevails in the East, were also typical of Christ ; and, whether designed to be so or not, they remarkably illustrate the security which is only to be had by belief in Him (see *e.g.*, Zech. ix. 12 ; Heb. vi. 18 ; Rom. viii. 1).

CHAPTER XXI.

Appointment of Cities for the Priests and Levites.[1]

Vers. 1-3 (*Demand of the Levites that Cities should be assigned to them*).—Ver. 1.—רָאשֵׁי אֲבוֹת, see on xiv 1. This application on the part of the chiefs of the Levites seems to have been made, not because the claims of the Levites had hitherto been overlooked (Calvin), but because now the fitting time had come for asserting them.

Ver. 2.—"*In the land of Canaan*": Not added to distinguish the Shiloh here mentioned from any other city of the same name, but in allusion to the letter of the instructions given by the Lord to Moses in Numb. xxxiv. 29, xxxv. 10. "*Jehovah commanded,*" etc., cf. Numb. xxxv. 1-8. מִגְרָשִׁים, see on xiv. 4.

Ver. 3.—It would seem from Numb. xxxv. 6 that the cities which had been appointed as cities of refuge were first assigned to the Levites, and that afterwards were added to them forty-two other cities. This distribution of the Levites among the rest of the tribes was a wise and merciful regulation, for thus

---

[1] A list of these cities is also given in 1 Chron. vi., which differs in many respects from that in this chapter. The discrepancy may, however, be accounted for partly from the springing up, in course of time, of new, and disappearance of old, towns; partly from changes in names; and partly from faulty readings. Moreover, though the number of cities mentioned in 1 Chron. vi. is only 42, yet in vers. 60-63 (Heb. 45-47) it is stated that the children of Aaron received 13, and the rest of the Kohathites 10; the Gershonites 13; and the Merarites 12 cities; and, therefore, in all there must have been 48 cities, as stated in Josh. xxi. 41.

the people could easily resort to them as their authorised instructors in religion, and more especially those who had fled to a city of refuge would have the benefit of spiritual admonition, instruction, and comfort.

Vers. 4-8.—In these verses we have an account of the number of cities assigned to the three great branches of the tribe of Levi, according to their respective families, with especial mention of the number assigned to the priests, who were of the Kohathite branch (ver. 4).

Ver. 4.—" *The families of the Q^ehathites* " : These were the families of Amram, Izhar, Hebron, and Uzziel (Exod. vi. 18), of which that of Amram was subdivided into the descendants of Moses and Aaron. To the line of the latter belonged the priesthood (Numb. xviii. 1-7), and to them were assigned thirteen cities out of the tribes of Judah, Simeon, and Benjamin ; God doubtless overruling the allotment, since by the position of those cities the priesthood would be established near the future Temple at Jerusalem. Hence, too, after the revolt of Israel, the priesthood and authorised worship would naturally remain in the tribes of Judah and Benjamin (2 Chron. xiii. 9-12). To the objection that thirteen cities were too many for the number of Aaron's descendants at this time, it has been well pointed out by Keil and others, that the appointment looked forward to the future increase of those descendants ; that already they were numerous, since Aaron at the time of the exodus was eighty-three years old, and his descendants might have entered upon the fourth generation seven years after his death ; also the cities were small, not exclusively inhabited by Levites, and many of them still in the hands of the Canaanites. Almost the same reply is applicable to the similar objection that the sum total of the Levites, viz., twenty-three thousand, did not require the allotment to them of so many as forty-eight cities.

Ver. 5.—" *The rest of the sons of Qʰhath*," *i.e.*, those who were sprung from Moses, Izhar, Hebron, and Uzziel. The rebellion of the non-priestly portion of the Qᵉhathites had resulted in the diminution of their numbers, cf. Numb. iii. 27 with Numb. xxvi. 57, etc., and hence ten cities sufficed for them.

Vers. 9-19 (*List of the Cities assigned to the Priests:* 1, *in Judah and Simeon*, vers. 9-16, *Nine Cities;* 2, *in Benjamin*, vers. 17-19, *Four Cities: Total, Thirteen Cities*).—Ver. 9.—יִקְרְאוּ, " *one calls* " : The indeter. 3rd pers. (§ 137, 3).

Ver. 10.—וַיְהִי לִבְנֵי־א׳, the nominative is either "the cities," supplied from the former verse, or " the lot," supplied from the parenthesis at the end of this verse. רִאשֹׁנָה, "*first*," an adv., the ancient form, but more commonly written רִאשׁוֹנָה, as in the margin.

Ver. 11.—" *The city of 'Arba'*," etc., see on xiv. 15. הָעֲנוֹק, more commonly read הָעֲנָק, xv. 13.

Ver. 12.—" *But the fields . . . they gave to Kalêbh*": In xiv. 13, 14, he is only said to have received the city, but from this verse we learn that he gave up the city to the Levites, but retained the fields and valleys belonging to it, except the necessary pasturage around the city for the cattle of the Levites (see Numb. xxxv. 2). Hence Keil infers that those who tilled these fields lived also in the Levitical city, and that the Levites had only certain dwellings assigned them in it, which were their inalienable property (Levit. xxv. 32-34).

Ver. 13.—"*Chebh-rôn, the city of refuge,*" etc. (cf. 1 Chron. vi. 57, Auth. Vers.): The words "*to be,*" inserted by the A. Vers. before "the city," etc., are not in the original. Chebh-rôn was already a city of refuge (see xx. 7, and note on ver. 3 above). On the words *miq-lat* and *ro-tse"ch*, see xx. 2, 3. "*Libh-nah,*" in the lowland (x. 29, xv. 42).

Vers. 14, 15 (The cities here mentioned were in the mountainous district of Judah, xv. 48-51).—Ver. 15. —"*Chô-lôn,*" written Chîlên 1 Chron. vi. 43, A. V. 58.

Ver. 16.—"*'A-yin*" (xv. 32), allotted to Simeon (xix. 7), in place of which is found 'Ashan, a city in the lowland of Judah (xv. 42; 1 Chron. vi. 44 [59]), which is probably the correct reading (Keil). "*Yuttah,*" in the hill country (see xv. 55), omitted in 1 Chron. vi. 44 (59). "*Bêth-shemesh,*" on the northern boundary of Judah (xv. 10). "*Out of those two tribes,*" viz. Judah and Simeon (ver. 9).

Vers. 17-19 (*Cities of the Priests in the Tribe of Benjamin*).—Ver. 17.—"*Gibh-'ôn*" (omitted in 1 Chron. vi. 45 [60]), see on ix. 3. "*Ge-bha',*" xviii. 24.

Ver. 18.—"*'A-na-thôth*" (possibly "echoes"), and "*'Al-môn*" (hiding-place), written 'Al-le-meth, 1 Chron. vi. 45 (60), are not found in the list of Benjamite cities (xviii. 21-28), perhaps being omitted as of little importance. Anathoth was the birthplace of the prophet Jeremiah (Jer. i. 1), and thither Abiathar was banished by Solomon (1 Kings ii. 26). It is now *Anâta*, about three or four miles N.N.E. of Jerusalem (Rob., *Bib. Res.*, i., 437-8). 'Almon is unknown, but is possibly Almît, about a mile northeast of Anâta (Grove).

Vers. 20-26 (*The Cities of the Non-Priestly Q^ehathites, viz., four from Ephraim, vers. 20-22, and four from Dan, vers. 23, 24, and two from West-Manasseh, ver. 25. Total, Ten Cities*).—Ver. 20.—The לְ before כְּמִשְׁפְּחוֹת means "as to" (Rosenm.), or here with יְהִי denotes possession, and the וְ before יְהִי has the force of "also." For the construction with a plural nominative see on xv. 4.

Ver. 21.—"*Shechem*," xvii. 7. "*Ge-zer*," x. 33, xvi. 3.

Ver. 22.—"*Qibh-tsa yim*" ("two heaps," from קָבַץ, to collect), unknown. It is read Yoq-nᵉ'am ("gathered by the people," from עַם and קָמָה, to collect), 1 Chron. vi. 53 (68), probably another name for the same place, and not to be confounded with Yoq-nᵉ'am in ver. 34. It would seem (says Grove) from 1 Kings iv. 12 to have been at the extreme east of the tribe of Ephraim (Art. "Jokneam," in Smith's *Dict. of the Bible*). Lieut. Conder suggests *Tell Abu Kabûs* (a name radically identical with Kibzaim), near Bethel, as a not impossible site. "*Béth-cho-ron*," whether upper or lower, or both, is not stated (see x. 10).

Vers. 23, 24.—On the four cities here named see xix. 42-45. The two in ver. 23, viz., 'Eltᵉqê' and Gib-bᵉthôn, are not mentioned in 1 Chron. vi. 53 (69).

Ver. 25.—"*Out of the half-tribe of West Manasseh.*" "*Ta'-nakh*," written Ta-'a-nakh (xii. 21): Instead of it we find 'A-ner in 1 Chron. vi. 55 (70), evidently an error (Keil). "*Gath-rimmon*" (xix. 45), but in 1 Chron. vi. 55 (70), בִּלְעָם, written יִבְלְעָם (Josh. xvii. 11), the correct reading, according to Keil, who thinks that Gath-rimmon may have crept into the text from the preceding verse; yet Gath-rimmon is the reading in the Vulg., Syr., Arab., and Chald. Targ. Possibly the town had both names.

Vers. 27-33 (*Cities of the Gerʻshunnites: Total, Thirteen Cities*).—Ver. 27 (*From the Half-Tribe of Manasseh in Bashan*).—"*Gô-lân*," see xx. 8. "*Bʻesh-tʻrah*," contract. in the Heb. from בֵּית־עַשְׁתָּרָה (so Winer), and, therefore, as בֵּית often falls away, undoubtedly the same as the Ashtaroth of Og (xii. 4, ix. 10); so it is written in 1 Chron. vi. 56 (71).

Vers. 28, 29 (*From the Tribe of Issachar*).—Ver. 28.—"*Qish-yôn*," see xix. 20. "*Da-bhʻrath*," xix. 12.

Ver. 29.—"*Yar-mûth*" and "*ʻÉn-gan-nîm*," xix. 21 (note).

Vers. 30, 31 (*From the Tribe of Asher*).—Ver. 30.—"*Mish-ʼal*," see xix. 26; written Mashal, 1 Chron. vi. 59 (74). "*ʼAbh-dôn*," perhaps the same as ʼEbh-rôn (xix. 28).

Ver. 31.—"*Chel-qath*," xix. 25. "*Rʻchôbh*," xix. 28; 1 Chron. vi. 60 (75).

Ver. 32 (*From the Tribe of Naphtali*).—"*Qe-dhesh in*[1] *Galîl*," cf. xix. 37, xx. 7. "*Cham-môth-dôr*," see note on xix. 35. "*Qar-tan*," an obsolete dual form (contrac. from קַרְתַּיִן) of קֶרֶת, for which occurs the later form, קִרְיָתַיִם (two cities), 1 Chron. vi. 61 (76); cf. דֹּתָן (2 Kings vi. 13), contrac. from דֹּתַיִן (Gen. xxxvii. 17). It is not mentioned among the cities of Naphtali (xix. 35, etc.), but is supposed by some to be identical with Rakkath (xix. 35). The name "Iscariot" has also been derived from it. (See the Art. on "Judas" in Smith's *Bib. Dict.*).

---

[1] The preposition in the Hebrew here includes the article, "in *the* Galil."

Vers. 34-40 (*Merarite Cities: Total, Twelve Cities*).—Vers. 34, 35 (*Out of the Tribe of Zebulun*).—Ver. 34.—"*Yoq-n^e'am*," see xii. 22, xix. 11; the name is omitted in 1 Chron. vi. 62 (77). "*Qar-tah*," perhaps the Qattah of xix. 15;[1] otherwise, like Dimnah (ver. 35), not mentioned in the list of Zebulonite cities in xix. 10-16, nor in 1 Chron. vi. Knobel, indeed, and others would identify Dimnah with Rimmon or Rimmono, xix. 13; 1 Chron. vi. 62 (77), but the text in Chronicles is undoubtedly corrupt, since it records only two names, Rimmon and Tabor. So Keil.

Ver. 35.—"*Na-ha-lal*," xix. 15; omitted in 1 Chron. vi. 62 (77).

Vers. 36, 37 (*Out of the Tribe of Reuben*).—Ver. 36.—"*Be-tser*," cf. xx. 8. For the three other cities see xiii. 18. Though these verses (36, 37) are omitted in some MSS. on the authority of Kimchi and the greater Masora, yet they are found in all the ancient versions, and in one hundred and forty-nine MSS. collated by Kennicott, and in forty collated by De Rossi. Also, if omitted, the cities of the Merarites would not be twelve as stated in vers. 7, 40, nor the total number of the cities of refuge forty-eight, as stated in ver. 41. Probably the omission arose from the similar ending of vers. 35, 37.

Vers. 38, 39 [Vers. 36, 37, in some Heb. MSS.] (*Out of the tribe of Gad*).—Ver. 38.—"*Ramoth in* (the) *Gil'adh*" (xx. 8), called Ramath-mizpeh (xiii. 26). "*Ma-ch^{a}nayim*" (xiii. 26).

---

[1] Such differences in writing or pronouncing a name are not uncommon (cf. Eshtemoh and Eshtemon, xv. 50, xxi. 14; Baalah and Balah, xv. 29, xix. 3).

Ver. 39.—"*Cheshbôn*," xiii. 17. "*Ya'-tsêr*," xiii. 25. The word כָּל־ before עָרִים is omitted in the Syr. and Arab. vers.

Ver. 40 (38 in some Heb. MSS.).—The word "so" (Auth. Vers.) in the first clause is not in the Heb., and the construction of the clause is broken. Render the last clause "*and their lot was twelve cities.*"

Ver. 41 (39).—"*Forty and eight cities*": According to the command which had been given (Numb. xxxv. 7). Note that $48 = 12 \times 4$, and twelve is significant of the Church (Rev. vii. 5-8, xxi. 12, 14), and four of universality (see, *e.g.*, Rev. vii. 1, "four winds," *i.e.*, winds coming from every quarter (cf. Jer. xlix. 36, 37 ; Dan. vii. 2). Hence Bishop Wordsworth well remarks here, "This dispersion of the ministry of the ancient Church into twelve times four cities, in all the tribes of the inheritance of Israel, which typified the whole earth regarded as a Church of God, evangelised by one and the same Gospel, was prophetic and figurative of the diffusion of the Apostolic Church of Christ into all parts of the world. It represented its catholicity and its apostolicity. The refuge provided in the cities of refuge, accessible to all Israelites, represented the one faith in Christ, the true Refuge, preached to all ; and the diffusion of the one tribe, that of Levi, teaching the same truths in all parts of the land of Canaan, represented the Christian ministry, bearing the same evangelical message, of Christ crucified, to all."

Ver. 42 (40).—עִיר עִיר. "*city, city*," *i.e.*, each city (§ 120, 5). After this verse the Sept. inserts a clause, partly repeated from xix. 49, 50, but with the additional statement, probably derived from a Jewish tradition, that Joshua buried in Timnath-serah the knives with which he had circumcised the people after the passage of the Jordan (see v. 2). This latter statement is also found in the Sept. Vers., at the end of xxiv. 30.

Vers. 43-45.—A conclusion to chaps. xiii.—xxi., and referring back, not only to xi. 23, but to i. 2-6, and connecting, as Keil says, the two halves of the book together.

Ver. 43.—"*He had sworn to give unto their fathers*": see Gen. xii. 7, xv. 18. Though many parts of the land were still occupied by the Canaanites (see xiii. 1, etc.), yet the whole territory had been apportioned out among the tribes of Israel, who had so far conquered the Canaanites that none of them, at the time here referred to, offered any further resistance; and when they subsequently gained ascendency, their success was due to the sloth and cowardice of the Israelites. God had never promised the latter to exterminate their enemies at once, but gradually (Exod. xxiii. 29; Deut. vii. 22), and on condition of their own fidelity to Himself (cf. note on xi. 23).

Ver. 44.—"*And Jehovah gave rest to them round about*" (*i.e.*, as long as Joshua and the elders, his contemporaries, lived, Judges i. 1, ii. 7) "*according to all which He had sworn,*" etc. (see Exod. xxxiii. 14; Deut. iii. 20, xii. 9, 10, xxv. 19). "*And there stood not a man,*" etc., cf. i. 5.

Ver. 45.—לֹא־נָפַל, lit., "*fell not,*" cf. xxiii. 14; more fully with the addition of אָרְצָה (2 Kings x. 10). מִכֹּל הַדָּבָר הַטּוֹב, "*of all the good word,*" comprising all the gracious promises which God had made to the Israelites (cf. 1 Kings viii. 56). For בֵּית, some MSS.

read בְּנֵי, Sept. τοῖς υἱοῖς. בָּא, "*came to pass*" (used also of the fulfilment of prophecy, see 1 Sam. ix. 6; Deut. xiii. 2 [3], xviii. 22; Judges xiii. 12). St. Paul assures the Christian believer that "all the promises of God in Christ are Yea, and in Him Amen, to the glory of God" (2 Cor. i. 20).

CHAPTER XXII.

The Dismissal of the trans-Jordanic Tribes to their own Inheritance, and their Erection of an Altar near the Jordan.

Ver. 1.—אָז, see on viii. 30. The time referred to was probably that when Joshua, having effected the conquest of Canaan, had portioned out the land, and had assigned to the Levites their cities, for thus in ver. 9 these trans-Jordanic tribes are said to have returned from *Shiloh*, where the children of Israel had assembled, in order that the distribution of their several inheritances might be completed (xviii. 1). For מַטֵּה many MSS. in Kennicott and De Rossi read בְּנֵי, which reading may have arisen from the occurrence of this latter term in vers. 7, 9, 10. On the distinction between the two words see on iii. 12.

Ver. 2.—Cf. Numb. xxxii. 20, etc.; Josh. i. 12-15.

Ver. 3.—זֶה used adverbially and = *now* (§ 122, 2, 2nd par., *b*). "*Ye have kept the observance of the commandment*," *i.e.*, ye have kept all which the commandment of the Lord required to be observed (cf. Gen. xxvi. 5; Levit. viii. 35).

Ver. 4.—לָכֶם לְכוּ, cf. vii. 10. For לְכוּ many MSS.

and editions read סְעוּ, as in Numb. xiv. 25; Deut.
i. 7, but this latter verb is not construed both with לְ
and –אֶל. אֹהָלִים may refer to their habits as pastoral
tribes (Stanley's *Sin. and Pal.*, viii., p. 326), though
they appear to have had also fenced cities (Numb.
xxxii. 17), and the Chald. Vers. here renders "cities,"
Sept. οἴκους. Being the ancient term for a "dwelling," the word may be here used generally for homes
(cf. Deut. xvi. 7; Judges vii. 8; 1 Sam. xiii. 2;
2 Sam. xix. 8).

Ver. 5.—Joshua here repeats the substance of the
commands given by Moses in Deut. vi. 5, x. 12, xi. 13,
22, xxx. 16, 20). אַהֲבָה. cf. xxiii. 11, is the infin.
with a fem. ending, or a verbal noun governing the
accus. (§ 133, 1).

Ver. 7.—The renewal here of the statement about
the inheritance of the two half-tribes of Manasseh may
be intended to give a completion, or finish, to this portion of the narrative. It was usual with the Hebrew
writers to repeat the mention of a fact rather than to
refer to it as already mentioned; see, *e.g.*, the oft-
repeated statement that the Levites had no share in
the land of Canaan (xiii. 14, 33, xiv. 3, xviii. 7).[1]
After נָתַן. understand אֲחֻזָּתוֹ. מֵעֵבֶר, "*on* (lit. "out of ")
the other side," *i.e.*, the side opposite to Bashan, which
was on the east of the Jordan. The Qᵉri has בְּעֵבֶר,
the more usual form. וְגַם כִּי . . . וַיְבָרְכֵם, "*and also when
. . . then he blessed them.*" As it is unlikely that
Joshua should, on account of his relationship to the
half-tribe of Manasseh (which was descended, like
himself, from Joseph) have blessed them apart from

---

[1] Cf. *Speaker's Com.*, and Keil *in loc.*

the other trans-Jordanic tribes (ver. 6), this statement may be another instance of the repetition alluded to above, and serves to introduce the further particulars mentioned in ver. 8.

Ver. 8.—נְבָכִים, from נָבַס, *i.q.* בָּנַס, to collect. The occurrence of this word here shows that it is not a word, as Gesenius (*Lex.*) says, of the later Hebrew.[1] The allusion is to the riches of which they had spoiled the Canaanites. With the command about the division of the spoil cf. Numb. xxxi. 25, etc.; 1 Sam. xxx. 23-25).

Vers. 9-12 (*The Erection of an Altar on the Banks of the Jordan by the trans-Jordanic Tribes, and the Offence thereby given to the other Tribes*). —Ver. 9.—Shiloh is here described as being "in the land of Canaan," in order to mark the antithesis between it and the land of Gilead, which is here put for the whole of the trans-Jordanic territory (cf. Numb. xxxii. 1, 29; Deut. xxxiv. 1; Judges v. 17, etc.). אֲשֶׁר נֹאחֲזוּ־בָהּ, "*in which they had been made possessors,*" lit. had been held fast or established: Cf. Numb. xxxii. 30, where the Niph. form is used in the same passive sense, whereas in Gen. xxxiv. 10, xlvii. 27, it is reflective, "to fix themselves firmly or settle."

Ver. 10.—גְּלִילוֹת הַיַּ, lit. *the circles* (cf. xiii. 2) *of Jordan*," *i.q.* כִּכַּר הַיַּרְדֵּן (Gen. xiii. 10, 11), or simply הַכִּכָּר (Gen. xiii. 12, xix. 17);[2] here that portion of the

---

[1] Though found in 2 Chron. i. 11, 12; Eccles. v. 18, vi. 2, and common in Aramæan, it cannot be inferred with any certainty that it therefore belongs to a later period of the Hebrew language (Keil, *Introd.*, p. 35).

[2] Both words probably relate to the windings of the stream (see Reland's *Pal.*, i., c. 43, p. 274). Of Geliloth Dean

Ghôr which was on the west bank of the Jordan (Keil and others). The words "*which are in the land of Canaan*" show that the altar spoken of at the conclusion of the verse must have been erected, not as Josephus (*Antiq.*, v., 1) says, on the eastern, but on the western side of Jordan. If on the eastern side, it could not so well have served for a testimony that the trans-Jordanic tribes had a part in Jehovah (see vers. 21-29). גָּדוֹל לְמַרְאֶה, lit. "*great as to appearance.*"[1]

Ver. 11.—אֶל־מוּל, lit. "*in the face or front of,*" "*in the fore-front of*" (Rev. Vers.). אֶל־גְלִילוֹת: The prep. here implies tarriance *in* after motion (Ges., *Lex.*, B., 47); cf. לְ. Ges., *Lex.*, B., and the use of εἰς and ἐς for ἐν, examples of which we have in the Greek Testament (see Matt. ii. 23; Mark i. 9; Luke xi. 7). אֶל־עֵבֶר בְּנֵי, "*at the side of the sons of Israel,*" or, "on the side that pertaineth to the children of Israel" (Rev. Vers.). עֵבֶר means a "side" in Exod. xxxii. 15, also several times in this book it is used in

---

Stanley says that the five times in which it occurs in Scripture, two are in the general sense of "coast" or "border" (Josh. xiii. 2; Joel iii. 4), "all the coasts of Palestine," and three especially relate to the course of Jordan (viz., Josh. xxii. 10, 11, Ezek. xlvii. 8). The word may perhaps find an analogy in the Scotch term "links," which is used of the snake-like windings of a stream, as well as with the derived meaning of a coast or shore. In later times no doubt the words were taken merely as provincial terms for "region," and as such were translated both in the Sept. and New Testament ἡ περιχῶρος, "the surrounding neighbourhood" (p. 284, note 5).

[1] Lieut. Conder would identify its site with the remains of an altar-like structure on a lofty conical peak, called *Kurn Surtabeh*, about twenty miles north of Jericho, in the valley of the Jordan, where the river, in its descent from its upper level, winds round several islets (*Pal. Explor. Fund, Monthly Statement*, Oct. 1874).

reference to the region on the west of Jordan (see v. 1, ix. 1, xii. 7, xxii. 7).[1]

Ver. 12.—וַיִּקָּהֲלוּ: This word seems to indicate that, after the land of Canaan had been apportioned, the cis-Jordanic tribes had dispersed to their several inheritances. "*To go up against them to war*": For, if their suspicions of the apostacy of the trans-Jordanic tribes had been correct, they would have been justified in so doing (see Deut. xii. 4, 13, xiii. 7, etc.).

Vers. 13-20 (*Before declaring War the Israelites send Ambassadors to demand an Explanation* [herein they obeyed Deut. xiii. 14]).—Ver. 13.—"*Pî-n^echas*" (mouth of brass), see Exod. vi. 25; Numb. xxv. 7, etc., xxxi. 6, etc. הכהן refers to Eleazar, see accents, and cf. Sept. and Vulg., though the title is given in

---

[1] The following remarks of Grove (in Dr. Smith's *Bib. Dict.*, iii., p. 1033) merit attention :—"The pile of stones which they (the eastern tribes) erected on the western bank of the Jordan to mark their boundary—to testify to after-ages that though separated by the rushing river from their brethren and the country in which Jehovah had fixed the place where He would be worshipped, they had still a right to return to it for His worship—was erected in accordance with the unalterable habits of Bedouin tribes, both before and since. It was an act identical with that in which Laban and Jacob engaged at parting,—with that which is constantly performed by the Bedouins of the present day. But by the Israelites west of Jordan, who were fast relinquishing their nomad habits and feelings for those of more settled and permanent life, this act was completely misunderstood, and was construed into an attempt to set up a rival altar to that of the Sacred Tent. The incompatibility of the idea to the mind of the western Israelites is shown by the fact that, notwithstanding the disclaimer of the two and a half tribes, and notwithstanding that disclaimer being proved satisfactory even to Phinehas, the author of Joshua xxii. retains the name Mizbèach for the pile, a word which involves the idea of sacrifice, *i.e.*, of slaughter (see Gesen., *Thes.*, 40?), instead of applying to it the term 'gal,' as is done in the case of the precisely similar 'heap of witness' (Gen. xxxi. 46)."

ver. 30 to Pinechas as the presumptive successor of Eleazar.

Ver. 14.—"*And* (they sent) *ten princes with him, a prince for each house of a father according to all the tribes of Israel*": The repetition of אֶחָד denotes distribution (§ 108, 4), and the tribes on the west of Jordan are enumerated as ten, because the half-tribe of Manasseh is reckoned as one. "*And each one was a head of their father-houses*": The expression בֵּית־אָבוֹת, instead of בֵּית־אָב, is a mode of forming the plural of compound nouns more usual in the Syr. (Ges., *Lex.*, 10, p. 116); the fem. plur. expresses *dignity* (§ 107, 3, *c*); hence we might here render "chief-houses." "*Among the thousands of Israel*": So Auth. Vers., but Rosenm. takes אֲלָפִים to denote "families" (cf. vii. 14, note), and renders "according to the families of Israel."

Ver. 16.—עֲדַת יְהֹוָה (cf. Numb. xxvii. 17, xxxi. 16; in Psalm lxxxii. 1, עֲדַת אֵל, "congregation of God"), appropriately so called, because it was by zeal for the honour of Jehovah that they were moved to make this remonstrance. מָעַל, see on vii. 1 : This term is applied especially to sins of unfaithfulness, such as idolatry, which rob God of the glory which is His due (see Levit. xxvi. 40; Deut. xxxii. 51). "*In that ye have built for you an altar that ye might rebel*"). etc. : מָרַד is a much stronger expression than מָעַל (Keil) ; it is used of rebellion against human rulers (Gen. xiv. 4 ; 2 Kings xviii. 7, 20, xxiv. 1, 20); but here, and in Ezek. ii. 3 ; Dan. ix. 9, of rebellion against Jehovah (Ges., *Lex.*).

Ver. 17.—אֶת־עֲוֹן, an accus. (§ 117, 2). Render "*Is there too little for us as regards the iniquity of*

Peor, from which we have not cleansed ourselves[1] *even unto this day?*" The reference is to Numb. xxv. 3, etc., and it is intimated that the Israelites were still in their hearts inclined to this sin of idolatry (xxiv. 14-23). "*And*[2] *the plague came upon the congregation of Jehovah*," *i.e.*, the whole congregation was involved in the punishment of the transgressors.

Ver. 18.—"*And* (yet) *ye are turning this day from* (following) *after Jehovah, and it shall come to pass ye rebel this day against Jehovah, and to-morrow He will be wroth with* (will break forth against) *the whole congregation.*" "*Ye rebel,*" *i.e.*, "if ye rebel . . . then," etc., cf. Gen. xxxiii. 13, "and (if) men should overdrive them," etc.

Ver. 19.—וְאַךְ, "*and truly,*" cf. Gen. xliv. 28 (Ges., *Lex.*). טְמֵאָה, "*unclean,*" because many of its inhabitants were heathen, and it had not the Tabernacle of Jehovah in it. "*Unto the land of the possession of Jehovah,*" cf. Levit. xxv. 23; Psalm lxxxv. 1. יָשְׁבָה, "hath dwelt and does still dwell" (§ 126, 3). הֵאָחֲזוּ, Niph. imper., "*take possession.*" אַל־תִּמְרֹדוּ: Here construed first with בְּ, and then with an accus. (cf. Job xxiv. 13, מֹרְדֵי־אוֹר, "*who rebel against the light*"). מִבַּלְעֲדֵי, "*besides,*" see § 154, 2, last par., cf. Numb. v. 20; Psalm xviii. 32 (Heb.).

Ver. 20.—This verse is connected with ver. 18, the preceding verse (19) being parenthetical. The argument is from the less to the greater. If by the sin of Achan alone wrath came on all the congregation,

---

[1] הִטַּהֵר Hithpael of טָהֵר, to be, or to become clean; the ה before ט assimilated (§ 54, 2, *b*).

[2] The ו should not be rendered "although," as in the Auth. Vers.

a fortiori might the like result be expected from the sin of two tribes and a-half. וְהוּא ... בַּעֲוֺנוֹ, "*and he was one man; he perished not* (alone) *in his iniquity.*" So D. Glass and Sept. (Alex.). Achan's sin caused the defeat before 'Ay (vii. 5), and the destruction of his children (vii. 24). For לֹא the Vulg. reads לוּ, utinam. גָּוַע, lit. "breathed out life": For the middle consonant see § 72, Rem. 10.

Vers. 21-31 (*The trans-Jordanic Tribes satisfactorily refute the Charge brought against them*). —Ver. 22.—Some (*e.g.*, Maurer here, and Dean Perowne on Psalm l. 1) render the three first words "*The God of Gods, Jehovah,*" but the Pesiq after the first and second nouns shows that in the opinion of the Masorets the nouns should be construed separately, *e.g.*, "*The Almighty, God, Jehovah,*" cf. Psalm l. 1, where אֵל, as here, is separated by the accent from אֱלֹהִים; also the Hebrew form of expression for "The God of Gods" would rather be אֱלֹהֵי הָאֱלֹהִים, as in Deut. x. 17; Psalm cxxxvi. 2. Probably, therefore, we have here three separate titles, rising in sublimity, to express the infinite majesty of the Deity, viz., *'El* = "The Mighty One;" *'Elohim* (perhaps from the obsolete rt. אָלָה, to worship, to adore, to fear) = "The Supreme Being worthy to be feared;" *Y*ᵉ*hovah* = 'The truly existing One, The covenant God." So Keil, Delitzsch, and Hengstenberg. הוּא יֹדֵעַ וגו, "*He knoweth, and Israel, he shall know; if in rebellion, and if in apostacy,*"[1] etc.: Supply עָשִׂינוּ אֶת־זֹאת, from ver. 24, the ellipsis being, as Keil remarks, in accordance with the broken speech of suddenly accused

---

[1] Sept. ἐν ἀποστασίᾳ.

innocence. The apodosis to the sentence beginning at אִם is contained in the closing words of ver. 23, "Let Jehovah Himself require it." The exclamation, "*Save us not this day*," at the end of ver. 22, is parenthetical, and a direct appeal to God for the purpose of asserting more strongly their innocence.

Ver. 23.—לִבְנוֹת, this and the following infinitives carry on the oath, *e.g.* (if we have done this), "to build for us," etc. אִם in adjurations has the effect of a negative particle; אִם לֹא of an affirmative (§ 155, 2, *f*.).

Ver. 24.—"*And if not from anxiety, for a reason,*" etc. דְּאָגָה, "fear, anxiety," rt. דָּאַג, *i.q.* דָּאַב, to melt, and hence "to be afraid," "to be anxious" (Ges., *Lex.*). דָּבָר, *a cause or reason*," cf. v. 4. לֵאמֹר, "*saying*" (or "thinking," Ges., *Lex.*, 2, p. 61). מָחָר, "*hereafter,*" cf. Josh. iv. 6, 21. מַה לָּכֶם, cf. 2 Sam. xvi. 10; Matt. viii. 29, τί ἡμῖν καὶ σοί; xxvii. 19; John ii. 4.

Ver. 25.—"*And* (shall moreover say) *Jehovah hath appointed the Jordan as a boundary between us and between you, ye sons of Reuben,*" etc. For brevity's sake no mention is made of the half-tribe of Manasseh. "*And* (so) *your sons shall make our sons cease from fearing Jehovah.*" יְרֹא is the m. Qal. infin. of יָרֵא, which with prefix לְ is generally contracted to לִרֹא (see 1 Sam. xviii. 29). In the Pentateuch the fem. form יִרְאָה is always used, *e.g.*, in Deut. iv. 10, v. 26, vi. 24, etc.

Ver. 26.—"*And so we said* (we thought) *let us do* (this) *for us to build the altar,*" etc.: A Hebrew mode of expression for "let us build," or נַעֲשֶׂה may be rendered "let us prepare" (see Ges., *Lex.*). Sometimes עָשָׂה is followed by the finite verb with וְ, as in Gen.

xxxi. 26. זֶבַח, a bloody sacrifice, which was not, like the holocaust, entirely consumed by fire.

Ver. 27.—"*But that it may be a witness*," etc. (Auth. Vers.), or, "it shall be a witness" (Rev. Vers.): So the altar built by Moses, and called Jehovah-Nissi (Exod. xvii. 15, 16), was not an altar for sacrifice, but a memorial altar. לְפָנָיו, "*before His face*," *i.e.*, before His tabernacle.

Ver. 28.—"*And we said that it shall be, when they shall say* (thus) *to us and*," etc. וְאָמַרְנוּ, "*then we will say*," either in our own persons, or in those of our descendants. אֶת־תַּבְנִית, lit. "*the structure*," or "*the building*," rt. בָּנָה, to build; then "*the pattern according to which a thing is made*" (Exod. xxv. 9, 40; 2 Kings xvi. 10); then, as probable here, "*the image or likeness of a thing*" (cf. Deut. iv. 16-18; Ezek. viii. 10); Sept. ὁμοίωμα. The Vulg. renders "Ecce altare," either having omitted אֶת־תַּבְנִית, or having understood it in its primary sense of a structure, as in Psalm cxliv. 12, a rendering adopted by Rosenmüller.

Ver. 29.—The words חָלִילָה וגו are rendered by Gesenius (*Lex.*, p. 280) "woe be to us (profane or accursed be it to us] *from Him* (*i.e.* Jehovah), *if we should sin against Jehovah*": Cf. 1 Sam. xxiv. 7 (Heb.); 1 Sam. xxvi. 11; 1 Kings xxi. 3. This is preferable to the rendering of Masius and others, "*Far be it from us to rebel*," etc., where לָנוּ is regarded as redundant. מִלְּבַד, "*apart from*," or "besides" (cf. Gen. xxvi. 1; Numb. xvii. 14 [Heb.]).

Ver. 30.—"*It was good in their eyes*," a Hebrew form of expression, well rendered as to sense by the Auth. Vers., "*it pleased them*," Sept. ἤρεσεν αὐτοῖς.

Ver. 31.—כִּי . . . יְהוָה, "*that Jehovah* (is) *in the midst of us,*" *i.e.*, is propitious to us, for to Him they justly attributed the preservation of the trans-Jordanic tribes from the iniquity of which they had suspected them. אֲשֶׁר, "*because*" (Ges., *Lex.*, B., 3, p. 89), more fully אָז יְדַעְתֶּם אֲשֶׁר, "*then*" = "therefore" (cf. Jer. xxii. 15; Psalm xl. 8; Ges., *Lex.*, p. 25), or "then (when ye acted as ye did) ye delivered," etc.

This satisfactory vindication of the two and a-half tribes from the charges brought against them teaches us how careful we should be in our judgment of others, lest we condemn those whom God approves. "Judge nothing before the time" (1 Cor. iv. 5); "Who art thou, that judgest another man's servant," etc. (Rom. xiv. 4, 13).

Vers. 32-34 (*The Return of the Ambassadors and the Naming of the Altar*).—Ver. 32.—וַיָּשִׁיבוּ, followed by an accus. of person and thing (cf. xiv. 7).

Ver. 33.—"*And they thought* (or spake) *no more of going up*": Cf. ver. 24, and for the omission of mention of the half-tribe of Manasseh in this and next verse, see ver. 25 (note).

Ver. 34.—"*And the sons of Reuben . . . named the altar, 'It is a witness between us'*": Though עֵד is supplied after קָרְאוּ in the Syr., Arab., and Auth. Vers., and in some MSS., it is not found in the Sept. and Vulg., nor in most MSS. The first כִּי is a sign of quotation, the Greek ὅτι in oratio directa, and may be omitted in English (see Ges, *Lex.*, B. c., p. 391). Thus the words contain both the name and the explanation, or a name not inscribed upon the altar, but intended to explain both its design and importance; they (the Eastern tribes) gave the altar the name of "*witness between us,*" because it was to be a witness that they also acknowledged and worshipped Jehovah as the true God (Keil). So the pile, which Jacob and Laban erected, was called Gal-'êdh, "the heap of witness" (Gen. xxxi. 47).

Note that in this chapter the testimony borne by Joshua to the courage and fidelity of the trans-Jordanic tribes, their zeal and that of the rest of the Israelites for the worship of Jehovah, the absence of any recrimination on the part of the trans-Jordanic tribes when vindicating their character from a false suspicion, and the readiness with which their apology was accepted, were all highly creditable, and seem to indicate that the nation at this time was under the influence of a truly religious spirit.

CHAPTERS XXIII.—XXIV.

Joshua's two farewell addresses: 1, to the rulers and authorities of Israel (chap. xxiii.); 2, to all the people (chap. xxiv.). The former address may be divided into two parts; in the first of which (ver. 2 *b*-11) Joshua encourages the rulers, etc., to persevere in the conquest of Canaan by promises of continued assistance from God; in the second (vers. 12-16) he warns them of the consequences of disobedience.

Both addresses (chaps. xxiii.-xxiv.) strikingly display Joshua's piety, zeal, and deep acquaintance with human nature. They may be compared with Moses's farewell addresses in the Book of Deuteronomy, to which reference in them is often made. Our heavenly Joshua, before He left this earth, gave a parting charge to His apostles (Acts i. 4).

CHAPTER XXIII.

Vers. 1-11.—Ver. 1.—וּגוֹ מִיָּמִים, "*from* (i.e., after) *many days*" (cf. Gen. iv. 3 ; Ezek. xxxviii. 8). "*After that Jehovah had given rest*," etc. (see xxii. 3, 4, xxi. 43, 44) : This clause appears to be in apposition to the foregoing, from which it is separated by a distinctive accent. The ו before יְהוֹשֻׁעַ should be rendered "and," not "that," as in A.V., for the apodosis begins at ver. 2. With the phrase זָקֵן וּגוֹ cf. xiii. 1. Here it indicates the still further advance of Joshua's age, so that he might any day anticipate his death (cf. ver. 14).

Ver. 2.—וַיִּקְרָא וּגוֹ, "*that Joshua called all Israel, its elders*," etc. The לְ after קָרָא need not be translated (cf. Gen. xx. 8 ; Levit. ix. 1, where it is untranslated in the Auth. Vers.). The terms "elders, heads," etc., are explanatory, being put in apposition to "all Israel." The place to which Joshua summoned them was either Timnath-serah (xxix. 50) or, more probably, Shechem (xxiv. 1), the centre of the land, and the place of the sanctuary. The זְקֵנִים were the representatives of Israel ; the רָאשִׁים were the heads of tribes, families, and houses, from whom were taken the judges and overseers (שֹׁטְרִים, i. 10), see on vii. 14. In the last clause the words "*I am old*," etc., imply a reason why he should lose no opportunity of exhorting them, nor they of attending to his counsel.

Ver. 3.—מִפְּנֵיכֶם, not, as Auth. Vers. and Rosenm., "*because of you*," i.e., on your account, but "*before you*," *i.e.*, driving them out before you; a constructio praegnans (Keil). "*For Jehovah, your God*, (is) *He that hath fought for you*": See the promise of Moses (Deut. i. 30, iii. 22). So in our Christian warfare the remembrance of what God has done for us in former times, and His promises for the future, should encourage and make us steadfast both in trust and obedience.

Ver. 4.—הִפַּ֫לְתִּי, see on xiii. 6, and cf. Psalm lxxviii. 55, where in like manner nations, instead of their land, are said to be allotted. בְּנַחֲלָה וגו, "*for a possession to your tribes.*" "*From the Jordan and all the nations which I have cut off, and the great sea towards the setting of the sun*": "The nations" are mentioned instead of their territory, because they were given to the Israelites to be destroyed; and "*the Jordan*" and "*the Great Sea*" mark the boundary of Canaan from east to west.

Ver. 5.—יֶהְדֳּפֵם, "*will expel them,*" from הָדַף, to thrust out (cf. Deut. vi. 19, ix. 4): Chateph-qamets is used instead of sheva (§ 60) on account of the weakness of the guttural ה (cf. Numb. xxxv. 20). On the form יְרִשְׁתֶּם see on i. 15.

Ver. 6.—וַחֲזַקְתֶּם, "*therefore* (and so) *be ye very strong*": The perfect is here used as an imperative, the preceding clause implying a cause (§ 126, Rem. 1, 2nd par.). With the exhortation cf. i. 7.

Ver. 7.—בּוֹא, followed by בְּ, means "*to hold intercourse with*" (Ges., *Lex.*, p. 106), cf. ver. 12. הִזְכִּיר בְּ, "*to make mention of,*" viz., as an object of religious affiance (cf. Isa. xlviii. 1; Psalm xx. 7 [8]). לֹא תַשְׁבִּיעוּ, "*cause ye not to swear,*" viz., "by the name of their gods." Swearing by the name of a god was always regarded as an evidence of belief in that god (see Deut. vi. 13, x. 20). עָבַד relates to outward worship by sacrifice and ceremonies; הִשְׁתַּחֲוָה, to the bending before God in prayer, and invocation of His name; the two are generally connected together, as here (cf. Exod. xx. 5, xxiii. 24; Deut. iv. 19, v. 9, etc.; Keil).

Ver. 8.—כִּי אִם, "*but*," after a neg. (cf. Psalm i. 2, 4). "*As ye have done unto this day*": An assertion to be understood in a general sense only, for there had been many individual exceptions. Note how by judicious praise Joshua encourages them to perseverance, lest they should lose a reward for the good which they had already wrought.

Ver. 9.—וַיּוֹרֶשׁ וגו, "*and Jehovah hath driven out from before you*," etc.: This was a fulfilment of Deut. iv. 38, vii. 1, ix. 1, xi. 23. וְאַתֶּם, "*and you*": Put absol. (§ 145, 2). "*No man hath stood*": A fulfilment of the promise in Deut. vii. 24, xi. 25.

Ver. 10.—יִרְדְּף, "*chaseth*": Cf. the promise in Levit. xxvi. 7, 8; Deut. xxviii. 7. The second clause of the verse is a repetition of ver. 3 *b*.

Ver. 11.—"*And take good heed to your souls*." לְנַפְשׁ here means "for the sake of your souls" (cf. Deut. iv. 15; Keil). "*To love Jehovah*," see Deut. vi. 5, x. 12, xi. 13: Likewise under the New or Christian Covenant love and obedience are united (John xiv. 15, xv. 14).

Vers. 12-16 (*Warning against Apostasy*).—Ver. 12.—"*But if ye do in any wise return*," viz., from following Jehovah (cf. xxii. 18). וְהִתְחַתַּנְתֶּם, "*and if ye make marriages with them*": This was prohibited (Exod. xxxiv. 12-16; Deut. vii. 3). חָתַן means primarily "to cut off," "to circumcise" (Ges., *Lex.*), and then, because marriage, like circumcision, was a kind of covenant, "to contract affinity with anyone;" cf. the meaning of the cognate word in Arabic, and see Hooker, *Eccles. Pol.*, v., 62, § 21, note 7 (end). In Hithpael it means to intermarry either by giving or receiving a daughter in marriage, and is here followed by בְּ, as in Deut. vii. 3 ; 1 Sam. xviii. 22, 23, 26, 27; Ezra ix. 14. וּבָאתֶם וגו, "*and ye come among them,*" *i.e.*, enter into fellowship with them (cf. ver. 7).

Ver. 13.—לְפַח : פַּח means a snare or net, rt. פָּחַח, to spread out, cf. παγίς, Luke xxi. 35 ; Psalm lxix. 23 (Heb.) ; Isa. viii. 14, where it occurs also with מוֹקֵשׁ, a trap, from יָקַשׁ, to lay snares. שׁוֹטֵט, "a scourge," from the Pilel of שׁוּט, to lash ; elsewhere the form שׁוֹט is used (see Prov. xxvi. 3 ; 1 Kings xii. 11, etc.). The expression "a scourge in your sides, and thorns," etc., is similar but stronger than that in Numb. xxxiii. 55. "Joshua crowds his figures together to depict the misery and oppression which would be sure to result from fellowship with the Canaanites, because from his knowledge of the fickleness of the people and the wickedness of the human heart in its natural state, he could foresee that the apostasy of the nation from the Lord which Moses had foretold would take place but too quickly ; as it actually did, according to Judges ii. 3, etc., in the very next generation" (Keil). "*Until your perdition from off the good land.*" אֲבָדְכֶם, Qal. inf. (short ŏ [ָ]), with suffix (§ 61, 1) ; with the language of this threat cf. Deut. xi. 17, xxviii. 21, in which latter place אֲדָמָה (properly ground in respect of culture) is used as here.

Ver. 14.—הַיּוֹם, "*this day,*" art. emphatic (§ 109),

meaning here that the time was close at hand (cf. Deut. ix. 1). "*The way of all the earth,*" cf. 1 Kings ii. 2. "*All the earth*" = all mankind, as in Gen. xi. 1; 1 Sam. xvii. 46; 1 Kings x. 24; 1 Chron. xvi. 23; Psalm lxvi. 4. "*Not one word* (דָּבָר) *hath failed*": Cf. xxi. 45; 1 Kings viii. 24, 56. So when through Christ, the glorious Antitype of Joshua, believers are put in possession of the heavenly Canaan, they will be able from their hearts to testify that not one word (promise) of God hath failed to be accomplished.

Ver. 15.—הָרָע ... כֹּל, "*every evil word,*" *i.e.,* every threatening, in allusion particularly to Levit. xxvi. 14-33; Deut. xxviii. 15-68, xxix. 14-28, xxx. 1-15. אֶתְכֶם, see Ges., *Gr.* (§ 117, 2). This is the original and regular form, which was contracted into אֶתְכֶם at a later period (Ewald, *Lehrb.,* § 264, *a*).

Ver. 16.—"*When ye transgress . . . and go and serve . . . then shall the anger of Jehovah,*" etc. The word הָלַךְ here denotes continuance and progress in impiety. The last clause of the verse is nearly a verbatim repetition of that in Deut. xi. 17.

CHAPTER XXIV.

Joshua's Second Farewell Address. This was spoken to all the Tribes of Israel in the Persons of their Representatives assembled at Shechem.

Vers. 1-15 (*Joshua rehearses the benefits which God had conferred upon their nation from its origin up to that time, and thereupon claims for God their hearty and entire allegiance; he leaves it, however, to their own choice to serve God or not*).—Ver. 1.—שְׁכֶמָה, "*to Shechem*," see on xvii. 7. A few MSS. of the Sept. have Shiloh for Shechem, but the Syr., Vulg., and the Chald. Targum accord with the Hebrew text. As Shechem was the place where Abraham and Jacob had erected an altar to God (Gen. xii. 6, 7, xxxiii. 18. 20), and close to which the solemnity recorded in Josh. viii. 30-35 had taken place, it was natural that it should have been chosen on this occasion as calculated, by its associations, to impress the minds of the Israelites (cf. Dean Stanley's *Sin. and Pal.*, p. 239). שֹׁטְרִים, see i. 10, xxiii. 2. יִתְיַצְּבוּ, "*presented themselves*," from יָצַב, "to place" (cf. Job i. 6). לִפְנֵי הָאֱ': This expression does not warrant the inference of Rosenm. and Knobel that the ark had been removed on this occasion from Shiloh to Shechem. Neither it, nor לִפְנֵי יְיָ, which occurs in reference to the Tabernacle (xviii. 6, xix. 51), need sometimes imply more than a general allusion to God's presence as giving solemnity to a place or ceremony (Hengstenberg, *Beiträge*, iii., p. 13, etc., quoted by Keil; cf. Judges xi. 11). It is, however, to be remarked that a sanctity attached to Shechem, because Joshua had erected an altar on Mount Ebal, near to it (see viii. 30).

Ver. 2 (*The first proof of God's favour—Abraham's call*).—"*All the people*," probably as many individuals out of each tribe attended as were able. "*God of Israel*," fitly so termed, since Joshua is about to rehearse the benefits which God had conferred on His people Israel from ancient times up to that present day, when He had put them in possession of the land of Canaan. "*The river*" (not "the flood," as in Auth. Vers.), *i.e.*, the Euphrates, called "*the* river," κατ' ἐξοχήν, as in Gen. xxxi. 21 ; Exod. xxiii. 31 ; see note on i. 4. The abode of their fathers was (1) Ur of the Chaldees ; (2) Charan of Mesopotamia (Gen. xi. 28, 31). מֵעוֹלָם, "*from time immemorial.*" תֶּרַח from תָּרַח, Chald., to delay (Ges., *Lex.*), Sept. (-)αρρα. He was the father of Abraham, Nachor, and Haran (Gen. xi. 27), but the two first only are mentioned here, because from them the Israelites were descended, viz., from Abraham on the paternal, and from Nachor on the maternal side (Gen. xxii. 23, xxix. 10, 16). "*And they served other gods:*" Perhaps the teraphim (penates) mentioned in Gen. xxxi. 19, 34. According to the Jewish tradition Abraham did not participate in this idolatry, and being persecuted in consequence was obliged to leave his native land (Targum Jonathan, on Gen. xi. 23), or rather was called away by God, that he might escape from the surrounding idolatry.

Ver. 3.—וָאוֹלֵךְ, "*and I led,*" lit. "I made to go." וָאֶרֶב, "*and I multiplied.*" אָרַב, Hiph. imperf. apoc., for which the Q°ri has the more usual form אַרְבֶּה. "*Isaac*" is explanatory of the foregoing word "seed," for in Isaac was his seed to be called (Gen. xxi. 12).

Ver. 4.—"*And I gave unto Isaac Jacob and Esau*" : In answer to Isaac's earnest prayer, and after he had been married twenty years (Gen. xxv. 21, 26 ; Psalm cxxvii. 3). "*And I gave unto Esau Mount Seir*"[1] : See Gen. xxxvi. 8 ; Deut. ii. 5, 12. Nothing is said

---

[1] = hairy, rough. It extended from the Dead Sea to the Elanitic Gulf.

here of the gift of Canaan to the posterity of Isaac, because Joshua assumes that as well known to the Israelites, and, therefore, only adds the statement in the last clause of the verse in order to introduce what follows in vers. 5-7.

Vers. 5-7 (*Second Proof of God's Favour, viz., the Deliverance from Egypt*).—Ver. 5.—"*And I smote Egypt,*" *i.e.*, its land and people. נָגַף is used of a plague, *e.g.*, that of frogs (Exod. vii. 27, viii. 2), and of the smiting of the firstborn of Egypt (Exod. xii. 23, 27). In Exod. iii. 20 נָכָה is used in the same sense. כַּאֲשֶׁר, "*according to that which*" (Auth. Vers.), or "*according to the plagues which,*" subaudi הַמַּגֵּפוֹת from the preceding אֲשֶׁר. The Sept. Alex. seems to have read בַּאֲשֶׁר, which it loosely renders ἐν σημείοις οἷς ἐποίησα, cf. the Vulg., "et percussi Ægyptum multis signis et portentis." "*And afterwards I brought you out,*" viz., out of Egypt, thus fulfilling the promise in Exod. iii. 20.

Ver. 6.—הַיָּמָּה, "*to the sea,*" *i.e.*, the Arabian Gulf, here called κατ' ἐξοχήν, הַיָּם, as in Exod. xiv. 2, but יַם־סוּף at the end of this verse (cf. ii. 10, note).

Ver. 7.—"*And they cried unto Jehovah*": See Exod. xiv. 10. "*And He put darkness*": The abrupt change from the first person in vers. 3-6 to the third person here is common in Hebrew (cf. Psalm xxii. 27 [Heb.], lxxxi. 16 ; Zech. xiv. 5). מַאֲפֵל, "*darkness,*" rt. אָפֵל, to set, to be obscure ; the noun is used here only, but the compound מַאְפֵּלְיָה, "the darkness of Jehovah," occurs in Jer. ii. 31. The allusion is to the pillar of the cloud (Exod. xiv. 20). "*And ye dwelt . . . many days,*" *i.e.*, for forty years (Numb. xiv. 33).

Vers. 8-10 (*Third Proof of God's Favour—the Conquest of the Land of the Amorites, and the Frustration of the Designs of Balak*).—Ver. 8.—וְאָבִיאָה, with ה parag., instead of the Qᵉri וְאָבִיא. וַתִּירְשׁוּ, "*and ye possessed*," Vulg. "et possedistis": See the history of this conquest in Numb. xxi. 21-35.

Ver. 9.—וַיִּלָּחֶם, "*and he fought*," not with weapons of war (see Judges xi. 25), but by employing Balaam to curse them, as said in the next clause.

Ver. 10.—וַיְבָרֶךְ בָּרוֹךְ, "*and he continued to bless*" (§ 131, 3, *b*). "*And I delivered you out of his hand*," *i.e.*, the hand of Balak,[1] who wished to destroy Israel, if he could (Numb. xxii. 6, 11).

Vers. 11-13 (*Fourth Proof of God's Favour—the Passage of the Jordan, and the Conquest of Jericho and of the Nations of Canaan*).—Ver. 11.—בַּעֲלֵי יְרִיחוֹ, "*inhabitants*[2] (not "lords," Knobel) *of Jericho*" (Ges., *Lex.*), Sept. οἱ κατοικοῦντες Ἱεριχώ (cf. Judges ix. 6; 2 Sam. xxi. 12). "*Fought*," *i.e.*, from the walls, for no mention is made of a battle outside the city. The same verb applies to the seven nations, or tribes, which are next mentioned, and which are not to be regarded as put in apposition to the inhabitants of Jericho, as though they had severally taken part with them in the defence of the city (Jarchi); rather ו should be supplied before הָאֱמֹרִי (Keil and Rosenm.).

Ver. 12.—הַצִּרְעָה, "*the hornet*": (Art. collec.) from צָרַע, "to strike down," with which is connected the idea of "to pierce" (Ges., *Lex.*); see the promise in

---

[1] = "the spoiler," from בָּלַק, to make empty.
[2] Owners or citizens.

Exod. xxiii. 28; Deut. vii. 20, where, as here, the word "hornet" is used not literally (Bochart and Rosenm.), but figuratively, to denote that effective terror (Keil) with which God inspired all the surrounding nations (Deut. ii. 25; Josh. ii. 11). In like manner, "bees" (or "wasps") are spoken of as the cause of terror (Deut. i. 44; Psalm cxviii. 12; cf. *Il.*, xvi., 259, etc.)[1] "*And it drave them out*": "Them" refers, according to the Auth. Vers., to "the two kings of the Amorites" mentioned in the next clause, but Keil and Rosenm. rightly understood ן before these words (cf. ver. 11). Not merely the seven tribes on the west side of Jordan, but the two kings of the Amorites on the east side, were driven out. "*Not by thy sword, and not by thy bow*," see Psalm xliv. 4 (Heb.), "they got not the land . . . by their own sword," etc.

Ver. 13.—"*In which ye did not labour*," i.e., to render it fruitful. יָגַע means "to labour with toilsome effort." זֵיתִים, lit. olive trees, though meaning here olive plantations, for which Hebrew has no one word; hence rightly, as to sense, the Auth. Vers. renders

---

[1] Though Bochart (*Hieroz.*, lib. iv., c. 13) has collected examples from ancient authorities of numerous bodies of men being driven away by noxious insects; and the Book of Wisdom (xii. 8, 9) supports this view of the expulsion of the Canaanites; yet the majority of commentators understand the term "hornet" to be used here (Josh. xxiv. 12) metaphorically. This view is confirmed by the fact that there is in the Book of Joshua no historical mention of the Canaanites having been thus driven out. Also in Exod. xxiii. 28 the word "hornets" is parallel with the word "fear" in ver. 27. And besides the examples given above of the use of the word "bees," the word œstrus, a gad-fly, is used poetically to denote madness or frenzy.

"olive-yards," Sept. ἐλαιῶνας, Vulg. oliveta. With this verse cf. the promise in Deut. vi. 10, 11.

Vers. 14, 15 (*An Appeal to the Israelites to renounce Idolatry, and to cleave to the Service of Jehovah—Joshua's own Resolve*).—Ver. 14.—וְעַתָּה, "*and now*," *i.e.*, on the ground of God's past benefits to your nation (cf. Psalm cv. 45, where, after having rehearsed God's mercies to the Israelites, the Psalmist declares the design of those mercies, viz., "that they [the Israelites] might observe His statutes and keep His laws"). יְראוּ, imper. of יָרֵא, but pointed like a verb, לָה for יְראוּ (cf. 1 Sam. xii. 24; Psalm xxxiv. 10 [Heb.]). עִבְדוּ, see on עָבַד xxiii. 7, Sept. λατρεύσατε. תָּמִים, prim. an adjec., "perfect, complete," but here used as a substantive, "integrity" (cf. Judges ix. 16, 19, where the Sept. renders it by τελειότητι). אֱמֶת, "sted-fastness," from אָמַן, to prop, to support, and hence faithfulness, truth, sincerity. God requires the same qualifications in His servants now (Matt. vi. 24; John iv. 23, 24). "*The gods . . . on the other side of the river*," see on ver. 2. "*And in Egypt*," see Ezek. xx. 7, 8, xxiii. 3, 8, 19.[1]

Ver. 15.—"*And if it is evil in your eyes*": Sept. εἰ δὲ μὴ ἀρέσκει ὑμῖν. בַּחֲרוּ לָכֶם, "*choose for your-selves whom ye will serve*" (cf. 1 Kings xviii. 21): We have not the liberty to choose whether we will serve or not; all the liberty we have is to choose our master (Bishop Sanderson, iii., 314). אֶת־אֱלֹהִים, *i.e.*, the teraphim or penates (ver. 2). The "*Emorites*" are probably put for the Canaanites generally, who

---

[1] The golden calf, or steer (עֵגֶל), was probably an imitation of Apis, or some other of the sacred bulls of Egypt.

were worshippers of Baal. The choice thus given to the Israelites was intended to test their sincerity, that they might not thoughtlessly pledge themselves to the service of God. "*But I and my house,*" etc.: As Joshua does not appear to have been married, his "house" probably refers to his servants (cf. "household" in Gen. xviii. 19).

Vers. 16-24 (*The Determination of Israel to serve Jehovah*).—Ver. 16.—חָלִילָה לָּנוּ (cf. xxii. 29), here followed by מִן with an infin. "*Far be it from us that we should forsake*" (Ges., *Lex.*), cf. Gen. xviii. 25, xliv. 7, 17.

Ver. 17.—הַמַּעֲלֶה, Hiph. part. with art., "*who brought up,*" answering to אֲשֶׁר הוֹצֵאתִי (Exod. xx. 2). "*The house of bondmen*": So in Exod. xx. 2. "*Those great signs,*" viz., those referred to in vers. 8-12.

Ver. 18.—גַּם־אֲנַחְנוּ, "*also we,*" in reference to Joshua's words (ver. 15), "I and my father's house."

Ver. 19.—לֹא־תוּכְלוּ, "*ye will not be able,*" i.e., without true conversion of heart. There is an implied allusion to their fickleness and proneness to rebel. קְדֹשִׁים, plur. adj., because Elohim is a plur. excellentiæ, denoting God in the fulness and multiplicity of the Divine powers (§ 108, 2, *b*; cf. Hosea xii. 1 [Heb.]; Prov. ix. 10). קַנּוֹא occurs here and in Nah. i. 2 only, *i.q.* קַנָּא (Exod. xx. 5, xxxiv. iv. 14; Deut. iv. 24, v. 9, vi. 15), a jealous God, who will not transfer to another the honour due unto Himself (Isa. xlii. 8, xlviii. 11). לֹא־יִשָּׂא, followed here and in Exod. xxiii. 21; Psalm xxv. 18, by a dat., but generally by an accus. of the thing; "*will not grant forgiveness to your transgressions.*"

Ver. 20.—כִּי, "*when.*" אֱלֹהֵי נֵכָר, "*strange gods*"

(lit. gods of a foreign country), so in Gen. xxxv. 2 ; Jer. v. 19. וְשָׁב, "*then He will turn*," *i.e.*, will assume a different disposition towards you. וְכִלָּה, "*and will consume you*," lit. "will finish" or "make an end of" you. "*After that He hath done you good*," *i.e.*, notwithstanding the past tokens of His goodness to you.

Ver. 21.—לֹא, "*nay*," as in v. 14.

Ver. 22.—After עֵדִים in the last clause is an ellipsis of אֲנַחְנוּ (we are) which is supplied in the Syr. and Arab. versions.

Ver. 23.—"*Put away the strange gods which are among you.*" Keil, after Levi ben Gerson, Augustine, and Calvin, takes בְּקִרְבְּכֶם to signify "within you," *i.e.*, in your hearts, because it is said in xxiii. 8 that the people had cleaved to the Lord "unto this day," and in xxiv. 31, that they "served the Lord all the days of Joshua." This meaning, however, seems forced, and it is, therefore, better to suppose that Joshua alludes to secret idolatry practised by individuals, though there was no national public recognition of strange gods. It is true that nothing is said of delivering up these idols to be destroyed, as was done in similar cases (see Gen. xxxv. 4 ; 1 Sam. vii. 4), but it would be rash to argue from the silence of the sacred narrative that no such surrender might have taken place.

Vers. 25-28 (*Joshua renews the Covenant, etc., and dismisses the People*).—Ver. 25.—"*Made a covenant*," *i.e.*, renewed the one which had been made at Sinai (Exod. xxiv. 3, etc.), and renewed by Moses in the plains of Moab (Deut. xxviii. 69 [xxix. 1, Auth. Vers.]). "*And he set for them* (*i.e.*, the people) *a statute and an ordinance.*" מִשְׁפָּט, prop. judgment, and hence a law or ordinance (Exod. xxi. 1, xxiv. 3 ; Levit. xviii. 4). There is a reference to Exod. xv. 25, and the meaning probably is that Joshua ratified the covenant as a Divine statute and ordinance, by which the Israelites were bound to obedience as a condition of receiving the blessings of the covenant.

Ver. 26.—אֶת־הַדְּבָרִים הָאֵלֶּה refers not only to the words spoken, but to all the transactions connected with the renewal of the covenant. "*The book of the law of God*," *i.e.*, the Pentateuch, which was laid up in the Holy of Holies, close by the ark of the covenant, probably in a chest (see Deut. xxxi. 24, 26). This was done not only for the safe custody of the book, and in testimony of its Divine authority, but as a protest against a breach of the covenant, of which the ark was a symbol, by idolatry (see Dr. Pusey, *On Daniel*, pp. 308, 309). "*Took a great stone and set it up*," cf. Gen. xxviii. 18 ; Josh. iv. 20-22 ; 1 Sam. vii. 12). הָאֵלָּה, "*the oak*" (Ges., *Lex.*); so Vulg., but Sept. "*the terebinth*" : The noun literally means "a thick tree," rt. אָלַל, properly to roll, hence to be round, thick (cf. אוּל and אֵלָה) ; the article probably alludes to the oak or terebinth of Moreh (Gen. xii. 6), where Abraham pitched his tent, and raised an altar, and where Jacob buried the idols of his household (Gen. xxxv. 4 ; see note on xxiv. 1). בְּמִקְדַּשׁ יְיָ, "*in the sanctuary of Jehovah*" : The allusion is not to the Tabernacle, for that was at Shiloh (xviii. 1), but to the spot sanctified by the altar erected by Abraham, and afterwards by Jacob. So Keil, Hengstenberg, and others.[1]

---

[1] Dean Stanley thinks that the place indicated was the same as that where Jacob buried the images and ornaments of his

Ver. 27.—"*For it hath heard*": An example of vivid personification (prosopopœia, cf. Deut. xxxii. 1; Isa. i. 2; Jer. ii. 12). "*Lest ye deny your God*," viz., in feeling, word, or deed (Keil). The same verb בִּחֵשׁ occurs in vii. 11.

Vers. 29-33 (*Death and Burial of Joshua and Eleazar, and mention of the Burial of Joseph's Bones*). —Ver. 29.—"*An hundred and ten years old*" (cf. Joseph., *Antiq.*, v., 1, 29): The same age as that of Joseph (Gen. l. 26).

Ver. 30.—"*Timnath-serach*," see note on xix. 50. "*On the north side of Mount Ga'ash*": The word גַּעַשׁ meaning "shaking," "earthquake," from גָּעַשׁ, "to push, to thrust," and in the pass. "to be concussed, to be moved" (Ges., *Lex.*), occurs again with הַר in Judges ii. 9, and with נַחֲלֵי (torrent-beds, or wadys of Gaash), in 2 Sam. xxiii. 30; 1 Chron. xi. 32. Eusebius and Jerome record the name (*Onomast.*, "Gaas"), but evidently had no knowledge of the situation. There is, however, a remarkable consent of Jewish, Samaritan, and Christian tradition, traceable from the fourth century downwards, which points to a village called *Kafr Hâris*, south of Shechem, as representing the burial-place of Joshua. Lieut. Conder ascertained that this tradition is still extant among the Samaritans, and, although it appears little understood by the peasantry, a sacred shrine exists outside the village of Kefr Hâris to which the name *Neby Lush'a* (no doubt a corruption of Yehusha or

---

Mesopotamian retainers (Gen. xxxv. 4), and that the tree or spot appears to have been known in the time of the Judges, as the traditional site of these two events, by the double name of "the oak of the enchantments" or "the oak of the pillar" (*Sin. and Pal.*, p. 142).

Joshua) is applied. Ancient tradition also places the tomb of Nun at this same village, and a second sacred place, called Neby Nûn, was found close to the supposed site of the tomb of Joshua (*Pal. Explor. Fund, Quarterly Statement*, 1881).

To this verse the Sept. and Arab. append the legend that the stone-knives, with which Joshua had circumcised the Israelites (chap. v.), were buried with him (cf. xxi. 42 [40]).

Ver. 31.—" *The elders*," *i.e.*, the rulers and leaders. יָדְעוּ, " had seen or experienced " : Cf. the statement in this verse with Judges ii. 7. The good example set by individuals in high station and authority may influence a whole people.

Ver. 32.—"*And the bones . . . Egypt*" (see Gen. l. 25 ; Exod. xiii. 19). "*Buried they in Shechem*," a place consecrated by Abraham's altar (Gen. xii. 7), the oldest sanctuary in the land. "*In a portion of the field*[1] *which Jacob had bought . . . for a hundred q'sî-tah*" (cf. Gen. xxxiii. 19). All the ancient versions, except Targg. Jerusalem and Jonathan, render קְשִׂיטָה, " a lamb," whence it has been thought to have been a coin bearing the impression of a lamb. But more probably the word signifies something weighed out, from קָשַׂט, an unused root, *i.q.* קָשַׁט, in Arab. " to divide," or "to distribute equally,"and, therefore, might denote money. Thus here Gesenius (*Lex.*) renders "a hundred measures, or portions of silver." This interment of Joseph's bones probably took place when the apportionment of the land had been completed,

---

[1] חֶלְקָה, a plot ; or portion, properly "a smooth piece" (cf. Gen. xxvii. 16, from חָלַק, to be smooth (Ges., *Lex.*).

but was not mentioned before, that the thread of the narrative might not be broken (Keil). To this day the tomb, whether correctly or not, is pointed out under the shadow of Mount Ebal (*The Land and the Book*, p. 473).

Ver. 33.—"'*El-'a-zar*": See note on xiv. 1. Whether his death was shortly before, or after, that of Joshua, Scripture does not tell us. Josephus says it occurred about the same time as Joshua's, twenty-five years after the death of Moses (*Antiq.*, v., 1, § 29). "*In the hill of Pî-n'chas*," or "*in Gibh-'ath-Pî-n'chas*," possibly a town so called. "This" (says Grove) "may be the Jibia on the left of the Nablûs [1] road, halfway between Bethel and Shiloh ; or the Jeba north of Nablûs (Rob., ii., 265, note 312). Both would be 'in Mount Ephraim,' but there is nothing in the text to fix the position of the place, while there is no lack of the name among the villages of Central Palestine" (Art. "Gibeah" in Dr. Smith's *Bib. Dict.*, I., p. 692). At the present day Samaritan, Jewish, and Christian tradition identifies the Gibeah of Phinehas with the village of *Awertah*, four miles south-east of Nablus, and here, or in the immediate vicinity, are shown the monuments of Phinchas and Eleazar. These were visited by Lieut. Conder and his fellow-explorers, and the former monument is described as bearing marks of great antiquity, and the latter as having been rebuilt (*Pal. Explor. Fund, Quarterly Statement*, 1881).[2]

---

[1] That is, Shechem.

[2] The tomb of Eleazar is "a rude structure of masonry in a court open to the air. It is 18 ft. long, plastered all over, and shaded by a splendid terebinth. That of Phinehas is apparently an older building, and the walls of its court have an arcade of round arches, now supporting a trellis, covered with a grape vine, and the floor is paved" (*Tent Work*, p. 41).

Here appropriately closes the Book of Joshua, but several editions and MSS. of the Sept. add some particulars relative to Pinᶜchas and the apostacy of the children of Israel after Joshua's death, which have been manifestly taken from Judges ii. 6, 11, and iii. 7, 12, etc., and are not found in any of the MSS. and editions of the Book of Joshua.

GEOGRAPHICAL NAMES.

(Spelt as in the Authorised Version.)

Abdon, xxi. 30
Abez, xix. 20
Achor, Valley of, vii. 24, 26, xv. 7
Achshaph, xi. 1, xii. 20, xix. 25
Achzib, xv. 44, xix. 29
Adadah, xv. 22
Adam, iii. 16
Adamah, xix. 36
Adami, xix. 33
Adar, xv. 3
Adithaim, xv. 36
Adullam, xii. 15, xv. 35
Adummim, xv. 7, xviii. 17
Ai, vii. 2-5, viii. 1-29, ix. 3, x. 1, 2, xii. 9
Aijalon,* xix. 42, xxi. 24
—— Valley of, x. 12
Ain, xv. 32, xix. 7, xxi. 16
Akrabbim, The Ascent of, xv. 3
Alammelech, xix. 26
Allon, xix. 33
Almon, xxi. 18
Amad, xix. 26
Amam, xv. 26
Ammon, xii. 2, xiii. 10
Amorite, ii. 10, iii. 10, v. 1, vii. 7, ix. 10, x. 5, 6, 12, xi. 3, xii. 2, xiii. 4, 10, 21, xxiv. 8, 12, 15, 18
Anab, xi. 21, xv. 50
Anaharath, xix. 19
Anathoth, xxi. 18
Anim, xv. 50
Aphek xii. 18, xiii. 4, xix. 30
Aphekah, xv. 53
Arab, xv. 52
Arabah, iii. 16, xviii. 18
Arad, xii. 14
Archi, xvi. 2
Arnon, xii. 1, 2, xiii. 9, 16
Aroer, xii. 2, xiii. 9, 16, 25
Ashan, xv. 42, xix. 7
Ashdod, xi. 22, xv. 46, 47
Ashdoth-Pisgah, xii. 3, xiii. 20
Ashdoth, x. 40, xii. 8
Ashdothites, xiii. 3
Asher, xvii. 10, 11, xix. 24, 31, 34, xxi. 6, 30
Asher, xvii. 7
Ashnah, xv. 33, 43
Ashtaroth (in Bashan), ix. 10, xii. 4, xiii. 12
—— (in Manasseh), xiii. 31
Ataroth, xvi. 2, 7
Ataroth-Addar, xvi. 5, xviii. 13
Avites or Avim, xiii. 3, xviii. 23
Azekah, x. 10, 11, xv. 35
Azem, xv. 29, xix. 3

Azmon, xv. 4
Aznoth-Tabor, xix. 34
Ba'alah, xv. 9, 10, xv. 29
Ba'alath, xix. 44
—— (Mount), xv. 11
Ba'alath-Beer, xix. 8
Baal-Gad, xi. 17, xii. 7, xiii. 5
Baal-Meon, xiii. 17
Balah, xix. 3
Bamoth-Baal, xiii. 17
Bashan, ix. 10, xii. 4, 5, xiii. 11, 12, 30, 31, xvii. 1, 5, xx. 8, xxi. 6, 27, xxii. 7
Bealoth, xv. 24
Beeroth, ix. 17, xviii. 25
Beer-Sheba, xv. 28, xix. 2
Beeshterah, xxi. 27
Bene-Berak, xix. 46
Benjamin, xviii. 11, 20, 21, 28, xxi. 4, 17
Beten, xix. 25
Bethanath, xix. 38
Bethanoth, xv. 59
Beth-Arabah, xv. 6, 61, xviii. 22
Beth-Aram, xiii. 27
Beth-Aven, vii. 2, xviii. 12 (wilderness of)
Beth-Baal-Meon, xiii. 17
Beth-Dagon, xv. 41, xix. 27
Beth-El, vii. 2, viii. 9, 12, 17, xii. 9, 16, xvi. 2, xviii. 13, 22
Beth-El (Mount), xvi. 1
Beth-Emek, xix. 27
Beth-Hogla, xv. 6, xviii. 19, 21
Beth-Horon, x. 10, 11, xvi. 3, 5, xviii. 13, 14, xxi. 22
Beth-Jeshimoth, xii. 3, xiii. 20
Beth-Lebaoth, xix. 6
Beth-Lehem (in Zebulun), xix. 15
Beth-Marcaboth, xix. 5
Beth-Nimrah, xiii. 27
Beth-Palet, xv. 27
Beth-Pazzez, xix. 21
Beth-Peor, xiii. 20
Beth-Shean, xvii. 11, 16
Beth-Shemesh, xv. 10, xxi. 16 (in Judah); xix. 22 (in Issachar); xix. 38 (in Naphtali)
Beth-Tappuah, xv. 53
Bethul, xix. 4
Beth-Zur, xv. 58
Betonim, xiii. 26
Bezer in the wilderness, xx. 8, xxi. 36
Bizjothjah, xv. 28
Bohan, Stone of, xv. 6, xviii. 17
Bozkath, xv. 39
Cabbon, xv. 40
Cabul, xix. 27

* Written also Ajalon.

Cain, xv. 57
Canaan, v. 12, xiv. 1, xxi. 2, xxii. 9, 10, 11, 32, xxiv. 3
Canaanite or Canaanites, iii. 10, v. 1, vii. 9, ix. 1, xi. 3, xii. 8, xiii. 3, 4, xvi. 10, xvii. 12, 13, 16, 18, xxiv. 11
Carmel (1, the mountain), xii. 22, xix. 26, (2, a town) xv. 55
Chephar Ha-Ammonai, xviii. 24
Chephirah, ix. 17, xviii. 26
Chesalon, xv. 10
Chesil, xv. 30
Chesulloth, xix. 18.
Chinnereth, xix. 35
Chinneroth, xi. 2
Chinnereth, Sea of, xiii. 27, or Chinneroth, Sea of, xii. 3
Chisloth Tabor, xix. 12
Dabareh, xxi. 28
Dabbasheth, xix. 11
Daberath, xix. 28, xxi. 28
Dan (1, the tribe), xix. 40, 47, 48, xxi. 5, 23; (2, the city of Dan), xix. 47
Dannah, xv. 49
Debir (1, in the highlands of Judah), x. 38, 39, xi. 21, xii. 13, xv. 15, 49, xxi. 15; (2, on the northern boundary of Judah), xv. 7; (3, connected with the boundary of Gad), xiii. 26
Dibon (on the east of Jordan), xiii. 9, 17
Dilean, xv. 38
Dimnah, xxi. 35
Dimonah, xv. 22
Dor, xi. 2, xii. 23, xvii. 11
Dumah, xv. 52
Ebal, Mount, viii. 30, 33
Eder, xv. 21
Edom, xv. 1, 21
Edrei, xii. 4, xix. 37
Eglon, xv. 39, x. 3, 23, 34, xii. 12
Egypt, ii. 10, v. 4, 5, 6, 9, ix. 9, xiii. 3, xxiv. 4, 5, 6, 7, 14, 17, 32
Egypt, River of, xv. 4, 47
Ekron, xiii. 3, xv. 11, 45, 46
Ekronites, xiii. 3
Eleph, xviii. 28
Elon, xix. 43
Eltekeh, xix. 44, xxi. 23
Eltekon, xv. 59
Eltolad, xv. 30, xix. 4
Enam, xv. 34
Endor, xvii. 11
En-gannim, xv. 34 (in the low country of Judah); xix. 21 (on the border of Issachar); xxi. 29 (allotted to Levites)
Engedi, xv. 62
En-haddah, xix. 21
En-Hazor, xix. 37
En-Rogel, xv. 7, xviii. 16
En-Shemesh, xv. 7, xviii. 17
En-Tappuah, xvii. 7
Ephraim, xiv. 4, xvi. 4, 5, 8, 9, xvii. 8, 9, 10, 17, xxi. 5, 20
Ephraim (Mount of), xvii. 15, xix. 50, xx. 7, xxi. 21, xxiv. 30, 33
Ephraimites, xvi. 10

Ephron, Mount, xv. 9
Eshean, xv. 52
Eshkalonites, xiii. 3
Eshtaol, xv. 33, xix. 41
Eshtemoa, xxi. 14
Eshtemoh, xv. 50
Ether, xv. 42, xix. 7
Euphrates, i. 4
Gaash, xxiv. 30
Gaba, xviii. 24
Gad, iv. 12, xiii. 24, 28, xviii. 7, xx. 8, xxi. 7, 38, xxii. 9, 10, 11, 13, 15, 21, 25, 30-34
Gadites, i. 12, xii. 6, xiii. 8, xxii. 1
Galilee, xx. 7, xxi. 32
Gath, xi. 22
Gath-Hepher, xix. 13
Gath-Rimmon (1, in Dan), xix. 45, xxi. 24; (2, in Western Manasseh), xxi. 25
Gaza, x. 41, xi. 22, xv. 47
Gazathites, xiii. 3
Geba, xxi. 17
Geder, xii. 13
Gederah, xv. 36
Gederoth, xv. 41
Gederothaim, xv. 36
Gedor, xv. 58
Geliloth, xviii. 17, xxii. 10, 11
Gerizim, Mount, viii. 33
Geshurites, xii. 5, xiii. 11, 13
Geshuri, xiii. 2
Gezer, x. 33, xii. 12, xvi. 3, 10, xxi. 21
Gibbethon, xix. 44, xxi. 23
Gibeah, xv. 57
Gibeath, xviii. 28
Gibeon, ix. 3, 17, x. 1, 2, 4-6, 10, 12, 41, xi. 19, xviii. 25, xxi. 17
Giblites, The, xiii. 5
Gilead, xii. 2, 5, xiii. 11, 25, 31, xvii. 5, 6, xx. 8, xxi. 38, xxii. 9, 13, 15, 32
Gilgal, iv. 19, 20, v. 9, 10, ix. 6, x. 6, 7, 9, 15, 43, xii. 23, xiv. 6, xv. 7
Giloh, xv. 51
Girgashites, iii. 10, xxiv. 11
Gittah-Hepher, xix. 13
Golan, xx. 8, xxi. 27
Goshen, x. 41, xi. 16, xv. 51
Hadattah, xv. 25
Halak, Mount, xi. 17, xii. 7
Halhul, xv. 58
Hali, xix. 25
Hamath, xiii. 5
Hammath, xix. 35
Hammon, xix. 28
Hammoth-Dor, xxi. 32
Hannathon, xix. 14
Haphraim, xix. 19
Havoth-Jair, xiii. 30
Hazar-Gaddah, xv. 27
Hazar-Shual, xv. 28, xix. 3
Hazar-Susah, xix. 5
Hazor (1, in North Palestine), xi. 1, 10, 11, 13, xii. 19, xix. 36; (2, in the South of Judah), xv. 23; (3, Hazor-hadattah), xv. 25
Hebron (1, in Judah), x. 3, 5, 23, 36, 39,

xi. 21, xii. 10, xiv. 13-15, xv. 13, 54, xx. 7, xxi. 11, 13 ; (2, in Asher), xix. 28
Heleph, xix. 33
Helkath, xix. 25, xxi. 31
Hepher, xii. 17
Hermon, Mount, xi. 3, 17, xii. 1, 5, xiii. 5, 11
Heshbon, ix. 10, xii. 2, 5, xiii. 10, 17, 21, 26, 27, xxi. 39
Heshmon, xv. 27
Hinnom, Valley of, xv. 8, xviii. 16; or Valley of son of Hinnom, xv. 8
Hittite and Hittites, i. 4, iii. 10, ix. 1, xi. 3, xii. 8, xxiv. 11
Hivite and Hivites, iii. 10, ix. 1, 7, xi. 3, 19, xii. 8, xxiv. 11
Holon, xv. 51, xxi. 15
Horem, xix. 38
Hormah, xii. 14, xv. 30, xix. 4
Hosah, xix. 29
Hukkok, xix. 34
Humtah, xv. 54
Ibleam, xvii. 11
Idalah, xix. 15
Iim, xv. 29
Iron, xix. 38
Irpeel, xviii. 27
Ir-Shemesh, xix. 41
Israel, Mountain or Mountains of, xi. 16, 21
Issachar, xvii. 10, 11, xix. 17, 23, xxi. 6, 28
Ithnan, xv. 23
Ittah-Kazin, xix. 13
Jaazer, xiii. 25
Jabbok, The Brook, xii. 2
Jabneel (1, on north boundary of Judah), xv. 11 ; (2, on boundary of Naphtali), xix. 33
Jagur, xv. 21
Jahaza, Jahazah, xiii. 18, xxi. 36
Janohah, xvi. 6, 7
Janum, xv. 53
Japhia, xix. 12
Japho, xix. 46
Jarmuth (1, in the lowlands of Judah), xv. 35, x. 3, 5, 23, xii. 11 ; (2, in Issachar), xxi. 29
Jattir, xv. 48, xxi. 14
Jazer, xxi. 39
Jearim, Mount, xv. 10
Jebusi, xviii. 16, 28
Jebusite, The, xi. 3, xv. 8, 63 Also, as a usual formula for the conquered people, iii. 10, ix. 1, xii. 8, xxiv. 11
Jehud, xix. 45
Jericho, ii. 1, 2, 3, iii. 16, iv. 13, 19, v. 10, 13, vi. 1, 2, 25, 26, vii. 1, viii. 2, ix. 3, x. 1, 28, 30, xii. 9, xiii. 32, xvi. 1, 7, xviii. 12, 21, xx. 8, xxiv. 11
Jericho, The plains of, iv. 13, v. 10
Jerusalem, x. 1, 3, 5, 23, xii. 10, xv. 8, 63, xviii. 28
Jethlah, xix. 42
Jezreel (1, in Issachar), xix. 18, also the Valley of Jezreel, xvii. 16; (2, in Judah), xv. 56
Jiphtah, xv. 43

Jiphtah-El, The Valley of, xix. 14, 27
Jokdeam, xv. 56
Jokneam, xii. 22, xix. 11, xxi. 34
Jokthe-el, xv. 38
Jordan, i. 2, 11, 14, 15, ii. 7, 10, iii. 1, 8, 11, 13-15, 17, iv. 1, 3, 5, 7-10, 16-20, 22, 23, v. 1, vii. 7, ix. 1, 10, xii. 1, 7, xiii. 8, 23, 27, 32, xiv. 3, xv. 5, xvi. 1, 7, xvii. 5, xviii. 7, 12, 19, 20, xix. 22, 33, 34, xx. 8, xxii. 4, 7, 10, 11, 25, xxiii. 4, xxiv. 8, 11
Judah, vii. 1, 16-18, xi. 21, xiv. 6, xv. 1, 12, 13, 20, 21, 63, xviii. 5, 11, 14, xix. 1, 9, xx. 7, xxi. 4, 9, 11
Judah upon Jordan, xix. 34
Juttah, xv. 55, xxi. 16
Kabzeel, xv. 21
Kadesh-Barnea, x. 41, xiv. 6, 7, xv. 3
Kanah, xix. 28
Kanah, The River, xvi. 8, xvii. 9
Karkaa, xv. 3
Kartah, xxi. 34
Kartan, xxi. 32
Kittath, xix. 15
Kedemoth, xiii. 18, xxi. 37
Kedesh (1, in the south of Judah), xv. 23 ; (2, in Issachar), xii. 22 ; (3, in Galilee, a city of Naphtali), xix. 37, xx. 7, xxi. 32
Keilah, xv. 44
Kerioth, xxv. 25
Keziz, The Valley of, xviii. 21
Kibzaim, xxi. 22
Kinah, xv. 22
Kirjath, xviii. 28
Kirjathaim, xii. 19
Kirjath Arba, xiv. 15, xv. 13, 54, xx. 7, xxi. 11
Kirjath-Baal, xv. 60, xviii. 14
Kirjath-Jearim, ix. 17, xv. 9, xviii. 14, 15
Kirjath-Sannah, xv. 49
Kirjath-Sepher, xv. 15, 16
Kishon, xix. 20, xxi. 28
Kithlish, xv. 40
Lachish, x. 3, 5, 26, 31, 33, xii. 11, xv. 39
Lahmam, xv. 40
Lakum, xix. 33
Lasharon, xii. 18
Lebanon, i. 4, ix. 1, xi. 17, xii. 7, xiii. 5, 6
Lebaoth, xv. 32
Leshem, xix. 47
Libnah, x. 29, 31, 32, 39, xii. 15, xv. 42, xxi. 13
Lo-Debar, xiii. 26
Luz, xvi. 2, xviii. 13
Maacahites, xii. 5, xiii. 11, 13
Maaleh Acrabbim, xv. 3
Maarath, xv. 58
Madmannah, xv. 31
Madon, xi. 1, xii. 19
Mahanaim, xiii. 26, 30, xxi. 38
Makkeddah, x. 10, 16, 17, 21, 28, 29, xv. 41
Manasseh, i. 12, ix. 1, xi. 12, xii. 6, xiii. 7, 29, 31, xiv. 4, xvi. 4, 9, xvii. 1-3, 5-12, 17, xviii. 7, xx. 8, xxi. 5, 6, 25, 27, xxii. 1, 7, 9-11, 13, 15, 21, 30, 31.

Maon, xv. 55
Maralah, xix. 11
Mareshah, xv. 44
Mearah, xiii. 4
Medeba, xiii. 9
Megiddo, xii. 21, xvii. 11
Me-Jarkon, xix. 46
Mephaath, xiii. 18, xxi. 37
Merom, The waters of, xi. 5, 7
Michmethah, xvi. 6, xvii. 7
Middin, xv. 61
Midian, xiii. 21
Migdal-El, xix. 38
Migdal-Gad, xv. 37
Misheal and Mishal, xix. 26, xxi. 30
Misrephoth-Maim, xi. 8, xiii. 6
Mizpeh, Land of, xi. 3; Valley of, xi. 8; in the lowlands of Judah, xv. 38; in Benjamin, xviii. 26
Moab, xxiv. 9
Moab, The plains of, xiii. 32
Moladah, xv. 26, xix. 2
Mozah, xviii. 26
Naamah, xv. 41
Naarath, xvi. 7
Nahallal, xix. 15, xxi. 35
Naphtali, xix. 32, 39; xx. 7 (Mount Naphtali); xxi. 6, 32
Neiel, xix. 27
Nekeb, xix. 33
Nephtoah, The water of, xv. 9, xviii. 15
Nezib, xv. 43
Nibshan, xv. 62
Nile, The (1, Shichor), xiii. 3; (2, River of Egypt), xv. 4
Ophni, xviii. 24
Ophrah, xviii. 23
Parah, xviii. 23
Perizzites, The, xi. 3, xii. 8, xvii. 15; also iii. 10, ix. 1, xxiv. 11
Philistines, xiii. 2, 3
Rabbah (in Eastern Palestine), xiii. 25; (in Judah), xv. 60
Rabbith, xix. 20
Rakkath, xix. 35
Rakkon, xix. 46
Ramah (1, in Benjamin), xviii. 25; (2, in Asher), xix. 29; (3, in Naphtali), xix. 36
Ramath-Mizpeh, xiii. 26
Ramath of the South, xix. 8
Ramoth in Gilead, xx. 8, xxi. 38
Red Sea, ii. 10, iv. 23, xxiv. 6
Rehob, xix. 28, 30, xxi. 31
Rekem, xviii. 27
Remeth, xix. 21
Remmon, xix. 7
Remmon-Methoar, xix. 13
Rephaim, Valley of, xv. 8, xviii. 16
Rimmon, xv. 32
River of Egypt, xv. 4, 47
Salcah, xii. 5, xiii. 11
Salt, City of, xv. 62
Sansannah, xv. 31
Sarid, xix. 10, 12
Sea, The Salt, iii. 16, xii. 3, xv. 2, 5, xviii. 19

Sea, of the plain, iii. 16, xii. 3
Secacah, xv. 61
Seir, (1, on the east of the Arabah), xi. 17, xii. 7, xxiv. 4; (2, on the northern boundary of Judah), xv. 10
Shaalabbin, xix. 42
Shahazimah, xix. 22
Shamir, xv. 48
Sharuhen, xix. 6
Sharaim, xv. 36
Sheba, xix. 2
Shebarim, vii. 5
Shechem, xvii. 7, xx. 7, xxi. 21, xxiv. 1, 25, 32
Shema, xv. 26
Shephelah, ix. 1, x. 40, xi. 2, 16, xii. 8, xv. 33
Shicron, xv. 11
Shihon, xix. 19
Shihor-Libnath, xix. 26
Shilhim, xv. 32
Shiloh, xviii. 1, 8-10, xix. 51, xxi. 2, xxii. 9, 12
Shimron, xi. 1, xix. 15
Shimron-Meron, xii. 20
Shinar, vii. 21
Shittim, ii. 1, iii. 1
Shunem, xix. 18
Sibmah, xiii. 19
Sidonians, xiii. 4, 6
Sihor, xiii. 3
Simeon, xix. 1, 8, 9, xxi. 4, 9
Socoh, xv. 35, 48
Succoth, xiii. 27
Taanach, xii. 21, xvii. 11, xxi. 25
Taanath-Shiloh, xvi. 6
Tappuah, xii. 17, xv. 34, xvi 8, xvii. 8
Tappuah, The Land of, xvii. 8
Taralah, xviii. 27
Telem, xv. 24
Timnah, xv. 10, 57
Timnathah, xix. 43
Timnath-Serah, xix. 50, xxiv. 30
Tirzah, xii. 24
Tyre, xix. 29
Ummah, xix. 30
Zaanannim, The plain of, xix. 33
Zanoah, xv. 34, 56
Zaphon, xiii. 27
Zaretan, iii. 16
Zareth-Shahar, xiii. 19
Zebulun, xix. 10, 16, 27, 34, xxi. 7, 34
Zelah, xviii. 28
Zemaraim, xviii. 22
Zenan, xv. 37
Zer, xix. 35
Ziddim, xix. 35
Zidon, xi. 8, xix. 28
Ziklag, xv. 31, xix. 5
Zin, xv. 3
Zin, The wilderness of, xv. 1
Zior, xv. 54
Ziph (1, in the south of Judah), xv. 24; (2, in the highlands of Judah), xv 55
Zorah, xv. 33, xix. 41

www.ingramcontent.com/pod-product-compliance
Lightning Source LLC
Chambersburg PA
CBHW031420230426
43668CB00007B/373